A Cook's Tour
OF SHREVEPORT

Favorite Southern Recipes

Junior League of Shreveport

In Celebration of the 80th Anniversary of the Junior League of Shreveport, it is our pleasure to offer this limited edition of the very popular, A COOK'S TOUR OF SHREVEPORT.

If you wish to order additional copies of A COOK'S TOUR OF SHREVEPORT, use the order blanks provided in the back of the book or write to:

Junior League of Shreveport-Bossier
Attn: Cookbook Chairman
2601 Line Ave.
Shreveport, LA 71104

Make checks payable to: THE JUNIOR LEAGUE OF SHREVEPORT-BOSSIER for $19.95 plus 8.6% tax and $4.50 for shipping.

Cover designed by Julie Sipple Dickinson and Jerry Wray.
Divider page artwork by Teri Tallant and Tina Mullins.
Coordination help provided by Gremillion & Pou Advertising, Inc.

First Edition	1964
Second Edition	1965
Third Edition	1967
Fourth Edition	1969
Fifth Edition	1971
Sixth Edition	1973
Seventh Edition	1975
Eighth Edition	1976
Ninth Edition	1978
Tenth Edition	1979
Eleventh Edition	1992
Twelfth Edition	2011

Title is used through the courtesy of Thos. Cook and Son.
"World's Oldest and Largest Travel Organization."

Manufactured by
Favorite Recipes® Press
An imprint of
FRP, INC
P.O. Box 305142
Nashville, Tennessee 37230
800-358-0560

Printed in China

Table of Contents

The Cookbook Committee sincerely appreciates the enthusiastic participation of the active and sustaining membership in testing recipes and compiling this book. In addition, many friends of the League have contributed very fine recipes which are included. It is truly A "COOK'S" TOUR OF SHREVEPORT.

Brand names have been used where necessary.

To order copies of A COOK'S TOUR OF SHREVEPORT, send a check for $19.95 plus 8.6% tax and $4.50 for postage to the following address:

Junior League of Shreveport-Bossier
Attn: Cookbook Chairman
2601 Line Ave.
Shreveport, LA 71104

JUNIOR LEAGUE PRAYER

Our Father,
We pray that we will never be so blind
That our small world is all we ever see,
Or so supremely satisfied that what we are
Is all we ever hope to be.
Grant us the joy of filling someone's need.
Make us gracious followers.
Make gracious those who lead,
And more than all, we pray, that through the years
We will remember there are
Always new frontiers.

There are no better words to describe what the Junior League of Shreveport has aspired to become.

WE PRAY THAT WE WILL NEVER BE SO BLIND THAT OUR SMALL WORLD IS ALL WE EVER SEE: With projects like C-BARC, adopted in 1956 to provide training and services for subjects capable of being placed in the community as self-supporting citizens, the establishment of the Council of the Aging in 1966, the Mollie Webb Speech & Hearing Center in 1973, and the Rutherford House in 1974 were just the beginning of many Junior League projects as we broadened our views of our community.

OR SO SUPREMELY SATISFIED THAT WHAT WE ARE IS ALL WE EVER HOPE TO BE: The Junior League expanded projects in 1989 by adding the VOA, Pregnancy Service Center and Call 3, and to the existing PAL program at the Shriners Children's Hospital an additional PAL Program at LSU-MC during the summer months.

GRANT US THE JOY OF FILLING SOMEONE'S NEED: Needs throughout the community have been met with projects like Schumpert's Adult Day Care Center, the McDade House, Literature-to-Life, Friend-to-Friend, and the LightHouse.

MAKE US GRACIOUS FOLLOWERS. MAKE GRACIOUS THOSE WHO LEAD: It was decided in 1990-1991 that we "focus" on a specific area. The membership selected Children and Youth to be our focus area for the next three to five years. Our projects in the community will try to follow along this focus area when we vote on new projects each spring.

AND MORE THAN ALL, WE PRAY, THAT THROUGH THE YEARS, WE WILL REMEMBER THERE ARE ALWAYS NEW FRONTIERS: The Red River Revel was established in 1976 as a week long multi-arts festival. It was the Junior League's Bi-centennial gift to the community. In 1989 it won the Presidential Award for Volunteerism. Over 180,000 people attend this week long celebration of the arts each year, and over 10,000 volunteers from Bossier and Shreveport participate in the Revel's success.

There are too many projects to list and too many names and faces to remember, but the Junior League has come a long way from 1933 when 98 young Shreveport women got together and decided to make a difference in their community. Now 78 years later, the Junior League of Shreveport is still—

MAKING A DIFFERENCE

MAKING IT COUNT

Party Fare

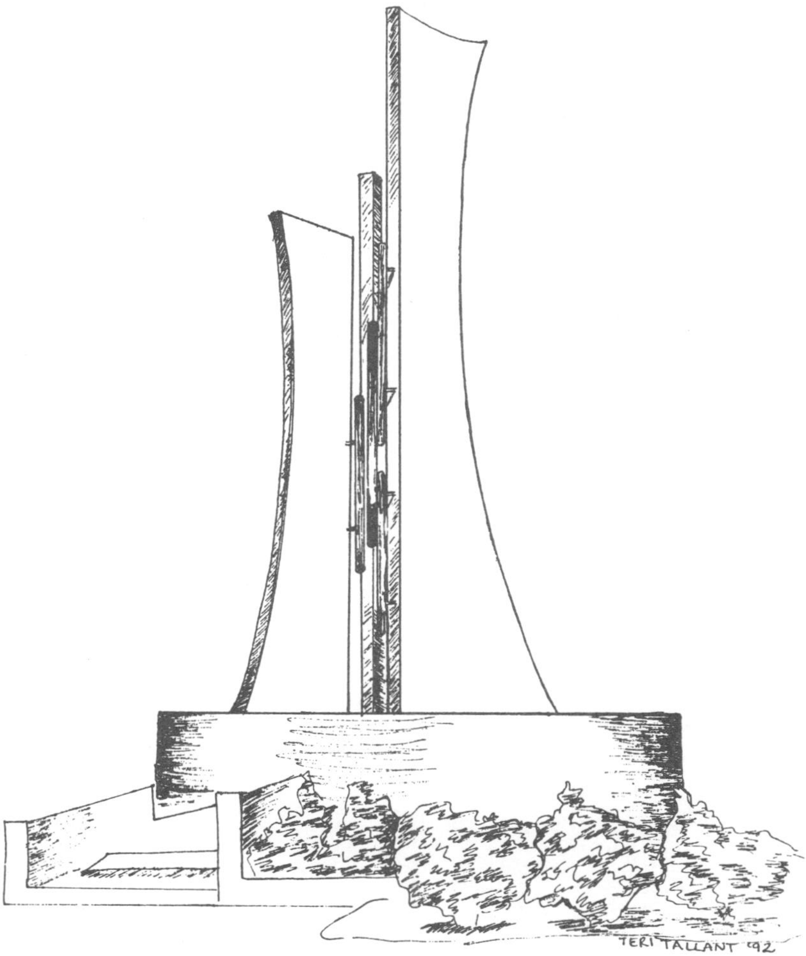

American Rose Center

AMERICAN ROSE CENTER

The American Rose Center features North America's largest rose garden with 118 acres of blooming beauty. The Center is headquarters for the American Rose Society. More than 20,000 roses are spectacularly planted in 60 individual gardens. Beautiful fountains, sculptures and the lovely chimes of the Windsounds Carillon Tower make the center a nature lover's delight. Special theme gardens include Fragrant Roses, Celebrity Roses, Thornless Roses, Royalty Roses, Single Petal Roses and the Green Rose, Black Rose and Blue Rose.

Each Christmas season, beginning the evening after Thanksgiving and continuing through Christmas Eve, the American Rose Center becomes a fantasyland of light. More than 600,000 lights make the center a winter wonderland. Light sculptures such as elephants, bears, rocking horses, the American Flag and the Statue of Liberty turn the center's gardens into a Christmas sensation, attracting visitors from throughout the nation. Area music groups perform each evening throughout the celebration.

BESSIE'S FRUIT PUNCH

1 quart ginger ale
1 12-ounce can frozen lemonade
1 12-ounce can frozen orange juice
1 46-ounce can orange juice
1 46-ounce can pineapple juice

Combine above ingredients. Use a block of ice in punch bowl. Will serve 50 people. Segments of fruit may be floated in bowl for decoration.

Mrs. A. Marvin Turner

AUNT SUSAN'S LEMONADE

1½ cups sugar
2½ cups water
Juice of 6 lemons
Juice of 2 oranges
1 cup fresh mint leaves

Boil sugar and water to form syrup. When cool, add juice of lemons and oranges. Pour liquid over mint leaves and let stand 1 hour. Strain into large pitcher. Place in refrigerator overnight. Serve ½ cup over crushed ice. Garnish with cherry or fresh mint leaves.

Mrs. Raymond Breazeale
Natchitoches, La.

FRENCH CHOCOLATE

3 squares unsweetened chocolate
½ cup water
½ teaspoon salt
¾ cup sugar
½ cup heavy cream

Grate chocolate. Add water and cook over low heat until thick, stirring constantly. Add salt and sugar; continue cooking 4 minutes. Fold in cream, whipped. Store in refrigerator.

To serve, spoon generous amount into each cup and fill with very hot milk. Stir well.

Mrs. Peyton Kelley

CAFE SOIREE

4 cups fresh dripped dark roast (or espresso) coffee
6 teaspoons sugar
1 inch stick of cinnamon
4 whole cloves
1 curl of orange peel
4 ounces brandy
Whipped cream

Mix seasonings; add hot coffee. Heat, but do not boil. Add brandy, strain and serve. Top with unsweetened whipped cream.

Serves 6 demitasse cups.

Mrs. Hank Bronner

EGGNOG

12 egg whites
8 egg yolks
12 tablespoons sugar
16 tablespoons bourbon (more if desired)
½ pint whipping cream
Nutmeg

Cream sugar and egg yolks together until well blended. Add the whiskey a little at a time. Fold in stiffly beaten egg whites. Then fold in whipped cream. Serve sprinkled with nutmeg.

Serves 16.

Mrs. Marion D. Hargrove, Jr.

SPICED TEA

Tie 2 teaspoons whole cloves in a piece of cheesecloth and boil in one gallon of water for ten minutes. Add 1⅞ cups sugar and four heaping tablespoons tea tied in cheesecloth. Steep until desired shade (5-6 min.) — fairly dark because the lemon juice lightens it considerably. Add juice of two lemons. This amount serves 24. It may be made ahead of time and reheated slowly.

Mrs. Randell Whitmeyer

SPICED TEA

½ pound orange pekoe tea
4 teaspoons packaged ground orange peel
2 teaspoons packaged ground lemon peel
2 4" cinnamon sticks, crushed
¼ cup whole cloves
1 teaspoon grated whole nutmeg
1 teaspoon slivered candied orange peel (¼ pound)

Toss all ingredients together in large bowl until well mixed. Makes about ¾ pound spiced tea. Brew as you would any tea.

Mrs. Clarence J. Edwards

IRISH COFFEE

½ jigger Irish whiskey per cup
Sugar to taste
Hot coffee
Heavy cream, whipped thick but not stiff

Into warmed cups place sugar and whiskey. Stir until dissolved, and fill with hot coffee. Gently drop whipped cream over the back of a spoon onto coffee.

Mrs. Charles Edward Porter

TOMATO JUICE COCKTAIL

Juice of ½ lemon
2 teaspoons sugar
1 teaspoon horseradish
½ teaspoon salt
Large can tomato juice

Mix, chill and serve. Makes 1 pitcher.

Mrs. Judith Wintle Taylor

FROZEN BACARDI COCKTAIL

2 cans frozen limeade
1 can frozen lemonade
½ cup grenadine
6 cups water
Fifth of white rum

Strain the ingredients and put in a plastic container. Cover and freeze at least 24 hours. Then stir the contents and return to freezer. Do not use for 48 hours after stirring.

Mrs. Darrell P. Miller

CHAMPAGNE PUNCH

1 cup sugar
2 bottles chilled sauterne
6 lemons
6 oranges
2 cups chilled brandy
1 block of ice made of 1 quart of water
3 bottles chilled champagne
3 more chilled bottles champagne

Stir the sugar and sauterne until the sugar is dissolved. Slice lemons and oranges and add to the sauterne mixture. Add the brandy, block of ice and 3 bottles of champagne. Just before serving, add the other 3 bottles of chilled champagne. At this time, you may also add a large 7-Up or ginger ale, if desired.

Mrs. Darrell P. Miller

MANHATTAN DAISY

½ gallon medium dry sherry
3 cups bourbon
1½ cups Italian sweet vermouth
4 dashes bitters
Peeling of ½ lemon and ½ orange

Mix ingredients and place overnight in refrigerator. Serve chilled from cocktail shaker (containing several cubes of ice) into cocktail glasses with cherry.

Makes about 42 cocktails.

Arthur F. Carr

MULLED CRANBERRY PUNCH

2 tablespoons whole cloves
1 tablespoon whole allspice
12 inches stick cinnamon, broken
½ to ⅔ cup sugar
¼ teaspoon salt
5 cups water
2½ cups grapefruit juice
2 1-pound cans (4 cups) jellied cranberry sauce, mashed

Tie spices in cheesecloth, add to other ingredients and bring slowly to a boil. Cover and simmer 5 minutes; remove spices. Pour into punch bowl. (If glass bowl, first heat with warm water; pour out water and place large silver spoon in bowl, then pour punch slowly down spoon.) Serve warm. This may also be served in a silver coffee or tea pot.

Makes about 20 half-cup servings. This punch is very good in the winter — especially at Christmas time because of its red color.

Mrs. T. J. Ostendorff, Jr.

CRANBERRY PUNCH

Sweet

For a sweet punch, mix equal parts of very cold cranberry juice and 7-Up. You may add a cup of light orange wine per punch bowl.

Tart

For a tart punch, mix equal parts of very cold cranberry juice and ginger ale. To this add 1 cup of sauterne or chablais per punch bowl.

This makes a beautiful clear red punch. Very colorful for the holidays.

Mrs. Vernon W. Woods

MINT DRINK

2 cups sugar
2 cups water
4 sprigs fresh mint
2 cups lemon juice
¼ teaspoon salt
1 quart ginger ale

In a saucepan, mix sugar and water. Add mint leaves and boil 5 minutes. Add lemon juice and salt. Chill. Add 1 quart ginger ale just before serving.

Makes 2 quarts.

Mrs. Peyton Kelley

WHISKEY PUNCH

Juice of 6 lemons (6 ounces)
Juice of 8 oranges (24 ounces)
1 small can pineapple juice (18-ounce)
2 bottles bourbon whiskey
2 large bottles ginger ale

Mix ingredients and pour over large piece of ice or 2 trays of cubes. Add more ginger ale and sugar to taste. Decorate with orange, lemon and pineapple slices.

Makes 45 servings of 4 ounces each.

Mrs. Marshall Martin

FRUIT PUNCH FOR 35

Mix:
4 packages lime Jello
2 cups cold water
2 cups hot water
2 cups sugar

Let this cool for one hour. Add:
2 quarts pineapple juice
3 pints lemon juice
2 quarts ginger ale

Serves 35 people.

Mrs. Max M. Morelock

BLACKBERRY DRINK

12 pounds blackberries
2½ ounces tartaric acid
Sugar

Crush berries and add tartaric acid to fruit. Let stand 36 hours in a crock. Strain berries through a thin bag, and then let drip through a thick bag. Measure juice, add same amount of sugar, and place in saucepan. Bring to a boil and let boil 5 minutes. Seal in jars.

To serve, dilute with water to taste and serve with lemon slices.

Mrs. P. A. Graham

ANTIPASTO

1 head cauliflower, separated into flowerets
1 green pepper, cut in strips
1 large carrot, cut in sticks
4 stalks celery, sliced
1 7½-ounce jar pickled sour onions
2 cloves garlic, pressed
½ pound button mushrooms
½-¾ cup oil
1½ cups wine vinegar
⅓ cup sugar
2 teaspoons prepared mustard
2 teaspoons salt
1 teaspoon oregano leaves
Pepper

Prepare vegetables. Mix marinade of remaining ingredients and pour over vegetables. Cover and chill at least 12 hours, turning occasionally. To serve, drain well. Garnish with olives, anchovies, pimientos, etc., if desired.

Mrs. Jack Stein

BELL PEPPER - CHEESE SPREAD

1 8-ounce package cream cheese (at room temperature)
1 green bell pepper, finely chopped
½ small onion, finely chopped
¼ teaspoon Worcestershire sauce
Dash Tabasco
1 tablespoon mayonnaise
Salt to taste (does not require much)
Lemon juice to taste

Mix all ingredients well and let stand overnight in refrigerator.

Mrs. Francis S. Randall

BOLOGNA STACK UPS

½ pound bologna
1 box cream cheese and chive dip, softened to room temperature

Spread cheese mixture between slices of bologna and stack. Chill. Cut into pie-shaped triangles and stick a toothpick in each.

Makes 8 triangles. It is best to double recipe.

Mrs. Melvin F. Johnson, Jr.

TEA OR COCKTAIL BISCUITS

2 sticks butter
2 3-ounce packages cream cheese
2½ cups flour

Have ingredients at room temperature. Blend well together and pat into a ball. Put in refrigerator or freezer.

When ready to use, roll out very thin. Cut with small cookie cutter and fill with orange marmalade. Place in 350° oven until slightly brown. Remove from cookie sheet and sprinkle with powdered sugar. Delicious hot or cold for tea or coffee.

For Hors d'Oeuvres — cut a little larger and fill with sharp cheese or Smithfield ham or chicken. Delicious hot.

Makes about 75 servings.

Mrs. Albert Sklar
Mrs. Conway Allen

BOEUF CHAUD-FROID

1 3-ounce package cream cheese, softened
4 green olives, chopped
1 tablespoon fresh horseradish
½ pound package dried beef

Blend cheese, olives and horseradish. Spread on small slices of beef. Roll and fasten with toothpicks. Brush with butter and broil until heated through. Serve immediately.

If preferred, rolls may be chilled until firm and served cold.

Makes 20 rolls.

Mrs. Gordon Lambert
Mrs. Melvin F. Johnson, Jr.

HOT BROCCOLI DIP

3 stalks celery, chopped medium fine
½ large chopped onion
1 small can mushrooms (pieces)
1 package frozen chopped broccoli
1 can cream of mushroom soup
1 roll garlic cheese

Saute celery, onion and mushroom pieces in butter or oleo. Cook broccoli as directed on package and drain well. Add mushroom soup to above ingredients. Melt cheese in double boiler. Combine all in chafing dish to serve.

Serves 12. This may also be served as vegetable. Freezes beautifully.

Mrs. Mike Tipps

CHEESE BALLS

12 ounces New York sharp cheese, grated
2 sticks margarine, melted
2 cups sifted flour
¼ teaspoon salt
¾ teaspoon red pepper
2 large jars small green stuffed olives

Mix grated cheese and flour. Add melted margarine and seasonings. Mix well, with hands if necessary. Make small balls, putting small olive in center. Cook at 450° for 5 minutes on bottom shelf of oven and 5 minutes on top shelf. Balls may be frozen.

Makes 4 to 5 dozen balls.

Frances Peyton
Mrs. C. Cody White, Jr.
Mrs. Charles McCall

MUSTARD CHEESE STUFFED CELERY

1 3-ounce package cream cheese
2 tablespoons mustard
1 large jar or 2 small (4-ounce) jars sharp cheese
1 cup finely chopped pecans, toasted in butter
2 tablespoons Worcestershire sauce
1 teaspoon Durkee's dressing
1 stalk celery
Paprika

Combine all ingredients except celery and paprika. Blend well by hand. Wash celery, crisp and cut into 1½-2-inch lengths. Stuff with cheese mixture. Sprinkle with paprika. This mixture may also be used on crackers. The cheese blend will keep well for several weeks in a covered jar in refrigerator.

Mrs. Kirke Couch

CHEESE CRACKER SNACKS

1 stick (¼ pound) butter or oleo
½ pound grated Cheddar cheese
½ package dry onion soup mix
½ teaspoon salt
1 cup flour

Bring butter and cheese to room temperature; mix well. Add rest of ingredients and blend. Shape into 1" rolls. Wrap in wax paper; chill. When ready to bake, slice into "cookies" which are about ¼ inch thick. Bake on ungreased baking sheet at 375°, 10 to 12 minutes, or until slightly brown.

These are good served with tomato juice or consomme.

Mrs. T. Haller Jackson, Jr.

CHEESE CRISPS

1 10-ounce package sharp cheese
1 stick margarine
1½ cups flour
Heaping teaspoon salt
1½ teaspoons baking powder
Red pepper and Tabasco to taste

Let cheese and margarine stand at room temperature. When soft, work together by hand. Add flour and other ingredients and continue mixing. Make rolls and place in refrigerator until chilled. Cut in very thin slices. Cook at lowest oven temperature possible.

Mrs. Edward P. Stiles

CHEESE HOOIES

1 pound butter
1 pound sharp American cheese
7 cups sifted flour
4 teaspoons salt
Cayenne — amount depending on personal taste

Grate cheese into butter and cream well together. Add salt and cayenne, then work in flour until well blended. This takes a good while, and a lot of "working." Knead on board until smooth. Roll into a long, thin roll and put into refrigerator to chill thoroughly. When chilled, slice in thin slices and bake on an ungreased cookie sheet in 350° oven until slightly brown, 8-10 minutes. Dust with powdered sugar.

These will keep indefinitely in a tightly covered container. Rolls of dough may be frozen and sliced as needed.

Mrs. Robert H. Nelson

CHEESE STRAWS

1½ sticks oleo
1 pound sharp cheese, grated
2 heaping cups flour (sifted)
1 teaspoon salt
1 teaspoon red pepper
Scant 1 tablespoon ice water

Allow oleo and cheese to soften at room temperature. Mix in rest of ingredients with electric mixer. Make strips with a cookie press on a cookie sheet. Sprinkle red pepper on top. Bake at 300° for 20 to 30 minutes.

Mrs. B. K. Eaves

CHEESE TOASTIES

Make a paste of:

1 cup grated cheese
⅛ teaspoon paprika
1 teaspoon mustard
½ teaspoon Worcestershire sauce
2 tablespoons milk

Remove crusts from ⅜" sliced bread. Toast on one side, then turn and spread first with deviled ham and then with cheese spread.

Mrs. John Davis

MINIATURE CHEESE PUFFS

Puff Pastry:
2 eggs (room temperature)
½ cup milk or water
¼ cup butter
½ cup sifted flour
⅛ teaspoon salt

Filling:
6 ounces cream cheese
6 ounces blue cheese
2 tablespoons brandy or water (approximately)

To make puffs: Place milk or water and butter in saucepan and heat to boiling point. Remove from fire and add flour and salt all at once. Quickly beat into a ball. Beat in eggs, one at a time. Beat hard. Chill dough ½ hour or longer. When chilled, drop with a demitasse spoon onto greased cookie sheets, making small bonbons. Leave 2 inches of space between each puff. Bake at 400° for 20 minutes, then reduce heat to 350° and bake 5 more minutes. Remove one puff from oven; if it is firm and doesn't fall, puffs are done. Cool, then cut slit in side.

To make filling: Soften the two cheeses at room temperature and mix together. Moisten slightly with brandy or water.

Fill puffs and store in refrigerator or freezer. At party time, heat briefly in oven. Serve piping hot.

Makes 4-5 dozen if small.

Mrs. John D. Harrell

SHARP CHEESE ROLL

1 4-ounce glass very sharp cheese
¼ pound blue cheese
4 3-ounce packages cream cheese
1 cup chopped pecans
1 teaspoon red pepper
1 tablespoon Worcestershire sauce
¼ teaspoon salt
Garlic salt as desired

Let cheese reach room temperature. Mix all ingredients, reserving ½ cup nuts. Make into roll and place in icebox. After it is firm, roll in rest of nuts.

Makes 2 dozen. Roll may be frozen and allowed to thaw an hour before serving.

Mrs. Albert Stephens, Jr.

JALAPENO DIP

3 tablespoons butter
1 heaping cup chopped onion
1½ cups tomatoes
4 chopped jalapeno peppers
1 pound grated sharp Cheddar cheese
Salt
Pepper

Brown onion in butter. Add tomatoes and salt and pepper to taste. Simmer until thick. Add the peppers and cook five minutes. Just before serving, heat sauce and stir in cheese until melted. Serve in chafing dish with crackers or large corn chips. Serves 10-12.

Mrs. William T. Murphy, III

CHILI CHEESE ROLL

1 ½-pound package pimiento cheese
1 ½-pound package Old English cheese
1 3-ounce package cream cheese
¾ cup finely chopped nuts
3 tablespoons mayonnaise
1 clove garlic, minced
Salt to taste
Red pepper to taste
Small amount of chili powder
Paprika

Soften cheese at room temperature. Blend with a fork, adding mayonnaise, red pepper, salt, nuts and garlic. Mix well. Shape in two log rolls about 8" long. Roll in chili powder and paprika. Wrap in waxed paper and chill 24 hours before serving.

Mrs. Campbell Tucker

CHILI DIP

1 large onion, chopped
1½ pounds ground meat
Salt to taste
1 teaspoon ground cumin
1 teaspoon chili powder
1 large can chili (all meat)
1 pound grated American cheese

Heat all ingredients and serve from a chafing dish with corn chips or tortillas.

Serves 20 (for before dinner snacking). To serve about 200 for a cocktail party use 6 times all the ingredients.

Mrs. Charles H. Jeter

CONSOMME MOLD

2 cans consomme
2 envelopes gelatin
2 3-ounce packages cream cheese
1 tablespoon sherry
1 tablespoon onion juice
¼ teaspoon red pepper
¼ teaspoon black pepper
½ teaspoon parsley, fresh or dried

Dissolve gelatin in ¼ cup cold water. Heat 2 cans consomme; add dissolved gelatin; stir well. Add any or all of the following seasonings to taste: lemon juice, onion juice, a dash of bitters, red pepper, ground black pepper, salt, dill seed, dried parsley flakes. Pour consomme into 1 quart mold (1 large or 2 smaller molds). Refrigerate until very firm. (Allow to harden overnight if possible.) Draw circle around center with knife; use spoon to scoop out center of mold. Melt this consomme very slowly. Meanwhile, have cream cheese at room temperature. Cream with fork, add onion juice, sherry, salt, pepper, and plenty of paprika to taste. Fill in cavity in consomme with cheese mixture. Pour cooled consomme over all. Either chopped pecans or chopped fresh green pepper may be added also. Return to refrigerator to set. Unmold and serve with crackers or as salad. Garnish with fresh parsley.

Serves 24 people.

Mrs. Willis L. Meadows

CHIPPER'S CHOICE POTATO CHIP "DUNK"

4 strips lean bacon
1 garlic bud
1 7-ounce can minced clams
½ teaspoon dried basil
2 teaspoons cornstarch
½ cup tomato puree
¼ teaspoon salt
⅛ teaspoon pepper
2 tablespoons Parmesan cheese
2 teaspoons parsley flakes

Cut bacon into ½ inch strips. Saute bacon and garlic (minced) over low heat until crisp. Drain off all but 2 teaspoons drippings. Add clams, basil and cornstarch. Blend well. Then add tomato puree, salt and pepper. Heat, stirring frequently, until mixture thickens. Stir in cheese and parsley flakes. Use clam juice to thin if needed. Serve hot in chafing dish or just **Hot** with chips.

Makes about 1¼ cups.

Mrs. John W. Paylor, Jr.
Mrs. Donald Ewing

CRAB DIP

2 8-ounce packages cream cheese
1 1-pound can white crab meat
1 teaspoon Worcestershire sauce
Juice of ½ lemon
6 or 8 chopped green onions (tops and bottoms)
Salt and red pepper to taste

Heat crab meat and lemon juice in double boiler and work in cream cheese. Add other ingredients. Place in refrigerator. Thin to desired consistency with milk or cream when ready to serve. Serve cold. Excellent with Melba toast rounds. Make this ahead for improved flavor.

Mrs. Clarence B. Erickson, Jr.

CORNED BEEF TOASTIES

1 can corned beef
½ pound New York State sharp cheese, grated
4 teaspoons mustard
Juice of one medium onion (grated)
2 to 4 tablespoons Worcestershire sauce
1 cup mayonnaise
Salt to taste

Finely mash corned beef. Soften at room temperature. Add grated cheese, onion juice, mustard, Worcestershire sauce, mayonnaise and salt. Mix thoroughly. Spread mixture between slices of bread. Trim edges of bread. Cut in quarters or triangles and place on cookie sheet or toast sheet and toast slowly in 250° to 300° oven, turning at intervals until crisp and lightly browned. Serve piping hot. The men love these!

Mrs. Silas W. Davis

HOT CRAB DIP

2 onions (chopped)
1 bell pepper (chopped)
5 stalks celery (chopped)
2 small cans crab meat
3 cans mushroom soup
½ cup Parmesan cheese
Worcestershire sauce, Tabasco, salt, pepper and parsley flakes to taste

Saute in saucepan onions, bell pepper and celery. Add crab meat and let all cook down. Add mushroom soup and cheese to mixture; season well and simmer for about 15 minutes. Serve in a chafing dish.

Serves a crowd.

Mrs. Albert L. Dietz, Jr.

COCKTAIL CRAB QUICHE

1 recipe pie pastry (frozen pastry shells may be thawed, rolled slightly thinner and cut for tart shells)
8 tablespoons Parmesan cheese, grated
8 tablespoons lump crab meat, flaked
8 tablespoons Swiss or Gruyere cheese, grated
2 eggs (separate 1 egg)
¾ cup light cream
½ teaspoon salt
¼ teaspoon pepper

Using two small muffin pans (twelve cups each), line each cup with pastry and brush with one lightly beaten egg white. Bake in 400° oven for 5 minutes. Into each cup, sprinkle 1 teaspoon Parmesan cheese, then add 1 teaspoon crab meat and 1 teaspoon Swiss or Gruyere cheese. Heat cream, add one egg and one yolk, beaten. Blend well, season with salt and pepper. Pour into tarts, dividing equally. Bake in 325° oven for 15-18 minutes, until lightly browned.

Makes 24 tarts.

Mrs. Gordon Lambert

CRAB MEAT AND CUCUMBER CANAPES

1 cup crab meat
Small amount mayonnaise
1 loaf bread
1 tablespoon butter
1 cucumber
Sprigs of parsley
Salt and pepper to taste

Shred 1 cup crab meat and mix enough mayonnaise with it to hold it together. Saute 3-inch rounds of bread in butter until lightly browned. Peel and thinly slice cucumber. Place a slice on each round of toast. Season with salt and pepper and spread on top of the cucumber a layer of crab meat mixture. Place the canapes in a pan and broil until light brown. Garnish with sprigs of parsley and serve hot.

Makes about 40 canapes.

Mrs. Robert Brown

HORSERADISH DIP

1 8-ounce package cream cheese
2 tablespoons milk
2 tablespoons prepared horseradish
¼ teaspoon Worcestershire sauce
Dash of salt
Paprika

Combine cream cheese and milk, blending until smooth. Add horseradish, Worcestershire sauce and salt. Mix well. Sprinkle with paprika and serve with corn chips.

Mrs. Marshall Martin

SMOKED ALMONDS

Soak 2 cups unblanched almonds in ½ cup liquid smoke for 20 minutes. Drain well. Spead almonds on a baking sheet and toast in a very slow oven, 250°, until crisp (about one hour). While nuts are hot, brush them with melted butter and salt to taste. Drain on paper towels.

Makes 1 pint smoked nuts. These keep well stored in tightly covered jar.

Mrs. Marshall Martin

CHICKEN LIVER PATE

2 pounds fresh chicken livers
1 pound butter (or ½ pound butter and ½ pound rendered chicken fat)
½ teaspoon nutmeg
1 teaspoon pepper
1 tablespoon salt
2 large onions chopped and put in blender with ½ cup red wine

Pat chicken livers dry. Saute slowly in butter. Cook about 15 minutes. With fork and sharp knife, cut into little pieces. Continue cooking until all signs of blood are gone. Add wine-onion mixture. Add seasonings. Cook 15 minutes more. Cool. Pack in small crocks. Pour additional melted butter over top. This keeps well in refrigerator or may be frozen.

Mrs. James R. Alexander

MARINATED MUSHROOMS

¾ cup salad oil
¼ cup olive oil
¼ cup tarragon vinegar

Mix above ingredients plus salt, garlic pod and parsley in blender. Pour over canned button mushrooms and slice onion on top. Let stand for several hours.

Mrs. Murphy Yearwood

MUSHROOM CANAPE

1 box mushrooms
2 to 3 tablespoons butter
2 tablespoons dry sherry
2 tablespoons bourbon whisky

Broil mushrooms without stems in butter in an iron skillet over very low heat. When heated through, add sherry. When practically finished cooking, add bourbon.

Mrs. Edward H. Jackson, Jr.

NOCHE SPECIALS

Cut tortillas into quarters and fry in deep hot fat until light brown and crisp on both sides. Drain and put about 1 teaspoon grated cheese and a slice of jalapeno pepper on each quarter. Place in hot oven until well heated and cheese begins to melt. Serve at once.

Mrs. Lyndon B. Johnson, LBJ Ranch, Texas

OYSTER ROLL

2 8-ounce packages cream cheese
2 cans smoked oysters
2 teaspoons Worcestershire sauce
Garlic (1 large or 2 small pods, pressed)
Onion (½ small, pressed)
Mayonnaise, 2 to 3 tablespoons
At least ⅛ teaspoon salt

Cream enough mayonnaise into cheese to hold it together. Add Worcestershire sauce, pressed garlic and onion. Combine well. Spread about ½ inch thick on wax paper. Chop oysters and spread them on top of cheese mixture. Roll as for jelly roll, using a knife to start it. Chill for 24 hours. Serve with toast rounds or crackers.

Mrs. Robert Kimmel
U. S. Forces in Europe

PARTY MIX

½ cup bacon fat
1 stick butter
1 teaspoon garlic salt
1 teaspoon celery salt
1 teaspoon savory
2 tablespoons Tabasco
2 tablespoons Worcestershire sauce

Mix the above and pour over:

1 cup pecans
1 can peanuts
½ box Wheat Chex
½ box Rice Chex
½ box Cheerios
1 box pretzel sticks

Toast in 275° oven for 1½ to 2 hours, stirring several times.

Mrs. William N. Penton

MEXICAN MEAT BALLS

Sauce:
- 2 1-pound cans tomatoes
- 2 teaspoons salt
- 1 onion, minced
- 2 tablespoons bacon drippings
- 2 tablespoons chili powder
- 1 cup water

Meat Balls:
- 2 pounds ground meat
- 1 cup corn meal
- 2 or 3 teaspoons salt (according to taste)
- 2 or 3 tablespoons chili powder
- ¾ cup sauce (enough to form meat into balls)

Combine all ingredients for sauce in saucepan, cover and cook slowly over direct heat, while you prepare meat mixture, for 20 to 30 minutes.

Combine all meat ball ingredients and make into balls either 2" in diameter for family or meal use, or into balls 1" in diameter for hors d'ouvres. Place meat balls in sauce, cover and simmer until done, 30 to 45 minutes. Serve plain or with spaghetti, macaroni, hot limp tortillas, or fluffy spoon bread.

Yields 2 dozen family meat balls or 4 dozen hors d'ouvres. This meat dish may be prepared in advance and re-heated, or frozen after cooking in sauce. Meat balls may also be frozen separately to be cooked later.

Mrs. Drew Liddell

SARDINE DIP

- 2 cans sardines
- 3 hard cooked eggs
- 1 tablespoon minced parsley
- 1 tablespoon minced onions
- 1 tablespoon prepared mustard
- ½ cup mayonnaise
- ½ cup creamy processed American cheese
- 1 tablespoon Worcestershire sauce
- Salt and pepper to taste
- ½ pint heavy cream

Drain and mash sardines. Put eggs through sieve. Combine all ingredients in double boiler or chafing dish. Add heavy cream until desired consistency is reached.

Mrs. Robert E. King

SLANG JANG

- 1 can cove oysters
- 1 small can tomatoes or fresh tomatoes in season
- 1 small onion chopped fine
- 1 small green pepper chopped fine

Mix together the above ingredients and cover with white vinegar. Season to taste.

Makes 8 medium servings. Slang Jang may be prepared and served immediately, but it is better to let it stand in the refrigerator overnight to chill.

Mrs. Paul E. Osburn, Jr.

SPINACH AND CRAB MEAT

2 packages frozen chopped spinach
Green onions and tops
Shredded Parmesan cheese
1 stick butter
Garlic powder
Salt and pepper
Tabasco sauce
White crab meat

Saute onions and tops, chopped fine, in butter. Cook spinach slightly; drain well. Add other ingredients to taste, and serve in chafing dish with crackers or party rye bread.

Served as cocktail, this yields 50 dips; on toast for luncheon, it serves about 8.

Mrs. Paul D. Abramson

MARINATED SHRIMP

10 pounds shrimp in shell or 6 pounds peeled and deveined shrimp
8 large lemons
6 large onions
1 pint sour cream
½ cup mayonnaise
3 teaspoons salt
1 teaspoon cayenne pepper

Boil shrimp in water seasoned with 2 teaspoons red pepper, 1 tablespoon salt, and 3 lemons cut in quarters. If using shrimp in shells, bring water to a boil and allow to cook 5 minutes. Then drain, cool and peel. When using peeled and deveined shrimp, put in cold water, allow to come to a boil and remove immediately.

To prepare marinade, slice onions and 8 lemons as thinly as possible. Mix sour cream, mayonnaise and seasonings. Place boiled shrimp, onions, lemons, and sour cream mixture in large covered bowl, being sure that all are thoroughly coated with sour cream mixture. Refrigerate and allow to marinate for 24 hours, turning occasionally. Before serving, remove lemon slices and some of the onions. Makes a delicious and attractive addition to a cocktail table, or may be served as a salad for luncheon.

Serves a large cocktail party or yields 12 luncheon salads.

Mrs. William Junkin

QUICK SHRIMP DIP

1 8-ounce can shrimp
Lemon juice to taste
1 teaspoon grated onion
Worcestershire sauce to taste
Mayonnaise

Drain shrimp and rinse well in cold water. Devein if necessary. Crumble shrimp very fine with fingers. Add other ingredients and mix until desired consistency is reached.

This may be served with chips as a dip, or with crackers as a spread. The amount of mayonnaise determines the thickness. Serves 6-8 people.

Mrs. Towner J. Pringle

MARINATED SHRIMP

2½ pounds shrimp
Celery tops
3½ teaspoons salt
¼ cup mixed pickling spices
2 cups onions, sliced
7 or 8 bay leaves

Marinade:
1¼ cups salad oil
¾ cup white vinegar
1½ teaspoons salt
2½ teaspoons celery seed
2½ tablespoons capers and juice
Tabasco to taste

Boil shrimp 10 minutes with celery, salt and spices. Drain, cool and devein. Alternate shrimp and sliced onions in shallow dish. Add bay leaves. Combine ingredients of marinade and mix well. Pour over shrimp and onions. Cover and store in refrigerator at least 24 hours. (The longer, the better.) Will keep 5 or 6 days.

Mrs. John W. Paylor, Jr.

SHRIMP PEANUT BUTTER

Cream together 2 tablespoons peanut butter and 2 tablespoons butter. Add 1 teaspoon curry powder and ⅛ teaspoon salt. Spread on rounds of white or whole-wheat bread. Split 6 cooked shrimp lengthwise and put half a shrimp on each round. Sprinkle with paprika, and serve very cold.

Mrs. Staunton B. Sample

SHRIMP DIP

1 cup peeled shrimp, chopped fine
2 8-ounce packages cream cheese
½ cup mayonnaise
1 tablespoon grated onion
½ cup bottled steak sauce with 2 teaspoons horseradish added
1 tablespoon Worcestershire sauce
1 or 2 dashes hot sauce
Pinch of salt

Whip ingredients in order given until light and creamy. Fresh vegetables are excellent with this dip.

Mrs. Robert E. King
Mrs. David Stell

"SAUCE FOR DUNKING"

½ pound butter, melted
ADD:
Juice of 1 lemon
1 tablespoon soy sauce
1 tablespoon Worcestershire sauce
1 tablespoon tarragon vinegar
3 dashes Tabasco

Heat all ingredients to simmering point. **DO NOT BOIL.** Serve hot as dip for shrimp or artichokes.

MAKE AHEAD SHRIMP DIP

3 cups mayonnaise (NOT salad dressing)
½ cup catsup
3 grated hard boiled eggs
½ large dill pickle, chopped fine
¼ cup finely chopped, stuffed green olives
½ cup celery, chopped fine
2 cups chopped cooked shrimp

Mix all above ingredients **the day before** serving to bring out shrimp flavor. If you do not, you will have to use more shrimp. More mayonnaise may be added later if it is too thick.

Mrs. Arthur James Ferguson

EASY HOT SHRIMP DIP

1 can frozen cream of shrimp soup
1 roll garlic cheese
1 can shrimp, drained
1 8-ounce can mushrooms, drained
Sherry

Melt soup and cheese in double boiler over low heat. Add finely chopped shrimp and mushrooms. Thin with sherry to desired consistency before serving. Serve in chafing dish.

Mrs. Raymond F. Kayser, Jr.

SAUSAGE ROLLS

2 cups flour
½ teaspoon salt
3 teaspoons baking powder
5 tablespoons shortening
⅔ cup milk
1 pound well seasoned sausage

Sift flour with salt and baking powder; cut in shortening until mixture resembles coarse crumbs; add milk all at once and mix. Divide dough into two parts; roll each out ¼ inch thick. Spread with sausage. Roll up as for jelly roll; repeat with remaining dough. Wrap in waxed paper and chill in refrigerator. When ready to serve, slice ⅓ or ¼ inch thick and bake in 400° oven for 5 or 10 minutes. Nice for morning parties.

Mrs. Harold Bicknell

HAM SANDWICH SPREAD

1 4½-ounce can deviled ham
3 chopped hard cooked eggs
½ cup celery, minced
⅓ cup onions, minced
3 tablespoons chili sauce
¼ cup mayonnaise
½ teaspoon salt
¼ teaspoon pepper

Combine ingredients. Mix well, chill and spread on buttered bread. Makes 1½ cups.

Mrs. Sidney E. Cook

CURRIED TUNA DIP

1 teaspoon instant minced onion
1½ teaspoons lemon juice
1 6½-ounce can tuna, drained
½ cup mayonnaise
¾ teaspoon curry powder
1 5-ounce can water chestnuts, drained and minced
Salt and pepper

Let onion stand in lemon juice five minutes. Combine remaining ingredients with lemon juice and onion, adding salt and pepper to taste. Heat in chafing dish and serve with favorite crackers.

Serves approximately 15 to 20.

Mrs. Matthew H. Miller

ZWEIBELKUCHEN (BACON AND ONION PIE)

16 strips bacon
4 large yellow onions, chopped
2 eggs plus 1 yolk
¾ cup sour cream
Salt and pepper to taste
Caraway seeds
2 8-inch pastry shells half baked at 400°

Fry bacon until very crisp. Drain, crumble, and set aside. In 3 tablespoons fat fry onions until soft and yellow. To onions add beaten eggs, and yolk, sour cream, salt and pepper. Add crumbled bacon. Pour mixture into pie shells and sprinkle with caraway seeds. Bake at 350° until centers are firm, 20-30 minutes. This may be prepared a day ahead but not baked.

Makes 2 8-inch pies.

Mrs. Melvin F. Johnson

CHRISTMAS TIDBIT SANDWICH

4 3-ounce packages cream cheese
Salad dressing, added to spreading consistency
2 teaspoons Worcestershire sauce
5 or 6 drops Tabasco
Garlic powder to taste
2 loaves extra thin sliced sandwich bread
3 jars sliced pimientos
3 large green peppers, sliced thin, lengthwise

Cream salad dressing into cream cheese until very smooth and easy to spread. Add Worcestershire sauce, Tabasco and garlic powder; mix well. Cut crusts off bread. Spread cream cheese on bread. Alternate 1 pimiento, 1 pepper slice, etc. until you have 3 of each on bread. Start rolling edges and hold pepper as you roll up sandwich. Wrap in waxed paper, twisting ends of paper tightly. Refrigerate overnight.

This mixture is sufficient for about 36 slices of bread. Will make 5 or 6 bite-size sandwiches per slice of bread.

Mrs. Tigner Walker

CRAB MEAT SANDWICHES

½ pound Swiss cheese
½ can ripe olives
2 7-ounce cans crab meat
Tabasco (a dash or so if desired)
1 teaspoon Worcestershire sauce
Salt to taste
Mayonnaise (to hold all together)

Grate cheese and chop olives. Mix all ingredients together and spread on buttered toasted bread or finger rolls. Heat and serve.

Makes 12 large sandwiches.

Mrs. Charles H. Jeter

CHICKEN AND NUT SANDWICHES

2 cups white meat of roast chicken
½ can French mushrooms (stems and pieces may be substituted)
½ cup English walnuts, chopped fine
Salt and pepper to taste
Melted butter
Whole-wheat bread

Mince chicken. Mix with mushrooms and nuts, and season with salt and pepper. Moisten with melted butter. Spread between slices of whole-wheat bread.

Makes approximately 12 sandwiches.

Mrs. Overton Brooks

WATER CRESS TEA SANDWICHES

½ cup butter
½ cup finely chopped water cress
1 teaspoon grated onion
1 teaspoon Worcestershire sauce
½ teaspoon salt
Dash Tabasco
Thinly sliced cucumber

Combine softened butter with next five ingredients. Spread on very thinly sliced rounds of white bread. Add a paper thin slice of cucumber to each sandwich and top with another bread round.

This makes about 3 dozen 1½-inch sandwiches.

Mrs. Sinclair Kouns

Grind up leftover meats, bind with gravy, and use to stuff undercooked oversized macaroni (manicotti) for an hors d'oeuvre. Add a cheese sauce and bake until hot and bubbly for main dish.

Pat cheese straw pastry into nut-sized rounds, insert an olive, a mushroom, water chestnut, etc., and enclose. Put them on a tin in your freezer. Bake in hot oven for 15 minutes for a quickie snack when company drops in.

Frozen juice cans make handy biscuit cutters for party sized tidbits.

Soups & Salads

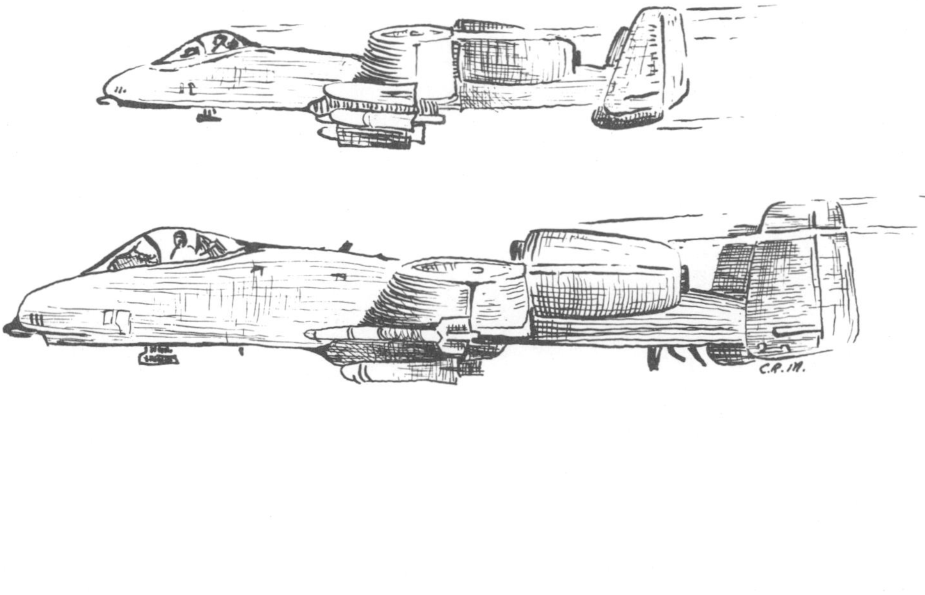

Barksdale Air Force Base

BARKSDALE AIR FORCE BASE

One of the largest air bases in the world and now headquarters of Air Force Global Strike Command, 8th Air Force, the Second Bomb Wing, and the Air Force Reserve's 307th Wing. The base has more than 11,000 feet of runways, 56 miles of paved roads and 4 million square feet of floor space. More than 8,000 military personnel and their families live and work on the base, which is also home to B-52 bombers, A-10 ground support fighters and a major training and air force combat exercise center. The 8th Air Force Museum is open to the public and offers an impressive collection of fighters, bombers and support craft from WWI to the present.

GAZPACHO (Famous Floating Salad from the Hills of Andalusia)

1 package tomato soup mix or can of tomato soup
5 cups water
1 cup V-8 juice (optional)
4 small tomatoes, peeled and chopped
¼ cup finely chopped green bell pepper
¼ cup finely chopped celery
⅓ cup herb or Italian dressing
1 small onion sliced and separated into rings
½ medium cucumber, thinly sliced
½ teaspoon salt
⅛ teaspoon pepper
Dash of garlic salt, Tabasco and Worcestershire sauce

Put soup mix or soup into medium saucepan. Stir in water, heat and bring to boil. Simmer 4 or 5 minutes. Pour into bowl and refrigerate until partially chilled. Add the balance of the ingredients, except cucumbers. Mix well. When thoroughly chilled, add cucumbers and serve.

Makes 8 to 10 servings. Delicious served ice cold as a salad, appetizer or soup.

Do not freeze.

Francis S. Randall

BLENDER GAZPACHO

2 cloves garlic
4 tomatoes
2 medium onions, chopped
2 green peppers, seeded
2 cucumbers
1 egg
¼ cup red wine vinegar
¼ teaspoon salt
Dash cayenne pepper
¾ cup tomato juice
¼ cup olive oil
2 tablespoons margarine
1 cup croutons

In electric blender combine garlic cloves, peeled tomatoes, 1 onion, 1 green pepper, 1 cucumber. Add next six ingredients, reserving croutons and margarine. Chill well. Brown croutons in margarine. Serve in soup plates garnished with remaining chopped vegetables and croutons.

Mrs. Podge Reed

QUICK CREAM OF CLAM SOUP

Heat 4 cups milk slowly and add 1 chopped onion which has been sauteed in 2 tablespoons butter. Add 1 tablespoon chopped parsley, 1 teaspoon celery seed, a pinch of saffron and salt to taste. When milk is hot, but not boiling, add 1 can minced clams and their liquor.

Mrs. Staunton B. Sample

CHINESE GULLA SOUP (Small Pot)

Chop fine so all together equals 1½ cups:

Green onion
Green pepper
Cabbage
Cucumber
Carrot
Celery
¼ cup oil
¼ cup soy sauce
2 pork chops or pork neck bones
Salt and pepper
1 teaspoon Accent
1 egg
1 teaspoon water
3 tablespoons flour

Heat oil, add chopped vegetables and cook until transparent. Add soy sauce and cook for 10 minutes, then add amount of water needed for desired dilution. Add pork, and season to taste. Cook for 2 hours. Mix with a fork: 1 egg, 1 teaspoon water, 3 tablespoons flour, and add to boiling soup. Serve immediately. For a change, add vinegar to make a sour soup.

Mrs. Robert Hase

CORN CHOWDER

1 ½-inch cube salt pork, cut small
1 small onion, sliced
4 potatoes, cubed or sliced
2 cups water
2 cups cream style corn
4 cups scalded milk
Salt and pepper
3 tablespoons butter

Saute pork in deep pan and add onion. Cook slowly for 5 minutes, stirring often. Remove the onion and pork, but crisp bits of salt pork and onion are delicious if left in. Add potatoes and water to fat. Cook until soft. Add corn and milk. Heat, season and add butter.

Serves 6 to 8 generously.

Charlotte Merriam

CUCUMBER SOUP

2 cups coarsely chopped cucumber
1 cup each chicken broth and light cream
¼ cup each of chopped chives and celery leaves
3 sprigs parsley
2 tablespoons each of soft butter and flour
Finely chopped cucumber and lemon rind, or chopped dill

In the container of a blender combine cucumber, chicken broth, light cream, chives, celery leaves, parsley, butter and flour. Cover the container and blend the mixture until smooth. Heat soup over low heat until it reaches a boil and season with salt and pepper to taste. Serve hot garnished with chopped dill, or serve cold garnished with finely chopped cucumber and grated lemon rind.

Serves 4.

Mrs. Charles Edward Porter

JELLIED GRAPEFRUIT AND AVOCADO BISQUE

2 avocados
¼ cup heavy cream
¼ cup grapefruit juice
1 teaspoon salt
½ teaspoon pepper
½ teaspoon chili powder
4 cups jellied chicken consomme
Whipped cream and grapefruit sections for garnish

Peel avocados and force pulp through a fine sieve. Add cream and grapefruit juice to pulp and blend until thick and smooth. Season with salt, pepper and chili powder. Combine pureed mixture and jellied chicken consomme and beat with a fork or in a blender. (If blended, allow to cool before serving). Serve the soup in chilled cups, garnished with whipped cream and grapefruit sections.

Makes 5 servings. An especially nice first course in summer, but good any time of year.

Mrs. J. Edward Lytle

BAKED ONION SOUP

3 pounds purple onions
6 beef bouillon cubes
1 loaf French bread
10 cups water
2-3 tablespoons salt
Parmesan cheese

Slice onions into rings and saute in butter for about 15 minutes until they soften. Melt bouillon cubes in one cup water and add to onion rings and 9 cups water. Slice bread and break into small pieces and submerge in water. Bring mixture to boil and cook over lowest possible flame for 5 or 6 hours. Can cook 9 or 10 hours and longer — cooking improves flavor. Toward end of cooking add salt. Ladle the thick soup into baking dishes. Sprinkle with thick layer of dry grated Parmesan cheese. Place under broiler until cheese melts and develops a gold crust.

Serves six.

Mrs. Claude Dinkins Smith

CREME VICHYSSOISE

1½ cups onions, chopped fine
3 cups boiling water
3 cups chopped Irish potatoes

Cook this together and then put through sieve or in blender. Add:

4 chicken bouillon cubes
1 cup light or heavy cream
1 teaspoon salt
5 tablespoons chives
3 tablespoons butter
1 cup milk
¼ teaspoon pepper
¼ teaspoon paprika

Serve either cold or hot with parsley sprinkled on top. Will freeze well.

Mrs. A. L. Wedgeworth, Jr.

SPLIT PEA POTAGE

½ pound split peas
1 small Irish potato cut in 1½-inch cubes
½ small onion cut in quarters
Ham hock or 5 or 6 pieces of ham cut in 1½-inch cubes
5 cups water
1½ tablespoons tomato catsup
1 tablespoon Worcestershire sauce

Rinse split peas and drain. Place above ingredients in boiler, cook for about 30 minutes and then season to taste with salt, pepper, and seasoning salt or garlic salt. (Cooking for 30 minutes allows you to see how salty ham is before seasoning.) Cook over low heat stirring frequently for 1 hour or until peas are mushy. If too thick add water. Fifteen minutes before removing from heat, add tomato catsup and Worcestershire sauce. Serve with piece of ham in each bowl.

Serves 6. Freezes well and may be prepared in advance. Add water and heat.

Mrs. Leroy Vogel

CRAB-SHRIMP-OKRA GUMBO

6-8 crabs, cleaned and halved
1-1½ pounds raw shrimp, cleaned and deveined
3 or 4 good sized onions
1 bunch green onions
1 bell pepper
1-1½ pounds okra, cut crosswise
1 cup finely chopped parsley
6 cloves garlic
4-5 bay leaves
1 teaspoon thyme
1 teaspoon black pepper
1 tablespoon salt
1-1½ tablespoons tomato paste
6 dashes Tabasco sauce
1 teaspoon Accent

First, have chopped and ready in 3 separate bowls: 1. green onions (tops), white onions, garlic, bell peppers; 2. okra; 3. parsley. Put 3 quarts water into large pot, add salt, pepper, bay leaves, thyme and crabs, and place on burner to bring to a boil. Into a large iron skillet or chicken fryer, put about ¾ cup salad oil and 6 tablespoons flour. Cook over slow heat, stirring constantly with wooden spoon until the mixture is thickened and very brown (about 20 minutes). Then add contents of bowl 1 and saute until limp. Add tomato paste. If too thick, add a cup or two of the boiling crab water. Then pour this into the pot of boiling crabs.

Now fry okra in a little salad oil until slightly brown, then add raw shrimp and saute for 5 or 10 minutes longer. Pour this into pot of boiling crabs. Let boil slowly for about 45 minutes or an hour. About 10 minutes before serving, add chopped parsley, Tabasco sauce and Accent.

Serves 12 generously.

Dr. E. C. St. Martin

CRAB BISQUE

1 can tomato soup
1 can green pea soup
1 cup chicken or beef bouillon
½ cup milk
½ cup cream
¼ teaspoon pepper
½ teaspoon salt
1 carton fresh crab meat (or 1 can)
3 to 8 tablespoons sherry

Mix all the liquid ingredients and the seasonings. 1 cup milk may be used in place of the chicken bouillon for a more creamy bisque. Just before serving add the crab meat to heat through. Keep it in large pieces to serve in each bowl.

Serves 4 to 6 generously.

Mrs. Robert E. King
Mrs. Campbell Hutchinson
Mrs. John Norris
Mrs. Robert S. Picard

CRAWFISH BISQUE I

5 pounds large crawfish
4 to 6 small red peppers
1 cup white wine
STUFFING FOR HEADS:
2 cups stale bread
1 tablespoon lard
1 onion, minced
2 tablespoons green onions, chopped
2 cloves garlic, minced
2 teaspoons parsley, minced
1 egg, beaten
Salt and pepper to taste
SOUP:
2 tablespoons flour
2 tablespoons butter
1 onion, minced
1 cup tomatoes
1 quart crawfish liquid
2 teaspoons minced parsley
1 sprig thyme
2 bay leaves
Salt and pepper
1 tablespoon Worcestershire sauce
½ cup sherry or white wine

Place crawfish in strong salt water for 30 minutes. Wash with plain water and plunge into boiling water, well seasoned with salt and red peppers. Add white wine. Boil 5 minutes. Cool and clean heads. Clean and grind meat from tails.

STUFFING: Drop bread in water and squeeze dry. Saute onions in lard. Add remaining ingredients except egg. Cook 5 minutes, stirring. Remove from heat and add egg. Stuff heads with mixture. Roll heads in flour and fry in deep fat until brown. Drain well.

SOUP: Brown flour in butter. Add remaining ingredients except Worcestershire sauce and wine. Boil 10 minutes, and then strain. Add Worcestershire sauce and crawfish heads. Simmer 15 minutes, add wine, simmer 3 minutes more and serve. Takes all day to prepare. Serve over rice with salad and French bread.

Makes 4 to 6 servings.

Mrs. Francis Kalmbach

SPLIT PEA SOUP

½ pound ham hock or link sausage
1 pound package of dried split peas
1 large onion, chopped fine
3 stalks celery, chopped fine
1 cup parsley, chopped fine
3 quarts water
1½ teaspoons salt
1 teaspoon black pepper
1 clove of garlic

Soak peas in water overnight. Drain well, discard water. Saute ham or sausage in heavy skillet to render the fat slightly, then remove the meat. In the rendered fat gently saute onion, celery and parsley until tender. Add water, drained split peas and garlic, pureed or finely chopped. Add ham or sausage when mixture begins to boil. Reduce flame, add salt and pepper, and cook for one and one half or two hours, or until peas have completely disintegrated. Correct the seasoning to taste, and serve with finely chopped parsley sprinkled on top of each bowlful.

Serves 6-8 generously.

Mrs. William J. Nesbitt

SPINACH SOUP WITH CHEESE

1 14-ounce package frozen chopped spinach
2 tablespoons butter
1 very small onion, grated or chopped fine
3 tablespoons flour
1 10½-ounce can chicken broth
2 cups milk
1 cup light cream
½ teaspoon salt, approximately
Dash of nutmeg (optional)
Roquefort or blue cheese, crumbled

Cook spinach, covered, until tender, then puree in blender. Melt butter, add onion and saute about three minutes. Blend in flour. Add broth and spinach and simmer about two minutes. Add milk and cream. Season with salt and nutmeg. Heat. Serve sprinkled with cheese.

Serves 5 or 6.

Laura Anne Brooks
Mrs. Melvin F. Johnson

SHRIMP SOUP

1 can frozen cream of shrimp soup
1½ cans milk
1 small tomato, finely chopped and peeled
½ cup crab meat (canned will do)
2 teaspoons good sherry
Whipped cream
Paprika

Heat soup, milk and tomato. Add crab, heat again. Remove from fire and add sherry. Chill thoroughly. Serve in soup cups with blob of whipped cream sprinkled with paprika.

Serves 4 as a luncheon dish, 6 as a first course. May be prepared the day before.

Mrs. Ned Wilson

BLACK-EYED PEA SOUP

½ pound dried black-eyed peas (wash and pick peas thoroughly)
1 large onion, chopped
1 can tomatoes (1½-2 cups)
Ham hock or ham seasoning or bacon drippings or margarine (optional)
Worcestershire sauce
Tabasco
Salt
Pepper

Soak black-eyed peas for 2 hours in water to cover. Bring to boil. Add onion, salt, pepper, tomatoes. and meat seasoning if desired. Cover and simmer for 1½ hours or until peas disintegrate. Cool; mash through sieve or put through blender (meat and all). Add Worcestershire sauce and Tabasco. Cook slowly for 20 minutes. If too thick, you may add water and seasonings to taste.

Makes 6 servings. May be prepared and kept for several days in refrigerator. A good source of protein.

Mrs. J. Bennett Johnston, Jr.

HOMEMADE VEGETABLE SOUP

1 can (No. 303) tomatoes (peeled)
1 can (No. 303) okra and tomatoes
3 pounds lean, boneless stew meat
1 medium size soup bone
2 large carrots
5 pieces of celery
1 cup fresh cut-up string beans or 1 can cut beans
2 medium or 1 large white onion
¼ head small cabbage
1 large white potato
¼ pound spaghetti
Salt and garlic salt to taste

Into a large heavy stewing pot place a gallon of cold water, soup bone and stew meat, which has been cut into small pieces. Add salt and garlic salt. Let these ingredients boil, skimming frequently until contents are clear. Grate or cut fine carrots, potatoes, and cabbage. Cut onions and celery fine. Break spaghetti into small pieces. Add spaghetti, vegetables, canned tomatoes and okra and tomatoes to meat. Cover and cook slowly until meat is very tender. Stir occasionally to keep from sticking. When done add pepper, and more salt, if desired.

This recipe will serve 10 or more. Serve with French bread, a salad, if you like, and apple pie makes a good dessert.

Mrs. F. H. Pinson

INSTANT VICHYSSOISE

1 package instant mashed potatoes (2 envelopes)
2 cups water (hot)
2 cups diced onions
1 stick butter
1 quart boiling water
3 tablespoons yellow base chicken stock (or 4 chicken bouillon cubes)
3 cups milk
1 teaspoon salt (no salt if you use yellow base chicken stock)
1 teaspoon white pepper
1 pint whipping cream
½ cup snipped chives
½ cup parsley

Mix together instant potatoes and water. Reserve. Cook onions in butter until soft and golden, but not browned. Add boiling water mixed with yellow base chicken stock or bouillon cubes. Cook 15 minutes. Add reserved mashed potatoes. Cook 5 minutes. Force through a sieve. Return to kettle. Add milk and seasonings. Bring to a boil, then simmer 5 minutes. Strain again through fine sieve. Chill. Add cream, parsley and chives. Serve very, very cold.

Mrs. James R. Alexander

WILD DUCK GUMBO

2 or 3 wild ducks, cut as for frying (use poule d'eau, bluebill, spoonbill, etc., rather than good roasting ducks)
½ cup flour
½ cup cooking oil
2 onions, chopped
4 celery stalks and tops, chopped
1 bell pepper, chopped
1 pod of garlic, minced
Few sprigs parsley, minced
2½ quarts warm water
2 bay leaves
1 teaspoon salt
2 tablespoons file'
Black pepper
Cayenne pepper
1 pint oysters
4 crabs or 1 cup crab meat
½ pound cooked shrimp

Using a heavy iron skillet or Dutch oven, make a roux by heating oil and adding flour. Blend and stir until flour is well browned. Add garlic, onions, bell pepper, celery and parsley, cook for five minutes; add duck, cook until lightly browned. Stir in water slowly, add bay leaves, salt and pepper to taste. Cover and simmer about two hours or until duck is tender. Add oysters and liquor, crabs, shrimp and file. Cook uncovered, thirty minutes. Correct seasonings as desired. Serve on plain or wild rice.

Main dish serves 6; first course, 10. May be prepared several days in advance and kept refrigerated or may be frozen after cooling.

. Mrs. Gordon Lambert

CRAWFISH BISQUE II

- 20 pounds fresh crawfish or about 3 pounds cleaned tails (be sure to get cleaned heads too for stuffing)
- 1 stick butter or oleo or ½ cup cooking oil
- ½ cup flour
- 2 cups chopped onions
- 1 cup chopped celery
- 1 cup chopped bell pepper
- 2 whole bunches green onions and tops, chopped
- ½ can whole tomatoes
- 1 tablespoon tomato paste
- 4 cloves garlic, minced
- 4 tablespoons chopped parsley
- 3 quarts water
- Salt, pepper and Tabasco to taste
- Thyme, Worcestershire sauce and bay leaves to taste
- ½ loaf French bread, toasted and pounded into crumbs
- 2 whole eggs

Scald crawfish. Peel crawfish tails, save meat and fat (yellow substance). Clean heads of foreign matter and save the head shells. Soak head shells in soda water until ready to use. NOTE: These are used later for stuffing and placing in each portion of bisque served. Make a roux with butter, oleo or oil or fat from crawfish, and the flour. Add 3 quarts of water, onions, celery, whole tomatoes, tomato paste, garlic, bell peppers, thyme, Worcestershire sauce, bay leaves and crawfish tails. Add Tabasco, salt and pepper to taste and simmer for 30 minutes or until tender. Add green onions and tops and parsley to bisque. Cool for about 15 minutes more.

Remove a portion (about ⅓) of the bisque mixture and mix with bread crumbs and beaten egg. (The amount mixed depends on the number of head shells to be stuffed.) Stuff heads with mixture and place in moderate oven until crisp and golden brown. Remove and add to bisque. Allow at least 6 heads per serving. Serve the bisque over steamed rice in soup bowls and place the stuffed heads as a crown on top of the bisque and rice. A green salad and light white wine round out an excellent meal.

Serves 8 to 12. May be frozen easily in well-covered plastic freezer containers. Heads and gravy may be frozen separately if desired.

P. J. Mills, Jr.

PAN ROAST OYSTERS

- 2 quarts oysters
- 1 quart cream
- 1 quart milk
- 3 sticks butter (not oleo)
- 1 bottle chili sauce
- 2 tablespoons Worcestershire sauce
- Salt and pepper to taste

Simmer butter, condiments and oysters together until oysters are plump. Heat milk and cream together and add to oysters. Bring just to boiling and serve on dry toast in soup bowls. To keep from separating, have both oysters and milk combinations the same temperature when putting together.

Mrs. Gene D. Scott

OYSTER BISQUE

1 pint oysters
1 chicken bouillon cube
1 teaspoon grated onion
1 large sprig parsley
1 bay leaf
3 tablespoons butter
4 tablespoons flour
1 quart half and half (cream and milk)
¾ teaspoon salt
Dash of pepper
½ pint whipping cream

Chop oysters fine (this releases all the flavor and makes a strongly flavored bisque) and pour oysters and liquor in a saucepan. Add bouillon cube, onion, parsley and bay leaf. Cook gently for about three minutes. Melt butter in top of large double boiler, add flour and stir until blended. Add half and half gradually and cook until thickened. Stir constantly. Add oyster mixture, salt, pepper, and then stir in whipping cream. Reheat and serve after removing parsley and bay leaf. This may be made ahead as it keeps nicely for two days.

Serves 6.

Mrs. Allen Dickson

MELL'S GUMBO

1 cup bacon fat
2½ cups flour
5 pounds shrimp, cleaned and shelled
5 pounds cracked crab or 2 pounds crab meat (the crab shells give marvelous flavor. If you don't want to work with live crabs, the boxed crab claws are a good substitute)
1 thick slice ham
1 whole bunch celery, chopped
2 large onions, chopped
4 to 5 pods garlic, chopped
Bunch of green onions
Parsley
Red pepper pods
Tabasco
4 or 5 cans tomato sauce
2 pounds okra, chopped
2½ tablespoons file dissolved in water

Make a dark brown roux using 1 cup bacon fat and 2½ cups flour in a very large pot or skillet. Add chopped celery, onions, garlic, okra and cook until tender. Transfer to soup pot or large (10 to 12 quart) pan. Add tomato sauce, ham, green onions, parsley, shrimp, crab, seasonings, and fill pot with water. Simmer as long as possible. Add file at last minute. **Do not let boil after adding file.**

Makes 10 to 12 quarts.

Mrs. D. Y. Smith

ANNIE LEIGH'S GUMBO

1 cup chopped onions
½ cup bell pepper
½ cup celery
2 tablespoons chopped parsley
1 large 3-pound hen, cut up
2 tablespoons fat, or more
Salt
Pepper
File
1 cup ham
1 pint oysters (or more)
1 can shrimp

Brown chicken in fat and remove chicken. Brown ham lightly in fat and remove ham. Flour all vegetables and brown in fat left in pan. Return chicken to pan and add boiling water (1 quart), salt and pepper. Add more water if needed. Simmer for an hour or so. (At this point you may remove bones from chicken and return chicken to gumbo). Before serving add oysters (let them curl), shrimp and ham. Then just before serving add 1 tablespoon file. **Do not let boil after this.** Serve in very large soup bowls with cooked rice on the side

Mrs. Thomas B. Wilson

FISH COURTBOUILLON

6 pounds red fish, cut in pieces of about 4 ounces each
2 cups flour
½ cup pure olive oil
¼ pound butter
4 pounds onions
1 bunch celery
1 head garlic
2 sweet peppers
1 bunch parsley
1 bunch onion tops
1 6-ounce can imported tomato paste
1 can tomato sauce
1 tablespoon Worcestershire sauce
1 lemon (four large slices)
2 (or 3) cups claret wine
Salt and red pepper to taste
Hot water
5 bay leaves

Make flour and olive oil roux. When well browned, add butter. When this is well browned, add onions, celery, sweet peppers and garlic which have been ground together. Add tomato paste and tomato sauce. Stir constantly throughout these steps to prevent burning.

Add about 3 quarts hot water. You may now add the following all at the same time: chopped parsley, cut-up onion tops, lemon, bay leaves, claret wine, Worcestershire sauce, salt and pepper, and about a spoonful of thyme if you have it. Let this cook slowly about 30 minutes. Add fish and it will be ready to serve in about 20 minutes. Cut large slices fresh French bread and serve with a bottle of imported white wine (chilled).

Serves 12 generously.

Mrs. E. C. St. Martin

SHRIMP SOUP de GUIGNE

1 cup cooked shrimp
2 tablespoons butter
1 small onion, chopped
Salt, pepper to taste
Pinch nutmeg
1 pint milk
1 pint cream
1 tablespoon sherry

Put shrimp and onion through a meat grinder or in blender briefly. Place in top of double boiler with butter and seasonings. Cook briefly, then add milk and cream and in about a half hour the sherry.

Mrs. Staunton B. Sample

SHRIMP MULL

2 No. 2 cans tomatoes
1 No. 2 can tomato soup
1 cup white salt bacon, diced
1 cup onion, chopped
¼ cup butter or margarine
2 cloves garlic, sliced
1 whole lemon, sliced thin
1 cup celery, chopped
1 teaspoon celery seed
15 drops Tabasco
1 bottle tomato catsup (regular)
2 tablespoons Worcestershire sauce
¼ teaspoon allspice
¼ teaspoon curry powder
5 pounds raw shrimp, peeled
1 cup sherry
¼ pound butter

In heavy kettle put 2 quarts water, canned tomatoes, and tomato soup. Simmer. Melt butter in skillet and brown bacon and onion in it. Add to tomato mixture. Add all remaining ingredients except shrimp, sherry and final butter. Simmer for 2 hours. Add shrimp and simmer for 1 hour. Add sherry and ¼ pound butter (optional). Thicken with cracker crumbs. Serve in soup bowls with rice.

Makes 8 generous servings, including seconds. I have frozen this after adding the shrimp and barely cooking it. When reheating add the sherry. Makes about 4 quarts for the freezer.

Mrs. James M. Turner

MELON-BALL COCKTAIL

1 teaspoon grated lemon peel
2 teaspoons grated orange peel
2 tablespoons lemon juice
⅔ cup orange juice
⅓ cup sugar
⅛ teaspoon salt
3 cups honeydew melon balls

Combine all above ingredients, except melon balls, in a small saucepan; bring to a boil, stirring until sugar is dissolved. Reduce heat; simmer, uncovered, 5 minutes. Chill syrup at least 2 hours. Divide the melon balls into 6 cocktail glasses. Add syrup, and garnish with sprigs of fresh mint. Cantaloupe or watermelon may be substituted for the honeydew.

Mrs. H. F. Falbaum

AMBROSIA MOLD SALAD

1 package orange-pineapple gelatin
1 tablespoon sugar
1 cup boiling water
¾ cup cold water
1 cup whipped cream
¾ cup mandarin orange sections
1¼ cup seeded halved red grapes
1 sliced banana
¾ cup fine grated coconut

Dissolve gelatin and sugar in boiling water. Add cold water. Chill until slightly thickened. Fold in whipped cream, then fold in remaining ingredients. Pour into either large mold or individual molds. Chill until firm.

Serves 8. Mrs. Claiborne Cook

APPLESAUCE SALAD

2 large oranges
Juice of 1 lemon
1 package strawberry gelatin
1 package lemon gelatin
1 No. 2½ can smooth applesauce

Dissolve strawberry and lemon gelatin together in 1 cup boiling water. Let cool; add 1 cup orange juice, the juice of 1 lemon, grated rind of 2 oranges and applesauce. Pour in molds to set. Note: If 2 oranges will not yield a cup of juice, add enough additional liquid to make full cup.

Serves 8 to 10. For party fare put spoonful of green colored mayonnaise on top with bit of parsley.

Mrs. Victor Luneborg

APRICOT SALAD IN GRAPEFRUIT CUPS

Scoop out 3 grapefruit. To 1 can apricots add equal amounts walnuts (or pecans) and grapefruit meat. Dissolve 1 package lime gelatin in 1 pint hot liquid (fruit juices and water). When cool add fruit and nuts. Put in grapefruit halves. Serve with nectar dressing.

Nectar Dressing

1 3-ounce package cream cheese
2 tablespoons honey or 3 tablespoons sugar
1½ tablespoons lemon juice
Rind of one lemon
¾ teaspoon salt
⅛ teaspoon red pepper
¾ cup cold salad oil

Mix all ingredients except oil, and then add this very slowly, one teaspoon at a time. Or mix ingredients in blender, then add oil while blending.

Serves 6. Mrs. Duncan Allen Brown

APRICOT PINEAPPLE SALAD

- 1 large can apricots, drained and finely cut
- 1 large can crushed pineapple, drained
- 2 packages orange flavored gelatin
- 2 cups boiling water
- 1 cup combined apricot and pineapple juice
- ¾ cup miniature marshmallows

Drain and chill fruit, reserving juice. Dissolve gelatin in boiling water. Add 1 cup juice, reserving rest for topping. Chill until mixture has congealed slightly. Fold in fruit and marshmallows. Pour into 9" x 11" shallow dish, chill until firm and spread with topping.

Topping

- ½ cup sugar
- 3 tablespoons flour
- 1 egg, slightly beaten
- 1 cup pineapple and apricot juice mixed
- 2 tablespoons butter
- 1 cup heavy cream, whipped
- ¾ cup grated American cheese

Combine sugar and flour; blend in egg, then gradually stir in juice. Cook over low heat until thickened, stirring constantly. Remove from heat, stir in butter. Cool. Fold in whipped cream and spread over gelatin. Sprinkle with grated cheese. Chill. Cut in squares and serve on crisp lettuce.

Mrs. John R. Mills

AVOCADO SALAD MOLD

- 1½ envelopes (1½ tablespoons) unflavored gelatin
- ½ cup cold water
- ¾ cup boiling water
- 2 tablespoons lemon juice
- 1¼ teaspoons salt
- 1 teaspoon grated onion
- 2 or 3 dashes Tabasco sauce
- 2½ cups sieved ripe avocado (canned frozen avocado may be used)
- 1 cup dairy sour cream
- 1 cup mayonnaise

Soften gelatin in cold water; dissolve in boiling water. Add lemon juice, salt, onion, and Tabasco. Cool to room temperature. Stir in avocado, sour cream and mayonnaise. Turn mixture into 6-cup mold or individual molds; chill until firm. Serve on lettuce leaf garnished with fresh fruits or tomatoes.

Makes about 8 servings.

Mrs. T. Haller Jackson, Jr.

AVOCADO SALAD

2 packages lime gelatin
2 cups boiling water
½ cup salad dressing
1 cup chopped celery
1 small grated onion
1 green pepper, minced
4 packages cream cheese, softened
2 or more mashed ripe avocados
Salt, lemon juice and Tabasco to taste

Dissolve lime gelatin in water and cool. Combine all other ingredients and add to lime gelatin. Pour into molds and chill.

Serves 16.

Mrs. Richard Langford

MOLDED BEET SALAD

1½ envelopes plain gelatin
¼ cup cold water
1 can beets and juice plus enough water to make 1½ cups liquid
6 tablespoons vinegar
½ cup sugar
½ teaspoon salt
2 hard boiled eggs, diced
2 stalks celery, diced
3 green onions, diced
1 tablespoon bell pepper, diced

Soak gelatin in cold water. Combine 1½ cups liquid, vinegar, sugar and salt. Bring this to a boil. Remove from heat and add gelatin mixture. Cool. Then add sliced beets, eggs, celery, onions and bell pepper. Pour into one large mold or individual molds. Slices of boiled egg may be put in mold first to make a design if desired.

Mrs. Edwin C. Horne

FRESH FRUIT SALAD

Fruit:
1 cup seedless grapes
1 cup diced banana
1 cup fresh or canned pineapple, diced
1 cup bing cherries, pitted
1 cup oranges, diced
1 cup cantaloupe balls
2 large plums, sliced
2 cups miniature marshmallows

Dressing:
2 egg yolks
2 tablespoons sugar
2 tablespoons orange juice
2 tablespoons vinegar
1 tablespoon butter
2 cups sour cream
Salt to taste

To make dressing, combine eggs and sugar. Mix well. Add vinegar and orange juice and cook over low heat, stirring constantly, until it thickens. Remove from heat. Stir in salt and butter and cool completely. Fold in sour cream. Chill. After the mixture has chilled, combine with marshmallows and fruits which have been thoroughly drained and refrigerate for 24 hours before using.

Mrs. Darrell P. Miller

BLUEBERRY SALAD

1 No. 1 can pineapple juice
1 No. 2 can blueberries, or frozen blueberries
2 packages lemon gelatin
1 large or 2 small bananas
½ pint whipping cream

Drain blueberries well. Combine blueberry juice and pineapple juice. Bring juice to a boil. Add gelatin. Let cool thoroughly. Add blueberries and mashed bananas. Add whipped cream and mold. Stir again when slightly thickened. Black cherries may be substituted for blueberries and nuts added, if desired.

Serves 10 or 12.

Mrs. Ray Oden, Jr.
Mrs. William Sherrill, Dallas, Texas

MINTED CANTALOUPE MOLD

2 envelopes plain gelatin
½ cup cold water
¾ cup hot water
¾ cup sugar
½ teaspoon salt
1½ to 2 tablespoons coarsely chopped fresh mint
¾ cup fresh strained lemon juice
¾ cup cantaloupe juice or cantaloupe juice and water
1 cup fresh orange juice, strained
2½ cups fresh cantaloupe balls
Fresh mint leaves for garnish
2 cups cantaloupe balls for garnish (if ring mold is used)

Soften gelatin in cold water and set aside. Mix hot water, sugar, salt, chopped mint, ¼ cup of lemon juice. Heat to boiling point. Strain and pour over gelatin; stir until dissolved. Strain cantaloupe juice from pulp around seeds. Pour into cup and add enough water to make ¾ cup. Add this to gelatin with remaining ½ cup of lemon juice and orange juice. Refrigerate, stirring often, until mixture is about as thick as egg whites and has begun to set. Fold in cantaloupe balls. Turn into 5-cup mold. Chill until firm. Unmold and garnish with mint leaves; if ring mold is used, fill center with 2 cups cantaloupe balls.

Serves 8.

Mrs. James McGregor

CHERRY SHERRY SALAD

1 package cherry gelatin
¾ cup boiling water
1 cup juice from fruit (pears or cherries)
¼ cup sherry wine
½ cup coconut cut extra fine
½ cup pecans cut extra fine
1 small can pears or jar of cherries (maraschino). These may be mixed.

Dissolve gelatin in boiling water and allow to cool. Pour sherry and juice over nuts, coconut and fruit. Let stand while gelatin is cooling. Then stir together with gelatin and pour into molds. Chill until firm. Serve as salad on lettuce or as dessert with ice cream or whipped cream.

Mrs. A. Glenn Flournoy

FROZEN FRUIT SALAD

- 1 cup mayonnaise
- 1 large or 2 small packages cream cheese
- ½-¾ cup sugar, depending on sweetness of fruit (canned or fresh)
- 1 can peeled apricots, mashed with juice
- 1 medium can crushed pineapple, well drained
- ⅓ cup maraschino cherries, chopped and little juice for color
- 1 banana chopped fine (optional)
- ⅓ cup chopped nuts (optional)

Blend in mixer the mayonnaise, cream cheese and sugar. When smooth, blend in apricots and juice. Stir in pineapple, cherries and any other fruits desired. Freeze in 2 small slightly oiled refrigerator trays. Takes 3 to 4 hours to freeze. When frozen firm, cover with foil or freezer wrap. Store in freezer. Keeps for several weeks. Remove and slice just before serving. It melts rapidly. Serve on lettuce with cherry on top.

Makes 10 to 12 servings. A nice accompaniment: small crackers brushed with melted butter, sprinkled with paprika and run under broiler just long enough to start browning. **Watch closely.**

Mrs. John Baird

TRIO MOLD SALAD

- 2 3-ounce packages cream cheese, softened
- 1 cup mayonnaise or salad dressing
- ¼ cup lemon juice
- ¼ cup granulated sugar
- ¼ teaspoon salt
- 2 cups canned pineapple tidbits, drained
- 2 cups diced orange sections, drained and snipped
- 1 cup snipped maraschino cherries
- 1 cup quartered, pitted, canned Royal Anne cherries
- 1 cup pecans, chopped
- 2 cups heavy cream
- Chicory
- Strawberries
- 1 cup heavy cream

Make, then freeze ahead, as follows: In large bowl blend soft cream cheese, mayonnaise, lemon juice, salt and sugar. Lightly mix in pineapple, orange sections, cherries, nuts and 2 cups cream, whipped. Pour into 10-inch by 4½-inch Bundt cake pan mold or mold of 3-quart capacity. Cover top of mold tightly with freezer wrap. Freeze.

To thaw: Unwrap mold; let stand in hot water 2 or 3 minutes, then unmold on serving plate. Thaw 1 hour in refrigerator.

To serve: Garnish salad with chicory and strawberries. Fill center with 1 cup cream, whipped. Use a sharp knife to cut it into wedges.

Serves 16.

Mrs. Jerry Waters

QUICK FROZEN FRUIT SALAD

2 packages cream cheese (small)
1 cup light cream
1 can mixed fruit, drained
¼ cup crushed pineapple
½ cup sliced peaches, drained
1 cup miniature marshmallows
1 banana, sliced

Combine cream cheese and cream in large bowl. Beat at medium speed until creamy. Add fruit and marshmallows to mixture slowly. Pour into two ice trays and freeze. Cut in squares and serve on lettuce with mayonnaise if desired. Other fruits (such as apricots) and of course fresh fruits are excellent for this salad.

Two trays serve 8 to 10. This is a good family salad as it can be made ahead with whatever fruit is at hand and there is usually another tray left for a later date.

Mrs. C. Walker Weston

"24 HOUR SALAD"

1 cup diced or crushed pineapple, drained
½ pound marshmallows (about 1 package "miniature" marshmallows)
1 can white cherries (pitted, "Royal Anne" type)
1 cup fresh or canned white grapes
1 cup broken nuts (pecans are best)
½ pint heavy cream, whipped
4 eggs, well beaten
Juice of 2 lemons
1 cup sugar

For dressing, cook last three ingredients in double boiler until thick. Then set aside and cool. Fold in ½ pint of heavy cream, whipped.

In a large mixing bowl mix fruit and nuts and fold into cooked dressing mixture. Add marshmallows last. Put into refrigerator for 24 HOURS. (Important!) This will "set" into an almost gelled consistency. Will keep a few days.

Serves about 10. May be used as salad or dessert.

Mrs. Hall S. Morehead
Mrs. John L. Rhea, Jr.

FROZEN CHERRY SALAD

2 3-ounce packages cream cheese
1 cup mayonnaise
1 cup heavy cream, whipped
½ cup red cherries
½ cup green cherries
2½ cups crushed pineapple
24 marshmallows, diced

Combine cream cheese and mayonnaise. Blend until smooth. Fold in whipped cream, fruit and marshmallows. Pour into 1-quart refrigerator tray or molds and freeze.

Mrs. Frank Green

FROZEN FRUIT ALASKA

1 large can fruit salad
1 medium can pitted black cherries
1 flat can pineapple, diced
1 cup diced marshmallows
1 small can salted almonds
Juice of one lemon
2 tablespoons sugar
2 tablespoons flour
1 cup heavy cream, whipped
¼ cup mayonnaise

Drain fruit and add lemon juice to fruit juice. Bring to a boil, mix flour and sugar and add to hot juice mixture which has been taken off fire. Return mixture to fire and cook until thick. Cool. Mix fruit, marshmallows and almonds with other ingredients. Fold in whipped cream. Pour into mold and freeze.

Mrs. W. T. Leeper

HEAVENLY SALAD

1 box lemon gelatin
1 box orange gelatin
1 No. 2 can crushed pineapple
3 small cans mandarin orange sections
1 large package miniature marshmallows
1 cup boiling water
½ cup chopped pecans (optional)

Combine boxes of gelatin. Add 1 cup boiling water. Add juices of pineapple and mandarins. Stir in fruit and marshmallows. Mold and refrigerate.

Topping

Whip one half pint of heavy cream. Add one cup mayonnaise and spread over top of salad. Decorate with grated cheese, nuts and cherries.

Serves 8 to 10.

Mrs. Harold K. Quinn

CONGEALED CRANBERRY SALAD

2 envelopes plain gelatin
½ cup cold water
1 8-ounce can crushed pineapple, drained
¼ cup lemon juice
1 can cranberries (whole or jellied as you prefer)
1 cup finely chopped celery
½ cup chopped nuts

Soften gelatin in cold water. Reserving pineapple, heat its juice, stir in the gelatin and water until completely dissolved, then add lemon juice and cranberry sauce. Cool and add pineapple, celery and nuts. Pour into ring mold or individual molds and chill until firm. Especially good with fowl.

Serves 8 to 10.

Mrs. W. T. Murphy, III
Mrs. Lane Sartor

BLACK CHERRY MOLD

2 tablespoons gelatin
½ cup cold water
½ cup boiling water
⅓ cup lemon juice
⅔ cup sherry or port wine
1 large can pitted black cherries
Cherry juice
¼ cup sugar
1 cup chopped pecans
Dressing:
2 3-ounce packages cream cheese
½ cup whipping cream, whipped
1 tablespoon sugar

Soak gelatin in cold water and dissolve in boiling water. Allow to cool. Drain cherries. Measure cherry juice and add enough water to make 2 cups. Add lemon juice, wine, cherries, diluted cherry juice, sugar and nuts to gelatin mixture. Mix well and pour in dampened ring mold. Refrigerate. Combine softened cream cheese with whipped cream and sugar for dressing. When ready to serve, unmold, and fill center with dressing.

Makes 8 servings. Mrs. Richard C. Eglin

RAW CRANBERRY SALAD

1 quart raw cranberries
2 oranges
1½ cups sugar
1 tablespoon plain gelatin
¼ cup cold water
2 packages raspberry gelatin
2¾ cups water
1 small can crushed pineapple, drained
1 cup chopped nuts

Day before: Put cranberries and both oranges (also use the peeling from one) through meat grinder. Add sugar and let stand overnight.

Soften plain gelatin in ¼ cup cold water. Make raspberry gelatin, using 1 cup boiling water and 1¾ cups cold water. Add plain gelatin to hot mixture, then add cranberry mixture, pineapple and nuts. Pour into 12" x 16" glass dish. Chill until firm.

Serves 15. Mrs. Robert A. Stacy, Jr.

PINEAPPLE CHERRY MOLD

1 small can sliced pineapple
1 medium can white cherries
½ cup pecans
¼ cup vinegar
½ cup sugar
Juice of 1 lemon
½ teaspoon salt
1 envelope plain gelatin

Mix juice of canned fruit, vinegar, lemon juice, sugar and salt in boiler over slow heat. Dissolve gelatin in ¼ cup water and put in boiler. Remove from heat and cool. Grease salad molds with butter and put fruit and nuts into molds. Pour contents of boiler into molds.

Makes 7 salads.

Sue Peyton

MOLDED HORSERADISH SALAD

1 box lemon gelatin
1½ cups water, boiling
½ cup mayonnaise
4 tablespoons horseradish (bottled or fresh)
¼ teaspoon salt
½ teaspoon paprika
6 tablespoons stuffed olives, sliced
½ cup heavy cream, whipped
Avocado

Dissolve gelatin in boiling water. Chill until thick and syrupy. Fold in rest of ingredients. Chill until thoroughly firm in oiled mold. Serve on romaine and garnish with slices of ripe avocado which have been marinated in sharp French dressing.

Mrs. W. J. O'Brien, Sr.

LIME CONFETTI SALAD

1 envelope plain gelatin
¼ cup cold water
1 package lime or lemon gelatin
1 cup boiling water
1 cup shredded cabbage
1 cup celery, sliced fine
1 flat can crushed pineapple
1 tablespoon grated onion
1 cup cottage cheese
1 cup mayonnaise
3 chopped carrots (optional)
2 tablespoons chopped green pepper (optional)
or
1 cup chopped sweet pickle (optional)
1 tablespoon vinegar or lemon juice
Salt to taste

Dissolve fruit gelatin in boiling water and plain gelatin in cold water, then combine. Chill until slightly thickened, then add all other ingredients and pour into mold. Chill until set.

Serves 8.

Mrs. George Conger
Mrs. Charles H. Jeter
Mrs. J. Craigo, Jackson, Miss.

RASPBERRY SALAD

4 packages raspberry gelatin
4 packages strawberry gelatin
8 frozen packages of raspberries
1 8-ounce package cream cheese

Dissolve gelatin in juice drained from frozen raspberries, adding water if necessary to make 16 cups. Let partially congeal. Add raspberries and small cubes of cream cheese. Put in salad molds and chill. Pour cream cheese mixed with cream and mayonnaise on top, to serve.

Makes about 30 molds.

Mrs. Lane Sartor

MANDARIN SALAD

- 1 package lemon gelatin
- 1 cup liquid (use juice from mandarin oranges and water)
- 1 tablespoon plain gelatin soaked in ¼ cup water
- 1 can concentrated frozen orange juice
- 1 flat can crushed pineapple
- 1 can mandarin oranges
- ¼-½ cup pecans

Dissolve gelatin in water and let set. Drain mandarin oranges well. Add enough water to juice to make one cup and bring this to a boil. Pour over lemon gelatin and then add plain gelatin mixture. Stir well until dissolved. Add thawed concentrated orange juice. Refrigerate and let thicken. Add oranges, crushed pineapple and pecans. Pour in molds.

Fills 8 square molds.

Mrs. William Lynch

FROZEN ORANGE MEDLEY

- 1 cup cottage cheese
- ⅛ teaspoon salt
- 1 cup pineapple, crushed or finely diced, and drained
- 1 cup Royal Anne cherries, pitted and drained
- 1 cup canned peaches, diced and drained
- 2 peeled oranges
- 8 marshmallows quartered (or the equivalent amount of tiny marshmallows)
- 1 cup whipping cream, whipped
- ½ cup mayonnaise

Mix all ingredients and freeze in shallow pan. When ready to serve, cut in squares, place on lettuce leaf and top with mayonnaise.

Makes 8 or 10 servings.

Mrs. W. J. Knighton

PINEAPPLE CINNAMON CROWN SALAD

- 1/3 cup red cinnamon candy (red hots)
- 1/2 cup hot water
- 2 packages lemon flavored gelatin
- 1 can (16-ounce) applesauce
- 1 can (13½-ounce) undrained crushed pineapple
- 2 tablespoons lemon juice
- 1/4 teaspoon salt
- 1/4 teaspoon nutmeg

Dissolve candy in water over low heat. Remove from heat and add gelatin. Stir until dissolved. Blend in other ingredients and pour into individual molds. Chill until firm.

Serves 8.

Mrs. Claiborne Cook

PINEAPPLE CHEESE SALAD

1 package lemon gelatin
1 pint hot water
1 cup chopped nuts
1 cup grated yellow cheese
1 small can crushed pineapple
1 cup whipped cream
1 small bottle stuffed olives, sliced

Dissolve gelatin in hot water. Place in refrigerator until nearly set. Whip until creamy, fold in whipped cream and other ingredients. Pour into large mold or individual molds.

Serves 12. Mrs. W. J. Dalrymple

FROZEN PINEAPPLE SALAD

1 package lime gelatin
1 3-ounce package cream cheese
½ pint whipping cream
1 cup chopped pecans
1 cup crushed pineapple

Drain ½ cup juice from pineapple. Bring to boil, add gelatin and dissolve. Stir in cheese, pineapple and nuts. Allow to cool but not congeal. Add whipped cream. Freeze. Cut in squares and serve.

Serves 5 to 6. Mrs. W. C. Hamel
Mrs. G. R. Shanley

RHUBARB SALAD

1 package frozen rhubarb
¼ cup water
3 tablespoons sugar
1 package raspberry gelatin
1 cup pineapple juice
1 apple chopped thin
¼ cup nuts if desired

Cook rhubarb in water with sugar added until tender, not stringy. While hot pour over gelatin. Stir until dissolved. Add pineapple juice. Refrigerate until syrupy. Add apple chopped thin and broken nut bits if desired. Refrigerate until firm.

Makes 6 to 8 servings. Mrs. Gerald LeVan

STRAWBERRY DELIGHT SALAD

1 large box strawberry gelatin
1 cup boiling water
1 medium can crushed pineapple
3 or 4 ripe bananas, mashed
½ cup pecans (optional)
1 small box frozen sliced strawberries, thawed

Combine gelatin and boiling water. Mash bananas well and add along with all other ingredients to gelatin. Mold and refrigerate.

Serves 8 to 10.

Mrs. John L. Gentry, Jackson, Miss.

RASPBERRY DELIGHT

1 package raspberry gelatin
1 dozen marshmallows
1½ cups boiling water
½ cup pineapple juice
1 3-ounce package cream cheese
1 cup crushed pineapple
½ cup nuts, chopped
3 level tablespoons salad dressing
1 cup whipped cream

Mix together gelatin, marshmallows, boiling water and pineapple juice. While this mixture is cooling, mix the cream cheese, crushed pineapple, nuts and salad dressing together. Then add these to the cooled mixture. Put in refrigerator and when thick enough (set to hold), fold in 1 cup whipped cream.

Serves 12.

Mrs. August C. Erickson
Mrs. A. Glenn Flournoy

SPANISH GELATIN

1 package lime gelatin
1 pint hot water, scant
½ cup bread and butter pickles, chopped fine
½ cup celery, cut fine
½ cup cabbage, shredded
2 or 3 pimientos
1 tablespoon lemon juice
1 tablespoon juice from pickles
½ teaspoon salt

Dissolve gelatin in hot water. Set aside to cool. Cut up other ingredients. Fill molds, then pour in gelatin.

Makes 10 servings; possibly 12 small servings. Nice with ham or pork.

Mrs. C. N. Frierson

PRESSED CHICKEN

1 5-6-pound hen, boiled in salted water along with favorite seasonings
8 eggs, hard cooked
3 envelopes plain gelatin dissolved in small amount cool broth
2 cups hot chicken broth
1½ cups diced celery
¾ cup mayonnaise
Small bottle stuffed olives
3 tablespoons India relish
1 teaspoon hot sauce
Salt and pepper to taste
Small bottle Durkee's salad dressing

Dissolve gelatin in cool broth, add hot stock, cut up chicken, sliced eggs, celery, mayonnaise, sliced olives, relish, hot sauce, salt and pepper, and salad dressing. Place in mold or square dish and place in refrigerator to congeal. Serve on lettuce leaf.

Serves 16.

Mrs. Grady L. Nelson

WALDORF SALAD MOLD

- 1½ cups cranberry juice cocktail
- 1 package lemon flavored gelatin
- ¼ teaspoon salt
- 1½ cups chopped, unpared Washington apples
- ½ cup chopped celery
- ¼ cup broken walnuts or pecans

Heat 1 cup of cranberry juice to boiling point; remove from heat and stir in gelatin until dissolved. Add remaining juice and salt. Chill until partially set. Stir in apple, celery and nuts. Pour into 6 individual molds or 1 large mold. Chill until firm.

Mrs. R. C. Basinger

TOMATO CHICKEN SALAD

- 1 can tomato soup
- 2 tablespoons plain gelatin
- ½ cup cold water
- 1 cup mayonnaise
- 1 8-ounce package cream cheese
- 1 cup diced celery
- 1 small bottle chopped stuffed olives
- 1 small onion, diced
- 1 can boned chicken or turkey

Dissolve gelatin in cold water. Heat soup, blend with gelatin. Add mashed cream cheese to warm soup. Add mayonnaise, celery, olives and onions and combine this with meat. Pour into mold and chill.

Serves 12.

Dressing

- 1 cup sour cream
- 1 tablespoon mayonnaise
- ½ teaspoon Tabasco

Mix these 3 ingredients and spoon over molded salad.

Mrs. B. S. Cheesman
Mrs. Sam W. Smith, Jr.

SALMON MOUSSE

- 1 envelope gelatin
- ¼ cup water
- 1 cup salmon
- ½ cup celery, chopped
- ½ cup bell pepper, chopped
- 2 tablespoons chopped olives
- 2 hard boiled eggs, chopped
- ¾ cup mayonnaise
- ½ teaspoon salt
- ¼ teaspoon paprika
- 1 tablespoon vinegar
- Dash cayenne pepper

Dissolve gelatin over heat in water. Mix remaining ingredients. Add gelatin and pour into mold. Put in refrigerator until firm.

Serves 6.

Mrs. Ernest A. Merklein, Jr.

TUNA MOUSSE WITH AVOCADO DRESSING

Tuna Mousse:
2 cans (6½- or 7-ounce) tuna
2 tablespoons lemon juice
1 teaspoon onion salt
2 tablespoons chopped pimiento
½ cup finely chopped celery
¼ cup finely chopped blanched almonds
½ cup mayonnaise
½ cup dairy sour cream
1 envelope plain gelatin
¼ cup cold water

Avocado Dressing:
1 avocado
½ cup dairy sour cream
1 teaspoon seasoned salt
Dash cayenne

Flake tuna, combine with lemon juice, onion salt, pimiento, celery, almonds, mayonnaise and sour cream. Mix thoroughly. Soften gelatin in cold water. Place over hot water and stir until dissolved. Stir into tuna mixture. Pour into 4-cup mold or small loaf pan. Chill until firm. Unmold and frost with avocado dressing or cut in slices and top each slice with a generous spoonful of dressing.

For dressing, cut avocado lengthwise into halves. Remove seed and skin. Mash thoroughly or press through sieve. Blend in sour cream, seasoned salt and cayenne.

Serves 6. Excellent for hot weather.

Eleanor Blatterman

TOMATO SOUP SALAD

1 cup mayonnaise
1 8-ounce package cream cheese
1 can tomato soup
2 envelopes plain gelatin
½ cup cold water
1 cup stuffed olives, chopped
1 cup chopped celery
Dash Tabasco
Salt, pepper to taste
½ teaspoon Worcestershire sauce
½ cup grated onion

Dissolve gelatin in cold water. Add ½ cup water to soup. Heat soup and add gelatin. Add cream cheese, celery, olives, mayonnaise, salt and pepper, Tabasco, Worcestershire sauce and onion. Rub mold with garlic. Pour mixture into mold and chill. Will set in about 30 minutes.

If a seafood salad is desired, add ½ pound chopped boiled shrimp to mixture just before pouring it into mold.

Serves 12 (approximately).

Mrs. C. F. Young
Mrs. John M. Crain
Mrs. Matthew H. Miller

INDIVIDUAL SHRIMP MOLDS

2½ cups boiled shrimp (small or medium)
1 pimiento, chopped fine
1 small bottle stuffed olives, chopped
¾ cup chopped celery
1½ teaspoons grated onion
1½ tablespoons gelatin dissolved in 2 tablespoons water
¾ cup mayonnaise
2 hard boiled eggs, chopped
Juice of one lemon
¼ cup pickles (dill or sweet)
Salt to taste
Pepper to taste

Soak gelatin in tap water, then melt in pan over hot water. Add lemon juice, then cool to lukewarm. Add salt, pepper and mayonnaise. Mix all other ingredients with this and pour into greased molds. Chill.

Serves 8

Mrs. Claiborne Cook

SPICY SHRIMP ASPIC

1 large can tomato juice
4 packages plain gelatin
1 to 2 cups finely chopped celery
1 very small green bell pepper, finely chopped
Parsley
3 pods garlic
1 tablespoon grated onion
1 tablespoon lemon juice
1 teaspoon Tabasco
1 teaspoon Worcestershire sauce
1 teaspoon salt
1 teaspoon black pepper
2 cans shrimp or fresh shrimp

Dissolve gelatin in a small amount of cold tomato juice. Simmer 3 pods garlic and some parsley in the rest of juice. Pour through strainer into gelatin. Cool and add all other ingredients. Taste and add any more seasoning needed. Pour into molds and refrigerate.

Serves 16. Mrs. Ed Minor

TOSSED BEET SALAD

½ cup French dressing
1 tablespoon prepared horseradish
1 can julienne beets
3 slices crisply cooked bacon
2 hard boiled eggs
1 medium head iceberg lettuce
Salt and freshly ground pepper to taste

Mix French dressing and horseradish. Chill 1 to 2 hours to blend flavors. Chill beets. Crumble bacon and chop eggs. Tear lettuce into bite-sized pieces. Add drained beets, bacon, eggs and dressing. Toss lightly until mixed. Season to taste with salt and pepper. May be garnished with sour cream, if desired.

Serves 6. Mrs. James B. Harris

DANISH CUCUMBER SALAD

2 medium-size cucumbers
1 tablespoon salt
1 cup water
¼ cup vinegar
1 tablespoon sugar

Peel cucumbers, slice paper-thin with potato peeler. Place in bowl and sprinkle with salt. Blend salt into cucumbers and let stand fifteen minutes. Put cucumbers in cheesecloth and wring out all juice.

Dressing

Combine 1 cup water, ¼ cup vinegar, 1 tablespoon sugar and add salt to taste. Place cucumbers in dressing and marinate for two hours in refrigerator. Serve with pork or poultry.

Shreveport Country Club

FIVE CUP SALAD

1 cup pineapple chunks
1 cup mandarin orange slices
1 cup very finely grated coconut
1 cup small marshmallows
1 cup sour cream
1 cup seedless green grapes may be added, if desired

Drain oranges and pineapple. Mix all ingredients, cover and chill overnight. Stir several times and return to refrigerator.

Important: This salad is best if you use the very finest grated coconut as this blends with sour cream.

Serves 8. This is delicious.

Mrs. Neil Dixon
Mrs. Bill Dowden, El Campo, Texas

GREEN SALAD WITH SHRIMP

Salad:
2 pounds cooked shrimp, peeled
3 or 4 avocados
Spinach
Romaine
Lettuce
10 or 12 strips cooked crisp bacon

Dressing:
2 cups salad oil
1 garlic clove, halved
1 teaspoon cracked pepper
½ onion, chopped fine
Salt to taste
3 tablespoons white vinegar
½ pint cottage cheese
1 teaspoon poppy seed
½ teaspoon cayenne

In a blender, prepare dressing a day ahead. Marinate shrimp and avocado in dressing overnight, treating avocado with lemon juice to prevent turning dark. Toss shrimp mixture and salad greens together. Crumble bacon on top.

Serves 4-6.

Mrs. James Galbraith

MARINATED ARTICHOKE HEARTS

2 packages (9-ounce size) frozen artichoke hearts
1 teaspoon salt

Marinade:
¼ cup lemon juice
¼ cup salad oil
¼ cup red wine vinegar
1 clove garlic, crushed
1 tablespoon finely chopped parsley
1 tablespoon finely chopped onion
½ teaspoon dried oregano leaves
½ teaspoon salt
¼ teaspoon pepper

Cook artichoke hearts according to directions on package, using 1 teaspoon salt in water. Drain and cool slightly. Make marinade in jar, shaking vigorously, or use blender. Pour over artichokes. Toss to coat well, cover and refrigerate several hours, or overnight, stirring occasionally. Add to a tossed green salad, or serve on lettuce leaves.

Serves 6.

Mrs. John R. Murphy

SOUR BEAN SALAD

3 1-pound cans baby limas, well drained
1 medium onion, thinly sliced
¼ cup chopped celery
1 cup sour cream
2 tablespoons vinegar
1 teaspoon sugar
1 teaspoon prepared horseradish
2 teaspoons salt
Pepper
¼ cup chopped parsley

Drain limas thoroughly. Add onion rings and celery to beans. Mix together sour cream, vinegar, sugar, horseradish, salt and pepper. Toss gently with bean mixture. Sprinkle with chopped parsley and serve very cold. This salad should be made several hours before serving.

Makes 6 to 8 servings.

Mrs. C. Walker Weston

CONGEALED CORNED BEEF SALAD

1 envelope plain gelatin
1½ cups tomato juice
1 can corned beef
¼ teaspoon salt
1 cup salad dressing
3 hard boiled eggs
1 tablespoon minced onion
2 cups celery

Dissolve gelatin in tomato juice. Combine rest of ingredients with this mixture, pour into greased molds and chill.

Serves 6-8.

Mrs. James B. Harris

BEANS VINAIGRETTE

3 cans small whole green beans
⅓ cup sugar
⅓ cup salad oil
½ cup wine vinegar
2 tablespoons soy sauce
1 dash Tabasco
2 tablespoons Worcestershire sauce
1 teaspoon salt
½ teaspoon paprika
½ cup chopped pimiento
3 or 4 chopped green onions
1 pod garlic, pressed
1 bell pepper, chopped
3 tablespoons sweet relish

Wash and drain beans, then place into casserole. Blend sugar, salad oil, vinegar, soy sauce, Tabasco, Worcestershire sauce, salt and paprika. Pour over beans. Mix pimiento, onions, garlic, bell pepper and relish. Stir into bean mixture. Let stand in refrigerator for at least 24 hours.

Makes 10-12 servings. Will keep for a long period of time.

Mrs. Peyton Kelley

CURRIED CHICKEN SALAD

2 cups cooked chicken, cut into bite-sized pieces
1½ cups chopped celery
1½ cups cooked rice (cold)
½ cup toasted almonds
¼ cup capers

Dressing:
½ cup sour cream
½ cup Italian style salad dressing
1 teaspoon salt
1 teaspoon curry powder

Combine chicken, celery, rice, almonds and capers. Mix dressing ingredients and pour over chicken mixture. Toss thoroughly. This salad is best prepared several hours before serving. Good served on sliced pineapple with toasted coconut curls sprinkled on top.

Makes 6 to 8 servings.

Mrs. John B. Entrikin
Mrs. E. E. Dilworth

GRAPEFRUIT SALAD

4 grapefruit
2 3-ounce packages cream cheese
Cream
Mayonnaise
½ jar crab apple jelly
Salt
Pepper
Tabasco

Peel and section grapefruit. Chill in refrigerator. Mash cream cheese and soften with cream and small amount of mayonnaise. Add jelly and whip until blended. Add salt, pepper and Tabasco to taste. Place slices of grapefruit on lettuce, pour sauce over and sprinkle with paprika.

Serves 4.

Mrs. Joe L. Hargrove

MARINATED GREEN BEAN SALAD

1 cup sour cream
¼ cup mayonnaise
1 teaspoon lemon juice
¼ teaspoon dry mustard
1 tablespoon prepared horseradish
¼ teaspoon onion juice
2 teaspoons chopped chives (optional)
3 cans green beans
1 onion
3 small tomatoes
2 tablespoons salad oil
2 tablespoons vinegar
Salt
Black pepper, cracked

Wash green beans, add thinly sliced onions and tomatoes cut in eighths. Marinate for approximately two hours in salad oil, vinegar, salt and black pepper. Blend remaining ingredients. Drain marinade from beans, onions and tomatoes and add enough of the sour cream mixture to coat the vegetables. Be sure not to use too much of the sour cream mixture. The vegetables are supposed to be coated, not drenched. This is good served in a salad bowl surrounded by salad greens. It is very popular with men and is an attractive looking addition to a buffet.

Serves 8. Mrs. William Junkin

WILTED LETTUCE SALAD

5 small heads Bibb or Boston lettuce
4 strips cooked crisp bacon
2 eggs, hard boiled
1 tablespoon vinegar
Dash of Tabasco
3 tablespoons olive oil
4 green onions
Salt and pepper to taste

Break lettuce into bite-sized pieces. Cut egg whites into lettuce; add chopped onions and tops. In a small bowl, mash egg yolks; add vinegar and Tabasco; pour over lettuce and mix until each piece is coated. Heat olive oil and pour over lettuce. Crumble bacon over all and mix well. Salt and pepper to taste and serve at once.

Serves 4. Mrs. Phil Foster

MACARONI SALAD

1 pound shell-shaped macaroni
1 bunch green onions, tops and bottoms chopped
1 whole medium onion, grated
1 can lobster
1 can crab meat
1 stalk celery, chopped
3 medium sized carrots, shredded
¾ bottle chili sauce
1 bunch parsley, chopped fine
1¾ cups mayonnaise (approximately)

Mix all ingredients. It is best to make day before serving. Excellent served with barbecue.

Serves 10. Mrs. John M. Crain

THE ORIGINAL CAESAR SALAD

2 or 3 medium heads romaine lettuce, chilled, dry, crisp
1 cup garlic-flavored olive oil (or salad oil)
2-3 tablespoons wine vinegar
Juice of 1 lemon
1 or 2 1-minute coddled eggs
Salt and freshly ground pepper
Dash Worcestershire sauce
5 or 6 tablespoons grated Parmesan cheese
1 cup Caesar croutons

One to several days before serving salad, prepare garlic-flavored olive oil by slicing 6 cloves of garlic lengthwise in quarters and letting stand in 1 cup olive oil.

Wash lettuce 24 hours ahead. Pat the leaves dry with a towel. Then wrap in fresh towels and refrigerate. The leaves will be dry and crisp next day.

For croutons, cut several slices of bread in 5 strips one way, then across 5 times to make squares. Spread on cookie sheet; pour a little garlic-flavored oil over them. Heat in extremely slow oven (225°) two hours. The croutons should be so dry they'd float on water. Sprinkle croutons with grated Parmesan cheese. Store in jar and refrigerate to keep crisp.

Now to make the salad: Break or tear romaine leaves in 2- to 3-inch widths. (Never cut the leaves, or they may take on an unattractive brown edge and wilt.) At last minute before serving, place romaine in chilled salad bowl. Drizzle garlic oil over it, then vinegar. (Oil is added first to coat the leaves, enabling salad to stay crisper.) Squeeze lemon over, using fork to help free juice. When adding these liquids, follow a Z-line for even distribution. Break in the 1-minute eggs. Grind a flurry of pepper over all. Season with salt and a dash of Worcestershire sauce. Sprinkle with cheese. Roll-toss 6 or 7 times, or until dressing is thoroughly combined and every leaf is coated. Add Caesar croutons; toss 1 or 2 times. Serve at once on chilled dinner plates.

Serves 6.

Mrs. Harland Hundley

COTTAGE CHEESE DRESSING

1 egg
½ cup salad oil, NOT olive oil
1 pound DRY cottage cheese or
1 pound creamed cottage cheese, drained
1 cup parsley, chopped
6 green onions, chopped
1 teaspoon salt
1 tablespoon lemon juice
1 heaping teaspoon thyme
Freshly ground black pepper

Put all into blender in order given. Blend until well mixed. Serve as a dip for raw carrots, cauliflower, beets and baby okra cooked whole for 10 minutes in boiling salt water, drained and chilled. Also good over a lettuce wedge or on Boston lettuce.

Mrs. Robert K. Butcher

GREEN VEGETABLE SALAD

- 2 No. 303 cans tiny whole green stringless beans
- 1 No. 303 can tiny early June peas
- 1 No. 303 can tiny green lima beans
- 1 8-ounce can mushrooms, buttons (optional)
- 6 eggs, hard boiled (or fewer)
- 1 cup chopped celery
- 1 teaspoon onion juice
- ½ cup French dressing
- 1 cup mayonnaise
- 1 teaspoon salt
- ½ teaspoon black pepper
- 3 dashes Tabasco

Drain and then marinate string beans, peas and lima beans in French dressing, onion juice and seasonings. Refrigerate 2 hours. Drain vegetables, add eggs, grated, mushrooms and celery. Refrigerate until just before serving. Toss gently with mayonnaise. This may be varied by adding fresh cucumbers, tomatoes or any desired vegetable. Good for outdoor patio parties.

Serves 12. Mrs. Bolinger Westbrook

CAESAR SALAD

- 2 cloves garlic
- ¾ cup salad oil
- 6 slices of white bread
- 4 quarts salad greens (although romaine is traditional, leaf lettuce alone or mixed with romaine may be used. Avoid using iceburg lettuce or endive.)
- 1½ teaspoon Worcestershire sauce
- ¼ cup lemon juice
- ½ cup blue cheese
- ¾ teaspoon salt
- ¼ teaspoon pepper
- 1 egg

Peel and slice garlic into salad oil, allowing it to stand for several hours. To make croutons, slice crusts from bread and cut into ½-inch cubes. Place on cookie sheet and brown in 300 degree oven for approximately one hour. Store in tightly sealed container when done earlier in the day. At serving time, tear greens into salad bowl. Add Worcestershire sauce, lemon juice, blue cheese, salt and pepper. Remove garlic from oil and pour half of oil into salad and half over croutons. Toss salad lightly. Break egg into salad and toss well. Add croutons and toss.

Serves 6. Mrs. T. O. Perry

To sweeten onions . . . slice them thin, separate into rings, place in large bowl, and sprinkle lightly with sugar. Cover with ice cubes and refrigerate for an hour or more.

NICOISE SALAD

Crisp lettuce leaves, preferably romaine
4 quartered small tomatoes
1 cup cooked green beans
2 sliced boiled new potatoes
2 quartered hard boiled eggs
Thin slices Spanish onion and bell pepper
8 anchovy fillets cut in small pieces
10 black Italian or Greek olives
1 can white tuna fish

Standard French dressing such as:
½ teaspoon prepared mustard
2 tablespoons red wine vinegar
6 tablespoons olive oil
Salt and freshly ground pepper to taste

Rub large salad bowl with garlic and place lettuce leaves in bowl. Arrange other ingredients on them. Over this pour French dressing. Toss salad thoroughly.

Serves 4 as main course — more as salad.

Mrs. Melvin F. Johnson

SHRIMP LOUIS

6-8 cooked shrimp per serving
1 hard boiled egg
Finely chopped chives
1 cup mayonnaise
¼ cup each of chili sauce and French dressing (made with tarragon vinegar)
2 tablespoons each of chopped parsley and chives
1 teaspoon each of horseradish and Worcestershire sauce
Salt and pepper

Combine mayonnaise, chili sauce, French dressing made with tarragon vinegar, parsley, chives, horseradish, Worcestershire sauce and salt and pepper to taste. Serve over 6 to 8 cooked shrimp on a bed of shredded lettuce. Top the shrimp with a slice or two of egg and finely chopped chives.

Makes 6 servings.

Mrs. Charles Edward Porter

Nasturtium leaves make a different and attractive garnish for a fruit salad.

TACO SALAD

1½ pounds ground beef
1½ cups onion, diced
1 cup celery, diced
1 cup bell pepper, diced
3 buds garlic, diced
1 pound Velveeta cheese
1 large head lettuce
2 large firm ripe tomatoes
1 large package corn chips
1 can Ro-tel tomatoes
Salt
Chili powder
Ground cumin

Brown the ground beef in small amount of oil. Saute vegetables until soft but not brown. Combine meat and vegetables and simmer together. Season with salt, chili powder and cumin. In top of double boiler melt cheese and add Ro-tel tomatoes. Cut lettuce coarsely and dice tomatoes, then put in large bowl. Add meat and vegetables and mix lightly. Add slightly crushed corn chips and toss. Top with hot cheese mixture. Serve immediately.

Serves 6-8.

Mrs. Stuart D. Lunn

CAPITAL DRESSING

1 pint vegetable oil
Juice of 3 lemons
3 large cloves garlic
Salt and pepper to taste

Combine these ingredients and store in refrigerator. This is a tart dressing, delicious over a lettuce and parsley salad, which has been sprinkled very generously with Romano cheese.

Mrs. Neil Dixon

BASIC FRENCH DRESSING

1½ cups salad oil (olive preferably)
½ cup wine vinegar
1 teaspoon dry mustard
Salt, pepper, monosodium glutamate

Place all ingredients in a bottle and shake well. Chill.
Makes 1 pint.

VARIATIONS

Barbecue

Add:
1 clove garlic, finely chopped
½ cup green pepper, finely chopped
¼ cup crisp bacon, finely chopped
2 eggs, well beaten
1 teaspoon barbecue sauce
1 teaspoon celery salt
Dash Tabasco
Dash Worcestershire sauce

Roquefort

Add:
½ cup crumbled Roquefort cheese
1 teaspoon Worcestershire sauce

Hollywood

Use grapefruit juice in place of vinegar

Indian

Add:
1 tablespoon curry powder
1 tablespoon chutney

Sour Cream

Add:
5 tablespoons sour cream
1 tablespoon chopped green onion

South Seas

Add:
1 tablespoon grenadine
1 tablespoon lime juice
1 tablespoon grated orange rind
Dash Tabasco

Mushroom

Add:
¼ cup diced raw mushrooms

California

Add:
1 tablespoon paprika
1 teaspoon chili powder
Chili sauce to taste

Cottage Cheese

Add:
3 tablespoons cottage cheese
1 tablespoon sweet relish

Italian

Add:
1 clove garlic, finely chopped
2 green onions, finely chopped
1 teaspoon anchovy paste
Dash Tabasco

Caper

Add:
1 tablespoon capers
1 hard boiled egg, finely chopped

Horseradish

Add:
2 tablespoons freshly grated horseradish
Chili sauce to taste

Caesar

Add:
Coddled egg
3 tablespoons Parmesan cheese

Tarragon

Add:
1 tablespoon chopped tarragon

Mrs. Whitney Boggs, Jr.

FROZEN FRUIT SALAD DRESSING

½ cup pineapple juice
¼ cup lemon juice
¼ cup orange juice
¼ teaspoon salt
½ cup sugar
1 tablespoon flour
2 eggs, separated
1 cup heavy cream, whipped

Mix flour, sugar and salt. Mix fruit juices with dry mixture and cook in top of double boiler for 20 minutes. Remove from fire and add well beaten egg yolks. Cook again for five minutes, stirring constantly. Remove from fire again and add to stiffly beaten egg whites, then cool. This may be kept in a jar in the refrigerator for future use. Before serving add whipped cream.

Mrs. Vincent S. Brennan

POPPY SEED DRESSING

1 cup white or tarragon vinegar
½ cup sugar
1 tablespoon paprika
1⅓ tablespoons dry mustard
1⅓ teaspoons ground ginger
1 tablespoon salt
Pinch each of cayenne and white pepper
¼ cup onion juice
½ egg
1⅓ cups honey
1 quart oil
⅓ cup poppy seed

Slowly bring to a boil the vinegar and sugar. Mix in other ingredients except last three. Cool a little, slowly add oil, honey and seeds. Chill well before serving. Very different when served on Waldorf salad.

The Shreveport Club

INSTANT GREEN GODDESS SALAD DRESSING

Combine 1 cup mayonnaise with 2 cups commercial Italian dressing. Add 1 bunch chopped green onions, 1 can anchovies along with juice, 2 tablespoons parsley flakes and 2 tablespoons chives. Pour this into blender and mix on high speed for about 5 minutes — or until well blended.

Makes 1 quart. Mrs. Ed Ligon

GREEN GODDESS DRESSING

- 1 clove garlic, minced
- ½ teaspoon salt
- ½ teaspoon dry mustard
- 1 teaspoon Worcestershire sauce
- 2 tablespoons anchovy paste
- 3 tablespoons tarragon vinegar
- 3 tablespoons minced chives
- ½ cup minced parsley
- 1 cup mayonnaise
- ½ cup sour cream
- ⅛ teaspoon black pepper

Combine all ingredients. Allow to stand for several hours before using.

Mrs. Jack Tullos, Jr.

GARLIC MAYONNAISE

- 1 egg yolk, hard cooked
- 1 whole egg, raw
- 1 teaspoon salt
- 1 teaspoon sugar
- 1 teaspoon dry mustard
- ½ teaspoon white pepper
- ½ teaspoon paprika
- 1½ cups good salad oil
- 3 tablespoons lemon juice
- 1 small clove garlic, crushed

Mash hard cooked egg. Blend in whole raw egg. Add dry ingredients. Mix well. Very slowly, drop by drop, add about ¼ cup oil, mixing on low speed of electric mixer. When emulsion is formed, add remaining oil in a thin stream, with mixer on medium speed. Slowly add lemon juice and crushed garlic. Continue mixing until thoroughly blended. Store in lower part of refrigerator. Will keep for a week. Should emulsion break, start over with one whole egg, and, bit by bit. add a little of the curdled mayonnaise until new emulsion is formed. Then add the rest, faster, as above.

Makes a good basic mayonnaise, omitting the crushed garlic.

Mrs. James R. Alexander
Mrs. W. J. Colbert

Chilled water chestnuts sliced very thin add an interesting touch to a tossed green salad.

AUNT HALLIE'S DRESSING

1 teaspoon dry mustard
1 teaspoon salt
1 tablespoon sugar
¼ teaspoon pepper
¼ teaspoon curry powder (optional)
1 teaspoon Worcestershire sauce
4 tablespoons tarragon vinegar
1 cup salad oil

Combine all ingredients except oil and shake well or beat in mixer or blender. Add oil a little at a time and continue to mix thoroughly. 1 clove of garlic may be left in overnight and then removed.

Mrs. K. J. Heddons
Henderson, Ky.

POPPY SEED DRESSING

Combine in blender:

¾ cup sugar
2 teaspoons powdered mustard
2 teaspoons salt
⅔ cup vinegar
½ cup minced onion

Add:

2 cups oil (slowly)
4 tablespoons poppy seed

Mrs. Saunders Gregg
Mrs. R. O. Smith

POTATO SALAD DRESSING

2 hard cooked egg yolks, mashed
3 raw egg yolks
1 pint salad oil
2 tablespoons onion juice
2 tablespoons vinegar
Salt
Pepper
Paprika
½ pint more salad oil
2 tablespoons cream

To the egg yolks slowly add 1 pint salad oil, onion juice, vinegar and salt, pepper and paprika to taste. Then add ½ pint more of oil and cream. Add cooked mashed egg yolks.

Mrs. Thomas B. Wilson

PELICAN ROQUEFORT DRESSING

12 tablespoons olive oil
2 tablespoons malt vinegar
2 tablespoons tarragon vinegar
½ teaspoon salt
¼ teaspoon freshly ground black peppercorns or whole pepper
4 tablespoons Roquefort cheese
2 cups mayonnaise
Dash paprika

Dissolve salt in vinegar. Add pepper and stir well, then whip in the olive oil. Blend mayonnaise with dressing and add crumbled cheese.

Serves 8. Mrs. Gene D. Scott

ROQUEFORT CHEESE SALAD DRESSING

3 ounces Roquefort or blue cheese
1 3-ounce package cream cheese
¾ cup salad oil
⅓ cup wine vinegar
1 6-ounce can evaporated milk
1 scant teaspoon salt
1 tablespoon minced onion
1 tablespoon parsley
1 teaspoon paprika (this is optional, for color)

Beat oil, vinegar, salt, onion and parsley until creamy and well blended. Soften cheeses and combine with milk. Combine all ingredients and beat. Chill.

Makes approximately 1 pint. Mrs. Mike Tipps

SINGAPORE DRESSING

To one quart French dressing add:

1 small orange, seeds removed
1 small lemon, seeds removed
1 apple, seeds removed
1 small onion, peeled
2 tablespoons brown sugar
2 teaspoons curry powder
½ cup vinegar
Salt, crushed black peppercorns, Tabasco, Worcestershire sauce

Pass the orange, lemon, apple (peel and all) and onion through the finest blade of your meat grinder. Mix curry powder and vinegar, bring to a boil, let simmer for one minute and cool. Now combine all the ingredients with the French dressing. Season to suit your own good taste with salt, crushed black pepper (use your pepper mill), Tabasco and Worcestershire sauce. Keep in refrigerator for future use.

E. Wirz, Chef, O'Hare Flight Kitchen, Chicago, Ill.

SOUR CREAM SALAD DRESSING

⅓ cup chopped green onions
2 cups mayonnaise
2 cloves garlic, pressed
2 tablespoons anchovy paste
1 cup sour cream
¼ cup cider or tarragon vinegar
2 tablespoons lemon juice
½ pound Roquefort (or blue) cheese, crumbled and beaten into sour cream

Mix all ingredients and add Worcestershire sauce and Tabasco to taste Keeps well in refrigerator.

Mrs. W. W. Lincoln

TETON SALAD DRESSING

1 cup sour cream
1 cup mayonnaise
1½ teaspoons lemon juice
1 clove garlic, minced
1 1½-ounce wedge blue cheese, crumbled
⅓ teaspoon celery salt

Combine all ingredients and blend well. May be made several days in advance.

Makes 2 cups. Mrs. A. L. Wedgeworth, Jr.

Cheese & Eggs

The Shreveport River Front

BARNWELL GARDEN AND ART CENTER

The Barnwell is one of the few combined art and garden centers in the Southwest. The South Wing houses a domed botanical garden conservatory dominated by tropical plants and seasonal and native plantings. Experience the feel and sound of the Fragrance Gardens, a special feature designed for the visually impaired.

BAKED OMELETTE

½ stick butter
6 eggs
¼ pound American cheese or
¼ pound diced ham
½ teaspoon salt
Pepper to taste

Melt butter in small casserole. Be sure that the sides are well buttered. Beat eggs until very fluffy. A blender helps. Fold in cheese or ham and seasonings. Pour into hot casserole and bake in preheated oven (375°) about 15 to 20 minutes, or until well set. Serve at once on hot plates. A dusting of chopped parsley or chives makes this an attractive dish for Sunday supper.

Serves 4. Mrs. Sinclair Kouns

WOODCHUCK

½ pound butter
6 tablespoons flour
1 pint milk
½ pound sharp New York cheese, diced
1 pound sauteed mushrooms
1 can tomato soup
1 tablespoon Worcestershire sauce
Salt, pepper, paprika, to taste
8 hard boiled eggs, sliced into thin strips

Melt butter; add flour and milk. Cook until smooth and thick, stirring constantly. Place in a double boiler and add cheese. Cook until cheese is melted, add mushrooms, soup, seasonings and eggs. Heat thoroughly. Serve on toast.

Serves 12. M. A. Prescott

EGGS BENEDICTINE

6 tablespoons butter
6 tablespoons flour
3 cups warmed milk
¾ teaspoon salt
Pepper
½ pound jar Cheez Whiz
½ pound Velveeta cheese
½ pound sharp Cheddar cheese, grated
1 dozen hard boiled eggs, mashed
1 large can mushrooms
Tabasco
1 teaspoon Worcestershire sauce
2 large cans Chinese noodles

Make white sauce using the first 5 ingredients: Melt butter, add flour, and mix until smooth. Add warm milk gradually until whole mixture is smooth and has thickened. Add salt and pepper. Add cheese, eggs, mushrooms, Tabasco and Worcestershire sauce. Serve hot from a chafing dish over Chinese noodles. Cooking time, 30 minutes.

Serves 20. Mrs. Boggs Creamer

CURRIED EGGS AND OYSTERS

6 eggs, hard boiled
1 pint drained oysters
Seasoning for eggs:
1 tablespoon butter
2 tablespoons mayonnaise
¼ teaspoon curry powder
¼ teaspoon dry mustard
1 tablespoon chopped chives
½ teaspoon salt
Pinch red pepper

Cream Sauce:
1 cup milk
2 tablespoons flour
1 cup hot milk
2 tablespoons butter
2 tablespoons sharp cheese
½ teaspoon curry powder
1 tablespoon sherry
Red pepper to taste
Salt to taste
3 tablespoons chopped parsley

Boil eggs. Cut in half, remove yolks, and fill cavities with a mixture of butter, mayonnaise, curry powder, dry mustard, chopped chives, salt and red pepper. Stuffing should be moist but slightly dry. Press yolks back into whites. Chill for several hours.

Make cream sauce by shaking 1 cup milk with flour in covered jar. Heat in top of double boiler. Add hot milk and cook until thick. Add butter and cheese. Season with red pepper, salt, chopped parsley, curry powder and sherry. Add oysters and stuffed eggs. Heat until oysters curl and eggs are hot. Serve on thin slices of dry toast. Serve with fruit cup or fresh fruit salad.

Makes 4 servings. Mrs. Walter T. Colquitt

EGG BRUNCH

4 slices bacon
½ pound dried beef (1 large and 1 small jar)
1 to 2 cans mushrooms (reserve some for top)
¼ cup butter
½ cup flour

1 quart milk
Pepper to taste
16 eggs
¼ teaspoon salt
1 cup evaporated milk
¼ cup butter

To make sauce, saute bacon until almost done. Add dried beef, mushrooms and ¼ cup butter. While still hot, add flour and milk. Add pepper, but no salt. Stir until thickened and smooth. Mix eggs with salt and evaporated milk and scramble in ¼ cup butter. Butter casserole. Place a small amount of sauce in bottom, then a layer of eggs, layer of sauce, another layer of eggs, and top with sauce. Garnish the top with mushrooms, if desired. Heat, covered, for 1 hour in a 275° oven. This may be fixed the day before, refrigerated and heated when needed. Makes a very excellent brunch dish.

Serves 12. Mrs. Charles H. Jeter

EGGS IN MUFFIN TINS

Into each compartment of a small muffin tin, put a small piece of butter, a pinch of fine bread crumbs, a little chopped parsley, a little chopped onion, salt and pepper to taste. Then break 1 egg gently into each, put into a 350° oven and let stand until set. Serve piping hot with English muffins and sausage.

Mrs. Whitney Boggs, Jr.

HUEVOS RANCHEROS (RANCH EGGS)

2 onions, minced
1 green pepper, chopped
2 tablespoons butter
¼ cup chili sauce
2½ teaspoons chili powder
1 tablespoon flour
½ teaspoon salt
½ teaspoon Tabasco sauce
½ cup water

Cook onion and green pepper in butter until clear. Add chili sauce. Mix chili powder and flour. Add a little water to make smooth paste. Add paste to onion mixture and stir until smooth. Add salt, Tabasco and rest of water. Serve hot over scrambled eggs.

Makes 6-8 servings. Mrs. Marlin W. Drake, Jr.

SOUFFLE VENDOME (SUNDAY BRUNCH)

3 tablespoons butter
3 tablespoons flour
½ teaspoon salt
Red pepper to taste
¾ cup warm milk
1 teaspoon dry mustard
3 tablespoons grated Parmesan cheese
4 egg yolks
4 beaten egg whites (not too dry)
4 to 6 teaspoons sour cream
4 to 6 eggs
3 tablespoons grated sharp Cheddar cheese

Melt butter. Add flour, salt and pepper, stirring. Slowly add warm milk, cook and stir until thick. Add mustard, Cheddar and Parmesan cheese. Add egg yolks one at a time, stirring after each one is added. Return to heat, bring to gentle boil, stirring constantly for one minute. Cool. Fold in beaten egg whites. Grease a single souffle dish, dust with a little grated Parmesan cheese. Cover bottom of dish with ½ cup souffle mixture. With back of tablespoon make 4 to 6 hollows in souffle; spoon one teaspoon sour cream into each hollow. Break one egg in each. Salt and pepper. Cover with rest of souffle mixture. Bake in 350° oven for 25-30 minutes until it is firm.

Serves 4. Mrs. W. W. Lincoln

EGGS A LA KING

1 can cream of mushroom soup
1 chopped green pepper
Oleo or butter
Chopped pimiento
Sliced boiled eggs

Heat soup. Dilute slightly with cream. Saute chopped green pepper in oleo or butter. Add to mushroom soup. Add chopped pimiento and sliced (or quartered) hard boiled eggs. Cook slowly 10 minutes. Serve on toast triangles or on top of ham slice.

Mrs. Morley Hudson

BACON-CHEESE SOUFFLE

½ cup butter
1 cup all-purpose flour
2½ teaspoons salt
¼ teaspoon pepper
⅛ teaspoon nutmeg
2 cups milk
½ cup heavy cream
2 cups grated natural Swiss cheese
½ cup snipped fresh chives
8 eggs, separated
About 9 slices white bread
6 lean bacon slices
1 small mushroom

About 2½ hours before serving: In large saucepan, melt butter. Stir in flour, salt, pepper and nutmeg. Slowly stir in milk and cream, blending well. Cook, while stirring constantly, until smooth and thickened. Blend in grated cheese (reserve 2 tablespoons) and snipped chives. Remove from heat, turn into large bowl, then stir in egg yolks one at a time. Let cool slightly. Start heating oven to 350°.

Butter a souffle dish, which measures 10 cups to brim. Line bottom of dish with about 3 bread slices cut to fit. Now cut 6 more bread slices in half lengthwise. Place them upright, and side by side, in a circle, around inner edge of dish. Lace a strip of bacon, in figure-eight fashion, around every two of these slices. Fold a 35-inch length of foil, 12 inches wide, in half lengthwise; wrap around outside of dish, so that a collar 3 inches high stands above rim; fasten with cellophane tape.

In large bowl, beat egg whites until stiff; then carefully fold into cooled cheese mixture; pour into souffle dish. Cut mushrooms into thin slices; lay some in a circle and one in the center on top of souffle mixture; sprinkle reserved grated cheese over top. Bake 1 hour and 40 minutes, or until golden. Carefully remove foil collar. Serve at once.

Makes 8 servings.

Mrs. James A. Latham

QUICHE LORRAINE

Crust:

1 cup flour
½ teaspoon salt
1 cup butter or oleo
3 to 4 tablespoons cold water

Sift flour and salt together; cut in butter or oleo. Add water and work into dough. Roll out on lightly floured board. Place in oblong ovenproof dish or pie pan.

Filling:

½ pound bacon, fried until crisp
1 pound Swiss or American cheese, grated
3 whole eggs, slightly beaten
2 cups milk or light cream
1 teaspoon salt
Red and black pepper to taste
Dash of Worcestershire sauce
Dash of Tabasco
1 medium onion
1 small can mushrooms (optional)
2 tablespoons butter

Crumble bacon into crust; cover with grated cheese. Mix eggs, milk (or cream), salt, pepper, Worcestershire sauce and Tabasco. Set aside. Saute minced onion and mushrooms in butter until onion is transparent. Add them to egg mixture. Pour it over cheese and bacon layers. Garnish with paprika. Bake in 400 degree oven 35 to 45 minutes. Allow to cool before serving for about 5 minutes.

Serves 4. Note: this makes a wonderful Sunday night supper, served with a fruit bowl.

Mrs. Phil Foster

CHEESE SOUFFLE

¼ cup butter or oleo
¼ cup flour
½ teaspoon salt
1 cup milk
½ pound grated sharp cheese
4 beaten egg yolks
4 beaten egg whites

Melt butter (or oleo) in top of double boiler. Add flour and salt. Blend well. Add milk; stir until thick and smooth. Add cheese; stir until melted. Add this mixture to the egg yolks. Fold in egg whites. Pour into greased casserole. Bake in oven (325°) for 1 hour and 15 minutes.

Serves 4 (approximately). This recipe may be varied by using 1 cup strained tomatoes instead of milk. Also 1 cup cooked corn or other vegetable may be substituted for the cheese. If canned corn is used, drain corn before adding it.

Mrs. W. J. Knighton
Mrs. Warren Ogden
Mrs. William McBride
Mrs. Vincent S. Brennan

CHEESE FONDUE A LA LAUSANNE

2 pounds New York State sharp cheese
2 pounds imported Swiss cheese
4 garlic buds, chopped
¾ bottle Chablis (or sauterne)
6 tablespoons cornstarch (approximately)
½ to 1 cup kirsch
Salt
Speck of pepper
Nutmeg (optional)
French bread, broken into bite-size chunks

Grate cheese. Rub fireproof bowl with chopped garlic buds. Remove garlic. Put bowl over burner on stove (low heat), adding 1 small water glass of wine for each serving. Heat wine. Add cheese. Keep fire very low. Stir constantly in figure 8 motion. After cheese is melted, put cornstarch in a cup with the kirsch and mix. Add mixture to cheese. Add salt, pepper and nutmeg. Rub chafing dish with garlic buds. Remove buds. Transfer cheese to chafing dish. Keep burner under chafing dish lit throughout meal. Spear a piece of bread with a fork and dip it into cheese.

This must be eaten immediately after preparation. When cheese has been heated for some time it tends to become stringy. May be used for a whole meal, served with a salad, and fruit for dessert.

Will serve 5 persons.

Linda Laskey

Breads

Cross Lake

CROSS LAKE

Situated on the west edge of Shreveport, boaters, water skiers, and anglers all enjoy this lake. Cross Lake provides outstanding fishing, swimming and boating facilities. Picnic and park facilities are available with the yacht club located nearby. Annual Regatta races are held during the Holiday in Dixie celebration.

BOB'S FRENCH TOAST

3 eggs
4 tablespoons milk
¼ teaspoon vanilla
2 tablespoons sugar
Powdered sugar

Mix first four ingredients thoroughly in shallow bowl. Dip each side of bread in batter (do not soak). Fry in ¼ inch hot shortening (450° in electric skillet) until brown crust forms on both sides. Butter and sprinkle with powdered sugar.

Serves 4. **Bob Stewart**

FRAULEIN DOUGHNUTS

1¼ cups milk scalded with 1 tablespoon sugar
1 cake yeast
4½ cups flour
¾ cup sugar
1 stick butter
1 egg
¼ teaspoon grated nutmeg

To make sponge, cool milk and sugar mixture and add yeast. Let dissolve. Stir 1½ cups flour into milk. Place the sponge in a warm place for about 1½ hours. Cream butter and egg together well. Add nutmeg, then combine with sponge. Add remaining flour to sponge. Work well. Place in a greased bowl. Let rise until doubled. Roll out and cut with doughnut cutter, or, cut in strips 1" x 4" and twist two together, spiral fashion, pinching ends, for crullers. Fry in hot (375°) deep fat. Drain on brown paper. Sprinkle with granulated sugar.

Mrs. Marshall Martin

POPOVERS

⅞ cup milk or ⅞ cup water plus ¼ cup non-fat dry milk solids
2 eggs
1 tablespoon soft butter or shortening
1 cup sifted flour
¼ teaspoon salt

Place all ingredients in glass container of electric blender in order given. Cover container and turn on blender, running until ingredients are thoroughly blended, about 20 seconds. **Pour into greased or ungreased cast aluminum or cast iron muffin pans or custard cups, filling not more than half full.** If custard cups are used, place them on a shallow baking pan **to place** in oven. Bake in preheated oven until puffed and brown, about 35 to 45 minutes. Pierce side of each popover with sharp knife to allow steam to escape, and serve immediately with butter and jam or marmalade. **Oven temperature: 425°.**

Makes 8 large popovers. **Mrs. T. O. Perry, Jr.**

GENUINE IMITATION HOMEMADE DONUTS

1 can refrigerated biscuits
2 tablespoons water
1 cup confectioners' sugar
¼ teaspoon vanilla

Open biscuits, cut each in half, pull halves out long and twist two halves together, pinching ends to hold. Fry in one inch of hot grease, turning once. Drain, and sugar with a mixture of cinnamon and sugar, or, dip in glaze of water, confectioners' sugar, and vanilla.

Makes 10 donuts. Mrs. John Gallagher

GOLDEN PANCAKES

1 slightly beaten egg
1 cup milk
¼ cup light cream
2 tablespoons butter
1 cup sifted flour
3 teaspoons baking powder
1 teaspoon sugar
¼ teaspoon salt

To egg, add milk, cream and butter. Mix well. Sift dry ingredients together. Add to first mixture. Beat with rotary beater until free of lumps. Cook on griddle until brown on bottom and top bubbly, then turn. Cook at 380° for 2-3 minutes.

Makes four generous servings. Mrs. B. S. Cheesman

SOURDOUGH PANCAKES

1 cup starter (or 1 yeast cake or 1 package of dry yeast)
2 cups flour (ideally ⅓ soya flour from health store and remainder all purpose)
Milk, enough to make a batter (about 1¼ cups)
Salt (a dash too much ruins action of starter)

Let above stand overnight (6-8 hours) in a warm room in a china or plastic bowl large enough to allow for increase in bulk. When it is ready to use, batter will look spongy and have pleasant yeast odor. Next morning, take out one cup of batter and put aside in a cool place as starter for next time. To remainder (about 2 cups of spongy batter) add:

2 eggs
3 tablespoons melted butter
1 teaspoon moistened soda
½ cup sugar

Mix well with fork to a smooth batter. If too thin, add a little spongy starter, but never flour. Cook on a hot griddle.

Serves 4. If made without starter, using one cake of yeast, there will be only about one cup of batter and the second part of recipe must be halved.

Dosite Perkins, Jr.

WAFFLES

1 cup sifted all purpose flour
1 tablespoon sugar
½ teaspoon salt
1½ teaspoons baking powder
1 egg, separated
1 scant cup of milk
2 tablespoons melted butter

Sift dry ingredients. Beat egg yolk in milk and add to dry ingredients. Beat until batter is smooth. Add melted butter, fold in stiffly beaten egg white.

½ cup broken nuts, ¼ cup crisply fried crumbled bacon, or ½ cup blueberries may be added before folding in egg whites. Serves 4.

Mrs. Dayton H. Waller, Jr.

BUTTERMILK BISCUITS

2 cups flour
3 teaspoons baking powder
½ teaspoon soda
1 teaspoon salt
7 tablespoons shortening
⅔ cup buttermilk

Sift dry ingredients. Cut in shortening. Add buttermilk. Pat out on floured board and cut. Do not roll with rolling pin. Cook in 450° oven 10-12 minutes.

Makes about 2 dozen. These may be made with sweet milk. Use same amounts and omit soda.

Mrs. Robert A. Stacy, Jr.

NEVER-FAIL BISCUITS

2 cups flour
2 tablespoons baking powder
2 tablespoons sugar
1 teaspoon salt
3 rounded tablespoons shortening
1 cup sweet milk

Sift dry ingredients; cut in shortening until mixture resembles coarse crumbs. Add milk, a little at a time, and mix just until dough follows fork around bowl. Turn out on floured surface and knead gently about ½ minute. Roll or pat dough out about ½ inch thick, and cut with biscuit cutter. Bake on ungreased cookie sheet in hot oven (450°) for about 13 minutes. If not brown enough, put under broiler for a few minutes.

Makes about 16 medium biscuits.

Mrs. Harman Chandler

CRUSTY BISCUITS

2 scant cups flour
1 teaspoon salt
4 teaspoons baking powder
½ cup shortening
¾ cup milk

Sift flour, salt and baking powder together. Add shortening and work in with pastry blender or two knives until consistency of coarse corn meal is attained. Add milk all at once, blend and place dough on lightly floured board. Knead lightly 15 times, then roll out to thickness of about ⅓ inch. Cut with standard biscuit cutter, place on greased baking sheet and bake in a preheated oven of 450° for 15 minutes or until lightly browned.

Yields approximately 30. Note: These biscuits are rather crisp, (tender on inside) less than an inch in height. Recipe may be doubled satisfactorily and kept in icebox for later use.

Variations

When using new "homogenized" flour, more milk must be added — approximately ¼ of a cup.

Bran biscuits: Substitute 1 cup 100% bran cereal for one cup of flour, but a little extra flour must be added in order to handle the dough. Use smaller biscuit cutter for these.

Cheese biscuits: Add ¾ cup grated mild American cheese to regular ingredients and cut with smaller cutter.

Sausage biscuits: Cook pan sausage thoroughly in patties ahead of time. Roll biscuits as thin as possible — not over ¼ inch thickness. Crumble sausage, thickly covering all dough. Fold dough in half and proceed to cut out biscuits with smaller cutter.

Mrs. Earl M. Harter, Jr.

OLD FASHIONED SHORTCAKE DOUGH

2 cups cake flour or 1¾ cup bread flour, sifted
3 teaspoons baking powder
1 tablespoon sugar
¼ cup butter
¾ cup rich milk or cream

Resift flour with baking powder and sugar. Cut in butter and add cream. Roll in large oval shape on floured surface or cut individual cakes. Bake at 425° for 12 minutes. Brush top with milk or melted butter to brown. Shortcake is traditionally buttered, covered with a layer of sliced, sweetened strawberries and garnished with whipped cream and a few whole berries.

Mrs. Earl M. Harter, Jr.

CORN BREAD

½ cup corn meal
1 tablespoon flour
⅛ teaspoon sugar
1 teaspoon baking powder
1 teaspoon salt
¼ teaspoon soda
½ cup buttermilk
2 tablespoons bacon drippings or cooking oil
1 egg

Sift meal, flour, sugar, salt and baking powder together. Dissolve soda in buttermilk. Add buttermilk and soda to dry ingredients, then add beaten egg. Pour hot bacon drippings into mixture. Pour into a small greased skillet which has been heated. Individual muffins may be made. Bake at 400° until brown, about 20 minutes.

Serves 4. Mrs. Grady L. Nelson

BUTTERMILK CORN BREAD

¾ cup corn meal
½ teaspoon salt
¼ teaspoon soda
¾ cup buttermilk
1 egg

Mix corn meal, salt and soda. Add buttermilk, then egg. Mix well. Place in skillet (small 6½-inch iron) 2 tablespoons bacon grease and heat. Pour ½ of grease into batter. Mix well, then pour batter into skillet. Leave skillet over burner on top of stove for 2 or 3 minutes, then place in hot oven (400-425°) for 20-25 minutes.

Makes 3 average servings. Mrs. B. S. Cheesman

HUSH PUPPIES

2 cups white corn meal
½ teaspoon salt
¼ teaspoon garlic powder
½ cup onions, finely chopped

Mix corn meal, salt and garlic powder together. Scald with boiling water and to this mixture add ½ cup chopped onions. Pinch off small amount and roll in your hand and place on tray. Cook in deep fat along with fish.

Smith's Cross Lake Inn

Story of Origin of the Hush Puppy

During the Civil War, after Sherman's march through Georgia, many of the homes were left without food except dry corn meal. Since they had no milk or shortening, they would scald the meal with hot water and bake it. One night as the old Negro mammy was cooking this bread for the family, all the dogs came to the back door with mournful howls from hunger, so she took a pone of this bread out of the oven and threw it to them, saying "Now, hush puppies!"; hence the name.

HUSH PUPPIES

3 level cups white corn meal
4½ cups water
7 teaspoons sugar
3 teaspoons salt

Add salt and sugar to water. Bring water to a hard rolling boil. Meal must be warmed to room temperature while dry. Pour boiling water into warm meal and stir briskly until mixture is smooth. After mixture is cool enough to handle, roll into balls approximately one inch in diameter. Cook in deep fat fryer at 350° until golden brown. May be prepared as much as 24 hours ahead of time and cooked just before serving.

Makes 3 to 4 dozen. Worm's Hilltop House

BUTTERMILK HUSH PUPPIES

1½ cups meal
1 tablespoon sugar
½ cup flour
2 teaspoons baking powder
½ teaspoon salt
1 egg, beaten
¾ cup buttermilk
1 small onion, grated

Mix all ingredients in order listed. Make into small balls (about 2 dozen) and fry in deep fat until golden brown.

Mrs. Francis S. Randall

SPOON BREAD

3 cups milk
1 cup white corn meal
2 tablespoons butter
4 eggs, separated
1 scant teaspoon salt
1 tablespoon sugar

Scald milk in double boiler. Remove from heat. Stir in meal carefully, to avoid lumping. Add butter and allow mixture to cool. Beat egg yolks, add salt, sugar and corn meal mush. Fold in well beaten egg whites. Pour mixture in buttered baking dish. Bake until done, about 45 minutes, at 350 degrees.

Serves 6-8. Mrs. Walter T. Colquitt

EGG BREAD

1 cup corn meal (fresh ground preferably)
½ teaspoon soda
½ teaspoon salt
1 teaspoon baking powder
1 quart buttermilk
3 large eggs, separated
1 stick oleo or butter

Sift corn meal, salt, soda and baking powder into mixing bowl. Add buttermilk and beaten egg yolks. Add hot melted butter and fold in blended egg whites, beaten until just frothy. Pour into hot buttered casserole. Bake at 350° for 45 minutes. Use as a starch. It is a spoon bread.

Serves 6 generously Mrs. William J. Norfleet

CORN MEAL ICEBOX ROLLS

1½ cups milk, scalded
⅓ cup sugar
½ cup butter or margarine
1 teaspoon salt
1 package or cake yeast, dissolved in ¼ cup lukewarm water
2 eggs
½ cup corn meal mixed with ½ cup cold milk
4 to 5 cups flour

Scald milk and add sugar, butter and salt. Let cool. Dissolve yeast in lukewarm water. Beat eggs. Add yeast mixture and scalded milk mixture to eggs. Add meal mixture. Stir in flour. Put dough in greased bowl, and allow to rise until double in bulk, covered with waxed paper and towel. Punch dough down. Make into rolls and allow to rise, or, place in refrigerator until ready to use. Will keep 2 to 3 days in refrigerator. Brush tops of rolls with melted butter after forming them. Makes a very delicate roll. Cook at 425° 12-15 minutes, depending on oven.

Makes about 5 dozen small rolls. Mrs. Walter T. Colquitt

COUSIN DEE'S BROWN BRAN ROLLS

½ cup 100% bran cereal
½ cup lard
½ cup boiling water
5 tablespoons sugar
Pinch salt
1 well beaten egg
1 yeast cake dissolved in ½ cup lukewarm water
3 cups flour

Mix bran, lard, boiling water. Add sugar, salt, beaten egg, dissolved yeast cake and flour. Cover in large bowl and let stand several hours in refrigerator. Shape in desired fashion and let rise about 2 hours. Bake at 400° about 20 minutes. Can stand in refrigerator overnight.

Mrs. J. B. McCullough

POTATO ICEBOX ROLLS

1 package or cake of yeast dissolved in ½ cup lukewarm water
¾ cup shortening
¾ cup sugar
1 cup mashed potatoes
7 cups flour
2 eggs, well beaten
1 cup scalded milk

Soak yeast in ½ cup lukewarm water, add to shortening and sugar. Cool and add mashed potatoes, flour, eggs and milk. Work until you can handle. Let rise 2 hours, then put in refrigerator. Make out rolls several hours before cooking so they can rise. Cook for about 10 minutes at 400°. May be kept in refrigerator for several days.

Makes about 2 dozen rolls. Mrs. J. S. Taylor

ROLLS

¼ cup sugar
1 cup lukewarm milk
1 cake compressed yeast
⅓ cup butter
4¾ cups flour
1 teaspoon salt
3 eggs, well beaten

Stir 1 tablespoon sugar into lukewarm milk and add the yeast to soften. Cream butter with rest of sugar. Add a bit of the flour, then alternate the milk mixture with the rest of the flour and salt. Add the beaten eggs. Do not use hands — mix with a spoon. When raised the first time, divide in half. Use plenty of flour when you pat out the dough. Shape as desired. Place in buttered pans, leaving room between each roll. Let rise until light and bake at 375° for 15 to 20 minutes or until nicely browned. Dough may be kept in refrigerator.

Mrs. Jackson B. Davis

FRENCH DINNER ROLLS

1 package yeast
1 tablespoon sugar
¼ cup warm water
1 cup milk
4 cups sifted flour
3 tablespoons butter
¼ cup sugar
1 teaspoon salt
1 egg, beaten
½ teaspoon lemon extract

Scald milk and set aside to cool. Dissolve yeast and sugar in water. Add warm milk and 1½ cups flour. Beat smooth, cover and let rise until light — 45 minutes in warm spot. Cream butter, sugar and salt. Add yeast mixture to butter mixture, add egg, flavoring and remaining flour. Knead until smooth and springy, at least 5 minutes. Let rise until double — 1 hour. Turn out and make into rolls (see below). Place on greased sheet or in muffin tins. Let rise until light — 30 minutes. Bake 15 minutes at 425°. Will freeze well after made into rolls and wrapped airtight. Allow 3 hours to thaw and rise in warm room. Will keep in refrigerator several days after rolls are made; allow 1½ hours to rise in warm room.

Makes about 3 dozen.

Butter Crisps

Roll dough into thin rectangle. Butter and cut into strips 1½ inches wide. Use pastry wheel or very sharp buttered knife. Pile strips on top of each other, 5 or 6 high. Cut down, making slices ½ inch thick. Put cut side up in muffin pans. Butter tops before last rising.

Scones or Napkin Rolls

Roll dough into circle as thin as possible. Butter, and cut into very small wedges — pie shaped — 1½ inches wide at outside edge. Roll up each wedge, starting at wide end. Put on greased sheet. Butter tops before last rising.

Mrs. T. Haller Jackson, Jr.
(nee Huldah Edens)

ELLEN'S ROLLS

1 yeast cake
2 tablespoons lukewarm water
2 eggs
½ cup sugar
1 teaspoon salt
1 cup sweet milk
½ stick butter
About 4 cups flour or enough to make stiff dough

Dissolve yeast in warm water. Beat eggs with sugar and salt. Scald milk and melt butter in milk. Combine ingredients and add flour. Let double in size. Knead, roll out, and cut. Twist shape is good. Place on greased pan and let rise one hour. Bake at 450° until lightly browned.

Mrs. James B. Haynes, Jr.

ROLLS

2 cups sweet milk
½ cup cooking oil or melted shortening
½ cup sugar
1 yeast cake
½ cup water
½ teaspoon sugar
1 egg
2 teaspoons salt
8 cups sifted flour

Scald sweet milk. Pour milk over shortening and ½ cup sugar. Let cool. Soak yeast cake in tepid water. Add ½ teaspoon sugar. To milk, shortening and sugar mixture add beaten egg and the dissolved yeast. Sift in 4 cups sifted flour and salt. Mix well. Then work in 4 more cups sifted flour. Knead lightly until all flour has been mixed in well. Set in warm place to rise. When double in bulk, work down to original size. Set in refrigerator. Dough will again double in bulk. When ready to bake, pinch dough into small balls about the size of a fifty cent piece, flatten and fold over to form pocketbook rolls. Place close together in greased pan and let rise in warm place for 1 to 1½ hours. Cook at 425° about 20-25 minutes. Dough may be kept in refrigerator for several days.

Makes about 6 dozen rolls. Mrs. T. Haller Jackson, Jr.

BUTTERMILK ROLLS

1 cake yeast
1 pint buttermilk
¼ teaspoon soda
¼ teaspoon baking powder
1 teaspoon salt
1 tablespoon sugar
3 tablespoons shortening
4 cups flour

Crumble yeast in small amount of buttermilk, stir until dissolved. Add remainder of milk. Mix soda, baking powder, salt, sugar, and shortening. Cream and add to buttermilk. Then add 3 cups of flour. Beat vigorously. Add rest of flour and roll out. Cut with biscuit cutter to make pocketbook or plain rolls. Cover and let rise from one to two hours. Bake at 400°.

Makes 2 large pans of rolls. Mrs. L. C. Allen, Jr.

EASY BUTTERMILK ROLLS

1 yeast cake
1 cup buttermilk at room temperature
2½ cups flour
½ teaspoon soda
1 teaspoon salt
1 teaspoon baking powder
1 tablespoon sugar
3 tablespoons shortening
Melted butter

Dissolve yeast cake in buttermilk at room temperature. Sift dry ingredients. Cut in shortening. Add buttermilk and yeast. Knead well. Roll out and cut with large round biscuit cutter. Dip each in melted butter and fold over. Let rise until double in size. Cook in 400° oven 15 minutes.

Makes 2 dozen. Mrs. Robert A. Stacy, Jr.

APPLE MUFFINS

1 egg, beaten
¾ cup milk
5 tablespoons bacon grease
1¾ cups flour
½ teaspoon salt
¾ cup sugar (scant)
2 teaspoons baking powder
¼-½ teaspoon nutmeg
½ teaspoon cinnamon
1 chopped apple

Mix egg, milk and bacon grease. Sift dry ingredients together and add to liquid mixture. Add apple last. Pour into muffin pans. Sprinkle additional cinnamon and sugar on top. Bake at 425° about 15 minutes.

Makes 1 dozen plus. Jack Burrows, Nacogdoches, Texas

NEW ENGLAND BLUEBERRY MUFFINS

¾ cup flour
1 teaspoon baking powder
¾ cup sugar
½ teaspoon salt
¾ cup blueberries
1 egg, well beaten
¼ cup milk
1 tablespoon butter

Mix and sift dry ingredients and add blueberries. Add milk to egg, then butter, and stir lightly into dry ingredients. Drop by spoonfuls in buttered muffin pans, and bake in a 400° oven for 25 to 30 minutes.

Makes 8 to 12 muffins. Mrs. Robert Ewing Brown

MUFFINS

2 cups flour
3 teaspoons baking powder
½ teaspoon salt
1 cup milk
2 eggs
1 tablespoon shortening

Sift flour, baking powder and salt; add milk, well beaten eggs and melted shortening. Mix well. Grease muffin tins and put 2 tablespoons of batter in each. Bake in hot oven (450°) 20-25 minutes.

Mrs. Marshall Martin

ORANGE MUFFINS

1 cup sugar
½ cup margarine
2 eggs
2 cups flour
1 teaspoon soda
½ teaspoon salt
1 cup buttermilk
1 orange
1 cup raisins
½ cup chopped pecans

Make a batter out of the first seven ingredients in the order they are listed. Grate orange rind, reserve juice. Add rind, raisins and pecans to batter. Pour in greased muffin tins. Bake at 350°. Combine juice of orange and ⅓ cup sugar. Bring to boil. Glaze muffins.

Mrs. Albert Weil

BANANA MUFFINS

1 cup sugar (white or raw)
1 cup margarine
1 cup mashed bananas (2 large)
4½ tablespoons buttermilk
2 eggs
1½ cups sifted flour
1 teaspoon soda
1 teaspoon cinnamon
1 teaspoon nutmeg
¼ teaspoon salt
1 teaspoon vanilla

Cream sugar and margarine. Add bananas, buttermilk and eggs, slightly beaten. Mix dry ingredients and fold into above mixture. Add vanilla. Pour into greased muffin pans and bake at 325° about 30 minutes.

Makes 14 to 16 medium size muffins.

Mrs. Norman Bills

COFFEE PECAN LOAF

2 cups sifted flour
2½ teaspoons baking powder
½ teaspoon salt
⅔ cup shortening
1 cup sugar
2 tablespoons instant coffee
3 eggs
⅔ cup milk
1 teaspoon vanilla
1 cup finely chopped pecans

Sift the flour, baking powder and salt into a bowl. In a second bowl cream the shortening with the sugar and powdered coffee. Beat in one egg at a time, until light and fluffy. Add the flour mixture, alternately with the combined milk and vanilla. Add finely chopped pecans. Pour into a well greased loaf pan (8" x 5" x 3"). Bake 55 minutes in a moderate oven (350°) or until cake tester inserted in the center comes out clean. Use sharp knife when slicing.

Mrs. Si Borden

NUT MUFFINS

2 cups flour
2 teaspoons baking powder
1 cup sugar
Cinnamon to taste
2 eggs, separated
½ stick melted butter
Nuts
¾ cup milk

Mix dry ingredients with beaten egg yolks. Add melted butter and milk, then fold in egg whites, beaten stiff, then the nuts. Bake at 400° for 25 minutes.

Mrs. Jack R. Lamb

BANANA NUT BREAD

1 cup sugar
½ cup butter
3 crushed ripe bananas
2 eggs, well beaten
2 cups flour
1 teaspoon soda
Pinch of salt
1 cup nuts

Cream sugar and butter together, and add crushed bananas, beaten eggs, sifted dry mixture and nuts. Bake in greased and floured loaf pan for about 1 hour at 300°. May be served with softened butter or cream cheese. Slice thin.

Mrs. David Walke
Mrs. Leroy Scott, Jr.
Mrs. H. W. Mulkey, Jr.

CRANBERRY BREAD

2 cups flour
1 cup sugar
1½ teaspoons baking powder
½ teaspoon salt
Juice and grated rind of 1 orange
2 tablespoons melted butter or shortening
1 beaten egg
½ cup chopped walnut meats
1-2 cups fresh cranberries cut in halves

Sift dry ingredients. Add combined juice, rind, melted shortening and enough water to make ¾ cup. Add beaten egg and mix. Fold in chopped nuts and cut up cranberries. Bake at 350° 50-60 minutes. (Waxed paper in pans is a help.)

Mrs. Robert G. Chandler
Mrs. C. M. Zaenglein

PEANUT BUTTER BREAD

2 cups flour
½ cup sugar
1 teaspoon salt
3 teaspoons baking powder
½ cup peanut butter (crunchy or smooth)
1¼ cups milk

Sift flour, sugar, salt and baking powder. Mix the peanut butter in with fork. Add milk and bake in a loaf pan 1 hour or more at 300°.

Mrs. Lea R. Hall

APRICOT NUT LOAF

1 cup sugar
2 tablespoons shortening
1 egg
¾ cup milk
¾ cup orange juice
4 teaspoons grated orange rind
3 cups flour
3½ teaspoons baking powder
1 teaspoon salt
1 cup finely chopped dried apricots
¾ cup chopped nuts if desired

Grease 9" x 5" x 2½" loaf pan. Mix thoroughly sugar, shortening and egg. Stir in milk, orange juice and rind. Sift together flour, baking powder, salt and add to above. Blend apricots and nuts and add to batter. Pour into prepared pan and let stand 20 minutes. Heat oven to 350°. Bake until toothpick thrust into center comes out clean.

Mrs. B. S. Cheesman

ORANGE BREAD

Rind of 2 oranges, candied
2 cups sugar
¼ cup water
1 egg
3 tablespoons melted butter
3½ cups flour
3 teaspoons baking powder
¼ teaspoon salt
1 cup milk or ½ cup milk and ½ cup orange juice
1 cup pecans (optional)

Cut orange rind (no white part) in strips with scissors. Use 3 oranges if small. Cover with boiling water three times, then cook with 1 cup of sugar and water, very slowly.

To make batter, beat egg, add other cup of sugar, butter, and add flour sifted with dry ingredients alternately with milk. Add nuts and candied orange rind with juice, cooled. Bake in loaf pan at 325° for one hour, then at 350° for about 15 minutes. Delicious toasted.

Mrs. Sam Haynes

PARMESAN ICING CRUST FOR BREAD

1 loaf Pullman (unsliced) bread
1 clove garlic, minced
½ pound butter
1 tall can Parmesan cheese

Remove crust from sides and top of bread, leaving only bottom and ends. Slice bread through to bottom. Add garlic to about four tablespoons butter. Apply with pastry brush between slices of bread. Add cheese to remainder of butter until good icing consistency is attained. Spread sides and top of bread, completely covering it. Wrap securely and close in foil. Bake 40 to 50 minutes in slow oven (300°).

Mrs. E. Rudolph Prince, McDade, La.

HERB BUTTER FOR BREAD

⅓ pound sweet butter (in the store this is labeled "unsalted butter" — do not use regular butter)
1 tablespoon (heaping) finely chopped chives or green onion, tops only
1 tablespoon finely chopped fresh parsley
1 level tablespoon Fines Herbes
Few drops of lemon juice

Cream all of the above together and let it set unrefrigerated for at least one hour. Butter slices of French bread and bake in 300° oven about 30 minutes. You may also use unsliced salt rising bread. Cut crust off all sides and ends. Cut in half lengthwise, then in 1-inch slices. Butter on two sides and bake.

Mrs. M. Allen Dickson

VIENNESE BUTTER FOR BREAD

½ pound butter
½ teaspoon rosemary
½ teaspoon thyme
½ teaspoon marjoram
½ teaspoon parsley
½ teaspoon celery salt

Melt butter, add above ingredients, and spread generously on French or Viennese bread. Cut loaf in slices but leave in loaf shape. Wrap in foil to warm in oven. Makes enough for 2 loaves of French bread.

Mrs. Edward N. Henderson

ANADAMA BREAD

1⅓ cups yellow corn meal
2 tablespoons salt
6 tablespoons shortening
1 cup unsulphured molasses or open kettle cane syrup
2 ounces yeast
12-14 cups all-purpose flour

Add the corn meal and salt to five cups cold water, cook and stir until thick to avoid lumps. Let mush cool to lukewarm, add shortening, syrup, yeast. Add flour gradually; knead when dough becomes too heavy to stir. Let rise in a greased bowl until double in size, in a warm place (about 80°). Punch down and let rest about ten minutes. Makes four to six loaves, depending on size of pans you are using. Grease bread pans well. Brush loaves with melted shortening and sprinkle with a mixture of 1 tablespoon each corn meal and salt. Let rise about 45 minutes, until double in size. Oven temperature: 350°; baking time: 1 hour.

Mrs. John G. Wafer, Jr.

EGG BREAD

¾ cup milk
1 cup water
2 yeast cakes
1 tablespoon salt
2 tablespoons sugar
3 tablespoons shortening
5 cups bread flour
4 egg yolks

Heat milk and water until lukewarm. Add yeast cakes and let rise. Then add sugar, salt and shortening, beaten egg yolks and flour. Beat, or knead by hand until batter is smooth. Oil top of batter and cover with damp cloth. Let rise, punch down and place in well greased pans. Let rise again and bake at 350° for 45 minutes to 1 hour.

Makes 2 small loaves.

For Herb Bread:

Add:
1 tablespoon grated Romano cheese
¼ tablespoon oregano

Mix this into dough before letting it rise second time.

Mrs. Otis C. Coles, Jr.

WHOLE WHEAT BREAD

1 package dry yeast
2 cups warm water
½ teaspoon sugar
3 cups whole wheat flour
3 cups white flour
½ cup sugar
½ cup wheat germ
1½ tablespoons salt
1 to 1⅓ cups dry milk (amount to make 1 quart liquid; look on the box. It varies with the brand of dry milk used, but use it dry)
2 beaten eggs
½ cup salad oil

Dissolve yeast in warm water with the touch of sugar added. Mix all the dry ingredients. Beat the eggs in the yeast mixture. Alternately mix salad oil and yeast-egg mixture into the dry ingredients. Knead out on floured board. You will need to use ½ to ¾ cup more flour (white) to work the dough until it is not gummy. Let rise to double size (3 hours or more, depending on heat in room). Work down and let rise again (will take shorter time). Knead down and form into loaves. Put in greased loaf pan. Let rise. Bake in a 325° oven for 35 to 45 minutes . . . until golden brown. Last 5 minutes of baking rub oleo over top.

Makes 2 large loaves or 4 small loaves.

Mrs. B. K. Eaves

BROWN BREAD

- 3 cups sifted graham flour
- 1 cup sifted white flour
- 2 cups buttermilk
- 1½ cups brown sugar
- 1 cup raisins
- 1 cup broken pecans
- 1 teaspoon soda
- ½ teaspoon salt

Mix ingredients. Grease and flour 4 1-pound baking powder cans. Fill cans slightly less than ⅔ full. Put lids on cans. Bake in 375° oven for 1 hour. This bread is good sliced and spread with butter. Freezes well.

Mrs. M. B. Chastain

COLQUITT HONEY BREAD

- 2 cups milk, scalded
- ½ cup honey
- 5 tablespoons margarine or butter
- 4 teaspoons salt
- 2 yeast cakes
- 2 cups lukewarm water
- 2 eggs
- 12 cups sifted flour, approximately

Scald milk. While hot, add honey, margarine and salt. Cool to lukewarm. Dissolve yeast in lukewarm water. Mix with milk mixture. Beat eggs until light, add water-yeast-milk mixture. Add flour. All this may be added with electric mixer except the last two or three cups — these will have to be stirred in by hand. Grease a large bowl lightly, place dough in, oil a piece of waxed paper and cover (oiled side down), then cover with a clean tea towel, place in a warm spot, free from drafts, and allow to double in size. This will take several hours. Punch down and let rise again (not so long). Turn out on floured board and knead until "springy." Shape into loaves and place in greased pans. Let rise to double in bulk and bake from 30-50 minutes in oven 350°. Turn out of pans, brush with melted butter, and cover with waxed paper and a cloth while cooling, if you want a soft crust (best for toast). Do not cover while cooling, if you prefer a crisp crust. Keep dough covered all the time it is rising to prevent crust forming.

This makes about 6 medium loaves. Keeps well in freezer if wrapped immediately after cooking in foil. A delicious "herb" bread is made with this basic recipe. Chop parsley, chives, add a little lemon juice, garlic juice, salt, oregano and soft butter. Roll dough out as for biscuits, spread with mixture, roll up like a French loaf and bake in shallow pan. Sesame seeds are good mixed into the dough. A sweet loaf may be made by rolling out dough, spreading with a mixture of cinnamon, sugar, grated orange rind, and butter. And this bread is easy to make.

Mrs. Walter T. Colquitt

WHITE CHEESE BREAD

2½ cups scalded milk
4 teaspoons soft butter
2 envelopes yeast
½ cup lukewarm water
7 cups flour
3 cups grated sharp cheese
1 tablespoon salt
2 tablespoons sugar

In a large warm mixing bowl combine milk, butter, salt and sugar. Let mixture cool to lukewarm. Dissolve yeast in water and add to milk mixture. Stir in 4 cups sifted flour and cheese. Add the remainder of flour, mixing with hands when dough becomes too stiff. Turn dough onto floured board and knead for 6 to 8 minutes, working ½ cup flour into dough. Put dough in buttered bowl and cover with warm towel for one hour or more. Punch down dough, knead, divide in half, and shape to fit pans. If small aluminum pans are used, divide into thirds. Allow dough to double in bulk in either two or three pans depending on size, covered with a hot towel. Bake in moderate oven at 350°, 35 to 40 minutes or until it shrinks from sides of pan. Cool by laying on side in pan covered with a warm towel.

Mrs. John D. Caruthers, Jr.

SWEDISH RYE BREAD

1 package active dry yeast or 1 cake compressed yeast
¼ cup water
¼ cup medium brown sugar
¼ cup light molasses
1 tablespoon salt
2 tablespoons shortening
1½ cups hot water
2½ cups sifted medium rye flour
3 tablespoons caraway seed or 2 tablespoons grated orange peel
3½ to 4 cups enriched flour

Soften active dry yeast in warm water, or compressed yeast in lukewarm water. In big bowl, combine brown sugar, molasses, salt and shortening; add hot water and stir until sugar dissolves. Cool to lukewarm. Stir in rye flour; beat well. Add softened yeast and caraway seed or orange peel; mix well. Reserve some of enriched flour for kneading, add enough of remainder to make a soft dough. Turn out on floured surface. Cover; let rest 10 minutes. Knead until smooth and satiny, about 10 minutes. Place dough in lightly greased bowl, turning once to grease surface. Cover and let rise in warm place until double (about 1½ to 2 hours). Punch down. Turn out on a lightly floured surface and divide into 2 portions. Round each piece of dough in a ball; cover and let rest 10 minutes. Pat balls of dough in 2 round loaves and place on greased baking sheet. Cover and let rise in warm place until almost double, about 1½ to 2 hours. Bake in moderate oven (375°) 25 to 30 minutes. For a soft crust, butter tops while hot. Grand for sandwiches or buffet suppers.

Makes 2 round loaves.

Mrs. Joe Warren, Midland, Texas

HOME MADE LIGHT BREAD

1½ cakes yeast
1 cup warm water
1 cup shortening
½ cup sugar
1 tablespoon salt
1 cup boiling water
2 beaten eggs
7 cups flour, sifted

Dissolve yeast in warm water, and put aside. Cream together shortening, sugar and salt. Add boiling water. Cool slightly and put in yeast mixture. Add beaten eggs and sifted flour. Put in greased bowl and let rise once. Knead in 2 minutes and put back in bowl; let rise again. Put dough in greased loaf pans; let rise again, and bake at 350° for 45 minutes.

Makes 2 loaves. Mrs. Fielder Calhoun

HERB BREAD

1 cup rolled oats
2 cups boiling water
2 packages active dry yeast
⅓ cup lukewarm water
2½ teaspoons salt
2 tablespoons soft butter
½ cup molasses (black strap makes a darker bread; regular molasses, a lighter bread)
About 6 cups enriched white flour
2 teaspoons leaf sage, crumbled
1 teaspoon leaf marjoram, crumbled
½ teaspoon caraway seed

Early in the morning (while getting breakfast), put rolled oats in large bowl and pour boiling water over them. About half hour later, while soaked oats are still warm, soak yeast by pouring on top of lukewarm water, letting stand about 5 minutes. Add to the soaked oats, the salt, molasses, butter and herbs. By now yeast is ready. Stir and add to above mixture. Next stir in 2 cups of flour, and then 2 more cups. This may be a little hard, but will gradually merge. The last two cups you knead in as follows. Leave your dough in bowl and scatter about half cup flour over it, and with the heel of your hand, press it in. Then shift it around with your fingers, turning it over occasionally, gradually adding flour. This will take 5 to 10 minutes. If it should be sticky, add more flour. When flour is all worked in, shape the dough into a mound in the center of the bowl. Cover with a clean dish towel, and let stand several hours. One hour more or less doesn't matter (no added heat from stove, just a warm room). When about twice the size you started with, cut it down with a knife a half dozen times, back and forth. Divide the dough and place in two well greased bread pans; shape the dough out to the end of the pans. Let the dough be fairly level and smooth on top. Cover and let rise again. It will come up more quickly (in about an hour, or maybe two). Bake in 325° oven on rack about 4 inches from the bottom of the oven. Bake about 50 minutes. If you forget to set the oven ahead of time, just put it in a cold oven and bake 60 minutes. Your bread pans should be about 9" x 5" x 3"

Makes 2 loaves. Mrs. O. B. Mobley, Jr.

MRS. BARKLEY'S BREAD

1 cake yeast
¼ cup warm water
1 scant tablespoon lard
1 scant tablespoon butter
¾ cup warm milk
1 teaspoon salt
1 scant tablespoon sugar
3 cups flour

Dissolve yeast in water. Melt lard and butter in milk. Do not let milk get hot. Add salt, sugar and yeast. Pour into big bowl. Put 3 cups flour in sifter and add enough to liquid in bowl to make a spongy dough. Knead well in bowl, cover with a towel and let rise in warm place until double in bulk, about 45 minutes. Punch down, add flour if sticky. Shape into a loaf and place in buttered bread pan. Cover with towel, let rise again about 45 minutes. Brush top with cream. Bake 45 minutes, or until brown, in 400° oven. Turn out at once to cool. Freezes well if not gone before you get there!

Mrs. J. B. McCullough

STICKY ROLLS

Roll dough
Softened butter
Brown sugar
Dark corn syrup
Pecans

Sticky rolls may be made from any roll dough by rolling it on a floured surface into a rectangular sheet. Spread with softened butter, sprinkle with brown sugar and roll like a jelly roll. Cut in ¾-inch pieces and place close together in a pan heavily greased with shortening and completely covered with a layer of syrup. Sprinkle syrup with a little brown sugar and pecans. Cut side of rolls should be down. Let rise to double in bulk. Bake at 400° for 20 minutes.

Mrs. John D. Caruthers, Jr.

COFFEE CAKE

½ cup butter
1 cup sugar
2 eggs
2 cups flour
2 teaspoons baking powder
Rind of 1 lemon, grated
Vanilla

Cream butter and sugar. Add eggs (beaten together) and flour, which has been sifted three times with baking powder. Fold in lemon rind and vanilla. Put in buttered oblong cake pan and spread with the following:

⅛ cup soft butter
½ cup sugar
1 cup pecans
2 heaping teaspoons cinnamon

Bake in 350° oven for 35-40 minutes. Serve hot or warm. The topping will "drip through the cake." This can be reheated quite successfully.

Mrs. Hurxthal Van Smith

ORANGE BOWKNOTS

Rolls:
1¼ cups milk, scalded
½ cup shortening
⅓ cup sugar
1 teaspoon salt
1 cake yeast
2 well beaten eggs
½ cup orange juice
2 tablespoons grated orange rind
5 cups flour

Glaze:
2 tablespoons orange juice
1 teaspoon grated orange rind
1 cup sifted confectioners' sugar

Combine milk, shortening, sugar and salt. Cool to lukewarm. Soften yeast in this mixture, add eggs, orange juice, orange rind and beat thoroughly. Add flour and mix to a soft dough. Cover. Let stand 10 minutes. Knead lightly on floured surface. Place in greased bowl and cover with a damp cloth. Let stand in warm place until double in bulk — about 2 hours. Punch down. Roll and cut in strips ½ inch wide and 10 inches long. Roll each strip lightly with palms of hands to smooth and shape. Tie each knot and arrange on a greased baking sheet. Let rise. Bake in hot oven (400°) 15 minutes. Spread with Orange Glaze: Blend orange juice, orange rind and confectioners' sugar.

Makes 18 bows.

Mrs. Harrel Mulkey, Jr.

SOUR CREAM COFFEE CAKE

"Batter" mixture:
1 cup butter
1 cup sugar
2 eggs
1 cup sour cream
2 cups flour
1 teaspoon soda
1 teaspoon baking powder
1 teaspoon vanilla extract
2 teaspoons almond extract

Cream butter and sugar together well. Continue creaming and add the eggs one at a time, mixing well. Sift flour, soda and baking powder and add to the mixture alternately with the sour cream. Then add the flavorings — mixing well.

"Crumb" mixture:
3 tablespoons butter
2 teaspoons cinnamon
3 tablespoons flour
½ cup brown sugar
½ cup granulated sugar

Mix together to make a crumb mixture.

Grease and flour generously a 9½" x 13½" pan or oversize loaf pan and pour one-half the batter mixture, spreading evenly. Sprinkle over this one-half the crumb mixture. Add the rest of the batter mixture and cover with the rest of the crumb mixture. Bake in a 350° oven for one hour or until tested done with a toothpick or cake tester. Serve from baking pan. Delicious when served warm. Freezes well after baking.

John L. Rhea, Jr.

GERMAN STREUSEL

1½ cups flour
3 teaspoons baking powder
¾ cup sugar
¼ cup shortening or margarine
1 egg
½ cup milk
1 teaspoon vanilla
½ teaspoon salt

Filling Mixture:
½ cup brown sugar (dark)
2 tablespoons flour
2 teaspoons cinnamon
2 tablespoons melted butter or oleo
½ cup chopped nuts

Sift flour, baking powder, salt and sugar together. Cut in shortening until mixture is like corn meal. Beat egg lightly and combine with milk and vanilla. Add to dry mixture and mix lightly. Do not use an electric mixer. Pour half of mixture into 8" x 8" square pan and top with half of filling. Pour remaining mixture into pan and top with remaining filling. Bake in 375° oven for 25 minutes or until straw inserted into cake comes out clean. Recipe may be doubled and baked in 9" x 12" pan.

To make filling, mix ingredients well and add more flour if too greasy.

Mrs. Elizabeth S. Paul

MARIE'S COFFEE CAKE

1¾ cups sifted cake flour
1½ teaspoons baking powder
½ teaspoon baking soda
½ cup butter
¾ cup granulated sugar
2 eggs
½ pint sour cream
1 teaspoon vanilla
½ cup raisins
½ cup walnuts
2 teaspoons cinnamon
½ cup sugar

Sift flour with baking powder and soda. Cream butter and sugar until light and fluffy. Add eggs one at a time and beat. Add flour mixture alternately with sour cream and vanilla. Put half of batter into baking pan. Top with mixture of the raisins, walnuts, cinnamon and sugar. Add rest of batter and bake for 45 minutes at 350°.

Mrs. Hines Scovell Vaughan

CINNAMON COFFEE CAKE

2 cups brown sugar
⅓ cup butter
1 cup milk
2 egg yolks
3 cups flour
3 teaspoons baking powder
2 egg whites
Cinnamon
Brown sugar

Cream brown sugar and butter. Add milk and beaten egg yolks. Add flour and baking powder. Fold in stiffly beaten whites. Pour into buttered pan. Sprinkle heavily with brown sugar and cinnamon. Cook at 350° for 45 minutes.

Mrs. C. C. Herrmann, Monroe, La.

Vegetables

HOLIDAY IN DIXIE

A treasure hunt, art shows, air shows, parades, sport tournaments, and Neighborhood Block Parties are just some of the features of this 10-day festival celebrating spring and the signing of the Louisiana Purchase in 1803. Barksdale Air Force Bases's Open House, the Doo-Dah Parade, and the Cotillion Ball are among some of the unique highlights of this festival.

ORANGE GLAZED APPLES

2 teaspoons grated orange rind
½ cup fresh orange juice
¼ to ½ cup sugar
4 cooking apples

Combine orange juice, rind and sugar. Pour into heavy iron skillet. Quarter apples and core, but do not peel. Put in skillet skin side up. Cover and simmer for 10 or 15 minutes until apples are tender but still hold shapes. Chill apples and juice and serve cold. Excellent with duck and also with turkey and dressing.

Mrs. Allen Dickson

BAKED CRANBERRY BANANAS

4 firm bananas (green tipped or all yellow)
Lemon juice (fresh)
Salt
¾ cup canned whole cranberry sauce

Preheat oven to 450°. Peel and slice the bananas in ¾" slices. Place in shallow well-greased pan or baking dish and pour 2 or 3 drops of lemon juice on each slice; salt lightly. Spread cranberry sauce over top of each slice, covering completely. Bake uncovered until the bananas are tender and easily pierced with a fork, about 10 to 12 minutes.

Serves 4. Serve hot with poultry, beef or ham. May be kept hot in chafing dish for a buffet supper.

Mrs. Martha Egger Jackson

CURRIED FRUIT BAKE

2 bananas
½ cup pitted black cherries
1 No. 303 can cling peaches
1 No. 303 can pineapple slices
1 No. 303 can pear halves
Small jar maraschino cherries
⅓ cup butter
¾ cup light brown sugar, packed
4 teaspoons curry powder

Day before: heat oven to 325°. Drain fruits after cutting in bite size pieces. Dry fruit on paper towels, then arrange in 1½ quart casserole. Melt butter, add sugar and curry powder. Spoon over fruit. Bake 1 hour uncovered. Let cool and then refrigerate overnight. When ready to serve, reheat casserole in 350° oven for 30 minutes.

Mrs. B. S. Cheesman
Mrs. Jackson Sibley
Mrs. Roscoe Rector
Mrs. Milton Friend

ARTICHOKES WITH CREAMY ANCHOVY SAUCE

4 artichokes
2 tablespoons lemon juice
Sliced onion
1 teaspoon salt
1 tablespoon anchovy paste
1 teaspoon paprika
2 teaspoons lemon juice
Salt and pepper
1 cup sour cream
Garlic salt

Wash artichokes, trim stems to 1 inch. Pull off tough outer leaves and snip off tips of remaining leaves. Place artichokes in 1 inch of boiling water to which 2 tablespoons of lemon juice or seasoned vinegar and sliced onion (just for seasoning) have been added. Sprinkle each artichoke with salt, cover tightly and simmer 45 minutes or until stems can be pierced easily with fork. Turn artichokes upside down to drain. Chill. Slice through center the long way, remove thistle (using ½ artichoke per serving), cover with sauce of blended sour cream, anchovy paste, lemon juice, paprika, salt, pepper and garlic salt. May be served hot as a vegetable.

Mrs. W. W. Lincoln

ASPARAGUS SOUFFLE

1 small can asparagus
Milk
4 tablespoons butter
4 tablespoons sifted flour
1 teaspoon salt
⅛ teaspoon pepper
4 eggs, separated

Put asparagus and juice through a course sieve or blender. Add enough milk to make 2 cups. Melt butter in top of double boiler, add flour and blend until smooth; then slowly add the liquid, salt and pepper. Beat egg yolks and add this to mixture in double boiler and stir constantly until mixture coats spoon well. Put this aside until cold. Beat egg whites until stiff and fold into asparagus mixture. Pour into large souffle dish and set in pan of hot water. Bake 50 minutes at 350°.

Serves 4 or 5.

Harriet Blish McGee

GREEN BEAN OR ASPARAGUS DELIGHT

1 tablespoon butter
4 cans cream of mushroom soup, undiluted
3 No. 300 cans asparagus spears or French style green beans
1 cup grated Longhorn mild cheese
1 can blanched sliced toasted almonds, or Ritz cracker crumbs

Grease casserole with butter. Cover bottom with 1 can mushroom soup. Place drained asparagus or beans over this and sprinkle with grated cheese and almonds or cracker crumbs. Repeat until casserole is full and top with mushroom soup. Bake 30 minutes at 325°.

Serves 8 generously.

Mrs. Arthur James Ferguson
Mrs. Albert Hand

STUFFED ARTICHOKES

6-8 artichokes
1 can Italian style bread crumbs
3 pods garlic, crushed
1 cup freshly grated Romano cheese
2 cups finely chopped parsley
¼ pound butter
1 cup cooking oil
1 lemon, thinly sliced
1½ teaspoons salt
1 teaspoon black pepper

Remove stems of artichokes, and trim the tips of leaves. Pound each artichoke on a board until the leaves open. Combine bread crumbs, cheese, garlic, parsley, salt and pepper. Stuff each leaf and the center of the artichoke. Top each artichoke with a large pat of butter and a thin slice of lemon. Pour over all the artichokes the cooking oil, then place in a large pot of lightly salted water that reaches about ½ inch high on the artichokes, or use a steamer. Cover and cook over medium heat, being sure that the water stays level by adding additional hot water as necessary. Artichokes should cook in about 1 hour, but the best test is to pull a large bottom leaf; when it pulls easily, the artichokes are done. May be served cold, but best hot.

Mrs. William J. Nesbitt

CORN AND ASPARAGUS CASSEROLE

2 12-ounce cans whole kernel corn
2 tablespoons butter
2 tablespoons flour
½ cup milk
½ cup liquid from corn
½ cup grated Cheddar cheese
1 egg, well beaten
1 tablespoon minced parsley
¼ teaspoon celery salt
½ cup blanched almonds, slivered and toasted
1 package frozen asparagus, parboiled

Drain corn; reserve liquid. Melt butter and blend flour. Slowly stir in milk and corn liquid. Bring to a boil, stirring constantly. Add cheese, egg, parsley and celery salt. Stir until well blended and mixture thickens. Add almonds. Remove from heat. Put a layer of corn, asparagus and then sauce in baking dish. Bake at 350° for 20 minutes.

Serves 6.

Mrs. Robert Roberts, III

GREEN BEANS AMANDINE

2 cans French style green beans
8-10 slices bacon
½ cup chopped onion
5 tablespoons vinegar
Salt
Pepper
3 tablespoons browned slivered almonds

Drain beans early in day and set aside. Fry bacon, dice and save. Brown onions in bacon fat, add beans, vinegar, salt and pepper. Heat these ingredients, then refrigerate all day. Just before serving add bacon and almonds and heat.

Serves 6.

Mrs. Frank M. Cook

PARTY BEAN CASSEROLE

4 packages frozen sliced green beans
1 8-ounce can mushrooms
1 medium onion, cut fine
1 stick butter
¼ cup flour
2 cups milk
1 cup light cream
¾ pound sharp cheese, grated
⅛ tablespoon Tabasco sauce
2 teaspoons soy sauce
1 teaspoon salt
1 teaspoon Accent
1 5-ounce can water chestnuts, sliced
¾ cup almonds, sliced

Cook beans and put in casserole. While beans are cooking, saute mushrooms and onion in butter. Add flour, milk, cream, cheese, seasonings, and water chestnuts. Pour sauce over beans in casserole and top with almonds. Bake at 350° for 20 minutes.

Makes 16 servings. Mrs. James Edwin Allen

HERBED STRING BEANS

4 slices bacon
1 small onion, thinly sliced
2 tablespoons chopped green pepper
1 No. 2 can string beans or 2½ cups cooked beans
2 tablespoons chopped parsley
⅛ teaspoon dried marjoram
Tiny pinch dried rosemary
¼ teaspoon Accent
Salt and pepper to taste

Dice bacon slices, fry slowly until crisp and remove bacon bits and reserve. Add onion and green pepper to bacon drippings and saute gently for about 5 minutes. Add beans (drained) and all other seasonings. Cover and simmer gently for 5 minutes. Turn the beans into a heated serving dish and sprinkle the bacon bits over the top.

Serves 3 to 4. May be done a day ahead and reheated.

Mrs. Edgar Galloway

SWISS BEANS

No. 2 can French cut green beans
½ pint sour cream
½ pound process Swiss cheese
2 tablespoons butter
2 tablespoons flour
Salt and pepper to taste
½ teaspoon sugar
1 teaspoon grated onion

Drain beans and place in buttered casserole dish. Melt butter, add flour until blended. Blend sour cream, stirring continuously, then add salt, pepper, sugar and onion. Fold sour cream mixture into beans and mix. Grate Swiss cheese and sprinkle over beans. Run into a 375° oven until cheese is melted.

Serves 4 or 5. Mrs. Campbell Tucker

GREEN BEAN CASSEROLE

1 can cream of mushroom soup
1 tablespoon Worcestershire sauce
1/8 to 1/4 teaspoon Tabasco
Garlic, small pod, chopped
1/2 pound grated Old English cheese
Buttered bread crumbs
1 No. 2 can French string beans
1/3 to 1/2 cup toasted slivered almonds
Red pepper to taste

Heat soup in double boiler. Add the Worcestershire sauce, Tabasco, red pepper, garlic and cheese. In 2-quart casserole place layers of beans, toasted almonds, cream of mushroom soup mixture. Top with buttered bread crumbs. Heat at 375° for 35-40 minutes.

Mrs. Charles Beaird

DILL GREEN BEAN CASSEROLE

2 cans Blue Lake whole green beans
1 slice bacon
1 teaspoon whole dill seed
6 tablespoons flour
8 tablespoons butter
1 cup bean juice
1½ cups milk
2 teaspoons grated onion
1 teaspoon cracked pepper
2 teaspoons Mei Yen seasoning
3 dashes Tabasco

Simmer beans, bacon and dill seed for 45 minutes. Refrigerate overnight. Make a sauce with butter, flour, bean juice and milk. Add seasonings and pour mixture over the beans which have been arranged in a casserole. Top with bread crumbs, dot with butter and heat at 350° until bubbling (30 minutes). Sauce may be prepared and poured over the beans the morning before serving.

Makes 8-10 servings. Mrs. L. R. Kirby

BAKED BEANS WITHOUT BAKING

3 regular or 1 extra large can pork and beans
2 tablespoons bacon drippings
1/2 onion, chopped
1/2 green pepper, chopped
1/2 cup catsup
2 heaping tablespoons brown sugar
Salt and pepper to taste

Brown onion and green pepper in bacon drippings. Add beans, sugar, catsup, salt and pepper. Let simmer for 30 minutes over medium flame.

Makes 6 to 8 servings. Mrs. G. R. Shanley

REAL CAJUN RED BEANS AND RICE

1 pound dried red beans soaked overnight
½ pound salt pork
2 quarts water
3 cups chopped Bermuda onions
1 bunch green onions, chopped
1 cup parsley, chopped
1 cup bell pepper, chopped
2 large pods garlic, crushed
1 tablespoon salt
1 teaspoon red pepper
1 teaspoon black pepper
3 generous dashes Tabasco
1 tablespoon Worcestershire sauce
1 small can (4 ounces) tomato sauce
¼ teaspoon oregano
¼ teaspoon leaf thyme (dried)
1 pound bulk sausage made into 8-10 tiny patties (optional)

Cook beans and pork in salted water slowly 45 minutes. Add vegetables, seasonings and tomato sauce. Cook slowly another hour, stirring occasionally. Add sausage — for extra body — and cook 45 minutes more. Cool, but do not necessarily refrigerate. Reheat and bring to a boil, then lower heat and simmer gently 30-40 minutes. Serve over boiled rice. Less pepper may be used for a tender palate!

Mrs. James R. Alexander

MEXICAN BEANS

2 pounds dried pinto beans or red beans
2 tablespoons salt
2 large onions, chopped
4 garlic pods
½ teaspoon black pepper
½ teaspoon comino seed
1 can roasted green chilies
1 can Taco sauce
1 No. 2 can tomatoes

Cook beans, onions and salt until beans are tender. Add all other ingredients and simmer about three hours.

Mrs. Mike Tipps

SCALLOPED BEETS

3 tablespoons flour
2 tablespoons melted fat
1 cup water
6 tablespoons lemon juice
½ cup vinegar
4 teaspoons sugar
2 cups sliced, cooked beets
6 strips bacon

Mix flour into fat, gradually add water, lemon juice and vinegar, stirring until smooth; add sugar and cook until thickened, stirring frequently. Arrange beets in greased baking dish, pour sauce over beets and lay strips of bacon on top. Bake in hot oven (400°) for 15 to 20 minutes, or until bacon is crisp.

Makes 6 servings.

Mrs. Hall S. Morehead

BROCCOLI SOUFFLE

1 package broccoli
5 tablespoons tapioca
1½ cups milk
4 eggs, separated
1 cup grated American cheese
2 onions, sauteed
Salt
Pepper

Cook broccoli, drain and chop fine. Add sauteed onions. Mix milk and tapioca and cook until thickened. Remove from the fire, add cheese and mix with broccoli. Add the beaten egg yolks to mixture. Beat the egg whites stiff, and fold into the mixture. Place in a 2-quart casserole. Put casserole in a pan of hot water 1 inch deep. Bake 1 hour in 300° oven.

Serves 6 to 8. Mrs. George N. Drake

CABBAGE STROGANOFF

(For those who don't like cabbage)

1 large firm head of crisp, green cabbage, slivered, with hard core discarded
1 teaspoon salt
1 inch water in bottom of large boiler
Butter
1 tablespoon sugar
1 tablespoon vinegar
1 cup sour cream

Boil slivered cabbage in salted water, tightly covered, for 5 minutes only. Drain in colander. Butter sides and bottom of casserole. Put hot cabbage in casserole. Add 2 tablespoons butter. Toss. Add sugar, vinegar and sour cream. Toss well. Bake uncovered in 350° oven about 20 minutes. Doesn't even taste like cabbage!

Mrs. James R. Alexander

CREOLE CABBAGE

1 medium head cabbage, cut in eighths
1 onion, medium, sliced crosswise
2 fresh tomatoes, diced
⅓ or ½ bell pepper, thinly sliced

Into an iron skillet put 2 tablespoons bacon grease. Let it become warm, not hot. Add cabbage and over it a layer of onion. Add the tomatoes and pepper mixed. Sprinkle with salt and pepper, then add 2 cups boiling water. Let come to a boil. Turn fire low and cover skillet. Let cook slowly 30 to 45 minutes, turning occasionally with a fork. Should be fairly dry.

Mrs. George Sproull

BRUSSELS SPROUTS, PARMESAN

1 package Brussels sprouts
1 or 2 garlic pods
¼ cup olive oil
Parmesan cheese

Thaw Brussels sprouts slightly. Dry. Pour olive oil in skillet, add garlic which has been put through press. Cook a few minutes. Add the sprouts and saute them for a few minutes. Put in casserole. Add a little water to skillet and pour over sprouts. Season with salt and pepper. Put cheese on top. Put tight lid on casserole. Bake at 350° until tender.

Serves 3. Mrs. Morley Hudson

SPICED CARROT STICKS

3 tablespoons butter or margarine
1 tablespoon cornstarch
1½ cups hot water
8 medium carrots cut in thin strips
1 teaspoon salt
Dash of pepper
4 whole cloves
2 bay leaves

Melt butter; add cornstarch and stir to smooth paste. Add water. Cook, stirring constantly until thick. Pour over carrots. Add remaining ingredients. Cover pan and simmer 5 to 6 minutes until carrots are tender. Remove cloves and bay leaves.

Mrs. George Sproull

BREADED CARROTS

2 pounds whole carrots, parboiled for 15 minutes in salted water
3 tablespoons melted butter
1 whole egg
1 tablespoon water
¾ cup bread crumbs
Salt and pepper to taste

Cut off ends and scrape skins off carrots. Beat egg. Add water and seasonings. Roll carrots in egg mixture, then in crumbs. Place in buttered flat pan, one layer only. Dribble melted butter over carrots. Bake 20-25 minutes in 375° oven or until delicately browned.

Mrs. G. Randell Whitmeyer

CARROTS DIVINE

1 pound package carrots
2 Bermuda onions
1 stick butter
½ teaspoon salt
½ teaspoon pepper
½ teaspoon dried parsley
¼ teaspoon powdered thyme

Peel and cut carrots into crosswise sections. Peel and slice onions into rings. Butter bottom and sides of casserole heavily. Put a layer of carrots, a layer of onions, dots of butter, carrots, onions and butter until all are used. Sprinkle parsley and seasonings. Cover tightly and bake at 350° about 1 hour. Needs no water. Butter melts and keeps from sticking.

Serves 4. Mrs. W. A. Stephens, Jr.

CARROTS JULIENNE

8 carrots
½ green pepper, chopped
1 minced garlic clove
3 sprigs parsley, cut up
¼ pound butter (not margarine)
Salt and pepper

Cut carrots into match stick size. Boil until tender; drain. Saute green pepper, garlic clove and parsley in butter. Make sure these are done. Add carrots to this mixture. Add salt and pepper. Heat thoroughly. Add more butter if desired.

Serves 6-8.

Mrs. Morley Hudson

CAULIFLOWER WITH CREAMED CORN AU GRATIN

1 head cauliflower
2 tablespoons oleo or butter
3 tablespoons enriched flour
1 cup milk
1 cup drained whole kernel corn
½ teaspoon salt
⅛ teaspoon pepper
½ cup shredded cheese

Cook whole head of cauliflower 15 to 20 minutes in boiling salted water. Do not overcook. Melt oleo (or butter) in saucepan over low heat or in upper part of double boiler. Blend in flour. Slowly add cold milk, stirring constantly. Cook until mixture is thick and smooth. Add corn, salt and pepper. Simmer 5 minutes, stirring constantly. Remove from heat. Gradually add cheese, stirring constantly until cheese is melted. Do not boil. Place cauliflower in serving dish. Pour corn mixture over cauliflower. Garnish with pimiento, if desired. Serve hot.

Serves 8 people using good sized cauliflower.

Mrs. K. J. Heddons
Henderson, Ky.

CAULIFLOWER CASSEROLE

1 head cauliflower, broken into flowerets
6 carrots, scraped and cut into rounds
1 box frozen English peas
2 cups rich cream sauce
1 cup bread crumbs

Cook cauliflower, carrots and peas separately. When vegetables are cool, drain and place in casserole in layers, covering each with bread crumbs and cream sauce, until casserole is full. Top with sauce and crumbs. Bake 30 minutes at 400°.

Serves 6.

Sherman, Chef of Charlton Lyons, Sr.

SAUCE PIQUANTE FOR CAULIFLOWER

4 tablespoons grated horseradish
1 tablespoon prepared mustard
½ teaspoon sugar
Pinch salt
2 or 3 grains cayenne
1 tablespoon vinegar

Combine ingredients and mix well. Pour over cooked cauliflower and serve immediately.

Mrs. James B. Harris

CELERY CASSEROLE

4 cups celery cut into 1" pieces
½ cup finely chopped blanched almonds
3 tablespoons butter
3 tablespoons flour
1½ cups chicken stock
½ cup cream
Salt and pepper to taste
New York State cheese
Bread crumbs

Parboil and drain celery. Put pieces in casserole with the almonds sprinkled over it.

Sauce: Melt butter and stir flour into it. Add stock, cream, salt and pepper, and cook until thick. Pour over celery mixture. Sprinkle grated cheese on top and sprinkle with bread crumbs. Cook at 350° 15 to 20 minutes.

Serves 6 or 8.

Mrs. Jackson B. Davis

CHILI RIENOS

2 cans green peeled chili peppers
⅓ pound sharp Cheddar cheese, grated

Batter:
1 egg, beaten
1 cup milk
¼ cup flour
Salt to taste

Split peppers and lay out on paper towels to drain. Roll peppers around small balls of grated cheese, about the size of a walnut. Place in single layer in baking dish. Make a batter of the four ingredients listed. Pour over the peppers and bake 25-30 minutes at 350°. A good accompaniment for meat.

Makes 6 servings.

Mrs. R. D. Lockhart, Barksdale Air Force Base

CORN SOUFFLE

6 ears corn
2 eggs
4 tablespoons milk
2 tablespoons butter, melted
1 teaspoon salt
¼ teaspoon pepper

Grate corn. Separate eggs and beat egg yolks. Add melted butter, milk, salt and pepper, and grated corn. Beat egg whites stiff. Fold into corn mixture. Bake in a buttered casserole, placed in a pan of hot water, in a 350° oven for a half hour.

Serves 6.

Mrs. William H. Waitz, Jr.
Haddonfield, N. J.

CORN PUDDING

3 packages frozen cream style corn
4 tablespoons flour
½ cup sugar
1 teaspoon salt
3 tablespoons melted butter
2 eggs
1 cup milk

Mix thawed corn, sugar, flour and salt together. Add butter, milk and beaten eggs. Pour in greased baking dish and bake uncovered at 350° for 1½ hours or until brown. Stir from bottom several times during first 30 minutes.

Serves 4. Mrs. Bob B. Slack

CORN CREOLE

1 onion, chopped
5 tablespoons bacon fat
1 clove garlic, chopped
1 can cream style corn
1 egg, beaten
2 cups milk
½ cup corn meal
¼ bell pepper, chopped (optional)
Red pepper
Black pepper
Salt
Bread crumbs
Butter

Saute chopped onion in bacon fat with finely chopped garlic. Add corn. Add egg, beaten with milk. Add corn meal and season to taste. Stir mixture until thick over a medium fire. Pour into a buttered casserole. Sprinkle top with bread crumbs and dots of butter. Bake 1 hour at 350°.

Serves 6-7.

Mrs. Carmen B. Montegut, St. Martinville, La.

EGGPLANT CASSEROLE

1 large eggplant
1 green pepper, diced
1 onion, diced
3 stalks celery, diced
3 tablespoons butter
1 hard cooked egg
3 cooked chicken livers
1 raw egg
2 tablespoons bread crumbs
Pinch cayenne
Salt and pepper
Cracker crumbs
Butter

Boil eggplant in salted water, drain and mash. Saute pepper, onion, and celery in butter. Add eggplant and cook 5 minutes. Grate egg, chop livers and add to mixture. Stir in raw egg, bread crumbs, cayenne, salt and pepper to taste and cook a few minutes. Sprinkle top with cracker crumbs and dot with butter. Bake 45 minutes at 375°.

Serves 4. Mrs. C. N. Frierson

EGGPLANT

1 cup cooked and drained eggplant
1 cup grated sharp cheese
3 cups corn flakes
¾ cup milk
2 hard cooked eggs, chopped
2 tablespoons butter
Salt and pepper to taste

Crush corn flakes and mix with other ingredients. Put in greased baking dish and bake until cheese is melted and casserole is heated thoroughly. Top with grated cheese.

Serves 6. Mrs. L. R. Kirby

EGGPLANT DRESSING

1 large eggplant, sliced and peeled
2 onions, chopped
¾ stick butter or oleo
1 large bell pepper, chopped
Salt and pepper
1 egg, beaten
3 tablespoons Worcestershire sauce
5 soda crackers, crushed
½ small can evaporated milk
3 hard cooked eggs, sliced
1 cup grated cheese

Saute pepper and onions in butter until golden brown. Peel and boil eggplant until tender. Drain and add salt and pepper to taste. Add beaten egg, Worcestershire sauce, onions, bell pepper, crackers and milk. Add sliced eggs and grated cheese. More cheese may be added to taste. Pour into casserole and cook in moderate oven until hot. Top with more grated cheese and brown. Serve while hot.

Serves 8 to 10. Mrs. Tigner Walker

EGGPLANT FRITTERS

½ cup eggplant
1 teaspoon baking powder
1 teaspoon salt
1 tablespoon sugar (heaping)
1 well beaten egg
½ cup milk
1 cup sifted flour (measure, then sift 3 times)

Peel and boil one medium size eggplant in slightly salted water. Boil until well done. Drain at once (do not let stand in water). Measure eggplant, let cool, then add other ingredients in order given. Drop by teaspoons in very hot salad oil. Use a small skillet. Too many cooked at one time seem to cool cooking oil and the oil should be kept the same temperature. Skim off any drippings of fritters in oil. The fritters will rise to the top almost immediately. Allow to fry a minute or two and take out. Drain on paper towels or brown paper. Serve immediately.

This recipe should make about 50 or 60 fritters. The fritters are best if they are small.

Mrs. Walter T. McCook

EGGPLANT CASSEROLE

1 medium eggplant, pared and sliced
1 cup ripe olives, cut up
½ cup chopped onions
¼ cup chopped green pepper
2 tablespoons butter
¼ teaspoon salt
⅛ teaspoon pepper
1 cup grated American cheese
Buttered bread crumbs

Boil eggplant in small amount of water. Saute onions and green pepper in butter. Add to eggplant. Blend in salt, pepper and cheese. Add olives. Pour in casserole. Cover with crumbs. Bake at 350° for 30 minutes.

Serves 6.

Mrs. W. B. Ogilvie

FRIED EGGPLANT

1 cup pancake batter or ½ recipe on packaged mix
1 large eggplant (approximately 2 pounds)

Peel and slice eggplant crosswise very thin. Plunge immediately into icy salted water with 1 tablespoon vinegar. Let set about 15-20 minutes. Drain and pat dry with towel. Dip into batter. Fry a few pieces at a time in 1 inch hot vegetable oil. Drain on absorbent paper. Salt liberally. Keep warm in very slow oven until ready to serve to retain crispness.

Mrs. James R. Alexander

CHEESE AND GRITS CASSEROLE

1 cup grits
1 teaspoon salt
3 cups boiling water
1 stick butter
1 stick sharp cheese
2 well beaten eggs
½ cup milk

Stir grits into boiling salted water. Add butter and cheese. Cook until blended. Add eggs and milk and bake at 325° until done.

Mrs. Saunders Gregg

BAKED GRITS

1 cup grits
2 eggs, beaten slightly
4 cups water
½ stick butter
1 roll garlic cheese, chopped
Dash garlic salt

Cook grits according to directions on the box. While hot, add cheese, butter and eggs. Place in buttered casserole and cook at 400-450° for 1 hour. Serve hot.

Makes 6 to 8 servings. Leftovers may be reheated in foil. May be prepared several hours ahead but cooked just before serving.

Mrs. Leroy Vogel

GRITS SOUFFLE

6 cups water
1½ cups grits
3 teaspoons salt
½ stick butter
1 cup grated cheese
4 eggs, separated
Salt and pepper to taste

Boil water, add grits and salt, allow to return to boil. Cover and cook over low heat for 30 to 40 minutes. Remove pot and stir in butter and cheese; stir well until blended. Cool to lukewarm, then add beaten egg yolks, then fold in beaten egg whites, and pour into a greased baking dish. Bake for 45 minutes in a 350° oven. May be seasoned with salt and pepper to taste.

Serves 8. Mrs. Kenneth Carstens

HOMINY

4 pieces bacon, fried crisp
2 large onions, chopped
1 green pepper, chopped
1 large can mushrooms, stems and pieces
1 large can white hominy, drained
1 can Ro-tel tomatoes
Salt and pepper
Worcestershire sauce
Tabasco sauce
Red pepper (if desired)
Grated American cheese

Saute onion and green pepper in bacon fat. Add drained mushrooms, bacon, hominy and tomatoes. Add seasonings to taste. Cook for 20 to 30 minutes, until all is tender. In greased casserole, alternate layers of hominy and cheese, ending with cheese. Bake 15 to 20 minutes at 350°.

Serves 6. Mrs. Donald Laskey

HOMINY CASSEROLE

1 15-ounce can hominy, drained
1 can cream of mushroom or asparagus soup
½ can water
½ pound mild Cheddar cheese, grated
1 can fried onion rings
Salt and pepper to taste

Heat soup, water, and hominy together. Grease a casserole and put a layer of hominy, soup, half of grated cheese, and ½ can of the onion rings. Repeat and end with onion rings on top. Put in 300° oven and heat until bubbly or about 20-30 minutes.

Serves 6. Mrs. T. Haller Jackson, Jr.
Mrs. W. G. McElroy

MACARONI AND CHEESE

2½ cups macaroni
¼ cup butter or oleo
¼ cup flour
2¼ cups milk
1 teaspoon salt
¼ teaspoon pepper
2 cups grated cheese

Cook macaroni in boiling salted water until tender. Drain. While macaroni cooks, melt oleo in saucepan and stir in flour. Add milk gradually. Cook, stirring constantly until sauce bubbles. Season with salt and pepper. In casserole, make alternate layers of macaroni and almost all the cheese. Pour hot sauce over the top and sprinkle with the remaining cheese. Cook in 375° preheated oven for 35 minutes.

Serves 8. Mrs. V. V. Thompson

CHEESE NOODLES

8 ounces noodles, cooked
1 cup cream style cottage cheese
¼ cup minced parsley
3 eggs, well beaten
1 pod garlic, minced
¼ cup blue cheese
¼ cup grated onion
¼ cup melted butter
Salt and pepper

Toss all together lightly. Bake in greased casserole at 350° for 30 minutes.

Serves 6. Mrs. Charles McCall

NOODLE PUDDING

1 3-ounce package cream cheese
2 tablespoons butter
2 eggs
1 cup milk
Salt to taste
Dash of pepper
1 5-ounce package fine noodles, cooked and drained

Cream butter and cheese. Add eggs, one at a time, then milk and seasonings. Combine this mixture with cooked noodles. Put in well buttered baking dish. Bake at 350° until top and sides are well browned, about 1½ hours. Very good with almost any meat dish.

Mrs. Jack Stein

OLD MAN'S OKRA

1 pound okra
Small lump butter
¼ cup milk
Salt and pepper

Select small tender okra; wash and boil in salted water 10 to 12 minutes or until tender. Drain well. Add butter, milk and seasonings. Put lid on and cook very slowly over low fire until milk is almost gone, then shake pan. Don't allow to boil after adding milk.

Mrs. A. H. Weyland

SAUTEED OKRA AND TOMATOES

1 pound fresh okra or 1 package frozen okra
1 large onion, chopped
1 can tomatoes
1 tablespoon bacon drippings
Salt and pepper

Saute chopped onion in bacon drippings until soft. Cut okra into ½-inch slices, crosswise, add to onions and cook until slightly brown. Add tomatoes and seasonings. Cover skillet and simmer from 20 to 30 minutes.

Makes 4 servings. Mrs. Scott Dunlop

NO-FUSS CURRY 'N ONIONS

1 pound small white onions
1 can cream of mushroom soup
⅓ cup milk
½ teaspoon curry powder

Peel the onions and cook in boiling, salted water for 20 minutes or until tender, then drain. Stir in mushroom soup, milk and curry powder. Heat slowly, stirring constantly, until bubbly hot and cream smooth. Serve at once.

Serves 6. Mrs. Whitney Boggs, Jr.

CHEESE AND ONION PIE IN CRUMB CRUST

30 saltine crackers, rolled fine
¼ cup butter, melted
2½ cups thinly sliced onion
1 tablespoon butter or margarine
½ pound grated sharp Cheddar cheese
3 eggs, slightly beaten
1½ cups milk, scalded
Salt and pepper to taste

Combine cracker crumbs and butter and press into 9-inch pie plate. Add onion rings, sauteed in butter until limp, and cover with grated cheese. 50 minutes before serving, combine eggs, milk and seasonings and pour over onion-cheese mixture. Bake in a preheated oven, 325°, until firm. Cut in wedges and serve. Perfect with steak or roast beef.

Mrs. John S. Hardy

BAKED ONIONS

Sweet Bermuda onions (1 per serving)
1 tablespoon butter (each)
2 dashes Worcestershire sauce
Seasoned salt

Peel outer layer from onions. Slit criss-cross a time or two in top of each onion. Push in butter. Add Worcestershire sauce and salt. Wrap in foil and bake in 375° oven 45 minutes or until tender. These are good served with steak and other meats.

Mrs. John J. Dailey

BREAKFAST ONIONS

24 small white onions
2 tablespoons butter
1½ tablespoons flour
Salt
Pepper
1 cup milk
½ cup sharp grated cheese
2 teaspoons vermouth
½ teaspoon Worcestershire sauce
¼ teaspoon Tabasco
¼ teaspoon mustard
1 cup salted peanuts or almonds, chopped

Pierce onions with ice pick (to keep whole while cooking), then peel. Cook in pressure cooker 2 to 4 minutes. Drain well and place in buttered baking dish. Melt butter in top of double boiler, add flour, salt and pepper. Blend well and add milk, stirring constantly until smooth, add cheese and cook until blended. Remove from heat and add vermouth and other seasonings. Pour sauce over onions and top with nuts. Bake 5 minutes at 450°.

Serves 6. Mrs. Arthur Carmody, Jr.

STUFFED ONIONS

6 Spanish onions
Cold cooked veal or chicken
¼ teaspoon salt
½ teaspoon pepper
1 teaspoon chopped parsley
¼ cup soft bread crumbs
¼ cup butter
1 tablespoon chopped cashew nuts
Buttered cracker crumbs

Parboil or steam onions about an hour. Remove from the fire and cut out a circular piece from the top of each. Then scoop out the inside to form cups. Chop fine or pass through a sieve the onion that has been taken out. Add an equal measure of veal or chicken chopped fine, salt, pepper, parsley, bread crumbs, butter and mix thoroughly. Put a spoonful of the mixture into each onion, then put cashew nuts in the rest of the mixture and finish filling the cups. Bake slowly one hour, basting three or four times with butter melted in hot water. Fifteen minutes before serving, sprinkle the top of each with buttered cracker crumbs, and return to the oven to brown. Serve surrounded with a cup of thin cream thickened with a tablespoon of butter and flour creamed together and seasoned with salt and white pepper.

Mrs. Charlotte Merriam

Try boiling small new potatoes in consomme with little green onions. Be sure to chop and include some of the green onion tops.

BLACK-EYED PEAS, BOWL GAME PARTY STYLE

- 4 pounds dried black-eyed peas
- 2 pounds dry salt pork with lean streaks
- 4 large onions, chopped
- 4 pods garlic, crushed
- 2 tablespoons salt
- 1 teaspoon black pepper
- 2 tablespoons Worcestershire sauce
- Tabasco to taste

Soak peas overnight. Add other ingredients, cover and cook slowly in a large kettle over low fire, about 4 hours. Add water if necessary to prevent sticking. To make a gourmet dish, serve with a relish of fresh chopped tomatoes; chopped fresh green peppers; chopped green onions; chopped celery; and a dressing of oil and vinegar.

Serves 40 or more hungry people! Mrs. B. L. Overton

HOLIDAY PEAS

- 2 cups medium cream sauce (season with sherry if desired)
- 1 can English peas
- ½ cup chopped green pepper
- 1 small can chopped pimiento
- 1 tablespoon Worcestershire sauce
- Salt and pepper to taste
- Grated American or sharp cheese

To cream sauce, add green pepper, pimiento, Worcestershire sauce, salt and pepper. Heat this mixture. Heat peas in their own juice; when hot, drain off juice and add peas to hot sauce. Sprinkle with grated cheese and serve.

Serves 4-6. Mrs. C. R. Minor, Jr.

PEAS AND CORN IN SOUR CREAM

- 2 boxes frozen English peas
- 2 boxes frozen whole kernel corn
- 1 cup chopped celery
- 1 cup chopped green onions
- ½ stick butter or margarine
- ¼ to ½ teaspoon thyme
- ¼ to ½ teaspoon summer savory
- Salt and cracked black pepper
- 1 pint sour cream

Steam frozen vegetables until done. Then drain thoroughly. Meanwhile, saute celery and onions in butter and add seasonings. Combine vegetables and butter mixture in a pan. Add sour cream and heat, but do not boil.

Serves 8 to 10. Mrs. Camp Flournoy
Mrs. Charles McCall

PEAS ORLEANS

1 17-ounce can early peas
2 tablespoons butter
1 tablespoon chopped fresh mint leaves or 1 teaspoon crumbled dried mint leaves
Rind of ½ medium orange, coarsely grated
Juice of ½ medium orange (about ¼ cup) — may substitute 3 tablespoons frozen undiluted orange juice
2 teaspoons sugar
⅛ teaspoon salt

Melt butter, add mint and orange rind. Simmer gently 3 or 4 minutes. Stir in orange juice, sugar and salt. Drain peas, add to sauce and mix lightly. Cover and cook until peas are hot. This is good with lamb and duck.

Serves 4 amply. Mrs. J. B. Haynes, Jr.

SCALLOPED POTATOES SUPREME

8 medium potatoes or 8 cups potatoes, sliced
¼ cup chopped green pepper
¼ cup minced onion
2 teaspoons salt
Dash of pepper
1 10½-ounce can condensed mushroom soup
1 cup milk

Alternate layers of potatoes, green pepper, and onion in greased baking dish; season each layer with salt and pepper. Mix mushroom soup and milk. Pour over potatoes. Cover and bake at 350° for 1½ hours.

Serves 8. Mrs. George Sproull

ROQUEFORT POTATOES

6 large baking potatoes
½ cup cream (light) and 1 stick butter
1 small wedge Roquefort cheese
1 teaspoon white pepper
2 teaspoons salt

Bake potatoes (well greased) in 375° oven for 1 hour, or until done. Scoop out potatoes quickly, and, while still hot, add butter and cream. Whip with electric mixer until creamy and smooth. Add seasonings. Add crumbled Roquefort cheese. Stuff back into shells. (May be frozen.) Bake about 20 minutes in 350° oven (a little longer if frozen), or until nicely browned around the edges.

Mrs. James R. Alexander

HASHED BROWN POTATOES

1½ pounds potatoes, pared and firmly cooked
½ medium onion, chopped fine
½ teaspoon salt
Pepper to taste
3 tablespoons butter
3 tablespoons bacon drippings

Grate cold cooked potatoes medium fine. Toss with onion, salt and pepper. (Pimiento and minced green pepper may be added.) Heat butter and drippings over moderate heat. Add potato mixture, pressing down well with wide spatula. Cook until crisp and brown on the underside, about 20 minutes; do not stir. Cut into pie-shaped wedges and turn out, brown crust side up.

Serves 6. Mrs. Ed S. Peterson

POTATO PUDDING

4 medium potatoes
1 onion
2 eggs
3 tablespoons flour
1 teaspoon baking powder
1 tablespoon butter
Salt and pepper to taste

Grate or put through fine blade of meat chopper, potatoes and onion. Add remaining ingredients and mix well. Turn into well buttered casserole and bake until well browned for about 1½ hours at 350°. Much like a potato pancake in taste and consistency.

Mrs. Jack Stein

SWEET POTATO BALLS

2 cups cold mashed sweet potatoes
½ teaspoon salt
½ teaspoon nutmeg
3 tablespoons brown sugar
Cooked ham, cut into ½-inch cubes
Prepared mustard
Crushed corn flakes

Combine mashed sweet potatoes, salt, nutmeg and brown sugar. Mix well. Roll each cube of ham in prepared mustard, then form potato mixture into a ball around ham. Roll in finely crushed corn flakes. Fry in preheated shortening until brown. Drain on absorbent paper. Serve at once.

Serves 6. Mrs. Andrew Querbes, III

SWEET POTATO RUM CASSEROLE

4 or 5 large sweet potatoes
1 tablespoon butter
1 cup chopped nuts (black walnuts are excellent)
1½ cups brown sugar
2 eggs, well beaten
4 ounces rum or bourbon

Boil potatoes with jackets on. Peel while hot, and mash or whip. Add other ingredients, put in orange cups or in casserole, top with marshmallows and bake in 325° oven for 25 to 30 minutes.

Mrs. George Sproull

RADISH CASSEROLE AU GRATIN

Radishes
Salt
Pepper
⅛ teaspoon Tabasco
¼ teaspoon Worcestershire sauce
¼ teaspoon mustard
1 cup cheese sauce
1 tablespoon dry vermouth
Croutons browned in butter

Cook radishes whole, in pressure cooker for 1 minute, or boil, in salt water until tender, and drain. Season. Place in buttered casserole. Add vermouth to good cheese sauce, and pour over radishes. Top with buttered croutons. Put casserole in 300° oven until thoroughly heated.

Mrs. Arthur Carmody, Jr.

SOUTH LOUISIANA RICE

3 cups water
2 cups rice
1 tablespoon salt
1 tablespoon oil

Combine all ingredients and bring to a fast boil. Stir well. Lower heat and cover, cooking very slowly for at least 45 minutes. Readjust cover and allow to steam 5-10 minutes. With a fork, separate rice as it is served. Never fails.

Mrs. James R. Alexander

14-MINUTE RICE

1 cup long grain white rice
2 cups cold water
1 teaspoon salt

Place ingredients in a 2-quart heavy saucepan. Bring to a vigorous boil. Turn the heat down as low as possible and cover with a tight fitting lid; leave over this low heat 14 minutes. Remove saucepan from heat and without removing the lid let the rice stand 10 minutes. This 10 minutes is important; after this, rice is ready for serving. This also works for smaller amounts of rice — ½ cup rice to 1¼ cups water, with ½ teaspoon salt.

Makes 4 to 6 servings.

Mrs. Sterling Bigner

RICE CASSEROLE

Small can mushrooms
Can onion soup
2 tablespoons margarine
½ cup raw rice

In skillet saute mushrooms and raw rice in margarine for about 5 minutes or until slightly brown. Then add onion soup and ½ can water. Stir and cover. Simmer for 20-25 minutes.

Serves 4.

Mrs. Edgar Galloway

GREEN RICE

- 4 cups cooked rice (1 cup uncooked)
- 3 eggs
- 1 cup milk
- ⅓ cup salad oil
- 1 tablespoon Worcestershire sauce
- ½ teaspoon Tabasco
- 1 teaspoon salt
- Cracked black pepper
- 1 bunch green onions, chopped (use tops, too)
- 1 green pepper, chopped
- 1 cup parsley, chopped
- 2 cups grated cheese
- Bread crumbs
- Parmesan cheese
- Paprika

Toss together thoroughly cooked rice and chopped vegetables. Beat eggs, then add milk, salad oil and seasonings. In large buttered casserole combine rice, egg mixture and cheese. Top with bread crumbs and Parmesan cheese; sprinkle with paprika. Bake in 325° oven for 50 minutes.

Makes 8-10 servings. Mrs. Camp Flournoy

DIRTY RICE

- 2 cups cooked rice
- 1 cup ground chicken livers and gizzards, combined
- 1 cup ground beef
- ½ cup ground onion and parsley
- 2 tablespoons butter or margarine

Saute beef, liver and gizzard mixture, onions and parsley in butter or margarine until onion is golden brown. Mix with cooked rice and season with salt and pepper. Should be well seasoned.

Makes 6-8 servings. Shreveport Country Club

CHINESE RICE

- 2 cups rice
- 2 chopped onions
- 2 cans sliced mushrooms
- ¼ pound butter
- 4 eggs
- 1 bottle soy sauce

Cook rice, using no salt. Put rice aside in bowl. In same pot, saute onions and mushrooms in butter. Mix this with rice. Scramble lightly 4 eggs mixed with a little water. Then mix all together and add 1 small bottle of soy sauce. Put in buttered casserole and cook 20 minutes in 350° oven.

Mrs. A. Lane Ellison

"DIRTY" RICE

1 12-ounce package brown rice
2 bell peppers
2 onions
4 ribs celery (tops and all)
½ pound chicken livers
⅛ pound ground beef or pork (optional, but good when cooked in large quantities)
1 clove garlic
4 tablespoons pecans or walnuts (optional)
2 tablespoons bacon drippings
Tabasco
Worcestershire sauce
Salt
Cayenne pepper
Black pepper

Boil rice according to directions on package. Drain. Brown rice has a slightly coarser grain than white. Chop onions, bell pepper, celery and garlic finely (use blender). In bacon drippings, saute chopped vegetables until the mixture cooks down, about 30 minutes. Add chopped chicken livers and ground meat and cook until done, then mash. The mixture looks "dirty" and soupy. Add remaining seasonings and nuts to taste, and mix with rice. May be prepared in morning and reheated. Additional water may be needed.

Makes 8 large servings. Mrs. J. Bennett Johnston, Jr.

WILD RICE CASSEROLE

½ pound wild rice
2 teaspoons salt
1 stick oleo or butter (¼ pound)
¼ cup flour
2 cups rich milk
2 8-ounce packages cream cheese
1 cup whole button mushrooms (more if desired)

Wash wild rice well, cover with water and add 1½ teaspoons salt, and cook until tender in top of double boiler. Add more water as necessary. It takes about 1 hour to 1 hour and 15 minutes to cook over low heat. When done, put into colander and allow to drain well.

Make cream sauce as follows: Melt oleo or butter in top of double boiler. Add flour and stir until it forms a thick paste. Begin to add milk very slowly. Stir constantly. Add the cream cheese; stir until melted and sauce is smooth. Add ½ teaspoon salt.

Butter a large casserole (at least 2-quart size) and alternate layers of rice, mushrooms and cream sauce, rice, mushrooms and cream sauce, etc., until dish is filled. Be sure to place generous amount of sauce on top. Bake in 325° oven about 30 minutes or until mixture is hot through, bubbles around edges and is golden brown on top.

Makes 12 to 14 servings. Mrs. T. Haller Jackson, Jr.

RICE DRESSING

6 tablespoons bacon drippings
2½ cups chopped onion
1½ cups chopped green onions and tops
¼ cup chopped bell pepper
1½ cups chopped celery and tops
1 teaspoon seasoning salt
1 teaspoon celery seed
1 teaspoon freshly ground black pepper
1 tablespoon Worcestershire sauce
1 tablespoon soya sauce
1½ cups dry rice
¼ cup chopped parsley

Saute all chopped vegetables in bacon fat. Add the dry seasonings. Cook the rice in the usual manner. For added flavor and vitamins, it may be cooked in stock. The rice should not be too moist. Then combine all and add the parsley. Taste and correct seasoning.

Serves 8. May be done ahead and heated when ready to serve. This is not meant to be used as stuffing, but as a vegetable.

Mrs. Gene Fleming

WILD RICE

½ pound butter
1 cup chopped onion
1 cup chopped green onion
1 large can stems and pieces mushrooms
1 cup chopped celery
1 tablespoon dried chicken stock
1 pound bacon
2 tablespoons chopped garlic
1 pound wild rice
2 cups water
1 tablespoon Worcestershire sauce
2 dashes Tabasco
Salt to taste

Saute onions, green onions, garlic, mushrooms in butter. Save liquid from mushrooms. Boil water, after adding chicken stock and celery. Combine with first mixture, then add juice from mushrooms, Worcestershire sauce, Tabasco and salt. Wild rice must be washed thoroughly, 4 to 5 times. Do so, then soak in hot water for at least one hour. Cook rice until done, but not soggy, for about 20 minutes. Drain in colander. Fry bacon until crisp. Add to sauce. Pour sauce over rice and keep warm. Do not combine sauce and rice until ready to serve.

Makes 16 generous servings as a vegetable.

The Shreveport Club

MAIN DISH RICE

2 tablespoons butter
1½ cups chopped onion
2 cups diced celery
¾ cup long grain rice, uncooked
½ teaspoon poultry seasoning
1 cup mushroom soup
1 cup chicken and rice soup
1 4-ounce can mushrooms, juice and all
¾ cup water
½ cup chopped nuts

Saute onion and celery in butter until transparent. Put in covered 2- x 14- x 7-inch buttered dish. Add rice, poultry seasoning, mushroom soup and chicken soup (undiluted), mushrooms and water. Bake at 325° for 1 hour 15 minutes. Stir in ½ cup chopped nuts. Bake 20 minutes longer. This makes a good main dish by adding cooked pork or chicken to it.

Mrs. Charles W. Lunan

BARLEY CASSEROLE

1 can mushrooms
4-5 tablespoons butter
1 large onion, chopped very fine
1 cup pearl barley
Salt, pepper
2-3 cups chicken broth

Heat butter in a skillet and add chopped onion. Cook 3 or 4 minutes; add mushrooms. Cook another 4 minutes, stirring occasionally. Add barley and brown it lightly, mixing well with the onions and mushrooms. Season to taste with salt and pepper and pour into a buttered casserole. Add enough boiling broth to cover the mixture and come ½ inch above it. Cover the casserole tightly and bake in a 350° oven for 25 minutes. Taste the barley for doneness. Add more broth, if necessary, and continue cooking until the liquid is absorbed and the barley tender. Serve as an accompaniment to any meat — wherever you would use wild rice.

Serves 6.

Mrs. James M. Turner

SPINACH CASSEROLE

3 packages frozen chopped spinach
1 8-ounce package cream cheese
2 eggs, separated
1 can mushroom soup
4 tablespoons Parmesan cheese
1 can French fried onion rings

Cook and drain spinach. Beat egg yolks, mash cream cheese and add both to hot soup. Add spinach, beaten egg whites and Parmesan cheese. Put in casserole, top with French fried onion rings and add a little cheese on top. Bake at 350° for 35 to 45 minutes.

Serves 8.

Mrs. George Drake
Mrs. William J. Peacock
Mrs. Donald Laskey

DEVILED SPINACH

2 packages frozen spinach
1 can either cream of vegetable soup, cream of celery soup or cream of cheese soup
1 cup chopped green onions and tops
½ cup chopped celery
2 tablespoons butter
1 can deviled ham
½ cup grated Velveeta cheese
Tabasco and Worcestershire sauce to taste
½ cup corn flake crumbs

Cook spinach according to package directions; drain well. Add soup to spinach. Saute onions and celery in the 2 tablespoons of butter. Add to spinach. Add ham, cheese, Worcestershire and Tabasco and mix thoroughly. Cover with corn flake crumbs and dot with butter. Heat in 350° oven about 10 minutes, or until casserole is bubbly.

Serves 4 to 6. Mrs. Phil Foster

CORN AND SPINACH PARMESAN

¼ cup minced onion
2 tablespoons butter
1 can (1 pound) cream corn
1½ cups chopped spinach, cooked
1 teaspoon vinegar
½ teaspoon salt
¼ teaspoon pepper
¼ cup fine bread crumbs
2 tablespoons Parmesan cheese
2 tablespoons melted butter

Saute onion in 2 tablespoons butter. Combine corn, spinach, vinegar, salt, pepper and sauteed onion. Turn into lightly greased shallow baking dish. Blend together bread crumbs, cheese and 2 tablespoons melted butter. Sprinkle over vegetable mixture. Bake in hot oven (400°) 15 to 20 minutes or until bubbly and brown.

Makes about 6 servings. Mrs. Hines Vaughan

STUFFED ACORN SQUASH

3 acorn squash, halved and seeded
1 pound pork sausage, cooked and drained
⅔ cup milk
1 teaspoon salt
¼ teaspoon pepper
1 teaspoon dry mustard
¼ cup sweet pickle relish
¾ cup quick or uncooked oats

Preheat oven to 425°. Place squash cut side down in shallow baking dish. (Pour a little water in dish.) Bake 30 minutes. Remove. For filling, combine sausage and other ingredients, mixing well. Spoon into centers and bake in a little water in 350° oven for 30 minutes.

Serves 6. Mrs. Judith Wintle Taylor

RED HOT SQUASH CASSEROLE

6 medium yellow squash, sliced
1 large onion, chopped
1 teaspoon salt
1 teaspoon sugar
¼ pound Velveeta cheese
2 tablespoons milk
2 Jalapeno peppers (without seeds)
Parsley flakes and/or paprika

Boil squash and onion in water with salt and sugar. Drain well in colander and pour into casserole. Make a sauce of Velveeta and milk and pour over squash; add finely minced Jalapeno peppers; mix well. Garnish with parsley and/or paprika. Heat in 350° oven for 10 to 15 minutes, or until thoroughly hot. Note: Bell peppers or chopped pepper relish may be used in place of the Jalapenos. This may be made early and heated immediately before serving.

Mrs. Phil Foster

YELLOW SQUASH SOUFFLE

8-10 yellow squash, diced
1 large onion, chopped fine
½ bell pepper, chopped fine
1½ cups medium white sauce (4 tablespoons butter, 2 tablespoons flour, 1¼ cups milk and 3 egg yolks)
¾ pound American cheese, grated
½ pound Roquefort cheese
1 cup mayonnaise
1 teaspoon salt
½ teaspoon pepper
3 egg whites

Cook squash, bell pepper and onion in small amount of water until just tender. Drain; set aside. Make white sauce. Add cheeses to sauce and blend until smooth. Cool sauce, add mayonnaise, squash mixture, seasonings and gently fold in stiffly beaten whites of eggs. Place casserole dish in a bain-marie, and cook in 350° oven for 40 minutes, or until browned nicely. Do not cover. Should be served immediately.

Serves 8 generously.

Mrs. William J. Nesbitt

YELLOW SQUASH PUDDING

2 pounds yellow squash
2 slices white bread
½ medium onion, chopped
1 cup milk
2 eggs
1 tablespoon butter
1 teaspoon sugar
¾ teaspoon salt
¼ teaspoon pepper

Boil squash in salted water until tender. Drain and mash. Add bread (broken into small pieces), onion, milk, eggs, butter, sugar, salt and pepper. Bake in oven in an uncovered greased casserole at 350° about 30 minutes, until firm and a delicate brown.

Serves 6.

Mrs. John R. Murphy

DILLY SQUASH

6-8 squash
1 large chopped onion
½ teaspoon dill weed
¼ stick butter
1 teaspoon sugar
2 beaten eggs
Beau Monde seasoning
Salt
Pepper

Boil squash, onion and dill weed in salted water until tender. Drain well and mash. Add rest of ingredients. Pour in casserole and top with bread crumbs. Cook in 300° oven for 45 minutes or until firm.

Mrs. Robert A. Stacy, Jr.

SQUASH LUCRETIA

2½ cups cooked squash
3 eggs, hard cooked and grated
1 cup grated cheese
½ stick butter or oleo
Salt and pepper to taste

Boil squash until tender. Drain. Add butter and mash. In a 1½-quart casserole, place layer of squash, then layer of eggs, then cheese, alternating until all ingredients are used. Bake in moderate oven (350°) 20 minutes until brown. Cracker crumbs may be added on top if desired.

Mrs. Ed J. Crawford, Jr.

TOMATOES OREGANO

6 large ripe tomatoes
Oregano
Garlic salt
Pepper
1 cup soft bread crumbs
1 tablespoon salad oil
1 teaspoon grated Parmesan cheese for each half tomato

Cut tomatoes in half. Place each half cut side up in baking dish. Sprinkle liberally with oregano, garlic salt and pepper. In a small bowl moisten bread crumbs with salad oil. Top each tomato with some crumbs and cheese. Bake at 350° 25 to 30 minutes.

Mrs. Paul R. Winder
Mrs. Walter McElroy

TOMATOES PROVENCAL

2 tablespoons melted butter
2 small cloves garlic, crushed
¼ cup chopped parsley
½ teaspoon salt
⅛ teaspoon pepper
Enough bread crumbs to absorb butter mixture
Fresh tomatoes, sliced about ¾" thick

Melt butter. Add garlic, parsley, salt, pepper and bread crumbs. Spoon this onto thick tomato slices. Broil 5 to 6 inches from heat until crumbs are golden (10 minutes).

Mrs. Marlin W. Drake, Jr.

STUFFED TOMATOES

6 tomatoes
3 stalks celery
3 sprigs parsley
2 small carrots
1½ cups raw spinach
1 large onion
1 small green pepper
3 tablespoons melted butter
¾ cup bread crumbs
⅓ cup milk
1 beaten egg
Parmesan cheese

Cut thin slice from tops of tomatoes and scoop out seeds and pulp. Salt shells and invert to drain for 15 minutes. Put celery, parsley, carrots, spinach, onion and pepper through food chopper. Then saute these vegetables in butter until onion is golden brown. Stir in bread crumbs, milk and egg. Salt and pepper to taste. Combine all ingredients, pack into tomatoes and sprinkle with grated Parmesan cheese. Place in buttered baking dish, and bake at 400° for 20 minutes.

Makes 6 servings. This may be prepared the day before baking to serve.

Mrs. Charles DeBardeleben, III

CREOLE ZUCCHINI

5-6 zucchini
Bacon drippings
1 large can tomatoes
1 large onion, chopped
½ teaspoon sweet basil
Seasoned salt
Pepper

Slice zucchini and boil in salted water until tender. Saute chopped onion in bacon drippings. Add tomatoes, basil, cooked zucchini, salt and pepper. Cook in uncovered iron skillet until most of the liquid is gone.

Makes 4 servings. Mrs. Robert A. Stacy, Jr.

ZUCCHINI SQUASH CIRCLES

6 small zucchini, cut in ¼-inch slices
1 medium onion, sliced and separated into rings
2 tablespoons butter or margarine
2 tablespoons water
1 teaspoon salt
½ teaspoon pepper
¼ cup grated Parmesan cheese

In a skillet, combine all ingredients except cheese. Cook, covered, 2 minutes; uncover and cook, turning frequently, about 10 minutes, or until tender. Sprinkle with cheese and toss to mix.

4 servings. Mrs. James M. Turner

ZUCCHINI-SAUSAGE TORTE

2 pounds zucchini
½ pound bulk pork sausage meat
¼ cup chopped onion
½ cup fine cracker crumbs
2 eggs, slightly beaten
½ cup grated Parmesan cheese
Pinch each of thyme and rosemary
Garlic salt, salt and pepper to taste
½ teaspoon Accent

Scrub zucchini and trim off ends; do not peel. Cook whole in boiling salted water 15-20 minutes, or until just tender. Drain thoroughly; chop coarsely. Cook sausage and onion together until sausage begins to brown, stirring with a fork to break sausage into bits. Add zucchini; add all remaining ingredients except about 2 tablespoons of the cheese; mix well. Turn into greased 9-inch pie plate and sprinkle with reserved cheese. Bake in moderate (350°) oven until firm and delicately browned (45 minutes). To serve, cut in wedges.

Makes 4 or 5 servings. Its flavor is excellent the next day, warmed over.

Mrs. J. B. McCullough

ZUCCHINI MAISON

6 medium size zucchini
¼ cup thinly sliced onion
4 tablespoons olive oil
2 tablespoons chopped parsley
2 ripe tomatoes, peeled and thinly sliced
Salt and pepper to taste
Parmesan cheese

Wash and slice zucchini about ½-inch thick and cook in boiling salted water, to cover, until tender. Saute onion in olive oil until yellow, add parsley and remove from heat. Drain zucchini, put in casserole in layers with sliced tomatoes and onion-parsley mixture. Sprinkle with salt and pepper and grated Parmesan cheese. Bake at 375° for 30 minutes.

6 servings. Mrs. Donald A. Raymond, Jr.

Bell peppers may be bought when in season and inexpensive, and may be chopped and frozen in plastic bags or cartons.

Use scooped-out firm tomatoes or bell peppers to fill with cheese souffle. Bake in flat casserole with a little water in the bottom at 350° for 30 minutes.

INDIAN CURRIED VEGETABLES

1 large eggplant
Salt to taste
Dash cayenne pepper
½ cup olive oil
3 yellow onions, peeled and cut in quarters
2 large carrots
4 outer stalks celery
2 leeks
Small jar button whole mushrooms
1 large green pepper, seeds removed, cut in eighths
Curry powder
2 tomatoes, skinned and cut in quarters

Cut stem off eggplant, then cut eggplant into 1½-inch squares. Put on a platter, sprinkle liberally with salt. Leave 20 minutes, then wash in cold water, drain well, and dry on paper towels. Heat oil in pan and fry eggplant quickly until golden brown. Remove. Cut carrots, celery and leeks in finger-length pieces. Put them, onions, mushrooms and green pepper in pan, adding a little more oil if necessary. Season with salt and cayenne pepper and a little curry powder. Cover pan and cook until vegetables are soft (about 45 minutes). Add eggplant and tomatoes; cook 15 more minutes. Serve in a casserole as a side dish.

Serves 8 people. Mrs. E. M. Adger, Jr.

PANTRY CASSEROLE

1 can English peas
1 large can green asparagus
1 can water chestnuts, sliced
1 large can mushrooms
1 can mushroom soup
5 or 6 cups grated Cheddar cheese
1 stick butter
4 or 5 slices old bread, with crusts removed and bread broken into small pieces

Drain all vegetables well. Butter a casserole and put a layer of peas, asparagus, water chestnuts and mushrooms in, and pour mushroom soup over. If you like hot seasoning, sprinkle this mixture with cayenne pepper. Cover with cheese. Melt butter and in it marinate bread. Spread bread over cheese. Bake in 350° oven until slightly browned, 30 to 45 minutes.

Makes 8 to 10 servings. Mrs. Mike Tipps

SUMMER GARDEN CASSEROLE

2 medium cucumbers
2 medium zucchini squash
1 sweet Bermuda onion
Italian seasoned bread crumbs
Italian seasoned cheese
½ stick butter

Butter a 2-quart casserole. Sprinkle with bread crumbs. Slice all vegetables about ¼-inch thick; do not peel cucumbers or squash. Put in casserole a layer of squash, sprinkle lightly with crumbs and dot with butter; then put a layer of cucumbers and more crumbs and butter; then onion and more crumbs and butter. Repeat this and top generously with cheese. Cover and bake 1 hour in 350° oven.

Mrs. W. J. O'Brien, Jr.

ANTOINE'S HOLLANDAISE

1 cup clarified butter
2 tablespoons tarragon vingear
1 tablespoon water
1 tablespoon minced onion
3 peppercorns
4 egg yolks
Juice of ¼ lemon

To clarify butter, slowly melt butter in a saucepan; let stand until clear layer can be skimmed off easily.

Put vinegar, water, onion and peppercorns in a saucepan. Cook over very low heat to reduce liquid to one teaspoon. Remove peppercorns. Cool, add egg yolks and beat slightly. Gradually add melted butter, beating constantly. Add lemon juice. Serve immediately.

Mrs. Robert Roberts, Jr.

BLENDER HOLLANDAISE SAUCE

3 egg yolks
2 tablespoons lemon juice
½ teaspoon salt
¼ teaspoon white pepper
Few grains cayenne
½ cup softened butter

Place all ingredients into glass container of blender. Cover and whirl until well blended. Then remove cover and gradually pour ½ cup boiling water into the center while blender is running. Put cover back on and blend about one minute, or until perfectly smooth. Remove to the top of a double boiler, and cook over hot water, stirring constantly, about 3 minutes or until the sauce looks like a soft custard. Keep warm over hot water, stirring occasionally. This is truly a never-fail recipe.

Makes about 1½ cups of sauce.

Mrs. John H. Hearne

FREEZER HOLLANDAISE SAUCE

¼ pound butter, softened but not melted
4 egg yolks, beaten slightly
4 tablespoons lemon juice
⅛ teaspoon salt
⅛ teaspoon Accent
Dash cayenne
4 tablespoons cold water

Combine all ingredients in the top of a double boiler and mix thoroughly. Place over hot, not boiling, water, not allowing water to touch bottom of the top pan. Stir constantly until mixture thickens. Remove from fire, use immediately or freeze for later use. If the sauce separates when reheated, add one tablespoon hot water at a time until the condition is corrected. The hot liquid from the vegetable to be served with the sauce may be used for this, if desired.

Mrs. Hugh C. Ilgenfritz

Seafoods

Louisiana State Exhibit Museum

LOUISIANA STATE EXHIBIT MUSEUM

Renowned for its towering murals and amazing dioramas depicting the history and life of Louisiana, the museum features exhibits of prehistoric Indian relics to space suits to thousands of elementary school children each year. Paintings in the art gallery are changed eight times a year.

SWEET-SOUR SHRIMP

1 pound shrimp, cleaned and cooked
6 tablespoons olive or salad oil
⅓ cup minced onion
½ cup green pepper, chopped
½ cup sugar
1 tablespoon cornstarch
1 teaspoon dry mustard
½ teaspoon Accent
¼ teaspoon salt
¼ cup vinegar
½ cup water
⅔ cup drained pineapple tidbits

Add onions and green pepper to oil in skillet — medium heat. Combine dry ingredients, add and blend in vinegar and water until smooth. Add to skillet with pineapple tidbits and cook until thickened and smooth. Toss shrimp into sauce. Serve with rice.

CRAYFISH ETOUFFE

30 pounds crayfish
1 stalk celery
6 medium onions, chopped
4 cloves garlic, chopped
1 bell pepper, diced
1 cup green onion tops, chopped
1 pimiento
Tabasco
4 tablespoons Worcestershire sauce
1 teaspoon Accent
Salt and pepper to taste
1 cup chicken fat or more, depending on amount of crayfish meat

Bring large kettle of water to boil, add salt and cook crayfish for 20 minutes. Peel tails. Save tails and fat and put in separate containers. Melt chicken fat and crayfish fat in large iron pot. Add celery, onions, bell pepper, garlic. Cook slowly until all is wilted. Add Worcestershire sauce, Tabasco and Accent. Blend, then add crayfish tails, salt and pepper. Cover and cook until tails are tender, about 15 minutes. Do not overcook. Add additional seasoning to taste, then pimiento for color. Turn off heat and allow to stand for 30 minutes. When reheating, use a double boiler. Serve over rice (about 4 quarts). 4 pounds peeled and deveined shrimp may be substituted for crayfish. ½ cup cooking oil may be susbtituted for 1 cup chicken fat.

Will serve about 15. Mrs. E. C. St. Martin

Use 1 tablespoon caraway seeds when boiling shrimp. The odor disappears!

SHREVEPORT CLUB CRAB ENTREE

4 tablespoons flour
4 tablespoons oleo or butter
2 cups milk
1 bay leaf
1 teaspoon chicken base
⅛ teaspoon white pepper
1 pound lump crab meat (use only fresh)
Parmesan cheese and mild yellow cheese, grated
Paprika

Heat the milk, bay leaf, chicken base and pepper. Make a white sauce by melting the oleo (or butter) in a saucepan, stirring flour in, adding the warm milk (bay leaf removed). (Chicken base is a chicken-flavored, greasy salt — use only enough to salt the white sauce properly.) In individual shells, casseroles, or one casserole, place the lump crab meat. Sprinkle Parmesan cheese over it. Cover with the white sauce. Sprinkle grated mild yellow cheese over the top. Then sprinkle a little paprika over the cheese. Bake until hot through, bubbly and cheese is melted. Cook at 350° for 20 minutes.

Makes 6 ladies' servings for a luncheon or 4 large servings. Can make the white sauce a day ahead. Can put cooled white sauce on crabmeat a little ahead of time — to 24 hours — with success.

The Shreveport Club
Mrs. James E. Smitherman, Jr.

FILLETS FLORENTINE

2 pounds spinach
Salt
4 tablespoons butter
½ cup water
½ cup white wine
3 peppercorns
1 small onion stuck with 1 clove
Sprig of parsley
4 fish fillets
2 tablespoons flour
¼ cup heavy cream
Few grains nutmeg
Few drops lemon juice
Grated Parmesan cheese

Cook spinach, drain and chop very fine. Season to taste with salt and add 2 tablespoons butter. Arrange on a well buttered baking dish and keep warm. Combine water with wine, peppercorns, onion and parsley. Bring to a boil and cook 5 minutes. Add fish fillets (1 to a person) and simmer for 5 minutes, or, until fish is cooked. Remove to a hot plate, let the liquid simmer 2 or 3 minutes longer and strain. Melt 2 tablespoons butter in a saucepan, or double boiler, and blend with flour, stirring constantly; gradually add the strained broth from the fish until thickened. Add cream, nutmeg and lemon juice. Place fillets on bed of spinach, cover with the sauce and sprinkle liberally with Parmesan cheese. Place the dish in a very hot oven (475°) for 5 minutes, or, until cheese is delicately browned.

Makes 4 servings. Mrs. G. Gardiner Green, Laurel, Miss.

FRIED CROSS LAKE CATFISH

(Cross Lake has a special Catfish — Blue Channel — feeding gives special flavor.)

2 8-ounce catfish
Milani dill sauce
Yellow corn meal
White corn meal
Salt

Dip catfish in Milani dill sauce, and roll in mixture of yellow corn meal, white corn meal and salt. Put on tray and place in icebox for several hours to set. Drop in deep fat fryer which is set at 350° and cook for 10-12 minutes, or, until golden brown and floats. Serve with tartar sauce, sliced onions and hush puppies.

Smith's Cross Lake Inn

CHOPSTICK TUNA

1 family size can tuna
2 cans mushroom soup
½ cup milk
2 large cans chow mein noodles
2 cups diced celery
1 cup green onion, chopped
1 cup salted cashew nuts (split)
1 can mandarin oranges, drained

Mix together the above ingredients, with the exception of the oranges. Cook in oven, 375°, 15 to 20 minutes. After baking, top with mandarin oranges, drained. Put the orange sections on just before serving.

Makes 8 medium servings.

Mrs. Paul E. Osburn, Jr.
Mrs. Gene Newton

SALMON AND NOODLE ONE DISH MEAL

4 tablespoons butter
4 tablespoons flour
¼ teaspoon dry mustard
¼ teaspoon paprika
1 teaspoon salt
3 cups milk
1 teaspoon Worcestershire sauce
1 tablespoon lemon juice
½ cup grated cheese
1 1-pound can salmon, drained and flaked
½ cup sliced stuffed olives
2 4-ounce cans sliced mushrooms
8 ounces noodles, cooked and drained
Buttered dry bread crumbs
8-10 canned asparagus tips
Parsley, pimiento and paprika

Melt butter, blend in flour, mustard, paprika and salt. Gradually add milk and cook, stirring until thickened. Stir in Worcestershire sauce, lemon juice and cheese, and stir until cheese is melted. Add salmon, olives and mushrooms. Combine noodles and sauce in lightly greased 2-quart casserole. Sprinkle with buttered bread crumbs and bake at 375° for 30 minutes. Garnish with asparagus, parsley, pimiento and paprika.

Serves 4-6.

Mrs. Ernest A. Merklein, Jr.

SALMON LOAF

1 1-pound can salmon (save juice)
2 tablespoons butter
¾ cup fine, dry bread crumbs
½-¾ cup milk, depending on dryness of salmon and crumbs
⅛ teaspoon pepper
4 egg yolks, beaten
1 small onion, grated
4 egg whites, beaten

Sauce:
1 tablespoon butter
2 tablespoons flour
1 cup milk
Juice from salmon
3 tablespoons catsup or chili sauce
1 tablespoon lemon juice
Tarragon
Hard boiled eggs (optional)

To make loaf: Drain salmon, chop and add ingredients in order given, lastly folding in stiffly beaten egg whites. Pour mixture into buttered loaf pan, set in pan of hot water and bake at 350° for 45 minutes, or until toothpick comes out clean when inserted in middle. Turn out onto platter. This mixture may also be baked in individual muffin tins, using a shorter cooking time.

To make sauce: Melt butter, add flour and cook until frothy. Add a good pinch of tarragon, add milk and blend until smooth. Add lemon juice, juice from salmon, salt, white pepper and catsup. One or more coarsely chopped hard boiled eggs may be added just before serving. Spoon over slices as served.

Makes 6 servings. Mrs. Robert K. Butcher

FAMILY SALMON LOAF

2 cups medium cream sauce (2 tablespoons butter, 2 tablespoons flour, 2 cups milk)
1 cup mild cheese, grated
⅓ cup finely chopped bell pepper
Salt and pepper
2 eggs
1 1-pound can salmon
1 cup cracker crumbs
½ cup finely chopped onion (optional)

Make cream sauce. Add cheese, bell pepper and season to taste. Mix raw eggs with salmon. Put layer of salmon, layer of sauce, layer of crumbs, etc., into buttered casserole. Bake 25 to 30 minutes, or until bubbly and slightly browned, in moderate oven, 350°.

Mrs. Marshall Martin

When freezing fish, pack them in a small amount of water in plastic milk cartons (½-gallon size) and seal with freezer tape. Fresh crabs, crawfish and shrimp may also be frozen this way.

LOUISIANA CRAB MEAT ROLL

Crepes:
2 eggs
¾ cup sifted flour
1 cup milk
1 teaspoon butter
Pinch of salt
Filling:
½ green onion, chopped
¼ bell pepper, chopped
1 tablespoon butter
Pinch of salt
½ cup white wine
½ pound crab meat
3 cups white sauce
American cheese, grated

For crepes: Mix eggs with flour. Add milk, butter and salt. Beat until smooth. Cook in 6-inch skillet. Cook until brown, then turn and brown other side. Makes 6 crepes.

For filling: Saute onion and bell pepper in butter until tender. Add wine. Add crab meat and 1 cup white sauce. Season with salt and pepper.

Place 2 tablespoons of filling in center of each crepe and roll. Cover each crepe with 3 tablespoons of cream sauce. Sprinkle each crepe with grated American cheese. Cook in 400° oven until cheese is melted and cream sauce is bubbling. Serve piping hot.

Serves 3 or 4.

Shreveport Country Club

CRAB MEAT AU GRATIN

4 tablespoons butter
3 tablespoons flour
3 cups milk
1 teaspoon Worcestershire sauce
Dash Tabasco
3 tablespoons chicken or beef broth or consomme
1 teaspoon salt
Dash of thyme (powdered)
2 beaten egg yolks
2 cans crab meat
1 pound grated cheese (medium sharp Cheddar is fine)
Bread crumbs
Butter

Make white sauce with first eight ingredients. Mix egg yolks, crab meat and cheese. Add sauce which is thick to crab meat mixture by mashing in with fork and let stand awhile. Cover with bread crumbs and dot with butter. Bake uncovered at 325° for about 30 minutes. Swiss cheese improves any seafood au gratin recipe. A small amount of Swiss cheese instead of Cheddar is very good in this.

Serves 8.

Mrs. Murff O Neal, Jr.

CRAB MEAT CALIFORNIA

- 1 small onion
- 1 small can mushrooms
- 3 tablespoons butter
- 1 can concentrated chicken soup
- Dash pepper
- Few drops Tabasco
- 1 teaspoon Worcestershire sauce
- ¼ cup light cream
- ½ can jumbo shrimp
- 1 7-ounce can solid pack tuna, crab, ham or chicken
- ½ can sliced ripe olives

Cook onion and drained mushrooms in butter until brown. Add soup and seasonings and simmer gently. Add cream, olives, shrimp and crab. Mix gently and heat. Serve over hot rice, canned Chinese noodles or toast points.

Makes 6 servings.

Mrs. Viva Begbie

IMPERIAL CRAB

- 1 pound fresh lump crab meat
- ½ teaspoon salt
- ⅛ teaspoon red pepper
- ½ cup special mayonnaise*
- ½ cup dry bread crumbs
- Paprika
- 1 heaping tablespoon capers

Combine crab meat, seasonings, mayonnaise and capers. Mix carefully with a fork to keep the crab meat in large pieces. Heap in greased crab shells, cover with bread crumbs and paprika. Bake in 350° oven for 25 minutes.

Serves 6. To serve cold, do not butter shells. Heap in shells, sprinkle with paprika and a sprig or two of parsley.

*Special mayonnaise:

- 2 teaspoons dry mustard
- 2 teaspoons salt
- 1½ teaspoons white pepper
- 2 teaspoons sugar
- 1 egg yolk
- 2 teaspoons lemon juice
- 1⅔ cups salad oil
- 2 teaspoons tarragon wine vinegar

Add dry ingredients, well mixed, to egg yolk, which has been beaten until almost white. Blend well. Add lemon juice and mix well. Add salad oil one teaspoon at a time, beating constantly, until ¼ cup oil has been used. Add remaining oil slowly, alternating last ½ cup oil with vinegar. Either an electric beater or blender may be used. Makes 2 cups. This separates easily if you stop, so don't answer the telephone when making it! This mayonnaise will keep well in refrigerator, but do not mix with crab meat until shortly before serving.

Mrs. Robert K. Butcher

HOT CRAB MEAT IMPERIAL CASSEROLE

1 large green pepper, diced
2 pimientos, diced
½ teaspoon salt
½ teaspoon freshly ground white pepper
1 tablespoon dry mustard
3 tablespoons mayonnaise
2 eggs, lightly beaten
3 tablespoons sherry
2 pounds fresh back fin lump crab meat
Paprika

Preheat the oven to 350°. Mix the diced pepper and pimientos. Add salt, pepper, mustard, mayonnaise, eggs and 2 tablespoons of sherry. Carefully fold the crab meat into the pepper mixture so as not to break the lumps of crab. Add the remaining tablespoon of sherry and place in a buttered casserole. Coat the top of the casserole with a thin layer of mayonnaise and sprinkle with paprika. Bake 15 minutes.

Makes 6 servings.

Mrs. Edward R. Jones

CRAB MEAT WITH BROCCOLI

1 package cooked broccoli
1 cup sour cream
1 can crab meat, frozen, or 2 small cans
1 onion, minced
⅓ cup chili sauce
2 tablespoons lemon juice
1 tablespoon lemon rind, grated
1 cup sharp cheese

Simply combine ingredients and warm in casserole until bubbly and serve. Crab tastes like fresh when seasoned this way. May be prepared the day before if necessary. Bake 20 to 30 minutes at 325°.

Serves 5.

Mrs. Robert E. King

CREAMED CRAB MEAT ON TOASTED BUN

1 can crab meat
1 cup grated sharp cheese
½ cup mayonnaise
Grated onion to taste
Worcestershire sauce, lemon juice, salt and pepper, paprika to taste

Mix in bowl and put on toasted bun (or English muffin). Run in broiler for 5 or 6 minutes until toasted around edges. Serve with congealed salad and iced tea for a nice lunch.

Makes 4 servings.

Mrs. John William Patton, Jr.

PARTY SANDWICH

2 7-ounce cans white tuna
½ can chopped ripe olives
4 hard cooked eggs, chopped
⅔ cup mayonnaise
Salt and pepper to taste

Icing:
3 jars sharp cheese spread
1½ cups soft butter
3 raw eggs
Bread

Wash and drain tuna and combine with olives, eggs and mayonnaise. Cut edges from bread and spread with this mixture as an ordinary sandwich. Beat cheese, butter and raw eggs at room temperature for 5 minutes. Use this to ice sandwiches like individual cakes. Refrigerate 12 hours. Bake 8 to 10 minutes in 450° oven. Serve on salad plates with fork. Excellent for bridge luncheons.

Mrs. Robert E. King

SEAFOOD CASSEROLE

2 slices bread soaked in ¾ cup water, set aside
½ cup chopped celery
½ cup chopped bell pepper
½ cup chopped onion, browned in butter and set aside to cool
2 cans king crab meat
1 small can shrimp
1 small can water chestnuts
½ cup mayonnaise
1 egg, beaten
½ pound grated sharp cheese
Dash Tabasco
1 tablespoon and 1 teaspoon Worcestershire sauce
1 cup crumbled potato chips

Combine all ingredients and mix gently. Before baking, crumble potato chips over top. Perfect for making the day before.

A perfect bread to serve with this is prepared by cutting hot dog buns in fourths. Spread with softened butter to which has been added ½ teaspoon thyme and ½ teaspoon savory to two sticks of butter. Spread on a cookie sheet. These bake at the same temperature (350°) and for the same length of time (30 minutes) as the casserole.

Serves 6 to 8.

Mrs. Lilbourn G. Morgan

CRAB AND SHRIMP ENTREE

1 pound can lump crab meat
1 pound cooked small or medium shrimp
1 cup toasted bread crumbs
2 small cans evaporated milk
1 teaspoon chopped onion
1 teaspoon chopped parsley
6 hard boiled eggs, chopped
1 cup mayonnaise
1 teaspoon garlic powder
Salt
Pepper
1 can sliced mushrooms
2 teaspoons lemon juice
2 teaspoons Worcestershire sauce

Mix all ingredients together. Put in large casserole dish or individual shells. Cook at 350° for 20 minutes. May be frozen before cooking.

Serves 10.

Mrs. Darrell E. George

DEVILED CRAB

1 chopped bell pepper
1 chopped onion
1 mashed garlic clove
3 chopped green onions (tops included)
2 stalks chopped celery
3 tablespoons chopped parsley
4 slices bread (soak in water and squeeze out)
½ cup grated sharp cheese
3 flat cans crab meat
⅓ cup mayonnaise
2 beaten eggs
1 tablespoon Worcestershire sauce
Juice of 1 lemon
Add to taste: seasoned salt, pepper and Tabasco

Saute bell pepper, onion, garlic, green onions, celery, parsley. Add to the remainder, mix well. Fill individual ramekins. Cook in 300° oven 30-40 minutes. May be made the day before serving.

Makes 8-10 ramekins. Mrs. Robert A. Stacy, Jr.

SHRIMP IN SOUR CREAM

1½ pounds shrimp
2 cups sour cream
¼ cup sherry
½ cup butter
2 green onions, minced
½ pound mushrooms, sliced
2 tablespoons flour
Salt and pepper to taste

Peel shrimp. Saute shrimp and onion in butter for 5 minutes until pink. Add mushrooms and cook 5 minutes longer. Blend in flour, salt, pepper, garlic salt, cayenne. Add sour cream gradually and cook until thick. Doesn't take long, stirring constantly. Remove from heat and stir in sherry. Serve on whole wheat toast or cup forms.

Serves 4-6. Mrs. W. W. Lincoln

SHRIMP OAKLEY

6 slices bread
½ pound Old English cheese
1 pound shrimp, shelled and cleaned
3 eggs
2 cups milk
½ teaspoon salt
¼ teaspoon red pepper
2 teaspoons dry mustard

Butter casserole. Break bread into pieces, and cube cheese the size of quarters. Place the bread, cheese and shrimp in layers in the casserole. Mix eggs, milk, salt and pepper and mustard together. Pour over the ingredients in the casserole. Cover and place in refrigerator overnight, or at least 3 hours. Bake for 1 hour at 375°.

Makes 4 luncheon servings. Mrs. Josephine B. Oakley

SHRIMP A LA DEWEY

2 bunches green onions, chopped fine
1 stick oleo
1 can whole tomatoes, cut up and drained
2 medium cans mushrooms, sliced
½ bunch parsley, chopped fine
3 pounds peeled raw shrimp; cook shrimp in shrimp boil until done
Salt
Worcestershire sauce
Accent
Black and red pepper
½ cup heavy cream or sour cream
¼ cup dry sherry or sauterne

Wilt onions in oleo, add tomatoes. Cook until tomatoes are blended. Add mushrooms, and cook a few minutes. Add parsley. Thicken with flour if necessary. Add cooked shrimp. Season to taste with salt, Worcestershire sauce, Accent, black and red pepper. Add cream and wine. More cream may be added if sauce is not sufficient. Serve in patty shells or on toast. For best results cook the day before serving so that seasoning will penetrate.

Serves 6 to 8. Mrs. Lawrence R. Burke

SHRIMP L'AIGLON

3-pound bag frozen, deveined shrimp
½ pound oleo
1 clove garlic, crushed
4 green onions, chopped fine
4-5 sprigs parsley
Dash nutmeg
3 lemons (may be 2, depending on amount of juice)
1 tablespoon Worcestershire sauce
Salt
Pepper
6 tablespoons bread crumbs

Make a paste of all ingredients except shrimp. Put shrimp in serving shells and cover with mixture. Bake at 450° 15 to 20 minutes. Serve immediately. May be fixed ahead. Best to keep the butter mixture separate and combine at the last minute. This can be broiled quite successfully.

Makes six servings in shells or ramekins.

Mrs. Keith O'Kelley, Ruston, La.
Mrs. John D. Harrell, Pensacola, Florida

KEY WEST SHRIMP SAUTE

8 raw jumbo shrimp per person
Garlic butter
Chopped parsley
Sherry

Peel and clean shrimp. Saute in garlic butter over medium flame for 5 minutes. Remove shrimp and increase flame. Add chopped parsley and sherry wine to garlic butter. Sear for 30 seconds. Pour over shrimp and serve.

Mrs. Jack C. Murrell

BROILED SHRIMP

2 pounds shrimp
1 stick oleo
1 bunch chives
1 cup sauterne
Salt and pepper

Put cleaned shrimp in ovenproof dish. Salt and pepper shrimp and add chives. Melt butter and pour over it. Put under broiler and cook until they turn pink. Then broil on other side. Now add 1 cup wine and cook 2 or 3 minutes. Serve in soup bowls and dip toast in the juice while eating.

This serves 4 people. Mrs. James A. Reeder

SHRIMP CURRY

2½ pounds shrimp
1 chicken bouillon cube
1 cup boiling water
5 tablespoons butter
½ cup minced onion
1 apple, peeled and chopped
4 tablespoons flour
3-4 tablespoons curry powder
1¼ teaspoons salt
1½ teaspoons sugar
1 teaspoon ginger
2 cups cream
2 teaspoons lemon juice

Cook and clean shrimp. Dissolve bouillon cube in water. Melt butter in double boiler top over direct heat. Add onion and apple. Simmer together. Stir in next 5 ingredients. Slowly stir in bouillon and cream. Cook over boiling water, stirring, until thickened. Add shrimp and lemon juice. Heat. Serve over rice with any or all of the following: chutney, tomato wedges, salted nuts, coconut, sliced avocado, chopped hard boiled egg, crisp bacon bits or canned pineapple.

Serves 6. May be frozen. May be prepared early in the day — except for adding shrimp and lemon.

Mrs. Francis Kalmbach

BASIC SHRIMP CREOLE

6 tablespoons bacon grease
4 onions
4 to 6 bell peppers
3 tablespoons flour
1 No. 2 can tomatoes
2 cans tomato sauce or paste
1 can tomato juice
Salt and red pepper
1 tablespoon file powder
3½ pounds boiled and peeled small shrimp

Heat bacon grease. Saute finely chopped onions and peppers until tender. Remove and drain grease back into skillet, then add flour and let brown. Add sauteed onions and peppers, tomatoes, paste, juice, seasonings, bring to a boil, then let simmer for several hours. Add shrimp just shortly before serving over boiled rice.

Serve 6 or 8. Mrs. Y. L. Forte

TEXAS STYLE SHRIMP CREOLE

- 2 onions
- 1 bell pepper
- 3 pieces celery
- Olive oil
- 1 can tomato paste
- 1 large can Italian tomatoes
- 3 cans tomato sauce
- 1 clove garlic
- 5 small bay leaves
- ⅓ can Ro-tel tomatoes
- Salt to taste
- 3 pounds shrimp, cooked and cleaned

Saute onions, bell pepper and celery in olive oil. Add tomato paste and cook 5 minutes. Add tomatoes, tomato sauce, garlic, bay leaves and Ro-tel tomatoes. Add salt to taste. Simmer several hours. Add shrimp the last 15 minutes. Serve over rice.

Mrs. William Wilkins

CREAM SHRIMP WITH CURRY

- 1½ pounds shrimp
- 1 cup chopped celery
- ½ cup chopped onion
- 4 tablespoons oleo or butter
- 4 tablespoons flour
- 2 cups milk
- 3 tablespoons soy sauce
- 3 tablespoons Worcestershire sauce
- 1½ tablespoons curry
- 1½ teaspoons salt
- Grated Parmesan cheese
- Bread crumbs
- Butter

Boil shrimp in salt water — about 5 minutes (clean). Saute celery and onion in oleo or butter until limp. Add flour, stir. Add milk slowly. Add next four ingredients. Cook slowly until it comes to a full boil. Now add shrimp, stir. Pour into greased baking dish; top with cheese, bread crumbs, 2 tablespoons butter. Bake at 350° for 40 minutes. Best if prepared a day or two before and reheated. Serve over rice or toast.

Makes about 4 servings. Mrs. N. E. Liles

CREOLE SHRIMP SPAGHETTI

- 4 tablespoons chopped onion
- ½ cup sliced celery
- 2 tablespoons butter, melted
- ¼ cup flour
- 1 teaspoon salt
- ¼ teaspoon pepper
- 4 cups cooked tomatoes
- 1 cup sliced mushrooms (fresh if possible)
- 1 teaspoon sugar
- 1 pound cooked shrimp
- 8 ounces spaghetti

Cook onion and celery in butter until tender. Stir in flour, salt and pepper. Add juice from tomatoes (2 cups) and stir until smooth. Crush tomatoes and add to sauce along with mushrooms and sugar. Simmer over low heat for 40 minutes. Add cooked shrimp. Serve over cooked spaghetti. Best if prepared ahead of time. May be frozen. Cook ½ hour to reheat. Add water if necessary.

Mrs. Robert Roberts, III

PAELLA

12 or more clams in shells, or canned may be used
2 large Spanish onions, chopped fine
6 tablespoons finely chopped parsley
1 cup cut-up chicken or turkey
¼ pound pepperoni, cut in small pieces
1 cup ground ham
½ cup olive oil
3 cloves garlic, chopped fine
1 pound scallops, sliced
1 pound shrimp, peeled and cooked
5 large tomatoes, peeled and diced, or 1 large can
2 cans pimientos
2 cups chicken stock
1 can crab meat, or fresh crab claws
1 pound rice
½ teaspoon powdered saffron

Saute in olive oil cut-up chicken, or turkey, and pepperoni. Remove and reserve. Saute shrimp, scallops and other seafood in same pan and remove. Drain off all but 2 tablespoons oil, add onions and half garlic and saute; add peeled tomatoes and pimientos and simmer for 5 minutes. Add chicken, pepperoni, seafoods, ground ham. Salt and pepper to taste and heat through. Mix remaining garlic, parsley and saffron in a cup of boiling stock or water and combine well. Slowly bring to a boil. Add rice and cook uncovered for 15 minutes, without stirring, then stir, using a wooden spoon, being sure nothing is sticking. Cook until rice is tender. Garnish with crab claws, steamed clams if available, and large shrimp; then put into warm oven to keep hot.

Makes 6 servings. Paella is traditionally cooked and served in a flat two-handled pan, from which it gets it name.

Mrs. Arthur F. Shuey

FINEGAN AND STEVENS SHRIMP TETRAZZINI

½ stick oleo
Chop and saute in oleo:
6 green onions
¼ cup bell pepper
1 cup celery
¼ cup parsley
Add next 7 ingredients for Sauce:
2 cans tomato soup
2 cans mushroom soup
4 tablespoons Worcestershire sauce
¼ teaspoon red pepper
½ teaspoon black pepper
¼ cup sherry
Juice of ½ lemon
1-pound package spaghettini
5 pounds fresh shrimp or 3 pounds cooked and peeled shrimp
Sharp grated cheese

Boil spaghettini in salted water. Drain well. Add cooked shrimp and sauce. Line greased casserole with rolled Ritz crackers. Add mixture, top with grated cheese and bake until brown.

Serves 12.

Mrs. C. S. Finegan
Mrs. Lawton Stevens

SHRIMP AU GRATIN

1 4-ounce can mushrooms
3 tablespoons chopped onion
3 tablespoons butter, melted
¼ cup flour
½ teaspoon salt
¼ teaspoon dry mustard
Dash pepper
1½ cups milk
1 cup grated cheese
1 pound cooked shrimp, peeled and deveined
¼ cup dry bread crumbs

Cook mushrooms and onion in butter until tender. Blend in flour and seasonings. Add milk gradually and cook until thick, stirring constantly. Add ¾ cup cheese and stir until melted. Stir in shrimp and pour into well greased casserole. Combine crumbs and remaining cheese, sprinkle over top. Dot with butter. Cook at 400° for 10 minutes.

Serves 4. Mrs. Ernest A. Merklein, Jr.

SHRIMP JAMBALAYA

2 teaspoons butter
1 onion, minced
1 green pepper, minced
1 clove garlic, minced
¼ cup pimiento, minced
1 cup rice, uncooked
½ cup mushrooms
1½ cups shrimp, cleaned
1 teaspoon salt
1 bay leaf
2 cups water
Red pepper, Tabasco and Worcestershire sauce to taste

Melt butter and add remaining ingredients. Cover. When steaming, turn heat to simmer and cook for 30 minutes.

Mrs. Hamilton Harper, Jr.

EGGPLANT WITH SHRIMP

1 large eggplant
1 large onion
½ cup water
1 stick of oleomargarine or butter
1 beaten egg
2 cups cracker crumbs
1 package (10 ounces) frozen cooked shrimp or 1 7-ounce can shrimp
1 cup grated sharp Cheddar cheese
Salt
Pepper
Tabasco

Peel and slice eggplant. Add chopped onion, water and butter. Cook until tender. Add egg, cracker crumbs, shrimp, cheese and season with salt, pepper and dash of Tabasco. Put ingredients in buttered casserole (1-quart size required). Top with small portion of grated cheese. Put in oven and cook until hot.

Mrs. Gilbert O'Brien

INDIVIDUAL SHRIMP-STUFFED EGGPLANT

- 2 cans small shrimp
- ½ cup chopped onion
- ½ cup chopped parsley
- ¼ cup chopped green pepper
- 2 cloves garlic, chopped
- ⅓ cup shortening, melted
- 1 cup canned tomatoes
- 3 eggplants (as small as possible)
- 2 whole bay leaves
- 1 teaspoon salt
- ½ teaspoon pepper
- ½ teaspoon crushed thyme
- ⅔ cup shrimp liquid
- 3 tablespoons butter
- ¾ cup dry bread crumbs

Drain shrimp and save liquid. Cook onion, green pepper, parsley and garlic in shortening until tender. Wash and cut eggplant in half lengthwise and scoop out pulp, leaving about ¼-inch thickness around shell. Turn shells upside down in pan of cold water to prevent discoloration. Chop pulp. Add tomatoes, seasonings, shrimp liquid, and chopped eggplant to onion mixture. Cover and simmer 10 minutes, or, until eggplant is tender. Remove bay leaves. Add shrimp. Combine butter and crumbs. Fill shells with layers of shrimp mixture and crumbs. Place in baking pan, adding a little hot water to prevent sticking. Bake in a hot oven, 400°, for 35 to 40 minutes, or until brown.

Serves 6. May also be used for tomatoes or mirliton.

Mrs. E. C. St. Martin

SQUASH SHRIMP CASSEROLE

- 8 pounds squash (yellow)
- 1½ cups onion
- 1½ cups celery
- ½ cup bell pepper
- 1½ packages prepared dressing mix
- 6 eggs
- 2 pounds shrimp

Cook squash in small amount of salt water until tender. In skillet cook in bacon drippings until tender: chopped onion, celery and pepper. In large mixing bowl combine cooked squash with liquid, sauteed vegetables, dressing mix, eggs, salt and pepper to taste. Mix well. Add to above mixture cooked shrimp. Divide into 2 or 3 casserole dishes. Top with buttered crumbs. Bake at 350° for 45 minutes. Good buffet dish.

Serves 25.

Mrs. C. Cody White, Jr.

DEVILED OYSTERS

1 tablespoon oleo
4 stalks celery
1 large onion
1 bell pepper
1 pint oysters
1 pint milk
Salt and pepper to taste
Tabasco to taste
½ small bottle Worcestershire sauce
¼-pound package of crackers

Cook celery, onion and bell pepper in oleo, until limp but not brown. Drain oysters and put in onion mixture. Cook until edges curl. Add milk and seasonings. Crumble crackers in until all the liquid is taken up. Pour into casserole and top with cracker crumbs. Dot with butter. Cook at 375° for 20 minutes. May be prepared early and heated in casserole later if desired, or it may be frozen.

Serves 4.

Mrs. W. M. Scott

SCALLOPED OYSTERS CASSEROLE

2 full cups celery, chopped
2 full cups onion, chopped
1 strip bell pepper, chopped
1 tablespoon parsley, clipped
1 scant tablespoon shortening
Salt
Pepper
2 cups milk
1 pint oysters
½ stick butter or oleo
1 box crackers
½ to 1 teaspoon Tabasco
2 teaspoons Worcestershire sauce
Black pepper to taste
Butter

Chop vegetables into bowl of cold water. Melt shortening in skillet and lift vegetables out of water into skillet. Salt and pepper while steaming. Steam for about 15 minutes. Do not brown or let fall apart, just let vegetables get tender. Scald milk (bring almost to a boil); then add vegetables to milk. Next drop oysters into hot milk a few at a time. Let oysters curl, then remove from fire and add butter. Break one package of the box of crackers into mixture. Season with Tabasco, Worcestershire sauce and black pepper. Pour into buttered casserole. Crush other package of crackers into crumbs by rolling with rolling pin between two sheets of waxed paper. Cover the top of casserole with these crumbs. Slice another ½ stick of butter or oleo into small strips and dot over casserole by sticking them down into the mixture. Bake in 450° oven until brown.

Serves, as a main dish, four to six; as a side dish, maybe more.

Mrs. J. S. Douglas

DEVILED OYSTERS

3 dozen large or 4 dozen small oysters
¾ cup cream (canned milk may be used)
7 tablespoons olive oil
1 tablespoon butter
2 egg yolks, well beaten
3 tablespoons minced parsley and green onion tops
1 bay leaf and dash of spice if desired
1 tablespoon flour
1 medium onion, minced
1 clove garlic, minced

Cook oysters in own liquor slightly. Drain and cut in small pieces, but do not mince. Fry onion, garlic in butter and oil. Add flour and cream a little at a time. Cook slowly 10 minutes. Stir in yolks; add oysters. Fill shells or ramekins. Dust with cracker crumbs. Put small lump of butter on each and bake at 350° 10 to 15 minutes. May be made the day before and kept in refrigerator until serving time.

Mrs. Vincent S. Brennan

TRADITIONAL SCALLOPED OYSTERS

4 tablespoons butter
1½ cups dry bread crumbs
1 pint oysters
1 cup cream (sweet)
1 tablespoon minced parsley
½ teaspoon celery salt
½ teaspoon paprika
Dash nutmeg
½ cup Parmesan cheese

Melt butter in pan, add bread crumbs and stir until well mixed. Place layer of crumbs in baking dish or ramekins. Draw liquor from oysters and mix with cream, parsley, celery salt, paprika, and nutmeg. Dip each oyster in mixture and place on buttered crumbs in dish. Sprinkle oysters with cheese and cover with balance of crumbs. Pour remaining cream mixture over oysters and bake at 400° until light brown.

Serves 4 or 5 people. Mrs. Otis C. Coles, Jr.

NEW ORLEANS OYSTER PATTIES

2 tablespoons bacon fat or oleo
1 pod garlic
2 stalks celery
3 green onions and tops, chopped fine
2 tablespoons flour
3 dozen oysters
2 tablespoons oyster liquid
Dash of Accent
Dash of cayenne pepper
Salt and pepper to taste
2 tablespoons parsley, chopped

Melt fat in pan. Add garlic, celery and onion; cook until soft. Blend in flour, oysters, oyster liquid, Accent, cayenne, salt and pepper. Cook on low heat, stirring constantly until oysters make more liquid. Simmer for 20 minutes. Add uncooked parsley and cool. Fill prepared patty shells and bake in 300° oven until heated, about 15 minutes.

This recipe fills 5 to 6 large patty shells. It is also delicious served in bite-sized shells as an appetizer.

Mrs. Louis Planchard

OYSTER PATTIES

4 dozen oysters, or 1 pint
¼ pound butter or oleo
1 medium onion, minced
1 bunch shallots, minced
5 tablespoons flour
2 tablespoons parsley, minced
1 tablespoon celery, minced
1 tablespoon bell pepper, minced
1 bay leaf
1 clove garlic, minced
1 teaspoon salt
Dash red pepper

Drain oysters, save liquid. Saute onions, celery, shallots, bell pepper, and garlic in butter until light brown. Add flour, stirring until well blended. Add oyster water, seasonings and 1 cup water. Let cook a few minutes, add oysters and cook until oysters curl around edges. Keep hot in double boiler or on asbestos pad. If it gets too thick, add a little milk. It should be creamy but not runny. Serve in patty shells.

Serves 4 to 6. Mrs. Andrew Querbes, Jr.

OYSTERS WITH BROWN RICE AND SAUSAGE

2 pounds hot sausage
2 cups minced onion
2 cups minced celery
6 cups cooked brown rice
2 pints fresh oysters
2 cups minced parsley

Crumble sausage into skillet and cook until done. Drain sausage while browning onion and celery in the skillet in which sausage was cooked. Drain grease from onion and celery after cooking. Mix sausage, onions, celery with rice which has been cooked according to package directions. At this stage dish may be kept for many hours. Forty-five minutes before serving add oysters. Bake about 30 minutes. Garnish top with parsley before serving.

Serves 12. May be used as side dish for duck as well as main dish. Good with tart flavor of cranberry sauce and grapefruit salad.

Mrs. B. T. Grainger

CREAMED OYSTER ROCKEFELLER

2 cups medium cream sauce
1 package chopped frozen spinach
1 tablespoon absinthe
1 teaspoon onion juice
Tabasco sauce
Worcestershire sauce
1 teaspoon sugar
2 tablespoons Parmesan cheese
Salt and pepper

Make cream sauce. Add frozen spinach to cream sauce in double boiler. Stir together until smooth. Add rest of ingredients and cook until thickness desired. Place portion of sauce over oysters (either on half shell or in ramekins) and broil in oven 370° for 10-15 minutes.

Mrs. Edgar Galloway

OYSTERS LORRAINE

6 large artichokes
1½ sticks butter
½ teaspoon salt
⅛ teaspoon pepper
1 tablespoon Worcestershire sauce
2 tablespoons fresh grated onion
1 pint large plump oysters

Steam or boil artichokes in salted water until tender. Scrape leaves; remove and reserve bottoms. Reserve 42 leaves that are extra pretty. Put scrapings in top of large double boiler with all other ingredients except oysters. Cook, stirring hard (or beat with mixer) until smooth and well blended. Add oysters. Stir gently, cooking only until oysters are plump and curled. Place reserved bottoms in individual ramekins (buttered lightly) and cover with scrapings and oyster mixture. Sprinkle with fine bread crumbs. Brown under broiler (or re-heat in hot oven about 20 minutes). Garnish with slices of lemons. Serve surrounded by reserved artichoke leaves. Squeeze a little lemon juice on leaves so that they do not turn brown.

Mrs. William Meyers, New Orleans, La.

OYSTERS BIENVILLE

1 dozen oysters on half shell
1 bunch shallots, chopped
1 tablespoon butter
1 tablespoon flour
½ cup chicken broth (bouillon)
½ cup shrimp, chopped (canned may be used)
⅓ cup mushrooms, chopped
1 egg yolk
⅓ glass white wine to taste
Ice cream salt
Cheese, bread crumbs

Place ice cream salt in pie plate or jelly roll pan. Place oysters on half shell on salt. Bake oysters in 350° oven until partially done (about 6-8 minutes).

Sauce: Fry shallots in butter until brown. Add flour and heat until brown. Add chicken broth, shrimp and mushrooms. Beat egg yolk with wine and slowly add to sauce, beating rapidly. Season to taste. Cook for 10 minutes over low heat, stirring constantly. Pour sauce over each oyster; cover with bread crumbs, paprika and grated cheese (which have been mixed). Place in oven to brown for about 12 minutes.

1 dozen oysters serve 2 people. Oyster shells may be placed on salt ahead of time. Sauce may be made early and kept in the refrigrator, and bread crumbs, paprika and cheese prepared and mixed ahead of time.

Mrs. Roger Gardner

SPANISH OYSTERS

1 clove garlic, chopped
1 cup onion, chopped
2 tablespoons butter or more
2 tablespoons flour
1 cup chopped green onion and tops, celery, parsley and bell pepper combined
3 tablespoons green tomato pickle
½ can tomato sauce
1 tablespoon Worcestershire sauce
Salt, fresh ground black pepper and red pepper to taste
1 pint small oysters (about 3 dozen)
Mushrooms and crab (optional)

Saute chopped garlic and chopped onion in butter. Add flour and brown. Add combined chopped vegetables. Cook. Add tomato sauce and green tomato pickle. Season with Worcestershire sauce, salt, pepper and red pepper. Drain oysters, retaining juice. Add oysters, and juice if necessary to make a moist mixture. Mushrooms and crab meat may be added. Cook at 325° for 20 minutes. Serve on croutons, or toast points. May also be put in buttered casserole and heated in oven, and served without toast. Excellent supper dish, or brunch casserole.

Serves 4, as main course.

Mrs. Melvin F. Johnson

OYSTER JAMBALAYA

½ pound red sausage, diced
5 onions, chopped
1 can tomatoes (2 pounds)
75 oysters
3 cloves garlic, minced
Salt and red pepper to taste
3 cups rice

Put sausage in deep iron pot to fry, putting a little oil in pot. Fry until browned; remove meat and put in onion; fry until light brown, then add a cup of hot water. Cook again until water is cooked out. Add tomatoes and cook down two or three times, by adding a little warm water now and then. It must cook long enough to get the sour taste out of tomatoes. Add oysters with liquor, which has been strained; also the fried sausage and the minced garlic. Add 4 cups hot water, season with salt and pepper and boil 5 minutes. Then add rice which has been thoroughly washed. Let come to a good boil and cover tightly. Put on low fire and cook 30 minutes without uncovering.

Makes 12 large servings, or more. For shrimp jambalaya, use 4 pounds shrimp, cleaned and peeled, and omit oysters.

Mrs. E. C. St. Martin

EGGPLANT OYSTER CASSEROLE

1 medium eggplant
1 teaspoon salt
40 square soda crackers
1 pint raw oysters
2½ cups milk
½ cup butter or margarine, melted
2 eggs, beaten
1 teaspoon salt
½ teaspoon pepper
½ teaspoon monosodium glutamate
2 drops yellow food coloring
1 teaspoon paprika

Peel and slice eggplant, place in saucepan, cover with water, add salt and boil slowly for 15 minutes. Drain and mash. In a buttered casserole, 7½" x 11½", put a layer of crumbled crackers, a layer of eggplant, a layer of drained oysters, repeating, and ending with a layer of crackers on top. Combine milk, margarine, eggs, seasonings and food coloring. Pour over eggplant and oyster combination. Let stand for 1 hour. Sprinkle paprika on top of casserole and bake at 350° for about 45 minutes.

Will serve 10-12 as side dish, 6 as main course.

Mrs. John L. Rhea, Jr.

OYSTERS ROCKEFELLER

1 package frozen chopped spinach, defrosted
6 small green onions
⅓ bunch parsley
4 to 6 slices crisp cooked bacon
½ cup lemon juice
2 slices bread (for crumbs), ½ in mixture, ½ on top
3 celery stalk tops
½ cup oleo
5 drops Tabasco
Salt
Pepper
1½ tablespoons Worcestershire sauce
1 to 2 ounces absinthe liquor

Combine all ingredients in blender. Spread on top of oysters on half shell. Pint oysters may be used, but fresh oysters on half shell are better, when available. This is enough sauce for about 40 half shells. Have shells on bed of rock salt. Bake in very hot oven, 450°, until done.

Serves 4. Mrs. Keith O'Kelley, Ruston, La.

SPINACH AND OYSTERS

1 package frozen spinach, half cooked and well drained
½ cup parsley
½ cup chives
1 teaspoon Tabasco
1 teaspoon Worcestershire sauce
Dash garlic salt
¾ stick butter, melted
1 pint oysters
½ to ¾ cup bread crumbs

Mix first seven ingredients together. Then fold in oysters and put into casserole with bread crumbs on top. Bake 30 minutes in a 350° oven.

Serves 4. Note: Parmesan cheese added to the bread crumbs makes this dish a little sharper and brings out the flavor.

Mrs. Don Ahearn

EGGPLANT AND OYSTERS BAPTISTE

2 large or 4 small eggplants
2 pints oysters
2 large bell peppers
1 white onion
1 bunch green onions
3 cloves garlic
6 sprigs parsley
3 sticks margarine
6 eggs
4 cups corn flakes
Salt and black pepper to taste
Red pepper and paprika to taste

Peel and cut the eggplant in pieces. Boil in salted water until tender. Drain and let cool. Barely scald oysters in unseasoned water. Drain. Melt margarine and stew finely chopped bell peppers, onions, garlic and parsley until they become tender and transparent, or about 30 minutes. Now add eggplant and season to taste. Beat eggs and slowly add to eggplant mixture. Finally add 3½ cups corn flakes. Mix well and add oysters. Pour in greased casserole. Sprinkle top with ½ cup corn flakes. Bake at 350° about 30 minutes.

This will serve around 10 people if used as an extra vegetable or 8 for lunch. This freezes nicely without oysters. Add them right before cooking time.

Mrs. William G. Scarborough

LOBSTER NEWBURG

¼ cup butter
Meat from 2 pounds boiled lobster, cut in pieces
¼ cup sherry
Rich cream sauce
Toast or patty shells

Melt butter and add lobster. Stir lobster lightly until coated. Add sherry and let stand while making rich cream sauce. Add lobster mixture and cook gently until very hot. Serve with toast or in patty shells.

Makes 4 servings.

Rich Cream Sauce

1 large onion, finely chopped
¼ cup butter
4 tablespoons flour
1 teaspoon salt
½ teaspoon curry powder
2½ cups light cream
1 tablespoon brandy (optional)
1 teaspoon paprika

Saute onion in butter until soft. Blend in flour, salt and curry powder. Remove from heat and add cream slowly, stirring constantly. Return to heat and cook slowly, stirring until it thickens. Add brandy and paprika.

Mrs. Clarence B. Erickson, Jr.

LOBSTER TAILS

2 fresh lobsters
8 ounces butter
1 clove garlic
1 teaspoon chopped parsley
1 pinch oregano
Juice of ½ lime
Lemon slices

Split lobsters and remove the tails from the shell. Remove spinal cords. Season to taste and dip in flour. Saute slowly in melted butter for 20 minutes, or until golden brown. Remove tails and simmer the garlic and parsley in the same butter. Add oregano and fresh lime juice. Pour over the lobster tails. Place sliced lemon on top and serve red hot.

Serves 4 to 6. Mrs. Jackson B. Davis

SEAFOOD NEWBURG

4 tablespoons butter
2 cups fish — lobster, shrimp, crab or a combination
2 tablespoons lemon juice
2 tablespoons butter
1 tablespoon flour
1 cup cream
Red pepper, paprika, salt, ground cloves
½ cup sherry
2 tablespoons brandy
3 egg yolks

Melt 4 tablespoons butter, stir in fish and lemon juice. Let this marinate while preparing sauce. In a double boiler melt 2 tablespoons butter, add flour, cream and seasonings. Add sherry and brandy, then beaten egg yolks. Add fish mixture. May be served over toast points from chafing dish or prepared in individual serving ramekins, and heated slightly in oven before serving. Toast points made from 2 or 3 day old salt rising bread, thinly cut, are excellent.

Makes 6 servings. Mrs. Melvin F. Johnson

FRUITS OF THE BAYOU

1 onion, chopped
Butter
1 can celery soup
1 can mushroom soup
1 pound boiled, clean shrimp
1 can crab meat
1 can lobster
Sharp cheese
Italian cheese
Cayenne pepper
Worcestershire sauce
Oysters

Simmer onion in butter. Add all ingredients, except oysters. Put in casserole or individual ramekins. Drain oysters well and add just before putting in oven to broil. May be served over rice, toast points, or in patty shells.

Serves 8. Mrs. Davidson H. Texada

SEAFOOD PROVENCAL

1 cup each chopped green pepper, onion, celery and parsley
Melted butter
1 can tomato soup
3 tablespoons butter
6 tablespoons flour
1 quart milk
½ pound New York State cheese
3 pounds shrimp
1 pint oysters
1 pound lump crab meat
2 boxes long spaghetti, cooked

Marinate green pepper, onion, celery, and parsley in melted butter for five minutes. Do not cook. Add tomato soup and cook for 5 minutes. In double boiler make white sauce of butter, flour and milk. When thick, add tomato mixture, then cheese, shrimp, drained oysters and crab meat. Add spaghetti and bake in moderate oven 50-60 minutes.

Serves 16. Mrs. Dudley R. Meier

TROUT MARGUERY

2½ to 3 pounds trout, skinned and deboned
5-6 tablespoons olive oil
1 cup water
3 egg yolks
1 stick melted butter
Juice of 1 lemon
12 large shrimp
2 truffles or 2 tablespoons chopped black olives
1 4-ounce can mushrooms (stems and pieces)
Salt, pepper and cayenne to taste.

Fold prepared fish and place in wide pan with olive oil and water. Bake in 475° oven 15 minutes. Remove. Put egg yolks in double boiler, gradually adding melted butter and lemon juice. Stir slowly until thick (do not let water boil . . . just like hollandaise). Cut shrimp, truffles and mushrooms into small pieces. Add to sauce. Salt and pepper fish to taste and pour sauce over fish. Pretty if you run it under the broiler for just a minute before serving. Also good with mashed potatoes piped around the edge of casserole or serving dish.

Mrs. Marshall Martin

TROUT VERONIQUE

Have fish market prepare fillets according to number of servings desired. Reserve bones and skin and simmer them with 1 onion, sliced, a sprig fresh parsley, the juice of 1 lemon, 1½ ounces of white wine and a little salt. A touch of thyme and bay leaf may be added. More wine may be needed. Simmer slowly 60 minutes, then strain. Prepare hollandaise sauce, using ¼ cup of above stock. Medium white sauce may be combined with hollandaise, ½ cup white sauce to 1 cup hollandaise. Salt fish and poach covered for 8-10 minutes in stock. Heat serving platter slightly. Saute green grapes in a little butter. Put fish on platter, top with sauce and garnish with heated grapes.

Makes 4 servings. Mrs. C. H. Webb, Jr., Jackson, Mississippi

BAKED STUFFED FLOUNDER

¼ pound butter
1 pound fresh crab meat
½ pound raw shrimp, peeled and deveined
1 cup finely chopped onion
½ cup snipped parsley
½ cup chopped green onion tops
1 teaspoon lemon juice
¼ teaspoon grated lemon rind
1 pound button mushrooms, or 1 6-ounce can button mushrooms, or 1 tablespoon mushroom powder
2 cups seasoned, fine bread crumbs
2 eggs
Salt, red pepper, black pepper to taste

Melt butter, add crab meat and shrimp. Cook over low heat until shrimp are pink. Add vegetables. Cook until onions are transparent and wilted. Add lemon juice and rind. Add mushrooms. Cook about 5 more minutes. Remove from fire. Add bread crumbs, beaten eggs and seasonings. Mix thoroughly, but gently. Have 8 nice flounder and have butcher make a good-sized pocket in each. Rub inside and out with salt and pepper. Fill cavities generously with stuffing. Arrange on large flat pan (or double layers of heavy duty foil), and bake uncovered in 375° oven. Baste well and often with:

¼ pound butter
1 teaspoon lemon juice
½ cup dry white wine

Do not attempt to turn flounder over. Lower temperature to 300° after 20 minutes. Cook 15-20 minutes longer.

Mrs. James R. Alexander

RED FISH HOLLANDAISE

2 quarts boiling water
1 package crab boil
Salt
Lemon rind
1 3- to 4-pound red fish

Sauce:
1 tablespoon butter
3 egg yolks
1 teaspoon cornstarch
1½ teaspoons lemon juice
½ teaspoon salt
Paprika

Put water on to boil with crab boil, salt and lemon rind. When boiling, drop in red fish fillets. Cook 20 minutes until tender, but not coming apart. For sauce, soften 1 tablespoon butter. Beat egg yolks and add butter. Add cornstarch and lemon juice. Just before serving add very, very slowly 1 cup boiling water. Cook over boiling water and stir until it thickens. Add salt and paprika. Pour hollandaise sauce over fillets and serve immediately.

Mrs. E. C. St. Martin

POMPANO EN PAPILLOTTE

3 pompano, medium-size trout or 6 frozen flounder fillets
Salt
2 cups water
2 green onions, chopped
6 or 7 tablespoons butter or margarine
2 cups sauterne, chablis or other white dinner wine
1 cup crab meat
1 cup small or diced cooked shrimp
1 teaspoon garlic puree or powder
1½ cups chopped red or white onions
1 bay leaf
Pinch thyme
2 tablespoons flour
2 egg yolks
Parchment paper or foil

Clean fish; cut into 6 fillets. Simmer heads and backbones in salted water to make 2 cups fish stock; set aside. Saute green onions and fillets in 2 or 3 tablespoons butter. Add wine; cover and simmer gently 5 to 8 minutes, or until tender. Drain, saving wine stock. Meanwhile, saute crab, shrimp and ½ teaspoon garlic in 2 tablespoons butter. Add chopped red onions and remaining ½ teaspoon garlic; cook 10 minutes. Add 1¾ cups fish stock, bay leaf and thyme; cook 10 minutes longer; remove bay leaf. In a large heavy skillet, blend together 2 tablespoons butter, flour and remaining ¼ cup fish stock. Add crab mixture along with wine stock. Cook, stirring constantly, until thickened. Beat egg yolks with some of the hot sauce; add to skillet, mixing thoroughly. Taste; correct seasoning. Chill sauce until firm. Cut 6 parchment paper or foil hearts (8" x 12"). Oil well. Place a tablespoon sauce on parchment, top with a fillet. Fold over; hand seal. Place on oiled baking sheet; bake in a hot oven (450°) until brown. Serve in paper hearts (Small paper bags tied close with string may be used in place of parchment hearts.) With this dinner I would prefer a turtle or onion soup, potatoes (souffle or French-fried) and green salad with olive oil and wine vinegar dressing.

Makes 6 servings.

Albert E. Moulin, Jr., Wine Advisory Board, New Orleans, La.

FILLET OF RED SNAPPER CREOLE

1 4-pound red snapper
1 large onion
2 large tomatoes
¼ cup diced green pepper
Salt to taste
Pepper to taste
Bay leaf
Parsley

Fillet snapper, wash, spread thickly with butter and sprinkle lightly with flour. Place in greased, shallow baking dish. Cover with thin slices of onion and top with thin slices of tomato. Sprinkle diced green pepper over all. Season with salt and pepper to taste. Add a crumbled bay leaf, cover, and bake at 350° 30 to 45 minutes. Garnish with fresh parsley.

Serves 6 to 8. Mrs. Oliver Moore

STUFFED BAKED RED SNAPPER

1 package herb bread stuffing
1 3-pound red snapper, dressed for stuffing
3 tablespoons butter
½ cup onions, chopped fine
¼ cup green pepper, chopped fine
2 cloves garlic, crushed
⅓ cup celery leaves, chopped
⅓ cup parsley, chopped
1 pound shrimp, peeled and deveined
¼ teaspoon Tabasco sauce
1 teaspoon salt
½ teaspoon black pepper
½ cup sauterne

Place stuffing in bowl and add 1 cup water. Stir with fork and let stand. Wash fish in cold water and dry. Saute vegetables in melted butter until onions look clear. Add shrimp and seasonings. Cover and cook over low heat for 10 minutes. Add to stuffing. Spread stuffing mixture inside fish. Place in greased roasting pan and put extra stuffing around fish. Bake for 25 minutes at 350°. Pour sauterne over fish and cook for 10 more minutes. Fish should be covered while baking. Serve on platter garnished with parsley.

One 3-pound fish will serve 3 people.

Mareom M. Giambra

GRILLED RED SNAPPER

3 pounds fillet of red snapper
Salt, white pepper and paprika
1 stick melted butter
2 cloves crushed garlic
Juice of ½ lemon

Heat a large griddle to smoking point. Grease liberally with olive oil and bacon fat. Season and sear the fish on both sides, turning carefully. Then cook quickly (about 3-5 minutes per side). Heat butter, garlic and lemon juice to bubbling and serve over fish.

Serves 6.

Carl W. Jones

BROILED FISH

8 to 10 portions of fish
Butter, salt and pepper to taste
½ cup Worcestershire sauce
½ teaspoon dry mustard
1 dash paprika
½ cup lemon juice
Butter
Parsley, minced
Green onion tops, minced

Place fish in baking dish. Season to taste and place a square of butter on each piece. Broil in the oven at 350-375° 10 to 12 minutes. Mix the sauce in a separate pan. Blend until the mustard is smooth. Stir well and pour over the fish. Cook 3 to 5 minutes more in oven. Sprinkle the minced parsley and green onion tops over the fish and serve.

Mrs. Jackson B. Davis

PEDRO'S TARTAR SAUCE

1 medium Kosher style pickle
1 medium onion
1 cup mayonnaise
3 dashes Tabasco
2 dashes Worcestershire sauce
Pinch red pepper

Grate pickle and onion. Set and let juice drain off well. Combine with mayonnaise and other ingredients. Best to let it set awhile in ice box. May add pinch of ground Natchitoches red pepper if you want it hotter.

Mrs. A. H. Weyland

TOMATO ZIP DIP

(A red sauce for shrimp)

1 cup chili sauce
¼ cup celery, finely chopped
½ teaspoon sugar
1 tablespoon horseradish
1 tablespoon lemon juice
¼ teaspoon Worcestershire sauce

Combine all ingredients in medium-size bowl. Stir well to mix. Cover; chill until serving time.

Mrs. John M. Campbell

SHRIMP COCKTAIL SAUCE

1 cup mayonnaise
¾ cup catsup
¾ cup chili sauce
2 tablespoons India relish
4 teaspoons Worcestershire sauce
2 teaspoons horseradish
1 teaspoon Tabasco sauce

Combine all ingredients and mix well. Chill. Keeps well in refrigerator.

Makes 1 quart.

Mrs. Robert K. Cooper

TARTAR SAUCE

4 egg yolks
1 teaspoon salt
1 teaspoon dry mustard
Juice of 2 lemons
2½ cups olive oil
½ cup chopped green onions
½ cup chopped pickles (squeeze all juice from pickles)
1 teaspoon capers
1 teaspoon chives

Place into the small bowl of electric mixer: salt, egg yolks and dry mustard. Mix thoroughly. Add olive oil gradually; beat continually until ¼ of the oil has been used, then add remaining oil and lemon juice a little faster than before until all has been used. Then add all of the remaining ingredients.

Columbia Restaurant

ROCKEFELLER SAUCE A LA REED

- 3½ pounds white onions, peeled
- 8 large garlic pods
- 1 pound oleo or butter
- 4 15-ounce cans spinach
- 20 ounces lemon juice (approximately 24 lemons) or four cans frozen concentrate
- 1 can parsley flakes
- 2 tablespoons celery salt
- 1-3 tablespoons Tabasco
- 2 tablespoons Worcestershire sauce
- 2 tablespoons salt
- 1-3 tablespoons red pepper

Chop onion coarsely and put through a food blender, if one is available. Chop fine if you do not have a blender. Put the garlic through a garlic press or chop fine and add to onion. Melt oleo (or butter) and add onion-garlic mixture and simmer for about one hour. Stir occasionally and keep over low heat. Put spinach through a blender or use cans of chopped spinach. Add the spinach and all the other ingredients to the cooked onion mixture and stir well. Cook the mixture for approximately 8 hours more, stirring occasionally. When mixture becomes thick enough to make large bubbles that burst and splatter, it will be done. It will be the consistency of thick paste.

Since this recipe takes so long, it might be done by cooking half the time one evening and finishing it the next day. Because it is highly seasoned, it keeps well. It will freeze nicely.

Dr. Carson R. Reed, Jr.

SPICY TOMATO SAUCE

Saute 1 onion, thinly sliced, in 2 tablespoons butter, add 2 fresh tomatoes, finely chopped, then juice of 1 or 2 lemons or a combination of lemon and lime. Season with salt, a tablespoon or more of sugar, ½ teaspoon dry mustard and allow to simmer a few minutes. A very good sweet-sour sauce for broiled or baked fish.

Mrs. Staunton B. Sample

REMOULADE

- 4 tablespoons olive oil or salad oil if preferred
- 2 tablespoons tarragon vinegar
- 1 teaspoon salt
- 2 tablespoons Creole mustard
- ½ teaspoon paprika
- 4 hearts celery, chopped fine
- 4 small green onions, minced
- 4 sprigs parsley, minced
- 10 tablespoons mayonnaise

Combine ingredients and let set 12 to 24 hours.

Mrs. Clarence B. Erickson, Jr.

REMOULADE SAUCE

2 hard boiled eggs, mashed fine
3 celery ribs, minced fine
1 tablespoon Worcestershire sauce
2 tablespoons sauterne
3 tablespoons prepared mustard
8 tablespoons Creole mustard (with horseradish)
1 teaspoon salt
1 teaspoon sugar
½ teaspoon red pepper
1 pint mayonnaise
1 small onion or clove of garlic, minced fine.

Combine the above ingredients and place in a jar. Will keep indefinitely in refrigerator.

Mrs. Clifford H. Irion, Benton, La.

Poultry & Game

Louisiana Downs

LOUISIANA DOWNS

Horseracing, "the sport of kings," comes to life in royal style at Louisiana Downs in Bossier City. One of the nation's top thoroughbred racetracks, Louisiana Downs features a four-level glass-enclosed grandstand and a variety of restaurants, bars, and seating areas, including elegant dining on the third (Clubhouse) and fourth (Sky Club) levels. The racing season runs from April through November, with off-track betting from January through April.

The Super Derby Festival is an 11-day festival leading up to the Super Derby thoroughbred horse race and benefiting area charitable organizations. It features big-name entertainment, a barbecue cookoff, sports tournaments, arts activities, a beauty pageant and a Taste of Shreveport with area restaurants providing delicious items to tantalize the tastebuds.

ARROZ CON POLLO (CHICKEN WITH RICE)

1 fat fryer (about 3 pounds)
Olive oil
1 large onion
½ large green pepper
2 large outer stalks of celery with tops
1 clove garlic
1 tablespoon fresh or dried chopped parsley
Pinch each of oregano, thyme, marjoram
1 can tomato paste
1½ cups raw rice
1 small can chopped pimiento
1 medium can green peas
2 dozen ripe black olives
1 can button mushrooms
Salt to taste

Fry chicken in a skillet with a little olive oil until yellow. Remove chicken and put in chopped onion, pepper, garlic, celery and leaves, parsley and cook until soft. Into a deep pot put tomato paste and enough water to make it about 4 inches deep. Add oregano, thyme, marjoram, the chicken, chopped cooked vegetables, salt and allow to simmer 2 hours or longer. About 1 hour before serving, remove chicken (keep warm) and bring liquid to a boil. Add rice. The liquid should cover the rice about 1 inch. Chop and add the pimiento to the rice and cover. Ten minutes before serving add peas, olives, mushrooms. The liquid from these may be added to make enough liquid to cook the rice if more is required. If not, add these drained.

Serves 6-8 (add 3 or 4 extra pieces of chicken for 8).

Mrs. William T. Murphy, III

CHICKEN AND ASPARAGUS

6 chicken breasts
2 cans asparagus (green tip)

Sauce:
1 medium onion, chopped
1 medium can mushrooms
½ cup butter or oleo
2 cans mushroom or cream of chicken soup
¾ can milk
½ pound sharp cheese
¼ teaspoon Tabasco
2 teaspoons soy sauce
1 teaspoon salt
½ teaspoon pepper
1 teaspoon Accent
2 tablespoons pimiento
½ cup chopped almonds

Boil chicken in seasoned water until done. Debone and tear in pieces. In 9" x 13" casserole put layer of asparagus. Cover with chicken pieces. Saute onion and mushrooms in oleo. Add remaining ingredients except almonds. Simmer until cheese melts. Pour cheese sauce over and top with chopped almonds. Cook at 350° until bubbly.

Mrs. Bruce Roberts

AZTEC CHICKEN

1 large fryer
Salt
Pepper
Flour
1 large onion
½ stick butter
No. 2 can tomatoes
No. 2 can corn, cream style

Disjoint fryer. Season with salt and pepper, roll in flour, and quick fry. Melt butter in skillet, cook chopped onion until clear. Add corn and tomatoes to butter and onion. Season with salt and pepper. Place fryer pieces in casserole, pour in sauce. Cover and cook in 350° oven until tender, about 45 minutes.

Mrs. John B. Hutchinson

BROILED CHICKEN IN WHITE WINE

2 broiler chickens, quartered
Salt and pepper
Approximately ¼ pound butter or margarine
1 onion, finely chopped
Pinch or two of rosemary
1 cup white wine

Salt and pepper chicken and brown in butter on top of stove. (Use a large iron skillet, with cover, or an iron roaster with cover or Dutch oven.) Sprinkle with onion, rosemary and add wine. Cover and bake 2 hours in oven at 275°.

Serves 4 people.

Mrs. Melvin F. Johnson

CHICKEN BECHAMEL

4 large chicken breasts, boned and halved
1 stick butter
1 onion, finely chopped
1 clove garlic
1-2 bay leaves
1 can bouillon or consomme
2 small cans mushrooms (stems and pieces)
½ to 1 cup white wine
Flour to thicken sauce
½ pint heavy cream or half and half
Salt and red pepper to taste

Melt butter. Brown chicken in butter. Remove to baking pan. Cook onion and garlic in butter until tender, add flour, bouillon, bay leaf, white wine and mushrooms. Simmer slowly until well heated. Add cream or milk, stirring until smooth. Season with salt and red pepper. Pour over chicken and bake at 350° for about 30 minutes. Serve with rice. Sauce, with chicken, may be frozen.

Makes 4 servings.

Mrs. Robert K. Butcher

STUFFED BROILED CHICKEN

4 broilers, split
1 pound fresh mushrooms
1 onion, chopped
2 cups cooked rice
Poultry seasoning
Salt and pepper
2 eggs, beaten
Butter
Juice of 1 orange

Broil chicken halves, breast side down for 15 minutes. Meanwhile, saute chopped mushrooms and onion in 3 tablespoons butter. Add to cooked rice which has been well seasoned. Add beaten eggs and pack into chickens. Turn skin side up and broil slowly for 30 minutes, basting with melted butter combined with orange juice. Serve with watercress and pickled pears.

Serves 8. Mrs. Allen Penniman

BAKED CHICKEN BREASTS

10 chicken breasts, boned
2 cups sour cream
1 tablespoon Worcestershire sauce
½ teaspoon Tabasco
1 clove garlic, crushed
2 teaspoons salt
1½ teaspoons paprika
Cup of fine bread crumbs

Mix sour cream and seasonings. Dip each piece of chicken in mixture, coating thoroughly, and put in a glass dish. Cover dish closely and refrigerate overnight. Next morning drop each piece of chicken into dish of bread crumbs. Shake each piece and place one layer deep in a baking pan. Cover pan closely and return to refrigerator for at least 1½ hours. Bake 75 minutes at 325°. After baking lift each piece onto platter and garnish with parsley.

Serves 10. May be frozen after being dipped in the sour cream.

Mrs. Camp Flournoy

COLD CHICKEN BAKED WITH HERBS

1 roasting hen
½ cup sauterne
½ cup olive oil
1 garlic clove, grated
1 small onion, grated
½ teaspoon each:
marjoram
rosemary
thyme
basil
tarragon

Mix all ingredients, except hen. Marinate hen overnight. Roast 2 hours in a 250° oven, basting frequently with marinade. Cool, but do not refrigerate. Serve sliced. The chicken should be golden brown on outside and very tender and juicy on inside.

Mrs. Robert K. Butcher

COMPANY CHICKEN BREASTS

8 chicken breasts, bones removed
1 quart water
2 teaspoons powdered chicken base or chicken bouillon cube
Oleo
Flour, salt and pepper for breasts
6 tablespoons flour
1 4-ounce can mushrooms or more
Salt and pepper
2 tablespoons sherry (optional)

Boil water, chicken base, bones and skin from chicken together for 30 minutes. Flour, salt and pepper the breasts and brown in oleo. Place browned chicken in casserole or baking dish. Pour off excess oleo. Brown the flour in the skillet. Pour in 3 cups of the broth from the chicken bones. Strain gravy. Season gravy with pepper, salt and add mushrooms and sherry. Pour gravy over chicken 30 minutes to 1 hour before ready to serve. Bake chicken and gravy in the covered casesrole. This will freeze; may be fixed a day or two ahead and kept in refrigerator.

Shreveport Club Chef
Mrs. James Smitherman, Jr.
Mrs. Daniel Shea, Dallas, Texas

OVEN FRIED CHICKEN

¼ pound butter
1 egg
½ cup sweet milk
1 cup flour, mixed with:
1 teaspoon baking powder
2 teaspoons salt
2 tablespoons sesame seed
2 tablespoons chopped pecans

Melt the butter in a flat pan. Make a batter of the egg beaten well and the sweet milk. Take pieces of frying size chicken and dip first in batter, then into flour mixture coating well. Swish in melted butter. Place on baking platter with skin side up and bake 30 minutes at 400°. Turn chicken over and cook until tender and brown.

Mrs. Hewitt H. Wheless

CHICKEN IN SOUR CREAM

1 cup sour cream
1 teaspoon paprika
1 teaspoon celery salt
1 tablespoon Worcestershire sauce
1 tablespoon lemon juice
2 cloves garlic
1 frying chicken, cut up, salted and peppered
Cracker crumbs

Combine first six ingredients and allow to mellow for about an hour. Then, dip chicken in mixture until well coated. Lay in shallow pan lined with foil. Sprinkle with cracker crumbs and cover pan with foil. Bake in 350° oven for one hour.

Mrs. Paul R. Winder

GOLDEN BROWN CHICKEN CASSEROLE

1 chicken, cut in serving pieces
1 stick butter
1 can mushrooms
1 tablespoon flour
2 tablespoons Worcestershire sauce
1 bay leaf
Lemon juice
1 can beef bouillon

Melt butter in skillet. Salt and pepper chicken and brown well in melted butter. Take out and put in large casserole dish. Brown mushrooms in same butter, and take out and place with chicken. Add the flour to the butter and mix well. Add Worcestershire sauce, bay leaf, lemon juice and beef bouillon. Pour over chicken and mushrooms, and cook for 1 hour in oven. The chicken and mushrooms get brown and the gravy thickens. This is excellent gravy for rice or mashed potatoes.

Serves 4. May be prepared a day ahead. Prepare and place in casserole. Next day, cook in oven until hot and bubbly.

Mrs. Harman Chandler

LUNCHEON CHICKEN RING

Chicken Ring:
1 chicken (5-pound hen), seasoned and cooked tender
2 cups soft bread crumbs
1 cup cooked rice
1 teaspoon salt
½ teaspoon paprika
¼ cup pimientos
2 well beaten eggs
¼ cup butter or chicken fat
1 pint milk or chicken stock

Remove meat from bone. Dice chicken. Combine all ingredients in order named. Pack mixture in large buttered mold or glass casserole and bake in slow oven 30 minutes. Serve with mushroom sauce.

Mushroom Sauce:
½ cup butter or margarine
2 cans mushrooms
½ cup flour
1 quart chicken stock
Salt and paprika
4 beaten egg yolks
1 tablespoon chopped parsley
1 tablespoon lemon juice
½ cup cream

Melt 4 tablespoons butter in frying pan. Add mushrooms sliced. Brown slightly for 5 minutes. Be careful not to burn. Place remaining butter in upper part of double boiler and add flour. Rub to paste, stir in hot chicken stock. Cook until thick and creamy. Add egg yolks, beaten with cream. Add salt, paprika, parsley, lemon juice and mushrooms. This dish is pretty baked in mold with mushroom sauce served in center and garnished with parsley and crab apples.

Serves 10.

Mrs. Max Morelock

LEMON CHICKEN BAKE

6 halved chicken breasts
Flour, salt and pepper
½ cup lemon juice
1 cup finely chopped celery
¼ cup water
½ cup butter

Remove skin from chicken breasts, wash and dry. Flour, salt and pepper them, then lightly brown the chicken on both sides in butter. Place chicken, bone side up, in shallow baking pan lined with foil. This makes a little hollow. Put 2 teaspoons lemon juice on each piece of chicken and sprinkle celery over all evenly. Put water and remaining lemon juice into frying pan with butter and brown crumbs. Pour sauce over chicken, fold foil loosely over top and bake at 250° for 1½ hours or until fork tender.

Serves 8-12. May be frozen and later warmed in foil.

Mrs. Vernon W. Woods

CHICKEN ENCHILADAS

4½-5-pound hen
30 soft tortillas
3 pints sour cream
Butter
2 large onions
Salt to taste
2 packages frozen chopped spinach
4 cans green chilies
1 cup spinach water
½ cup milk
Monterrey Jack cheese, about 12 ounces

Cook the hen until tender. Shred or chop the meat. Make a sauce of the sour cream, onions (sauteed in butter first), salt, cooked and drained spinach (reserve juice), chilies, spinach water and milk. Mix some of the sauce with the diced chicken. Fill and roll the tortillas. Cover with grated Monterrey Jack cheese and top with remaining sauce. Bake until hot through at 350° (about 30 minutes).

Mrs. Charles H. Jeter

CHICKEN PIE

1 4-pound fowl
1 onion
Celery
Parsley
Pepper and salt to taste
1 large can sliced mushrooms
¼ cup butter
3 tablespoons flour
3 hard cooked eggs
Recipe of short pastry

Boil fowl in water and cover until tender with celery, onion, parsley, salt and pepper. Remove from stock (saving stock) and separate from bones. Saute mushrooms in butter, add flour and about 3 cups of the stock. Alternate layers of chicken, eggs, and thickened stock until casserole is filled. Strip with crust and brush with melted butter. Bake in oven at 400° for 30 minutes.

Mrs. Bert Kouns

DUTCH CHICKEN PIE

- 1 large or 2 small chickens (white meat only)
- 3 tablespoons butter
- 3 cups stock in which chicken was boiled
- 1 small onion
- Several stalks celery
- 1 cup cream or whole milk
- Salt to taste
- Pepper to taste
- Parsley

Batter:

- 2 tablespoons butter
- 1 teaspoon salt
- 1 egg, beaten
- 1 cup rich milk
- 2 cups flour
- 2 teaspoons baking powder

Boil the chicken and cut in large pieces. Cook butter, stock, onion and celery in a double boiler until reduced to 2 cups. Then add the cream or milk and season to taste with the salt, pepper and parsley. Pour over chicken. Make the batter as follows: Sift together the salt, flour and baking powder. Stir in butter, beaten egg and milk. Pour over the chicken and sauce which are already in the baking dish. Bake at 400° until brown.

Mrs. Vincent S. Brennan

CHICKEN LIVERS A LA CARTE

- ½ cup butter
- ½ cup chopped green pepper
- ½ cup chopped green onion
- ½ cup finely sliced white onion
- 1½ cups chicken livers
- 4 tablespoons chopped mushrooms
- ½ cup lima beans, drained
- ¼ cup sliced pimiento
- Salt and cayenne to taste

In a 9-inch skillet melt butter and saute green pepper, green onion and white onion. Add chicken livers and saute until browned, about 8 minutes. Add mushrooms, lima beans, pimiento, salt and cayenne. Heat through. Serve over hot rice.

Makes 2-3 servings.

Mrs. Marlin W. Drake, Jr.

CHICKEN PAPRIKA

- Chicken breasts, 1 per serving
- Butter
- Salt to taste
- Paprika
- Lemon juice
- Worcestershire sauce

Remove bones from chicken. Fold skin of chicken under and fasten with toothpicks. Melt butter and, with pastry brush, spread over chicken. Add salt to taste, then cover heavily with paprika. Place chicken in roasting pan, skin up. Melt more butter, add lemon juice and small amount of Worcestershire sauce for basting. Cook chicken in oven 300-325° until tender, about 45 minutes to 1 hour, basting every little while. Breast may be stuffed with small amount of dressing and cooked the same way.

Mrs. Walter Chandler

CRISP BAKED FRYER

1 fryer, 2½ or 3 pounds
1 large or 2 small lemons
Seasoned salt
Seasoned pepper
Oleo at room temperature
Water (in bottom of pan)

Preheat oven to 400°. Wash chicken and dry. Cut into quarters. Squeeze lemon juice on both sides of chicken. Salt generously. Place chicken in baking pan, skin side up. Pan should not be more than 2 inches deep for skin to be crisp. Pepper skin side only, and spread oleo on chicken generously. Add enough water to cover bottom of pan — about ¼-inch deep. More may be added during cooking if this dries. Place in hot oven to brown, then turn heat down and continue to cook until tender. Cook uncovered. Baste with juice in bottom of pan several times while cooking. Bake at 400° for 30 minutes, then 300° for 45 minutes. Pour remaining juice over chicken. Chicken is excellent reheated, uncovered, next day.

Mrs. Martha Egger Jackson

CHICKEN MARENGO

2 2½-pound broilers, cut up
½ cup flour
1 teaspoon salt
1 teaspoon pepper
½ cup olive oil
4 small white onions
1 small clove garlic
1½ cups sliced mushrooms
2 teaspoons minced parsley
1 cup dry white wine
1 tablespoon brandy
1 tablespoon tomato paste
1 tablespoon flour

Dust pieces of chicken with seasoned flour. Heat oil and saute chicken until golden brown. Remove and keep warm. Make roux with 1 tablespoon flour. Add onions, garlic, mushrooms, parsley. Cook a few minutes, then add wine and brandy and tomato paste. Mix and blend, allow to simmer about 10 minutes. Put chicken in sauce, cover, cook 30 minutes or until tender. Serve in sauce over rice.

Serves 8.

Mrs. Lane Sartor

GENEVA CHICKEN LIVERS

1 cup wild rice
4 cups water
1 pound fresh mushrooms
1 pound chicken livers
¼ cup butter
4 tablespoons flour
2 cups chicken broth
½ teaspoon salt or more to taste
¼ teaspoon pepper or more to taste
¼ cup sherry

Boil rice in water 30 to 40 minutes. Drain and steam until dry and fluffy. Saute mushrooms and livers in butter. Sprinkle with flour and mix well. Add chicken broth and cook until thickened. Season with salt and pepper. Add sherry. Serve over wild rice.

Serves 4.

Mrs. Jack Murrell

CHICKEN FONDUE

1 3½-pound hen
1½ pints milk
6 eggs
1½ pints chicken stock
1 1-pound loaf white bread
Salt
Pepper
½ cup grated American cheese
2 pimientos
Finely chopped parsley

Place chicken in pot and cover with water. Simmer until tender (use a carrot, a stalk of celery and a small onion to flavor the stock). Let chicken cool. Drain off stock.

Remove crusts from bread and break into pieces. Soak the bread in stock for 1 hour. Remove the bones from the chicken and cut the meat into small pieces. Beat eggs well and add the milk. Pour milk and eggs over chicken and then add the chicken stock mixture, mixing well together. Season with salt and pepper. Pour into baking dish. Sprinkle with grated cheese and bake in a 350° oven for 30 minutes. Garnish with strips of pimiento and chopped parsley.

Makes 6 servings. Mrs. Jackson B. Davis

CHICKEN ROYALE

4 whole chicken breasts
¼ cup flour
½ teaspoon salt
¼ teaspoon paprika
Black pepper to taste
1 herb stuffing recipe
½ cup oleo or butter, melted
Chopped parsley
1 recipe sour cream mushroom sauce

Herb Stuffing Recipe:
2 cups dried bread crumbs
1 tablespoon chopped onion
½ teaspoon salt
¼ teaspoon poultry seasoning
¼ cup hot water

Sour Cream Mushroom Sauce:
½ pound fresh mushrooms, cut in half
½ cup minced onion
2 tablespoons butter
2 tablespoons flour
½ cup cream
½ cup sour cream
½ teaspoon salt
½ teaspoon pepper

Cut the chicken breasts just enough to fold them. Combine flour and all seasonings in paper bag and shake chicken in it. Mix together all ingredients for herb stuffing and fill the cavity of each breast with it. Hold stuffing in by closing opening with toothpicks. Dip chicken in melted butter. Bake in casserole at 325° for 45 minutes. Then turn over and bake until tender. Sprinkle with parsley and serve with mushroom sauce.

To make mushroom sauce, cook mushrooms and onion in butter until tender. Cover. Cook 10 minutes over low heat. Stir in flour. Add sour cream and cream. Add seasonings. Makes 1½ cups.

Serves 4. Mrs. Jackson B. Davis

SAVORY SUPPER CHICKEN

- 3 chicken breasts, halved
- 1 cup flour, seasoned with salt and pepper
- 2 cups salad oil
- 3 cups hot water
- 2 bay leaves
- 1 teaspoon kitchen bouquet
- 1 can condensed cream of mushroom soup
- ½ (soup) can of sherry
- 1 small package toasted slivered almonds (optional)

Put seasoned flour in paper bag with chicken breasts and shake well. Heat oil in heavy skillet and brown chicken on both sides. Remove from oil. Pour off all but 4 tablespoons oil. Decrease flame and add 4 tablespoons leftover seasoned flour, stirring until light brown in color. Add 3 cups hot water. Continue stirring. Add soup thinned with sherry. Add bay leaves and kitchen bouquet. Simmer gently 10 minutes. Pour over chicken in deep pan, cover and simmer 45 minutes. Garnish with toasted almonds if desired.

Serves 6. Mrs. David Key

RICE AND CHICKEN OR RICE AND PORK CHOPS

- 2 cups instant rice or regular rice
- 1 stick oleo
- 1 package onion soup mix
- 6 or 8 pork chops or 1 cut-up chicken

Wash regular rice and put in casserole, or put 2 cups of instant rice as is in casserole, melt oleo and pour over rice. Prepare soup mix as directed and pour over rice and oleo and stir lightly. Lay pork chops or chicken pieces on top and place in 400° oven. Cook 1 hour for chicken and 1½ hours for pork chops. Mushrooms make a nice addition if chicken is used.

Serves 6. Mrs. Larry H. Teague

SOUTH LOUISIANA CHICKEN SAUCE PIQUANTE

- 5 cooking spoons cooking oil
- 3 cooking spoons flour
- 4 large onions, chopped
- 1 can sweet peas
- 1 can mushrooms
- 1 hen
- 1 large can tomatoes
- ½ pod garlic
- Red pepper and salt to taste

Brown flour in oil, then add onions and cook to a golden brown. Add tomatoes. Let this fry until well cooked, then add chicken cut into pieces and enough water to make gravy. Add garlic and seasonings. Cover and cook slowly until chicken is ready to leave the bone. Just before serving add mushrooms and sweet peas. Chicken may be cooked before making gravy, and taken off bone. This cuts cooking time.

Serves 6. Mrs. Gene St. Martin

SAUTEED CHICKEN SUPREME

2 broilers (cut into serving pieces)
1 stick butter
2 tablespoons hot brandy
1 teaspoon tomato paste
2 tablespoons flour
1 cup chicken stock (bouillon)
1 carton sour cream (¾ to 1 cup)
2 tablespoons grated Parmesan cheese
1 grated lemon rind
Salt, red and black pepper to taste

Brown chicken all over in hot butter (slowly to prevent sticking). Pour over the brown chicken the hot brandy. Remove chicken from the pan and stir in tomato paste and flour; then pour on stock. Stir over fire until mixture comes to a boil; then beat in slowly with a whisk, sour cream, grated cheese, grated lemon rind, salt and pepper. Place pieces of chicken back into sauce and simmer gently for 40 minutes. Remove and arrange on serving dish. Pour some sauce over and pass the rest of the sauce in gravy boat.

Serves 4 to 6 depending on size and number of pieces of chicken. Always serve this with rice. Gravy is delicious!

Mrs. Roger Gardner

CHICKEN SAUCE PIQUANTE

2 frying size chickens, cut up
4 Bermuda onions
2 bunches green onions
2 cans mushrooms
2 large bell peppers
6 stalks celery
4 or 5 cloves garlic
3 cups chopped fresh parsley
2 small cans tomato sauce
3 or 4 bay leaves
Salt and pepper to taste
3 or 4 tablespoons flour
Water

Brown 2 chickens in cooking oil. In another pot saute finely chopped green onions, bell peppers, garlic, celery and parsley in small amount of cooking oil. Drain oil from chicken and add sauteed vegetables to chicken. Add tomato sauce, sliced Bermuda onions, bay leaves, salt and pepper. Add water to cover chicken and flour dissolved with water for thickness, mixing all ingredients thoroughly. Cook down over moderate flame until desired thickness is reached. Add mushrooms and serve over rice.

Mrs. John Hearne
Mrs. B. F. O'Neal, Jr.
Robert A. Taliaferro

SICILIAN CHICKEN SAUTE

- 3 tablespoons butter or margarine
- ¼ cup olive oil
- 2 bunches green onions with tender tops, chopped fine
- 3-pound chicken cut in pieces for frying
- 1 teaspoon salt
- ½ teaspoon pepper
- ½ cup marsala wine
- 2 peeled, seeded and diced tomatoes
- 4 sprigs parsley, chopped
- ½ cup chicken stock

Heat butter and olive oil in heavy iron pot. Add chicken and onions. Brown slightly on all sides. Season with salt and pepper and marsala wine. Simmer until wine is reduced to half. Add tomatoes, parsley and chicken stock. Cover and continue cooking for 30-45 minutes, or until chicken is tender, adding more stock if necessary. Arrange on a platter and pour remaining sauce over chicken. Serve with rice, a crisp green salad, and French bread for a real treat, from the old country.

Makes 4 servings. Mareom M. Giambra

CHICKEN AND PASTA

- 1 large hen (4½-5 pounds) or 3 2-pound fryers or 6 1-pound Cornish game hens
- Pieces of celery and green onions
- Salt and pepper
- 2 sticks butter
- 1 cup cooking sherry
- ½ cup water
- 1 teaspoon salt
- 1 teaspoon cracked red pepper
- 2 cartons fresh mushrooms or 1 large tall can whole button mushrooms
- 1 teaspoon oregano
- 1 pound rich Italian noodles
- 1 tablespoon salt
- 2 ounces olive oil
- ½ stick melted butter
- 4 ounces grated Parmesan or Romano cheese
- 2-3 cloves garlic, crushed

Stuff inside of well salted and peppered fowl with pieces of celery and green onions. Truss. In heavy kettle, melt butter. Keep fire low. Brown birds just until golden. Transfer to covered roaster. Salt and pepper liberally (with red pepper this time). Sprinkle with oregano. Pour melted butter over. Add sherry and water. Cover and bake at 350° until tender (game hens, about 45 minutes; fryers, about 1 hour and 15 minutes; hen, about 3½ hours). Baste often with pan juices, every 10-15 minutes. (This much may be done well ahead of time.) Add mushrooms during last 15 minutes of cooking. In large kettle of boiling salted water, add noodles. Boil 10 minutes. Drain in colander. Have ready a large casserole with olive oil, melted butter, grated cheese and crushed garlic. Add drained pasta. Toss well until coated with sauce. Serve with chicken and mushrooms, and pass pan drippings for gravy. Pass additional grated Parmesan or Romano cheese and coarse ground red pepper.

Serves 6. Jerome Cargill

CHICKEN LASAGNA

Sauce 1:
2-2½ pounds chicken breasts
1 can Italian peeled tomatoes
2 cloves garlic
1 bay leaf
Pinch thyme
Pinch rosemary
Dash cayenne
3 tablespoons olive oil
½ teaspoon sugar
½ teaspoon salt or to taste
½ pound lasagna noodles or broadest you can find

Sauce 2:
1½ cups chicken broth (about)
2 tablespoons flour for each cup broth
Salt and pepper to taste
4 tablespoons chopped parsley
¼ teaspoon monosodium glutamate
¼ teaspoon soy sauce
½ pound Mozzarella cheese
Parmesan cheese

Cook chicken in water, onion, garlic and celery until tender. Keep broth. Cut chicken in thick slices, not chunks. Combine tomatoes, garlic, bay leaf, thyme, rosemary, cayenne, olive oil, sugar and salt. Cook in covered pan until thick. Simmer 25 to 30 minutes. Boil noodles in salted water 10 minutes. They should be chewy, or al dente, as the Italians say. Drain in colander. Run cold water with a few spoons of vinegar over noodles; then use plain cold water. Place on towel to dry. Measure chicken broth and thicken well with flour, beat with fork and keep from lumping over low heat until thick. Add second group seasonings. Now you are ready to make lasagna. In a large ovenproof baking dish pour a thin layer of tomato sauce. Cover with wide noodles placed side by side. Then add layer of large pieces of chicken. Cover with thin slices of Mozzarella cheese, then a layer of the chicken gravy. Repeat until all is in the dish. Cover heavily with Parmesan cheese. Cook at 375° for 30 minutes or until top is good and brown.

Mrs. A. H. Weyland

CHICKEN WITH NOODLES

1 large fowl, cut in pieces
6 cups cooked noodles
½ pound mushrooms, sliced
½ teaspoon salt
Dash of pepper
3 tablespoons butter
1 cup chicken broth
1 cup milk, scalded
½ cup bread crumbs, buttered

Simmer chicken until tender. Remove meat from bones. Place hot noodles, chicken and mushrooms in alternate layers in greased casserole, using ½ of each. Repeat layers with remaining amounts. Add salt, pepper and butter to hot broth and milk and pour over filled casserole. Cover with crumbs and bake, uncovered, in moderate (350°) oven about 20 minutes, or until browned.

Makes 6 to 8 servings.

Mrs. Hall S. Morehead

COUNTRY CAPTAIN

- 1 3-pound chicken (young and tender)
- 2 tablespoons butter
- 1 onion
- 1 green pepper
- 1 clove garlic
- 1 cup water
- 1 teaspoon salt
- ½ teaspoon pepper
- ½ teaspoon curry powder
- 2 cans tomatoes
- ½ teaspoon chopped parsley
- ¼ teaspoon powdered thyme
- ¼ pound almonds
- 3 tablespoons dry currants
- 3 tablespoons small seedless raisins
- 1 pound rice

Fry chicken dusted with flour. Set aside and keep warm. Melt butter in a skillet, add sliced onion, green pepper and garlic. Brown slowly 10 minutes. Add water, salt, pepper, curry powder, tomatoes, parsley and thyme. Stir well. Put chicken in casserole. Mix the sauce with it and cook in oven 45 minutes at 325°. While cooking, brown almonds. Wash currants and raisins. When chicken is done, mix almonds and raisins in with the sauce. Have 1 pound of rice cooked. Put chicken in center of platter with the rice around it. Pour sauce over rice.

Mrs. Jerry Howard

HUNGARIAN CHICKEN

- 1 young chicken (4-5 pounds) cut up fairly small
- 1 package spaghetti
- 4 onions, chopped fine
- 2 green peppers, chopped fine (1 may be red)
- 1 heaping tablespoon flour
- ½ teaspoon cinnamon
- ½ teaspoon ground cloves
- 1 teaspoon salt
- 1 teaspoon paprika
- 1 cup canned tomatoes

Place onions, peppers, tomatoes, spices, seasoning and a large piece of margarine in bottom of large kettle. Dredge chicken in flour and lay on top. Cover and cook very slowly for 4 hours. Boil spaghetti, put on large serving platter and lay pieces of chicken on it. Thicken sauce remaining in kettle with 2 tablespoons flour rubbed smooth in a little water. Pour over all.

Serves 6-8.

Mrs. Wesley E. Wheless, Jr.

CREAMED CHICKEN FOR 16

- Breasts of 2 (6-pound) hens
- 4 cans cream of celery soup
- Chicken broth
- ½ cup milk
- 3 small jars pimiento, drained
- 4 hard cooked eggs, chopped
- 4 large cans Chinese noodles

Cook chicken until tender. Cut up in small pieces. Heat soup slowly with small amount of chicken broth and the milk. Add pimiento, eggs and chicken. Serve over noodles.

Serves 16. May be made ahead and reheated.

Mrs. Hubert L. Joyner

CHICKEN SPAGHETTI

3 medium sized hens (4-5 pounds)
2 stalks celery
1 onion, quartered
1 tablespoon salt
1 teaspoon pepper
2 sprigs parsley
3 pounds ground meat
½ pound butter
1 large bunch celery, chopped
3 large bunches shallots
1 cup parsley, chopped
5 cloves garlic, minced
½ large bell pepper, chopped
2 No. 2 cans tomatoes
3 medium cans mushrooms
Salt, red and black pepper to taste
1½ pounds New York State cheese, grated
2½ pounds spaghetti
¾ pound Italian cheese, grated (Parmesan)
Hot sauce, if desired

Boil chicken day before with celery, onion, salt, pepper and parsley. Strain stock, dice chicken and store in refrigerator. Next day skim grease from stock. Saute ground meat in butter with celery, shallots, parsley, garlic and bell pepper. Add stock, tomatoes, mushrooms. Simmer four hours on very slow fire in heavy pot. Add chicken, New York cheese and boiled spaghetti. Let stand. Heat before serving. Add Italian cheese as desired.

Serves 30. Mrs. William H. Phillips, Sr.

CHICKEN SPAGHETTI

1 large hen (6-7 pounds), boiled with about 4 bay leaves, cooled and taken off bone
1 pound package spaghetti, boiled in plenty of salted water

Saute:
2 onions (in butter or oleo)
2 pods garlic

Add:
2 small cans tomatoes
Salt to taste
Worcestershire sauce
Dash of Tabasco
Pepper
1 quart chicken broth
2 scant tablespoons flour

Cook down slowly to a thick sauce about 30 to 45 minutes. Take out bay leaves.

¾ pound grated American cheese
2 cans mushrooms (pieces)
2 cups ripe olives

Put cut up chicken, spaghetti, mushrooms and olives and American cheese in layers in a baking dish and add sauce. (I put about 2 layers of each, adding the sauce with each layer.) Bake 1 hour (may be less) in slow oven (325°).

Mrs. Ralph F. Pullen

CHICKEN SPAGHETTI

1 large hen
1 large onion, chopped
2 tablespoons butter
1 small can corn
1 small can mushrooms, chopped
1 can tomato soup
Celery salt
Comino seed
1 package spaghetti
Parmesan cheese
Salt, red and black pepper to taste

Boil hen in large pot with seasonings of your choice. Save stock. Mince and fry onion in butter. Mix and cook together corn, mushrooms and soup. Season with celery salt, comino seed, salt and pepper. Add cut up chicken and onion and simmer slowly. Add spaghetti which has been boiled in the chicken stock and drained. Mix all together and season to taste. If more liquid is desired, use stock. Sprinkle with cheese.

Mrs. Glenn Davis

CHICKEN-SPINACH DISH

Brown Sauce:
2 tablespoons butter
2 tablespoons flour
1 thick slice onion
1 beef bouillon cube dissolved in ½ cup boiling water
½ cup white wine

Melt butter in saucepan. Sizzle until brown. For added flavor put onion slice in the butter until brown, then remove onion. Stir in flour until smooth. Slowly add bouillon and wine, stirring over low heat until thickened. Salt and pepper to taste. Add tabasco if desired. Makes 1 cup. May be cooked ahead and warmed for later use.

Chicken-Spinach Dish:
4 whole chicken breasts
2 packages of leaf spinach (frozen)
1 package fresh mushrooms
1 cup brown sauce

Carefully bone chicken breasts; one breast per person. Season with salt, pepper, and Accent and saute in butter until tender and brown on both sides (15 to 20 minutes). While breasts are browning cook spinach according to instructions on box. Saute fresh mushroom caps in butter until tender. Drain spinach and place on platter. Top with breasts of chicken. Cover with mushroom caps and pour hot brown sauce over the whole dish.

Makes 4 servings.

Mrs. P. J. Mills, Jr.

CHICKEN TETRAZZINI

1 5-pound hen
1 package spaghetti
1 can mushrooms
1 bell pepper
1 large onion
½ cup flour
1 quart milk
1 8-ounce package Old English cheese
1 8-ounce package American cheese
Parmesan cheese

Boil hen in water seasoned with onion, celery and salt. Reserve broth. Saute bell pepper and onion. Saute mushrooms. Make cream sauce of flour and milk. Add cheese cut in small pieces and stir until cheese melts. Add sauteed onion, pepper and mushrooms. Cut chicken in bite-size pieces and add to sauce. Boil spaghetti in chicken broth. Add sauce mixture. Put in casserole. Top with Parmesan cheese. Bake in 350° oven 45 minutes.

Mrs. William Wilkins

CHICKEN CASSEROLE

2½ cups diced chicken
1 cup finely sliced celery
¼ cup chopped green pepper
½ cup chopped toasted almonds
1 teaspoon salt
½ teaspoon pepper
3 tablespoons grated onion
3 tablespoons lemon juice
1 cup mayonnaise
1 teaspoon Accent
1 cup grated Cheddar cheese
Mushrooms
Pimiento
Parmesan cheese
Potato chips

Combine all ingredients except cheese and potato chips in casserole. Grate cheese on top, then add ¼-inch layer potato chips, crushed. Sprinkle Parmesan cheese on top. Bake 30 to 40 minutes in a covered casserole at 350°. Take cover off the last few minutes of baking.

Serves 8 to 10.

Mrs. Charles H. Jeter

HOT CHICKEN SALAD

2 cups chicken, cut up
½ cup almonds, chopped
1 cup mayonnaise
2 tablespoons lemon juice
2 cups celery, thinly sliced
1 cup potato chips
2 teaspoons onion, grated
1 teaspoon salt
½ cup grated cheese, American or Swiss

Mix all ingredients except cheese and potato chips. Pile lightly in individual baking dishes or a casserole. Sprinkle with crushed potato chips and cheese. Cook at 400° about 25 minutes. ½ cup chopped green pepper makes a nice addition. May be prepared the day before.

Mrs. T. Haller Jackson, Jr.
Mrs. Hubert L. Joyner
Mrs. Kenneth Hickman
Mrs. Stanley Clark

HERBED CHICKEN EN CASSEROLE

3 large chicken breasts, cut in half
Salt and pepper
¼ cup butter or margarine
1 can condensed cream of chicken soup
¾ cup cooking sauterne
1 5-ounce can water chestnuts, drained and sliced
1 3-ounce can broiled sliced mushrooms, drained
2 tablespoons chopped green pepper
2 tablespoons chopped celery
¼ teaspoon crushed thyme

Lightly season chicken with salt and pepper. Brown slowly in butter. Arrange chicken, skin side up, in 11½" x 7½" x 1½" baking dish. Brown green pepper and celery in drippings. For the sauce, add soup to drippings in skillet; slowly add sauterne, stirring smooth. Add remaining ingredients. Heat to boiling. Pour sauce over chicken. Cover with foil and bake in 350° oven 25 minutes. Uncover; continue baking 25-35 minutes or until chicken is tender.

Serves 6. May be prepared early in the day.

Mrs. Frank Cook

CHICKEN AND WILD RICE CASSEROLE

1 cup wild rice, uncooked
½ cup chopped onion
½ cup butter
¼ cup flour
1 6-ounce can mushrooms
1½ cups light cream
3 cups diced chicken
¼ cup diced pimiento
2 tablespoons parsley
1½ teaspoons salt
¼ teaspoon pepper

Prepare 1 cup of wild rice. Cook ½ cup chopped onion in ½ cup butter until tender. Remove from heat. Stir in ¼ cup flour. Drain mushrooms. Save liquid. Add enough chicken broth to mushroom liquid to make 1½ cups. Stir slowly into flour mixture. Add cream. Cook and stir until thickened. Add rice, mushrooms, chicken, pimiento, parsley, salt and pepper. Place in greased 2-quart casserole. Cook at 350° for 30-45 minutes.

Makes 6 servings. May be prepared the day before.

Mrs. Frank Cook

CHICKEN-SAUSAGE-RICE CASSEROLE

2 pounds sausage
2 large onions
1 large bell pepper
1 bunch celery
2 cups raw rice
3 packages dehydrated chicken noodle soup
½ to 1 cup slivered almonds

Put sausage (cut in chunks) into a frying pan and brown. Dip sausage out with slotted spoon and place in large bowl. Set aside. Add to frying pan and drippings cut up onions, pepper and celery. Saute. Cook rice as usual (Do not use "instant" rice.) Add sauteed vegetables, rice and nuts to sausage. Mix. Prepare soup by direction on box, using only **one-half amount of water** called for on package. Add soup to sausage mixture, place all in baking dish, and bake for 1 hour at 350°. If desired, remove from oven 10 minutes before done, cover with Cheddar cheese, and finish baking.

Serves 12. May be frozen successfully.

Mrs. John L. Rhea, Jr.

TURKEY OR CHICKEN CROQUETTES

4 tablespoons butter or margarine
5 tablespoons flour
1 cup milk
½ cup chicken stock
3 cups finely chopped or ground turkey or chicken
1 teaspoon onion, grated
1 tablespoon chopped parsley
½ teaspoon salt
¼ teaspoon pepper
1 egg
1 tablespoon water
Dry bread crumbs or cracker meal

Make a thick cream sauce, with butter, flour, milk and stock. Cool. Add turkey or chicken, onion, parsley, salt and pepper. Shape as desired. Beat egg and add water. Dip croquettes in egg and roll in crumbs. Set aside in refrigerator for one hour or longer. Fry in deep fat until a delicate brown. Drain on absorbent paper. Serve hot. May be served with a hot mushroom sauce. A good way to use leftover turkey.

Serves 4. Mrs. John R. Murphy

"CALL IT WHAT YOU LIKE"

For each portion remove crust and cut diagonally one piece of white bread. Toast well. Place halves on ovenproof plate. Cover toast with either chicken or turkey sliced very thin. Cover with your favorite medium cream sauce and sprinkle with sliced fresh mushrooms, Parmesan cheese and paprika. Edge the cream sauce with four cubes of fresh tomato. Place under broiler until sauce starts to bubble. Remove and cross with partly cooked bacon. Return to broiler until plate is very hot. Garnish with a sprig of parsley or with pimiento.

Mrs. Jack C. Murrell

TURKEY HAWAIIAN

2 eggs, beaten
½ cup flour
½ teaspoon salt
3 tablespoons water
2 cups cooked cubed turkey
Fat for frying
13½-ounce can pineapple chunks
2 tablespoons cornstarch
1 tablespoon butter
1 tablespoon chicken stock base, or bouillon cube
1 each green and red pepper, cut in eighths
1 tablespoon soy sauce
1 8-ounce can onions, drained

Combine eggs, flour and salt with water; beat until smooth. Add turkey and stir until all pieces are coated well. Drop into hot shallow fat and brown on all sides. Keep warm. Drain pineapple juice into saucepan, blend in cornstarch, add butter, pineapple and remaining ingredients. Simmer for 5 minutes, stirring frequently. Add turkey and serve at once.

Makes 4 servings. Mrs. Tom Stagg

CHICKEN CHOP SUEY

1 1-pound can (2 cups) bean sprouts
½ cup onion slices
2 tablespoons butter or margarine
1½ to 2 cups diced cooked chicken or turkey
1 cup celery slices
1 5- or 6-ounce can (about ⅔ cup) water chestnuts, drained and sliced
½ cup chicken broth or 1 chicken bouillon cube dissolved in ½ cup water
2 tablespoons cornstarch
¼ teaspoon salt
¼ teaspoon monosodium glutamate
¼ cup water
2 tablespoons soy sauce
4 cups hot cooked rice (or fried chow mein noodles)
½ cup slivered blanched almonds, toasted

Drain bean sprouts, reserving liquid. Cook onion in butter until tender but not brown; add chicken, celery, water chestnuts, broth and bean sprout liquid; heat to boiling. Combine cornstarch, seasonings, water and soy sauce; stir into chicken mixture. Cook, stirring constantly, until thick. (Cooks fast, just 15 minutes.) Add bean sprouts and just heat through. Serve with hot rice and almonds. Pass bottle of soy sauce.

Makes 4 to 6 servings. Mrs. John H. McKee

TURKEY WITH RICE AND OYSTER DRESSING

16-18-pound turkey
Salt and pepper
Gin and lemon juice
1 cup melted fat (½ cup butter, ½ cup bacon fat)
¼ cup melted fat
1 cup water
1 cup red wine

Wipe inside of turkey with damp cloth. Salt and pepper cavity liberally. Rub with gin and lemon juice. Fill with **Stuffing** (recipe below). Skewer or sew vents. Place turkey on rack in roaster. Pour over turkey 1 cup melted fat. Cover turkey completely with **Pastry** (recipe below). Drizzle ¼ cup melted fat over pastry. Add 1 cup water and 1 cup red wine to bottom of pan. Bake in 300° oven for at least 6 hours. Baste frequently with pan juices. Legs should be wobbly when bird is thoroughly done. Pastry will be almost black. Remove to platter and make **Gravy** (recipe below). Then remove and discard pastry.

Stuffing:
Liver, gizzard, heart, 3 or 4 extra chicken livers
1 stalk celery
Neck
Eggs from turkey (if hen)
3 cups water
1 teaspoon salt

Cook over moderate heat until gizzard is tender. Reserve liver, gizzard and 1 cup broth for gravy.

2 cups unwashed rice
3 cups cold water
1 tablespoon salt
1 tablespoon salad oil

Put all together and bring to a rolling boil. Immediately lower heat to lowest possible flame and place over asbestos pad. Cover and simmer for 45 minutes. Readjust cover to allow steam to escape for 5 more minutes. Turn off fire.

3 tablespoons bacon fat
2 tablespoons flour
Remaining broth and chopped giblets (approximately 2 cups)
1 pint oysters and liquor
1 cup parsley
1 cup Bermuda onions
1 cup celery
1 bunch green onions
½ cup bell pepper
½ stick margarine
Salt and pepper

Heat bacon fat in Dutch oven. Add flour to make roux. Add broth and giblets. Cook 10-15 minutes. Cool a little. Add oyster liquor. Combine rice, finely chopped vegetables, melted margarine and cooked roux. Snip oysters in 2 or 3 pieces and add to mixture. Salt and pepper to taste.

Pastry:
3 cups unsifted flour
1 teaspoon baking powder
1 teaspoon salt
½ teaspoon dried thyme
½ teaspoon dry mustard
½ cup salad oil
¼ cup cold water

(Continued on next page)

Mix dry ingredients. Add oil and water. Mix lightly and roll thin on floured board. Cover buttered turkey.

Gravy:

Pan juices
Reserved broth and chopped liver and gizzard
½ cup wine
1 cup chopped green onion tops
Buerre manie (1 teaspoon flour and 1 teaspoon butter mixed together with fingers)

Add broth and giblets to pan juices. If sauce is too thin add a buerre manie. Stir all brown bits from bottom of pan. Add wine. Cook 5 minutes. Add onion tops, chopped fine.

Mrs. James R. Alexander

OYSTER STUFFING FOR TURKEY

3 dozen oysters (2 pint cans)
½ loaf stale bread
2 tablespoons butter
1 tablespoon bacon drippings
3 large onions, chopped fine
Celery, chopped fine
1 tablespoon each chopped parsley, thyme, bay leaf
Salt and pepper to taste

Drain oysters and use liquor to moisten stale bread. If there is not enough oyster liquid, pour a little water over oysters in colander and use this. Squeeze stale bread quite dry. Chop oysters. Add onion and celery to bacon drippings and fry to golden brown. Add seasonings and mix well. Add butter, blending all thoroughly, and add chopped oysters. Stir and cook for 5 minutes, remove from fire and stuff turkey. This is sufficient to stuff a 10-pound turkey.

Mrs. Paul R. Winder

CORN BREAD DRESSING

2 9-inch pans baked corn bread
6 slices white bread
2 cups chopped celery
3 cups chopped onion
½ pound butter or margarine
2-3 cups turkey stock (chicken broth may be used)
2 eggs
2 hard cooked eggs
Cooked giblets, if desired

In an iron skillet, saute onion and celery until yellow and limp. Crumble corn bread into onion mixture. Tear bread up in fine pieces and add. Add stock until mixture is moist but loosely packed, about 1½ to 2 cups stock. Add chopped hard cooked eggs and slightly beaten eggs. Season well with salt and pepper. Pack into buttered baking dishes, cover with foil and bake about 45 minutes at 325°. More stock may be needed if dressing becomes dry. Giblets may be added to dressing or used in gravy. This will make enough dressing to serve with a 10-12-pound turkey.

From the recipes of Mrs. J. A. Bell

FRENCH BREAD DRESSING

1 stalk celery, chopped
1 bunch green onions, chopped
1 large onion, chopped
2 cloves garlic, minced
1 bunch parsley, chopped
1½ loaves stale French bread
1 box frozen chicken livers
2 boxes frozen chicken gizzards (also liver and gizzard from fowl you are cooking)
3 sticks butter
2 eggs
Salt and pepper to taste

Boil livers and gizzards until tender, drain, cool and chop. Save stock. Saute onions, garlic, celery and parsley in butter until tender. Put seasonings through vegetable grinder. Put chopped livers and gizzards through meat grinder. Soften bread in stock and put through grinder. Combine above ingredients, add eggs and salt and pepper. Bake in casserole in 350° oven for 30 minutes. If dressing seems dry, it may be softened with drippings from fowl before baking. When combining ingredients you should have one third seasoning, one third bread and one third meat.

Serves 8. This dressing may be made ahead of time and frozen. Be sure to thaw before baking.

Roch H. Pedarre, Baton Rouge, La.

COMPLETE INDIAN DINNER

Coconut Sambal

2 fresh coconuts, grated
3 medium, firm tomatoes
1 medium onion, chopped
1¼ teaspoons salt
½ teaspoon black pepper
Pinch sugar
1 tablespoon vinegar
¼ cup water

Seed tomatoes, and remove pulp, drain, then chop fine, and combine with grated coconut and chopped onion. Add to the mixture the seasonings, adjusting to taste.

Lime Pickle

2 pounds limes (lemons may be substituted if necessary)
2 tablespoons salt
2 teaspoons dry mustard
1 teaspoon cayenne pepper
1 clove garlic, crushed
½ teaspoon ginger
1 cup salad oil

Wash limes, dry; slice them crosswise into ⅛-inch slices. Arrange in a single layer on a cookie sheet. Combine salt and other ingredients except oil, mixing well. Sprinkle over limes, let stand 1 hour. Heat oil until smoking, allow to cool slightly. Pack lime slices into 2 hot sterilized pint jars. Cover with oil, making certain there are no air bubbles. Cap immediately. Let stand at room temperature for at least 4 days before using. Serve with any spiced meat. Makes 2 pints.

Shrimp Curry

2 pounds shrimp, shelled and cleaned
2 large onions, chopped fine
4 tablespoons butter
2 cloves garlic, chopped fine
2 tablespoons tomato puree
2 tablespoons curry powder
4 tablespoons coconut milk* (if available)

Melt butter in skillet, saute chopped onion and garlic until they begin to change color, but do not let them brown. Add curry powder, stirring well, and cook for 3-4 minutes over a slow fire. Add a little water if too dry. When the "raw look" disappears, add 2 tablespoons tomato puree, mixed with a pint of water. If available, add coconut milk*. Add salt and lemon juice to taste, and let the sauce simmer until a richness appears in the curry. Add shrimp to the sauce. Do not let the curry boil. Cook about 30 minutes after adding shrimp.

*To make coconut milk: Cover 4 tablespoons grated coconut with boiling water. Allow to stand 20 minutes, then squeeze the milk out of the coconut. (Use a strainer.)

Chicken Korma

2 disjointed chickens or selected pieces
2 cloves garlic, chopped
4 tablespoons onions, finely chopped
Marinade:
1 pint sour cream
2 tablespoons ground coriander
2 tablespoons grated coconut
2 scant teaspoons ground turmeric
1 teaspoon ground cumin seed
1 teaspoon ground red pepper

Marinate the disjointed chicken in the sour cream mixture for at least 1 hour. Saute the chopped onions and garlic in butter. Add the chicken and the marinade. Mix well and simmer until the chicken is done. Add salt and lemon juice as necessary.

Rice

4 cups long grain rice
6 cups water
2 cloves
2 bay leaves
2 bouillon cubes
2 generous pinches turmeric
2 pinches comino
1 tablespoon salt

Combine all ingredients in a large casserole, with a tight lid, and cook at 350° until the rice is fluffy and the grains separate. Stir when half done and re-cover. Serve on a large platter garnished with raisins which have been sauteed in butter and toasted coconut snips.

Lentils prepared according to package directions are served also.

A good hot **chutney** is always served as a condiment.

A flat crisp bread is traditionally served. Tortillas which have been toasted, or sesame wafers would be good.

These recipes, used as a complete meal, will serve 8 people.

Mrs. C. L. Stacy, Jr.

JAN GARBER CHICKEN

Saute favorite pieces of chicken, which have been salted and peppered, in 2 tablespoons butter. (No flour.) Add 1 cup or more chicken bouillon, ½ bay leaf, a fresh tomato, diced, and 1 teaspoon Worcestershire sauce. Cover and cook slowly about ½ hour. Add 1 teaspoon cornstarch (mixed with a little water) to thicken gravy. Serve over rice or grits. 1 tablespoon cooking sherry may be added. May be prepared well ahead of time.

Mrs. David Comegys

DOVE SAUCE PIQUANTE

(For 16-18 Doves)

- 4-5 tablespoons fat
- 3 tablespoons flour
- 2 large or 3 small Bermuda onions, chopped fine
- ½ can tomato paste (approximately 3 tablespoons)
- Doves, cleaned well and wiped dry, salted and peppered liberally, inside and outside
- 2 bell peppers, finely chopped
- 1 bunch green onions, chopped (white and green parts)
- 1 small can chopped black olives
- 1 5-ounce can mushrooms and juice
- 2 cups hot water
- 2 tablespoons Worcestershire sauce
- ½ teaspoon Tabasco
- ½ teaspoon black pepper
- 1 teaspoon salt
- 3 crushed garlic cloves
- ½ cup fresh snipped parsley (or 1 tablespoon dried)
- ¾ cup dry red wine

Heat fat in large kettle. Make sure it covers the bottom of the vessel well. Add flour. Brown slowly, but get the roux a deep, rich brown. Add onions. Stir until limp and transparent. Keep fire low. Add tomato paste. Stir until well blended — about 5 minutes. Add doves. Stir the roux over and over them, and cook uncovered 20-30 minutes, or until each dove is slightly browned. Add bell peppers, green onions, olives, mushrooms and juice. Stir well to blend. Add water and seasonings. Let it come to a full boil. Then lower fire to simmer. Add garlic and parsley. Cover and let cook 2½ to 3 hours. Stir from the bottom every 30 minutes. Add wine. Cook another 45 minutes to an hour — very slowly, covered. They are done when they start to fall apart. Serve over rice.

Makes 6 servings.

Mrs. James R. Alexander

BAKED QUAIL

6 dressed birds
Salt and pepper
3 dozen peeled grapes
½ lemon
6 slices bacon
¼ cup melted butter

Sprinkle salt and pepper inside each bird. Fill each cavity with peeled grapes. Rub outside with half lemon, then sprinkle with salt and pepper. Wrap a bacon slice around each bird, securing with toothpicks. Place quail in pan, add melted butter, cover and bake at 450° about 30 minutes. If birds are not tender, add ¼ cup water and steam at a lower temperature (375°) for an hour or less. Baste with melted butter every 10 minutes. Young birds require a short cooking period, while older ones need a little more cooking to make them tender.

The following relish is a fine acompaniment for the quail:

Ginger-Orange Relish

2 tablespoons prepared mustard
½ teaspoon ginger
1 cup orange marmalade

Combine and serve chilled.

Mrs. E. Newton Wray

COMPANY QUAIL

8 quail (if frozen, thaw in milk to cover)
1 stick butter (or margarine)
Flour, salt
1 cup water, very hot
2 chicken bouillon cubes (or 1 tablespoon yellow base chicken stock)
1 teaspoon dried powdered mushrooms
1 teaspoon dried parsley
4 tablespoons Madeira or dry sherry
White pepper to taste

Wipe birds dry with cloth. Sprinkle liberally with flour and lightly with salt. Pat it in. Heat skillet or Dutch oven. Lower fire to medium and add 1 stick butter. When melted and foamy, quickly saute the birds on both sides. Meanwhile, mix together water, bouillon cubes, mushroom powder and parsley. Shake well to blend in a jar. When birds are browned, pour mixture over, lower fire (use asbestos pad, if possible) and simmer very slowly, covered, for one hour, or until really tender. Then add wine and cook 5 minutes with cover off. Serve birds, reduce sauce a minute or two longer, spoon sauce over birds, and pass extra sauce.

Serves 4.

Mrs. James R. Alexander

ROAST WILD DUCK

1 duck
2 tablespoons dry mustard
1 teaspoon salt
½ teaspoon black pepper
½ raw apple
½ onion
¼ raw potato
1 clove garlic
1 piece celery
1 slice orange
½ cup water
¼ cup sherry or red wine (optional)

Wash duck thoroughly and let stand in pan of cold water, containing 2 teaspoons baking soda and 2 teaspoons salt, for 20 minutes. Wash duck again. Combine dry mustard, salt and pepper in bowl. Pat each duck inside and out generously with mixture. Cube vegetables, mix and fill cavity of duck. Place duck, breast side up, in a Dutch oven or roasting pan. Pour water in pan but do not splash duck. Cover. Baste duck every ½ hour. Add wine after 1 hour. Cook at 325° for 2 hours. 1 duck serves two, depending on size of duck. May be prepared in advance. Use gravy over wild rice or white rice or a mixture of the two. Mushrooms may be added to gravy.

Mrs. Robert U. Goodman

WILD DUCK A LA FAUVETTE

2 wild ducks
2 tablespoons butter
2 tablespoons sherry
2 tablespoons tomato paste
3 tablespoons flour
1½ cups strong bouillon
½ cup dry red wine
Salt and pepper to taste
½ pound mushrooms, sliced
1 bay leaf
2 cups cooked wild rice

Halve ducks, removing wings (and backbone if you can manage it). Melt butter in Dutch oven and brown the halves thoroughly, turning often, until they are very dark. Pour sherry over them. Remove ducks to stir sherry into pan juices. Lower heat. Add tomato paste. Stir in flour gradually, stirring to make smooth. Gradually add bouillon, warmed previously, seasonings and red wine. Bring mixture to boiling point and add ducks. Add sliced mushrooms and crumbled bay leaf. Cover and cook over very low heat for 1 hour or until tender. Place ducks on platter with mound of wild rice between them. Skim grease from sauce, reheat and pour over all.

Serves 4. Garnish platter with red spiced crab apples.

Mrs. W. W. Lincoln

DUCKS DELUXE

4 wild ducks
2 apples
1 large onion
4 large celery stalks, with tops
1 tablespoon pickling spice
Cinnamon sticks
1 clove garlic for each duck
1½ cups sherry wine
4 carrots
1 green pepper
2 oranges
Salt and pepper

Cut vegetables and apples in large chunks, add pickling spice. Stuff the well-cleaned ducks with this mixture. Coat stuffed ducks with flour; sprinkle top with powdered cinnamon; place on rack in baking pan and add enough water to pan to prevent burning. Tuck sliced oranges and cinnamon sticks around ducks; cover and bake at 350° for 3 hours, basting occasionally. Remove top of baking pan and brown ducks for 30 to 40 minutes under high heat, basting about 3 times with the sherry. When browned, remove ducks and pour fat off drippings in pan; add flour to thicken and more water, if necessary, for gravy.

From Teal Lodge, Aransas Pass, Texas
By Mrs. Mike W. Tipps

DUCK STEW

2 large ducks
Salt
Red pepper
Black pepper
½ cup oil
4 large onions
5 garlic cloves
3 stalks celery with leaves
1 bell pepper
1 to 2 pints water
2 bunches green onions
½ bunch parsley

Cut ducks into pieces. Then salt and red and black pepper it. Put a large pot on the fire with ½ cup of oil in it and heat until very hot. Then brown the duck in hot oil. Remove duck from oil and allow to cool. Cut up onions, garlic cloves, celery, bell pepper, and add to above oil. Return duck to oil, add these ingredients and cook over medium heat for 15 minutes, stirring fairly constantly. Then add one to two pints of water, cover and cook slowly about 2½ hours or until tender. Check occasionally and add a cup of hot water when needed. About 15 minutes before serving, add green onions and parsley cut fine. Serve over rice.

Makes 4-6 servings.

Mr. Paul F. O'Brien, Jr.

DUCK A LA TEXAS

6 wild ducks
2 apples
2 oranges
2 large stalks celery
2 large onions
2 strips bacon for each duck
1 cup fresh orange juice
1 cup red wine

Clean ducks and rub inside and out with salt and pepper. Stuff with apples, oranges, celery and onions chopped in rather large pieces, leaving the peeling on the apples and oranges. Stuff ducks full so that they stand out plump and round, then tie the opening with kitchen string. Put in an electric cooker or oven on rack in large open cooker. Lay 2 strips of bacon on each duck and cook 30 minutes at 500°, then turn to 375° for two to three hours (depending on size of the ducks). During this last cooking process, the ducks should be basted with the orange juice mixed with red wine. When ducks are done, remove from pan and make gravy from the drippings.

Mrs. Joe J. Fisher, Jasper, Texas

FROG LEGS OVER CHARCOAL

Frog legs (allow at least 2 pairs per person)
Milk
Salt, black and red pepper and Accent
Flour
Cooking fat

Sauce: Combine and heat:
1 stick butter, melted
½ teaspoon Tabasco
2 tablespoons lemon juice
1 teaspoon Worcestershire sauce
1 crushed clove of garlic

Buy frozen frog legs and thaw them in milk, almost to cover. While thawing, move them around so all get thoroughly soaked. Drain. Shake well in paper bag containing flour, salt, pepper and Accent. (For each cup of flour, use 1 teaspoon of each seasoning.) Let them rest a while in the bag, and then shake again. They should be thoroughly coated with the flour mixture. Meanwhile, make good, hot fire outdoors with charcoal. Put large heavy kettle half filled with grease on grill, and when kitchen match ignites in grease, it is hot enough to fry frog legs. (Temperature — about 375°). Fry them quickly — about three or four minutes (or a little longer, depending on size), and drain on absorbent paper. Have sauce ready and serve frog legs on large platter with sauce drizzled over liberally.

James R. Alexander

SQUIRREL

Allow at least ½ squirrel per person. Clean and quarter squirrel, then season thoroughly with salt, pepper and flour. Cover bottom of cast iron pot with fat, and brown pieces of squirrel in fat. Chop up one onion for each squirrel and add to pot after browning squirrel. Then add 1 cup water and a stalk of celery (if desired), cover the pot and cook on top of stove or in oven for about an hour, or until tender. Use a low fire. After 30 minutes of cooking, add some red wine to the pot. Use about ¼ cup wine per squirrel.

Mrs. W. J. Atkins

TURTLE SOUP

2-3 pounds turtle meat
3 tablespoons flour
2-3 tablespoons cooking oil
1 cup chopped celery
1 cup chopped onions
½ cup chopped green pepper
2 cloves chopped garlic
4 medium size bay leaves
1 small lemon, sliced
1 cup tomato sauce
1 tablespoon Worcestershire sauce
¼ teaspoon each of allspice, sweet basil, marjoram, sage, rosemary and thyme
Salt, pepper, Tabasco to taste
½ cup dry sherry
2 tablespoons chopped parsley
3 hard cooked eggs

Boil fresh turtle meat in enough water to cover completely. To the water add 2 stalks celery, 1 small onion, salt and pepper to taste. While cooking, remove white bubbles from top of water. When tender remove meat from broth, strain broth and save. Remove tough outer portion from meat, if any remains, de-bone and cut into bite-size pieces. Replace meat in broth and set aside. Make a roux using 3 tablespoons cooking oil and 3 tablespoons flour and cook until brown, stirring constantly. Add broth, meat and then celery, onions, green peppers, garlic, tomato sauce, bay leaves, salt, pepper, Tabasco, Worcestershire sauce, and lemon slices and stir. Cook in an uncovered pot for 20 minutes. Then add spices to taste (approximately ¼ teaspoon of each depending on taste). Add more water if needed. This soup should be thin but never watery. Then cook for another 30 minutes. Before serving, add parsley and approximately ½ cup dry sherry. Place hard cooked egg slices in soup bowls and pour hot soup over egg. Serve immediately, making sure each bowl has a serving of turtle meat along with the broth. Do not include egg in soup when preparing for freezer. Add egg after thawing and when ready to serve.

Mrs. P. J. Mills, Jr.

VENISON EXTRAVAGANZA

8 pounds venison ham (approximately)
Wine vinegar
1 pound salt pork, cut in match-size strips
½ cup parsley, snipped extra fine
½ cup flour
1 teaspoon salt
1 teaspoon cracked black pepper
1 cup vegetable oil
Flour, about 2 tablespoons
1 cup chicken broth
1 cup dry red wine
1 cup water
1 cup onion, chopped
1 cup green onions, chopped
½ cup bell pepper, chopped
½ cup brandy
1 pound fresh button mushrooms

Marinate venison for several hours in wine vinegar. Wipe dry. With a larding needle, if possible, or an ice pick, force holes into venison at fairly regular intervals and insert strips of salt pork which have been rolled in parsley. Be sure some of the salt pork is as close as possible to the bone, for venison is extremely lean. Trim off protruding ends of pork. Beat ½ cup flour mixed with salt and pepper into roast. Use all of it. Heat oil in iron pot to smoking point. Carefully brown venison on all sides. Use tongs to turn so juices will not be released. Remove venison. Add to oil about 2 tablespoons more flour. Stir until roux is deep, rich brown. Add chopped vegetables. Cook until onions are transparent. Add broth, wine and water. Cook 10 minutes. Lower fire to simmer, and gently add venison ham to sauce. Cover and simmer about 2 hours, or until done, turning ham occasionally. Remove ham to platter. Strain gravy; boil it up and add brandy. Simmer a minute or two. Add mushrooms. Cook slowly 5 more minutes. Serve sauce over sliced venison.

Mrs. James R. Alexander

Warm some currant jelly in half as much port wine and serve hot with roast duck or other game.

Mrs. Staunton B. Sample

VENISON STEAK

1 pound venison steak, tenderized by pounding
Worcestershire sauce
Flour, salt and pepper
1 tablespoon salad oil
1 large onion, chopped
1 bouillon cube dissolved in two cups water
1 cup water mixed with 1 tablespoon flour
1 tablespoon parsley flakes
Monosodium glutamate

Place venison in a pan in your refrigerator and sprinkle generously with Worcestershire sauce. This helps to remove to a limited degree the strong odor of deer meat. Do this the night before cooking steaks. Remove all fat from steaks. Boil 2 cups of water in another pan and dissolve bouillon cube. Also mix 1 tablespoon flour in 1 full cup of water. Chop onion. Sprinkle steaks with flour, salt and pepper. Put salad oil in skillet and brown onions. When onions are light brown, add steaks to skillet and brown on both sides. Turn fire down and add bouillon mixture, flour and water mixture and parsley flakes. Sprinkle steaks generously with monosodium glutamate. Simmer steaks over a low fire for at least an hour or until tender. Add water when necessary. If you plan to have company and have deer meat be sure to have three or four skillets on hand, and use at least 4 or 5 pounds of deer meat steaks.

1 pound will serve 2 people.

Mrs. Arthur James Ferguson

Meat

LOUISIANA STATE FAIR

The thrill of midway rides, the aroma of cotton candy and the sounds of nationally-known performers attract more than 600,000 people each year to the Louisiana State Fair, the single largest annual attraction in the state. Professional cowboys vie for titles in the Louisiana Rodeo Cowboys Association Championship Finals. Boys and girls participating in their school Four-H clubs participate in the annual live-stock show, and all the exhibit halls are filled with fun, interesting and educational displays.

BEEF A LA BOURGUIGNONNE

1 tablespoon butter
1 cup diced salt pork
3 pounds cubed round, top sirloin or rump of beef
1½ dozen small onions
6 medium carrots, cut in bite-size pieces
½ stalk celery, bite-size pieces
2-3 chopped shallots
1 clove garlic, crushed
2 tablespoons flour
2 cups red wine
1 cup broth
Bouquet of herbs: 3 sprigs parsley, 2 pieces celery, bay leaf and pinch of thyme
½ pound sauteed mushrooms (optional)

Fry salt pork (or bacon) in a tablespoon of butter until cubes are golden brown. Remove pork cubes. In the same fat, brown cubed beef, searing on all sides. Season lightly with salt and pepper and add flour. Set pan in the oven until the flour is golden brown; add wine and broth. The meat should be completely covered. If more liquid is needed, keep the same proportion of 2 cups wine to 1 cup broth. Add carrots, celery, shallots, and salt pork along with bouquet of herbs. Cook until meat is tender and about half done. Reduce heat until liquid is just simmering and cook covered until meat is tender and sauce reduced — about 2½ hours. Shake the pan occasionally to prevent meat from sticking. Put in a deep pot and let the grease rise, then skim it off. Remove bouquet of herbs. Saute onions and place on top. This may be served as is, right from the casserole, or you may finish it with the ½ pound of mushrooms. Small boiled potatoes sprinkled with parsley are very good with it.

Serves 12.

The Shreveport Club

WOOD CHUCK

1 cup chicken, ham, beef, or tuna fish, cooked
2 cups white sauce
1 can cream of mushroom soup
1 can mushrooms
1 can pimiento
½ bell pepper
1 package pimiento cheese
6 hard boiled eggs
Chinese fried noodles

Mix diced cooked meat, white sauce, mushroom soup, mushrooms, chopped pimiento, chopped bell pepper, and pimiento cheese. Heat thoroughly. Before serving add eggs cut in quarters. Then serve on Chinese fried noodles.

Serves 6.

Mrs. George Hodges
Mrs. Scott Dunlop

McCAIN MEAT LOAF

1½ pounds ground beef
1 medium onion
1 medium bell pepper
1 tablespoon catsup
2-3 slices Old English cheese, broken in bits, or equivalent thereof
1 piece of bread, broken in bits
1 egg, raw
Dash of salt
Dash of pepper
Juice of ½ lemon
Dash Worcestershire sauce
Dash A-1 sauce

Dice onion and bell pepper. Cook in frying pan with a little bacon grease, stirring occasionally until onion is clear; pepper, soft. Drain off liquid. Add onion and bell pepper and all above ingredients to meat. Blend well until everything is thoroughly mixed with meat. Pour part of following sauce over meat loaf, saving rest of sauce to reheat and pour over at serving time. Bake in 350° oven 1 hour.

Sauce

2 cans tomato paste plus 2 cans water or 2 cans tomato sauce plus can of water
Juice of ½ lemon
Dash Worcestershire sauce
Dash A-1 sauce
1 tablespoon catsup
Dash salt
Dash pepper

Serves 2-3 people. (Use 2 pounds meat for 4 people.) This may be frozen if desired.

Mrs. K. J. Heddons
Henderson, Kentucky

MEAT LOAF, BARBECUE STYLE

1½ pounds ground beef
1 cup bread crumbs
1 onion, minced
1 egg
1½ teaspoons salt
¼ teaspoon pepper
2 8-ounce cans tomato sauce
½ cup water
3 tablespoons brown sugar
3 tablespoons vinegar
2 tablespoons prepared mustard
2 teaspoons Worcestershire sauce

Mix together beef, crumbs, beaten egg, salt, pepper and ½ can of tomato sauce. Form into loaf and put in shallow pan. Combine rest of sauce and remaining ingredients. Cook at 350° for 1 hour, 15 minutes. Baste often, using all of sauce.

Serves 4 to 6.

Mrs. Tandy Lewis

SWEDISH MEAT BALLS WITH SOUR CREAM

Meat Ball Mixture:
Bread crumbs
½ cup milk
1½ pounds ground meat
1 onion, chopped
2 tablespoons margarine
2½ teaspoons salt
¼ teaspoon pepper
2 teaspoons nutmeg
2 teaspoons paprika
1 teaspoon dry mustard
1 teaspoon dried mixed herbs
3 beaten eggs

Sauce:
1 tablespoon margarine
4 tablespoons flour
¼ teaspoon crushed garlic
2 teaspoons tomato paste
1 teaspoon beef concentrate
2 cups bouillon (add enough water to make 2 cups liquid)
1 teaspoon aromatic bitters
½ pint sour cream
Buttered noodles

Mix together meat ball ingredients and form into approximately 48 small meat balls. Brown them in a skillet using ¼ cup of margarine. For the sauce, remove meat balls from skillet and add margarine to drippings; blend in flour, then crushed garlic. Add tomato paste, beef concentrate and bouillon water. Add bitters. Stir sauce over low heat until it thickens. Put meat balls back in sauce. Just before serving, add sour cream. Boil noodles according to directions on package. Add a little butter or margarine. Put meat balls over noodles or serve separately.

Makes 8 servings. May be prepared the day before. May be frozen without noodles. Add sour cream after thawing.

Mrs. Carson R. Reed, Jr.

MEAL IN A DISH

⅓ cup chopped onion
⅓ cup chopped green pepper
1 pound hamburger
1 large can creamed corn
3 fresh tomatoes
1 package flat egg noodles
Butter
Salt and pepper

Make buttered bread tufts as follows: Melt a small amount of butter in skillet. Pull bread into small pieces 1" x 1" and toss until coated.

Brown onion and pepper in pan, add meat. Divide mixture and place half in casserole, season. Cover with layer of cooked noodles (½ total amount). Add layer of corn, then layer of sliced tomatoes, dot with butter. Add remainder of meat and noodles. Top with buttered bread tufts. Cover and bake in moderate oven (325°) about 1 hour.

Mrs. Gene Scott

NATCHITOCHES MEAT PIES

Meat Filling:
- 1½ pounds pork
- 1½ pounds baby beef (have butcher grind pork and beef together twice)
- 1½ tablespoons flour
- 2 medium white onions, ground
- 4 buttons garlic, put through a press
- 1 teaspoon baking powder
- 2 tablespoons cold water (if needed)
- ⅔ cup chopped green shallot tops
- ¼ cup chopped parsley
- ¼ cup white part of shallots, chopped

Cook meat until mealy. Add flour, onions, garlic and baking powder. If sticky, add water. Add chopped green shallots, parsley and white part of shallots. Season highly with salt, red and black pepper. Cook until done, stirring often. Chill meat before placing on pastry rounds. Be sure that the same amount of meat and gravy goes into each pie.

Pastry:
- 4 cups flour, unsifted
- 2 teaspoons baking powder
- ¼ teaspoon salt
- ½ cup shortening, melted
- ¾ cup milk
- 2 whole eggs, beaten

Place flour, baking powder and salt in bowl. Cut in shortening with a teacup saucer. Add milk and eggs. Form dough into a ball. Roll out a portion of the dough on a lightly floured board. Cut into rounds the size of a saucer. Place a generous tablespoon full of the meat mixture on one side of the pastry round. Dampen pastry on pie edge. Fold pastry over meat and seal edges with a floured fork. Fry in deep hot shortening until golden brown.

Makes about 24 pies. To freeze: wrap pies individually or freeze until firm on cookie sheets, then place frozen pies in a plastic bag. To serve: let frozen pies defrost and fry in deep hot shortening until golden brown. These are a real treat for lunch with a green salad or for dinner with French-fried onion rings, a broccoli casserole and salad.

Mrs. C. Vernon Cloutier

HONG KONG HAMBURGER

- 2 tablespoons shortening
- 1 onion, chopped
- 1 pound ground beef
- 6 eggs, well beaten
- 1 teaspoon salt
- ¼ teaspoon pepper
- 1 No. 303 can bean sprouts, drained

Saute onion in melted shortening until transparent. Add beef and brown. Mix egg, salt, pepper and bean sprouts, then add to meat mixture. Pour into greased 9" x 13" baking pan and bake 20-25 minutes at 350°. Serve with soy sauce if desired. Children love it.

Makes 6-8 servings.

Mrs. Charles H. Lewis, Jr.

TATER-TOP CASSEROLE

- 2 tablespoons butter
- 1 medium onion, chopped
- 1 pound ground beef
- 1 tablespooon A-1 sauce
- 1 teaspoon salt
- 2 cups cooked green beans
- 1 can condensed tomato soup
- Mashed potatoes; 4-6 servings (either instant or leftover)

Saute onion in butter until tender but not brown. Add ground beef, A-1 steak sauce and salt. Brown lightly. Stir in soup and beans and pour the mixture into a 1½ quart casserole. Top with mounds of mashed potatoes and bake in a moderate (350°) oven for 25 minutes or until potatoes begin to brown.

Serves 6.

Mrs. R. D. Fletcher

CHINESE BEEF

- ½ cup oleo
- Small bell pepper, chopped
- 3 stalks celery, chopped
- 1 large onion, chopped
- 1 2-ounce can mushrooms (save liquid)
- 1 pound lean ground beef
- 1 small chopped garlic clove
- 3 tablespoons soy sauce
- Salt and pepper
- 2 cups cooked rice
- 2 eggs, beaten well
- 1 peeled and quartered tomato
- ½ head thinly sliced lettuce

Saute until tender in oleo, bell pepper, celery, onion. Add mushrooms, saving liquid, then add beef; brown with garlic clove. Add soy sauce, mushroom liquid, salt and pepper. Mix with rice and eggs. Cook in oven until bubbling; top with lettuce and tomato. Replace in oven until lettuce wilts and tomato shrivels. Bake at 350° for 30 minutes.

Serves 4.

Mrs. Robert King

HAMBURGER PATTIES WITH TOMATO-CHEESE TOP

- 1½ pounds ground beef
- ½ cup soft bread crumbs
- ¾ teaspoon seasoning salt
- ½ teaspoon pepper
- 1 beaten egg
- Prepared mustard
- 6 slices onion
- 6 slices American cheese
- 1 can tomato soup

Combine first 5 ingredients and shape into 6 patties. Place in shallow baking dish. Spread each pattie with mustard, then onion slice with cheese on top. Pour tomato soup over all. Bake 40 minutes at 350-400°.

Serves 6.

Mrs. Robert A. Stacy, Jr.

TALLERINI

1½-2 pounds ground round steak
2 tablespoons salad oil
1 large onion, chopped
2 cloves garlic, minced
1 can enchilada sauce
1 can tomato paste
1 can cream style corn
1 can whole pitted ripe olives (optional)
1 pound American or Cheddar cheese, cubed
1 large or 2 small (6-ounce) packages egg noodles
Dash chili powder, Tabasco or red pepper
Salt and pepper to taste

Lightly brown meat in oil. Add onion and garlic; cook until wilted, stirring constantly. Add sauce, paste and uncooked noodles. Lower heat, cover and cook slowly until noodles are tender (about 10 minutes). If necessary, add olive juice and small amount of water to keep from getting too dry. Turn heat off, add corn, cheese, olives, chili powder, Tabasco, or red pepper, salt and pepper to taste. Place in casserole and reheat at 300°. Easily frozen.

Mrs. Gerald LeVan
Mrs. John Davis

BEEF BALLS PAR EXCELLENCE

Beef Balls:
1 pound ground beef
½ cup crushed corn flakes
¼ cup minced onions
¼ cup milk
1 teaspoon salt
½ teaspoon monosodium glutamate
¼ teaspoon pepper
⅓ cup flour
3 tablespoons fat

Sauce:
⅓ cup butter
½ pound mushrooms or 1 large can, drained
1 can cream of celery soup
2 tablespoons milk
1 teaspoon Worcestershire sauce
1 cup sour cream

Beef Balls: Mix all ingredients together except flour and fat. Shape into 1" balls. Coat with flour. Brown in fat over medium heat. Drain.

Sauce: Cook mushrooms in butter until brown. Blend remaining ingredients (except sour cream) and add to skillet and heat. Remove from heat and add sour cream in small amounts. Heat thoroughly and pour in chafing dish. Dip with Melba toast or serve with buttered noodles if used for dinner dish.

Mrs. Leo A. Bird

HARVEST FESTIVAL STEW

2 onions, chopped
1 green pepper, chopped
3 tablespoons butter
2 pounds beef, cut in 1" cubes
Seasoned flour (flour, salt and pepper)
3 cups beef bouillon
2 dashes Tabasco
1 teaspoon paprika
1 teaspoon salt
¼ teaspoon pepper
1 cup sour cream
1½ cups carrots
1½ cups green beans
1 cup potatoes, cubed
Dumpling batter
3 teaspoons caraway seeds

Saute beef cubes sprinkled with seasoned flour in 3 tablespoons butter along with onions and green pepper. Add beef bouillon, Tabasco, paprika, salt and pepper. Cover and simmer 1½ hours. Then, lower heat and add sour cream. Add carrots, green beans and potatoes. Cook 25 minutes. Make a dumpling batter (use box recipe). Add caraway seeds to batter and spoon on top of stew. Cover and cook over low heat 25 to 30 minutes.

Serves 8. Mrs. R. F. Kayser, Jr.

TEXAS BEEF STEW

½ cup water
½ cup vinegar
¼ cup catsup
1 teaspoon chili powder
2 bay leaves
½ teaspoon black pepper
1 tablespoon Worcestershire sauce
1 minced garlic clove
2 large onions
2 teaspoons salt
2 pounds round steak cut into 1" strips

Mix the above ingredients to form a marinade for the meat. Let meat stand in marinade for several hours. Turn frequently. Put meat and marinade in Dutch oven. Cover and simmer very slowly for about 1½ hours, or until meat is tender.

Serves 4. Mrs. T. Haller Jackson, Jr.

SHISH KEBOB

Allow about ¾ pound of meat per person. Steak quality beef may be used, but I prefer a combination of loin of pork and leg of lamb. Have the butcher bone the meat. Cut in cubes of about 2 inches. Place on skewers as follows: a cube of meat, a piece of onion, a section of tomato, meat, onion, green pepper and so on until the skewers are full. Season very heavily with garlic, salt, thyme, pepper and oregano. If you use what you think is far too much salt, they will be about right as during the broiling over charcoal, much of the salt drips away. Use very firm, barely ripe tomatoes. Cut onions in eighths and separate layers before placing on skewers. Serve with tossed salad with Greek olives and Greek feta cheese. Add a rice pilaf and your meal is complete.

Mrs. George Caragonne, Houston, Texas

BURGUNDY BEEF

5 pounds heavy chuck, cut in 2" cubes
10 small white onions, sliced thin
2 tablespoons flour
Marjoram
Thyme
Tarragon
Salt
Pepper
Beef bouillon (1 cup made with 2 bouillon cubes)
1 cup dry red wine
1 pound fresh mushrooms, sliced

Brown meat in small amount of fat that has been rendered from fat trimmed from meat. Brown in heavy Dutch oven over high heat until each piece is almost black on all sides. Remove to lid of pan as pieces brown. When all meat is well browned, simmer sliced onions in remaining fat until soft. Return meat to Dutch oven and sprinkle all with flour and a good dash of the spices. Add wine and bouillon, stir well, cover and simmer slowly for 3-4 hours. Don't boil. More wine and bouillon may be added. Add sliced mushrooms 1 to 2 hours before done, depending on size and freshness. The result should be a very dark brown. This may be made the day before and freezes well.

Serves 6-8. Mrs. Robert K. Butcher

ROLLED ROUND STEAK

2 round steaks, totaling 3 pounds, or 1 large steak
Salt, pepper, paprika
¼ pound sliced mushrooms
2 onions, thinly sliced
Bread crumbs
½ cup melted butter or bacon drippings
1 tablespoon water
1 egg
1 garlic clove, crushed
Stuffed green olives
¼ cup butter or bacon drippings
1 cup dry red wine

Pound round steak until thin. Rub in salt, pepper, paprika. Overlap steaks on meat board, making one large steak. Spread steaks with sliced mushrooms, and cover with thinly sliced onions. Sprinkle fine bread crumbs over all. Combine melted butter or bacon drippings, boiling water, egg, garlic. Dribble this over bread crumbs. On long side of steak arrange a row of stuffed olives. Begin to roll the meat around the olives. Tie roll firmly; flour outside. In roaster, brown meat in butter or bacon drippings. Sprinkle lightly with salt, pepper and paprika. Add wine. Roast meat in 350° oven for about 2 hours. Serve hot or cold.

Serves 6. Mrs. Melvin F. Johnson

BEEF STEW SICILIAN

- 2 pounds lean beef, cut in ½" pieces
- 1 tablespoon butter
- 1 tablespoon olive oil
- 1 small red onion, sliced
- 2 cloves garlic, chopped
- 2 tablespoons diced bacon
- 1 cup claret wine
- 1 tablespoon tomato paste
- Pinch oregano
- Salt and pepper

Heat butter and olive oil and saute onion and garlic. When slightly brown, add bacon and cook for one minute. Put in beef and brown well on all sides. Add salt and pepper, a good pinch of oregano and claret wine. Simmer until wine is reduced to half and stir in tomato paste, adding enough water to cover the meat. Cover pot and simmer slowly until meat is tender and the sauce, thick and rich, 1 hour or more depending on quality of meat.

Mareom M. Giambra

GOURMET BEEF AND ARTICHOKES

- ½ stick oleo or butter
- 2 jars dried beef
- 2 pints sour cream
- 3 tablespoons flour
- 2 packages cooked frozen artichokes (or 2 cans)
- Dash Worcestershire sauce
- 3 tablespoons grated Parmesan cheese
- ½ cup dry white wine
- 1 medium can mushrooms
- Dash of pepper and Tabasco
- 2 packages English muffins, halved

Saute beef in butter and sprinkle with flour. Stir well, add sour cream. Milk may be added if mixture is too thick. Add other ingredients and serve over toasted English muffins. Very nice in chafing dish for brunch or luncheon.

Serves 6-8. Mrs. James Galbraith

BOILED BEEF WITH HORSERADISH SAUCE

- 2 pounds boneless beef stew (large chunks)
- 1 onion
- 2 carrots
- 2 stalks celery
- 3 sprigs parsley
- 2 teaspoons salt

Horseradish Sauce:

- ½ cup tomato catsup
- 2 teaspoons horseradish
- 1 teaspoon vinegar
- ¼ teaspoon salt

Mix and chill horseradish sauce until ready to use. Bring 1 quart water to boil. Add meat, vegetables, salt and fresh ground pepper to taste. Boil for 2 hours. Remove meat from water and serve with Horseradish Sauce.

Serves 6. Mrs. Lilbourn G. Morgan

STEAK ON THE ROCKS

1 rib-eye or club steak per person
Pepper
Salt
Melted butter
5 pounds charcoal for first 2 pounds of meat

Allow meat to come to room temperature before cooking. Sprinkle with fresh ground black pepper only. Prepare a glowing charcoal fire, using 5 pounds of charcoal for first 2 pounds of meat, ½ pound for each additional pound of meat after that. The object is to arrange the coals so that the meat is directly touching them. Put on steaks to be well-done first. Let flames come up around meat. A word of caution: it takes only a short time to cook meat this way. Put on medium and rare steaks when you turn over the well-done meat. Turn meat only once. The rare meat takes very little time, and should be turned after 1 minute. Remove steaks to a hot platter, spread with a little butter and salt to release sealed-in juices. Very good.

Harold K. Quinn

SAUERBRATEN

4-5 pound roast (I use eye of round)
2 cups vinegar
2 cups water
1 large onion, sliced
¼ cup sugar
2 teaspoons salt
10 peppercorns
3 whole cloves
2 bay leaves
1 lemon, cut into ¼ inch slices
2 to 3 tablespoons butter
For gravy:
¼ cup butter
¼ cup flour
3 cups liquid (reserved cooking liquid and enough marinade or hot water to equal 3 cups)
½ cup thick sour cream

Wipe meat and place in deep bowl. Combine vinegar, water, onion, sugar, salt, peppercorns, cloves, and bay leaves in saucepan and heat without boiling. Pour over meat. Cool and add lemon. Cover and set in refrigerator. Marinate for 4 days, turning once each day. Remove meat from marinade, drain and strain marinade. In heavy kettle with tight fitting cover melt 2-3 tablespoons butter over low heat. Brown meat slowly on all sides. Slowly add 2 cups reserved marinade. Bring liquid to boiling. Reduce heat, cover tightly and simmer 2½ to 3 hours or until tender. Add more marinade if necessary. Liquid should at all times be simmering, not boiling. Remove to warm platter. Pour cooking liquid from kettle and set aside for gravy.

For gravy: melt butter in kettle. Blend in and brown flour. Remove from heat and gradually add liquid. Return to heat, boil and cook rapidly, stirring constantly until thick. Remove from heat. With wire whisk, stir in sour cream, adding very small amounts at a time. Cook over low heat 3 to 5 minutes.

Serve with potato pancakes.

Mrs. Jerome Ferguson, Jr.

SUKIYAKI

2 tablespoons fat
2 or 3 pounds sirloin tip, cut paper thin
1 onion, diced
½ bottle soy sauce
1 large can mushrooms
Pepper
⅛ teaspoon nutmeg
2 cans water chestnuts
4 tomatoes, quartered
4 bell peppers, cut in rings
1 can bean sprouts

Brown meat and onions in fat. Add soy sauce, mushrooms, pepper, nutmeg, chestnuts and simmer an hour covered. Ten minutes before serving, turn heat up high. Add tomatoes, bell pepper, bean sprouts. Cover and cook 5-7 minutes and serve over rice. Be sure vegetables cook only a short time, to preserve crispness. This is the Japanese style.

Makes 6 servings. Mrs. Kenneth Williams

KOSHER CORNED BEEF

4 pounds brisket (stab with ice pick all over)
½ box pickling spices
3 cloves garlic
2 tablespoons saltpeter
6-7 tablespoons salt
Black and red pepper to taste (about 1 teaspoon black, ¼ teaspoon red)

Place brisket in deep dish. Make brine with all the other ingredients. Pour over meat. Add enough water to cover meat. Cover and place in refrigerator for 14 days or leave in cool place for 10 days. Remove from brine and boil in water until tender.

Mrs. Drew Liddell

BEST BEEF BRISKET

3 pounds fresh boneless beef brisket
1½ teaspoons salt
Dash pepper and paprika
1 bay leaf
3 medium onions
6 medium potatoes
½ teaspoon salt
Dash pepper

Trim excess fat from meat. Place in Dutch oven with tight fitting lid. Sprinkle with 1½ teaspoons salt, dash of pepper and paprika. Add bay leaf. Cut onions in thick slices and arrange over meat. (Do not add water.) Cover and bake in slow oven 3½ to 4½ hours until very tender. Last hour of baking, arrange potatoes, pared and halved, lengthwise around meat. Sprinkle potatoes with ½ teaspoon salt and dash of pepper; cover and continue to bake until done, turning and basting potatoes every 15 minutes. (If meat and potatoes need more browning, uncover last 30 minutes, turning and basting potatoes.) Skim off excess fat. Serve with juices or thickened gravy. To carve, cut across the grain, slanting knife slightly and making thin slices. Pass prepared horseradish.

Makes 9 servings. Mrs. Jerome H. Ferguson, Jr.

GRAVIED ROUND STEAK

2 pounds round steak ½" thick, cut into individual serving pieces
Salt to taste
Pepper to taste
Flour
2 onions
4 tablespoons parsley
1 teaspoon thyme
1 teaspoon salad herbs
1 teaspoon oregano

Salt, pepper, flour and brown meat. Place in layers in a heavy baking pan and cover each layer with chopped onions, parsley, oregano, thyme and salad herbs. Cover almost to top with liquid consisting of ⅔ wine and ⅓ water. Bake in a 300° oven, covered, for 3 hours.

Mrs. Roscoe Rector, Barksdale Air Force Base

BEEF STROGANOFF

3 tablespoons flour
1½ teaspoons salt
¼ teaspoon pepper
1 pound top round steak or sirloin steak (1" thick)
1 cut garlic clove
¼ cup butter
½ cup minced onion
¼ cup water
1 can cream of chicken soup
1 8-ounce can mushrooms
1 cup sour cream

Combine flour, salt and pepper. Rub meat with garlic. Pound flour into both sides of meat. Cut meat into bite-size pieces. Melt butter and brown meat in it. Add onion, saute until golden. Stir water into mixture. Add soup and mushrooms. Cook, uncovered, over very low heat for 1 to 1½ hours. Just before serving stir in sour cream. Good over rice or noodles.

Serves 4. If freezing, do not add sour cream until thawed and heated again.

Mrs. Francis S. Randall

CHUCK ROAST DELIGHT

3- or 4-pound chuck roast
Salt to season
Flour to coat
1 package dehydrated onion soup mix
Potatoes
Carrots

Salt, flour and sear roast. Place in ovenproof dish. Add 2 tablespoons water, 2 tablespoons oleo and sprinkle onion soup over it. Cover tightly with foil and bake 2 hours at 350°. During last 45 minutes of cooking, add precooked potatoes and carrots. Use canned small potatoes and canned whole carrot pieces, if desired. Thicken liquid for gravy.

Mrs. John W. Paylor, Jr.

EASY CHUCK POT ROAST

4 pound chuck roast
1 can cream of mushroom soup
1 package dried onion soup
¼ cup water
1 tablespoon Worcestershire sauce
Salt and pepper to taste

Place roast on foil strip large enough to wrap around the roast later, in roasting pan. Salt and pepper according to personal taste. In bowl to the side add water to mushroom soup and onion soup and beat until well blended. Add Worcestershire sauce. Pour this mixture over roast and wrap the roast well in the foil. Bake at 325° for 3 hours. It bastes itself and you have gravy, too.

Serves approximately 8.

Mrs. Dalton Pittman

POT ROAST — BARBECUE STYLE

½ cup finely chopped onion
½ cup finely chopped green pepper
2 finely crushed garlic cloves
½ cup red wine
1 8-ounce can tomato sauce
½ teaspoon paprika
½ cup vinegar (or a little more)
Pinch whole mixed pickling spices
Pot roast (or any inexpensive cut of roast)
2 tablespoons shortening or drippings
¼ cup tomato catsup
1 tablespoon Worcestershire sauce
1 teaspoon mustard

Combine onion, green pepper, garlic, red wine, tomato sauce, paprika vinegar and generous amount of pickling spices. Pour over meat and marinate in refrigerator at least overnight, turning the roast several times. Heat shortening in heavy skillet or Dutch oven. Remove meat from marinade. Brown on both sides in hot fat. Blend catsup, Worcestershire sauce and mustard into remaining marinade; pour over meat. Cover pan and simmer until meat is tender, about 2 to 2½ hours. Gravy may be thickened, if desired, with a little cornstarch mixed with water.

Mrs. Bob B. Slack

MARINADE FOR ROAST

2 cloves garlic
½ teaspoon cracked pepper
Dash cayenne pepper
⅛ teaspoon ground cloves
2 tablespoons wine vinegar
¼ cup olive oil or cooking oil

Mince garlic. Add dry seasonings and wine vinegar with garlic. Mix well and rub into meat. Place in shallow bowl and splash olive oil over meat. Turn meat to cover all sides. Cover and keep at room temperature for 2 hours. Cook on outdoor grill.

Mrs. J. Claiborne Cook

BEEF STROGANOFF

1½ pounds beef sirloin or 1½ pounds tender round steak, cut in thin strips or 1" cubes
6 tablespoons butter
2 tablespoons olive oil
2 onions, minced
1 8-ounce can mushrooms, drained
Dash Worcestershire sauce
1½ cups sour cream
Salt and freshly ground pepper
Chopped parsley
¼ cup dry sherry

Melt 4 tablespoons butter in heavy skillet. Add 1 tablespoon olive oil to keep butter from burning. Saute beef quickly, turning to brown evenly. Remove meat to hot platter to keep warm. Add remaining butter and olive oil to skillet. Add onions and mushrooms. Saute until onions are clear, not brown. Return beef to skillet and blend with onions and mushrooms. Add wine and Worcestershire sauce. Cook over very low heat about 5 or 10 minutes. Add sour cream last. Do not let boil after cream is added or it will curdle. Stir sauce until well blended and heat thoroughly. Season with salt and pepper. Serve over rice topped with chopped parsley.

Serves 4 generously. Mrs. John C. Miles

MARINADE FOR 6-8 POUND BRISKET ROAST

2 cups burgundy, heated with the following:
2 tablespoons salt
1 tablespoon whole cracked black pepper
1 bay leaf
1 large garlic clove
2 tablespoons mixed pickling spices
1 tablespoon celery seed
2 tablespoons sugar
½ teaspoon cloves
1 teaspoon curry powder
Tie together: 1 large carrot, 1 piece celery, 2 or 3 green onions and parsley
Onions

Cover roast with sliced onions held on with tooth picks. Let roast soak in marinade for several days, turning once or twice daily. Drain and dry the roast, brown well in its own fat, return the marinade to the pan, adding one or two cups of water or stock and cook like a pot roast 5-6 hours on top of stove. Toward the end when done, remove roast and cook a short time in oven to crisp. Drain liquid and make gravy from it, after skimming off fat. Serve with noodles or potato pancakes. One or two knuckle bones cooked along with the roast will make the liquid jell when cooled. The fat should be skimmed off when jelled.

Mrs. Melvin F. Johnson

YORKSHIRE PUDDING

(To be served with roast beef)

- ⅞ cup flour
- ½ cup milk
- 2 eggs
- ½ cup water
- Roast drippings

Sift flour into bowl; beat in milk. Beat eggs separately until fluffy, then stir into the flour mixture. Add water. Beat well. Let stand 1 hour, then beat again. Pour hot drippings from roast into a 10" x 10" pan (3 or 4 tablespoons of drippings). Heat pan. Pour in pudding mixture and bake at 400° for 20 minutes. Reduce heat and bake 10 more minutes at 350°.

Mrs. Thomas B. Wilson

BARBECUED BEEF BUNS

Combine:
- 4 cups 2" strips cooked beef (leftover roast)
- ¼ cup vinegar
- 1½ cups water
- ¼ cup sugar
- 4 teaspoons prepared mustard
- ¼ teaspoon pepper
- 1 tablespoon salt
- ¼ teaspoon cayenne pepper
- 2 thick slices lemon
- ½ cup butter or margarine

Simmer above mixture uncovered 20 minutes. Then add:

- 1 cup catsup or chili sauce
- 3 tablespoons Worcestershire sauce

Simmer 10 minutes and serve on toasted buns.

Makes 12-15 servings and freezes well.

Mrs. Douglas Attaway

DEVILED CORNED BEEF BUNS

- 4 hot dog buns
- ½ cup shredded corned beef
- ½ cup grated American cheese
- ⅓ cup chopped stuffed olives
- ¼ cup catsup
- 2 tablespoons minced onion
- 1 tablespoon Worcestershire
- 1 teaspoon minced bell pepper (optional)

Split buns, remove soft centers. Combine all other ingredients and fill buns. Wrap each roll in waxed paper; twist ends. Put in paper bag and heat in 325° oven for 20 minutes.

Serves 4.

Mrs. W. E. Wilson

REUBEN SANDWICH

Boiled corned beef
Good rye bread
Butter
Sauerkraut
Thousand Island dressing
Swiss cheese

Slice and butter the bread. Place beef on bread. Then place some well-drained sauerkraut and Thousand Island dressing on it. Top with Swiss cheese and broil. Suggestion: serve with beer!

Mrs. William Garland, Barksdale Air Force Base

CALAVISITAS

1 pound zucchini squash
¾ pound cubed beef
¼ pound cubed pork (very good with all pork)
1 onion, chopped
1 clove garlic, crushed
3 tablespoons olive oil
2 chopped roasted green chilies
1 large tomato, peeled and chopped
2 or 3 ears of corn, cut from cob
Salt and pepper to taste

Brown meat, onion and garlic in oil. When almost done add squash, tomato, corn, chilies, salt and pepper. Cover and simmer slowly until corn is tender (about 15 minutes).

Serves 4. Mrs. R. F. Kayser, Jr.

JAIL HOUSE CHILI

3 pounds diced lean beef
¼ cup liquid shortening
1 quart water
8 chili pods or 6 tablespoons chili powder
3 teaspoons salt
5 cloves finely chopped garlic
1 teaspoon ground cumin
1 teaspoon marjoram
1 teaspoon red pepper
1 tablespoon sugar
3 tablespoons paprika
To thicken:
3 tablespoons flour
6 tablespoons corn meal
1 cup water

Heat oil in large pot, add meat and sear over high heat, stir constantly until meat is gray but not brown. Add water and cover, cooking over low fire for 1½ to 2 hours. Add remaining ingredients, except thickening, and cook at a bubbling simmer for 30 minutes. Add thickening which has been previously mixed with 1 cup of water. Cook about 5 more minutes and stir to prevent sticking. More water may be added for desired consistency. If meat is very fat, skim off fat before adding thickening. This is rather hot chili. For milder flavor, cut the chili powder and red pepper in half but add 2 more tablespoons paprika for color.

Serves 6. The Editors

PEDERNALES RIVER CHILI

4 pounds chili meat
1 large onion, chopped
2 cloves garlic, chopped
1 teaspoon ground oregano
1 teaspoon comino seed
2 tablespoons chili powder
2 cans Ro-tel tomatoes
Salt to taste
2 cups hot water

Put chili meat, onions, and garlic in large heavy boiler or skillet. Sear until light colored. Add oregano, comino, chili powder, tomatoes and hot water. Bring to a boil, lower heat and simmer about 1 hour. Skim fat off as it cooks out.

Serves 8. Mrs. Lyndon B. Johnson, LBJ Ranch, Texas

CHILI

2 pounds lean ground beef
2 large onions
2 pods garlic
Salt and pepper
1 large can tomatoes
1 can tomato sauce (Spanish style)
3 to 5 tablespoons chili powder to taste
1 tablespoon cumin
2 cans kidney beans or pinto beans

Brown meat, add chopped onions, crushed garlic, salt and pepper and cook in covered skillet for about an hour. When done, pour into colander; with paper towels, press out all fat. Mix tomatoes, tomato sauce, chili powder and cumin in deep pot; add meat mixture. Combine thoroughly, add beans. (If canned beans are used, drain well before adding.) Mix well, cover and cook very slowly for about 3 hours, stirring occasionally.

Serves 4. Mrs. Phil Foster

QUICK CHILI PIE

1 can chili
1 small can corn
1 medium onion
Bag of corn chips
4 ounces Cheddar cheese, sharp

Line bottom of pan with corn chips. Mix corn, chili and chopped onion together. Pour ½ of this over chips. Add ½ of the grated cheese, add rest of chili, corn and onions. Cover the top with chips and rest of the cheese. Cook at 350° for 20-30 minutes.

Mrs. Paul Wear

HOT TAMALE PIE

1 cup corn meal
4 cups boiling water
½ teaspoon salt
¼ cup bacon drippings
1 pound ground round steak
½ pound ground pork
1 large onion, chopped
1 clove garlic, minced
2 tablespoons chili powder
1 green pepper, chopped
1 teaspoon salt
½ teaspoon pepper
1 can tomatoes or 1 can tomato sauce

Make a mush by adding corn meal to boiling water, add salt. Spread mush over bottom of greased casserole. Saute meat, onion, garlic, green pepper in bacon drippings. Add seasoning and canned tomatoes. Allow to simmer a few minutes. Pour meat mixture over mush layer in casserole. Pour remainder of mush on top. Place in moderate oven of 350° to bake for 1 hour.

Will make 6 servings. Mrs. Grady L. Nelson

MEXICAN CASSEROLE

2 No. 2 cans chili (no beans)
1 package frozen tortillas, thawed
1 large onion, chopped
¼ pound mild Cheddar cheese, may use more if desired

Line bottom of 8" x 10" casserole (which has been greased) with overlapping strips of tortillas. Heat chili (with no water) in saucepan. Pour ½ of chili over tortillas, then sprinkle half of onions and grated cheese over chili. Repeat this process, beginning with tortillas, chili, onion and top with remaining cheese. Pour about ¼ cup of water around the edges to prevent drying out. Cook at 325° 45 minutes to 1 hour. May be prepared early in the day.

Serves 4. Mrs. Robert Potts

SWEET 'N SOUR MEAT BALLS

1 pound ground beef
½ cup prepared bread crumbs
1 teaspoon salt
½ teaspoon pepper
1 egg, beaten
¼ cup milk

Sauce:
½ cup chopped onion
8 tablespoons sugar
¼ teaspoon pepper
½ cup catsup
6 tablespoons vinegar
2 teaspoons Worcestershire sauce
1 cup water

Mix beef, bread crumbs, salt, pepper, egg and milk. Form into small balls and brown in skillet in oil to cover the bottom of the skillet. Drop the brown meat balls in the hot sauce which has been made ahead. Simmer on top of the stove until the sauce is thick and clear and the meat balls are tender. Stir often. Serve with rice, creamed potatoes or buttered noodles.

Serves 6. Mrs. John B. Entrikin

LIVER AND ONIONS

2 pounds calf liver, sliced approximately ¼ inch thick, dredged in seasoned flour

Brown quickly over medium flame in 3 tablespoons (or enough to cover bottom of skillet) bacon fat. Set browned liver aside. Add 2 tablespoons flour to pan drippings. Stir while roux browns. Add:

1 large onion, sliced
1 bell pepper, thinly ringed
½ teaspoon dried parsley
2 cups hot water
2 tablespoons Worcestershire sauce
2 tablespoons catsup
Salt and pepper to taste
1 bay leaf
1 dash Tabasco (optional)

Push vegetable rings to one side of skillet. Slip liver into gravy. Rearrange vegetable rings. Cover and cook 30 to 45 minutes (depending on tenderness of liver) over slow fire. Remove bay leaf before serving. Serve with grits.

Serves 6.

Mrs. James R. Alexander

MEAT BALLS AND SPAGHETTI

(A very old Italian recipe)

1½ pounds ground chuck
1 cup Italian grated cheese
8 small crackers (soaked in water and squeezed)
3 large eggs
2 teaspoons salt
1 teaspoon pepper
2 dashes Tabasco
1 large bunch green onions
2 large cloves garlic, minced
1 cup parsley, chopped fine
½ cup olive oil
2 8-ounce cans tomato puree
2 pints water
1 teaspoon salt
½ teaspoon red pepper
1 teaspoon oregano

Combine first seven ingredients. Make into small meat balls — about 1½ inches in diameter. Brown meat balls and onions in olive oil. Remove meat; add tomato puree and water. Add garlic and seasonings to taste. Cook one hour or until reduced to about one half. Add meat balls. Simmer 1 hour. Serve over cooked, drained and buttered spaghetti. Pass additional cheese.

Mrs. James R. Alexander

MEAT BALLS

- ½ pound heavy lean beef
- ¼ pound veal
- ¼ pound lean pork
- 2 tablespoons chopped onions, browned in 1 tablespoon butter
- 1 small garlic clove, put through press
- 1 egg, beaten
- ½ cup whipped cream, or sour cream
- 1½ tablespoons sugar
- 1 pinch allspice
- Salt, fresh ground pepper, cayenne
- Worcestershire sauce
- 2 tablespoons butter

Grind together first three ingredients (quite fine). Mix well all ingredients and make in small balls. Saute in 2 tablespoons butter very slowly over medium heat. Do not disturb. After 20 minutes set in medium oven (325°) for another 20 minutes. Add a little cream to make a thin gravy and add chopped dill.

Makes 6 servings.

Mrs. Melvin F. Johnson

SPAGHETTI

- 2 pounds ground top round (ground twice)
- ¼ pound butter
- 2 large cans tomatoes
- 3 cans Italian tomato paste
- 3 cans water (paste cans)
- 6 medium size onions, chopped
- 1 small bunch parsley
- 4 buds garlic, chopped fine
- 1 or 2 cans mushrooms
- 2 bell peppers, chopped
- 1 pound sharp grated cheese
- Seasoning to taste:
- Salt
- Black pepper
- Red pepper and/or Tabasco
- 1 tablespoon Worcestershire sauce
- 1 teaspoon mustard
- Grated peel of 1 lemon

Brown meat and onions in butter. Add chopped parsley, tomatoes and tomato paste, water, chopped pepper and garlic. Cook 1 hour, making thick sauce, adding mushrooms, cheese, lemon rind and seasonings during the last 15 minutes. This recipe makes a good "Friday" spaghetti by omitting the meat and adding a half pound or more of grated cheese, 1 more chopped green pepper and doubling the mushrooms.

Serves 10-12.

Mrs. Arthur Carmody, Jr.

MORE

1½ pounds ground beef
½ pound pork sausage
¼ cup diced onions
1 pint tomatoes, canned or fresh
1 small can Spanish style tomato sauce
½ teaspoon salt
½ teaspoon Accent
⅛ teaspoon pepper
1 tablespoon dried parsley
1 teaspoon celery seed
1 cup pitted ripe olives
½ cup chopped mushrooms
⅛ teaspoon oregano
⅔ pound spaghetti, cooked until tender in 4 quarts salted water
½ pound Cheddar cheese, grated

Brown beef, sausage and onions in frying pan. Add remaining ingredients, except for spaghetti and cheese, and simmer slowly 15 minutes. Combine with the spaghetti, mix well, and pour into casserole. Cover with grated cheese and bake at 350° until cheese melts and ingredients in dish are thoroughly heated.

Makes 8-10 servings.

Mrs. T. O. Perry

SPAGHETTI AND MEAT BALLS

For Sauce:
2 tablespoons olive oil
2 onions, chopped
2 cloves minced garlic
2 No. 303 cans tomatoes
1 cup water
2 leaves basil
½ teaspoon thyme
2½ teaspoons salt
¼ teaspoon pepper
¼ teaspoon crushed red pepper
1 6-ounce can tomato paste

For Meat Balls:
½ pound hamburger
½ pound ground pork
2 onions, minced
1 clove garlic, minced
¼ cup chopped parsley
½ cup bread crumbs
1 egg
2 teaspoons salt
½ teaspoon pepper
2 tablespoons olive oil

For sauce, cook onions and garlic in oil until yellow; add tomatoes and simmer uncovered for 20 minutes. Add water, parsley, seasonings and paste and bring to a boil. Add meat balls, cover and simmer for at least 2 hours. Add more seasoning if desired.

For meat balls, combine all ingredients except oil and mix thoroughly. Add a little water if it seems too dry. Shape into small balls and brown slowly in hot oil. Serve over hot drained spaghetti and sprinkle with cheese.

Makes 6 good sized servings. Freezes well, and since it takes time to prepare, I double or triple amounts and freeze the rest.

Mrs. Thomas E. Stagg

JOHNNY BIZETTI

1 16-ounce package noodles
2 large onions, diced finely
1 green bell pepper, chopped
2 pounds ground chuck
2 cans tomato soup
1 large can whole kernel corn
1 medium can large sliced mushrooms
1 small bottle stuffed green olives
2 cups (1 pound) grated sharp cheese
1 package slivered almonds

Saute onions and green pepper. Add and brown meat. Boil and drain noodles. Mix all ingredients, saving part of the cheese and all of the almonds to sprinkle on top. Salt and pepper to taste. Put in greased casserole dish and heat. Bake at 350° about 1 hour.

Makes about 8 servings. May be frozen before cooking.

Mrs. Michael W. Eiser

LASAGNE

Meat Sauce:
1 pound ground meat
1 pound Italian sausage
1 clove garlic, minced
1 tablespoon whole basil
1 teaspoon salt
1 onion, chopped
1 1-pound can (2 cups) tomatoes
2 6-ounce cans (1⅓ cups) tomato paste
Worcestershire sauce
Seasoned salt
Pepper

Brown meat slowly; spoon off fat. Add remaining ingredients. Simmer uncovered ½ hour. Stir now and then.

Lasagne: Cook 10 ounces green spinach noodles in large amount boiling salted water. This may take 15 to 20 minutes. Drain; rinse in cold water.

Cheese Filling:
3 cups fresh ricotta or creamy cottage cheese
½ cup grated Parmesan or Romano cheese
2 tablespoons parsley flakes
2 beaten eggs
1½ teaspoons salt
½ teaspoon pepper
1 pound Mozzarella cheese, shredded

Mix above ingredients in a bowl.

Place cooked noodles in a 13" x 9" x 2" baking dish; then cheese filling; then meat sauce. Repeat layers. Bake in moderate oven (375°) 30 minutes. Before serving, let stand 10 minutes — filling will set slightly.

Makes 12 generous servings. Any left over may be frozen. If left in icebox, it is better the second day. May be prepared and placed in refrigerator day before and cooked before serving. Takes only about 45 minutes to put it all together, cooking sauce and noodles included.

Mrs. Ralph F. Pullen

LASAGNA

For Sauce:
¼ cup olive or salad oil
2 medium size onions, chopped
2 cloves garlic, minced
2 pounds ground beef
3 No. 2 cans tomatoes (about 7 cups)
2 6-ounce cans tomato paste
½ cup water
½ cup chopped celery (optional)
¼ cup chopped parsley or flakes
1½ tablespoons salt
2 teaspoons sugar
¼ teaspoon pepper
2 bay leaves
1 teaspoon dried basil

Heat oil in large kettle. Add onions and garlic, saute five minutes. Add ground beef, saute until brown, breaking up meat as it cooks. Stir in remaining ingredients. Bring mixture to a boil, reduce heat and simmer 3 hours, stirring occasionally. Remove bay leaves, skim off fat, or let cool and remove fat.

1 pound lasagna noodles
1 tablespoon salad or olive oil
5 cups sauce
2 cups (1 pound) cottage cheese or ricotta cheese
2 8-ounce packages Mozzarella cheese, thinly sliced
½ cup Romano or Parmesan cheese, grated

Lightly oil baking dish (13" x 9" x 2" or a smaller and deeper dish). Boil noodles, stirring frequently to prevent sticking, about 15 minutes or until almost tender. Drain and cover with cold water while filling baking dish. Line bottom of dish with single layer of noodles, spoon over ¼ of sauce and cottage or ricotta cheese, top with ¼ of Mozzarella and Parmesan cheese, repeat to make 4 layers ending with cheese on top. Bake at 350° for 30 minutes.

Serves 8 very generously.

The sauce recipe above makes 2 times the amount needed for amount of noodles, etc. given here. So to serve 15, make the 10 cups of sauce and double the noodle part, i.e., use 2 pounds noodles; also double cheese. Sauce may be made a day ahead of time.

Mrs. Thomas B. Wilson

HAWAIIAN PILAF

1 pound pork sausage
½ bell pepper, chopped
2 packages dry noodle soup
1 cup uncooked rice
5 cups boiling water
½ cup blanched almonds
1 onion, chopped
2 cups celery, diced

Fry sausage, add onions, celery, pepper and other ingredients. Mix and bake 50 to 60 minutes uncovered in 375° oven.

Mrs. R. O. Smith

PILAF

1 pound ground meat
2 tablespoons hot grease
1 large onion
1 green pepper
1 or 2 cloves garlic
1 cup chopped celery
1 can tomatoes
1 cup uncooked rice
1 can mushrooms and juice

Brown meat in hot grease. Add chopped onion and green pepper and brown. Then add chopped garlic, celery, tomatoes, rice, mushrooms and juice. Season mixture with salt and pepper and cover skillet with a tight lid. Cook on high heat until mixture begins to steam. Remove cover and cook in moderate oven (350-400°) for one hour.

Serves 6. This pilaf may be prepared in advance. Take from skillet and place in casserole in the refrigerator and reheat.

Mrs. Claude Cunningham

WALTER'S ITALIAN PIZZA

1 cake yeast
2 tablespoons lukewarm water
1 cup boiling water
2 tablespoons shortening
3 cups flour
1½ teaspoons salt
Yellow corn meal

Filling:
Olive oil
½ cup grated Parmesan cheese
¾ pound diced Mozzarella cheese
2 large cans Italian style peeled tomatoes, drained
3 large cloves garlic
2 teaspoons oregano
2 tablespoons olive oil
2 pounds Italian sausage

Dissolve yeast in lukewarm water. Pour boiling water over shortening and salt. Cool to lukewarm; add yeast; add half of flour and beat. Add remainder of flour; beat smooth. Divide dough in half and roll on a well floured board into large circles. With a pastry brush, brush two 14" pizza pans with olive oil and sprinkle with yellow corn meal. Pinch edge of dough around edge of each pan. Brush dough with olive oil. Partially cook Italian sausage and remove from cases. Sprinkle dough with Parmesan cheese; arrange diced Mozzarella on top. Cover with tomatoes mixed with garlic (run through garlic press), salt and pepper. Sprinkle with oregano. Drizzle on 2 tablespoons olive oil. Sprinkle with pieces of sausage. Bake in hot oven (450°) until crust is brown.

Yields 2 pans — 8 slices. This may be made in the morning and cooked late in afternoon before serving. May be frozen. Keeps indefinitely.

Mrs. Hugh C. Ilgenfritz

SPANISH RICE

¼ cup salad oil or shortening
1 cup raw rice (plus 1 cup hot water and 1 teaspoon salt)

Sauce:
2 tablespoons salad oil
1 clove garlic, crushed
1 pound ground beef
1 large can tomatoes (plus 1 cup hot water)
¼ cup chopped onion
¼ cup chopped green pepper
2½ teaspoons chili powder
2 teaspoons salt
1 cup grated cheese

Heat oil in skillet; add rice, cook slowly until brown. Add 1 cup hot water and 1 teaspoon salt and let simmer. In another skillet, heat oil, add garlic and meat, and stir with fork until meat is broken up and thoroughly cooked. Add tomatoes, one cup hot water, onions, green pepper, chili powder and the rest of the salt. Cook 5 minutes longer and add to rice. Mix well and pour in a baking dish. Cover with cheese and bake 1 hour or until cheese is toasted (350°).

Serves 4 to 6. Mrs. John L. Rhea, Jr.

DAUBE GLACE

3 pound roast beef (less tender cut may be used)
2 tablespoons shortening
1 tablespoon salt
6 cups water
1 onion, chopped
1 cup celery, chopped
1 green pepper, chopped
2 bay leaves
4 sprigs parsley
1 tablespoon gelatin softened in ¼ cup cold water

Rub salt into roast and sear dark brown in shortening. When browned pour off all grease. Add water and onion, cover tightly and allow to boil slowly. After about an hour, add celery, green pepper and bay leaves. Continue cooking until meat is very tender and can be pulled apart with a fork. Add parsley, minced fine. Remove from heat and add gelatin to the liquid. Shred the meat into fine particles and mix with liquid. When the mixture is cool, pour into a mold and chill. Red pepper and Worcestershire sauce may be added if more seasoning is desired. Place in the refrigerator overnight. Unmold and slice with a very sharp knife.

I have made this daube and molded it in the sides of plastic egg cartons so that I could unmold as many as I needed, place on round crackers and serve as hors d'oeuvres. However served, I find this daube glace most successful when highly seasoned.

Serves 12. Mrs. Roger Gardner

DAUBE GLACE

- 2 pounds beef round with bone
- 4 calves' feet (fresh pig's feet may be used)
- 4 large onions
- 4 cloves garlic
- 1 teaspoon crushed thyme
- ½ stalk celery
- 2 tablespoons parsley
- 3 whole carrots
- 10 ounces claret wine
- 1 or more teaspoons salt
- ¾ teaspoon pepper
- ¼ teaspoon red pepper
- 2 bay leaves
- 2 packages gelatin
- 2 tablespoons lemon juice

Marinate daube overnight in refrigerator in wine mixed with seasonings. Next day place daube and marinade in large pot and cover with cold water. Let come to a quick boil, then reduce heat and simmer for 3 to 4 hours, or until bones can be removed from beef and calves' feet. Remove from heat, skim off fat. Cut carrots in fancy slices and place around sides and bottom of mold. Remove all bones, fat and gristle from meat. Put beef, whole or cut-up and meat from calves' feet into mold. Strain juice, add gelatin, dissolved in ½ cup water. Taste for sufficient seasonings. Add 2 tablespoons lemon juice. Pour liquid over meat in mold. Set in refrigerator to congeal, preferably overnight. Turn out on platter, decorated with lettuce leaves. Serve with homemade mayonnaise. Horseradish added to the mayonnaise is delicious. A good main meat dish for a buffet supper.

Makes 6 servings. Mrs. J. Edward Lytle

LEFTOVER HAM CASSEROLE

- 1 can string beans
- 2 cups diced ham
- 2 hard boiled eggs
- 2 tablespoons butter or oleo
- 2 tablespoons flour
- 1 cup milk
- 2 tablespoons chili sauce
- Dash curry powder
- Dash dry mustard
- Salt and red pepper to taste

In casserole put layer of drained string beans, layer diced ham, layer sliced hard boiled eggs. Repeat. Melt butter (or oleo) in saucepan over low heat, gradually blend in flour, slowly add cold milk, stirring constantly until mixture is thick and smooth. Remove from flame, add 2 heaping tablespoons chili sauce, curry powder, dry mustard. Taste. If you taste chili sauce or curry predominantly, add the lesser ingredient until neither flavor predominates, and you have acquired a new flavor. Pour sauce over ingredients in a casserole. Heat in 350° oven until hot and sauce is bubbling for 20 to 30 minutes.

Serves 4-6. Mrs. K. J. Heddons

TERIYAKI KEBAB

2" cubes beef, shrimp, lamb or chicken
Tomatoes
Potatoes
Onions
Stuffed olives

Marinade:
¾ cup canned pineapple juice
2 tablespoons soy sauce
2 tablespoons lemon juice
1 garlic clove

Marinate meat for 2 hours in above sauce. Place on skewers alternating with any of the following: tomatoes, parboiled potatoes, parboiled onions, stuffed olives and broil about 10 minutes, basting with marinade.

Mrs. Joe Warren, Midland, Texas

TENNESSEE OR VIRGINIA COUNTRY HAM

This is a recipe for cooking one of those delectable country hams. To glaze you need prepared mustard, pepper, brown sugar and cloves. Soak a 20- to 24-pound ham overnight in cold water. Next day scrub, trim, wipe dry and unjoint at first joint. Put into large kettle or roasting pan, flesh side up, with enough water to cover well. Bring water to a boil, then reduce heat and simmer 4 or 5 hours, or 20 minutes to each pound, until tender. Remove from fire and let it cool in the water it has been cooked in. Remove skin and trim off excess fat layers. Sprinkle this surface lightly with black pepper, cover with prepared mustard, then put a layer of brown sugar and stick with cloves. Bake until glaze is light brown (350°).

Note: If you like, it is also good when a clove of garlic, 2 bay leaves and a tablespoon of sherry are added to the kettle of water.

Mrs. Jack McLean

BAKED HAM WITH ORANGE SAUCE

1 8-10-pound ham
¼ cup brown sugar
1 tablespoon dry mustard
1 cup liquid honey
½ cup orange juice
Whole cloves

For uncooked ham place fat side up on rack in roasting pan. Bake in 325° oven 25 minutes per pound. Combine brown sugar, mustard, honey and orange juice and allow to stand several minutes. Remove rind one hour or more before total baking time. Score fat; insert a whole clove in each section. Pour sugar mixture over ham. Baste frequently with this mixture during last hour. Drain sauce from ham and chill. Remove solidified grease from top of the sauce. Heat before serving. Cooking time will naturally be greatly reduced with a precooked ham. This will perform wonders with a picnic ham or a whole Canadian bacon.

Mrs. T. O. Perry

HAM AND ASPARAGUS MORNAY

2 boxes frozen asparagus, cooked and drained
12 thin slices cooked ham
1½ cups chicken broth
¼ cup butter or oleo
3 tablespoons flour
½ teaspoon dry mustard
½ cup light cream
½ cup grated Parmesan cheese
1 egg yolk, beaten

Arrange 4 pieces asparagus on each slice of ham. Roll up, place in shallow pan and pour ½ cup chicken broth over all. Cover with foil and heat 15 minutes at 350°.

Sauce: Melt butter, stir in flour and mustard, slowly add 1 cup chicken broth and cream, stirring constantly until thick. Add egg yolk which has been mixed with a little of sauce first. Stir in cheese. Place hot ham rolls on serving platter and cover with sauce.

Mrs. Donald Laskey

HAM LOAF WITH MUSTARD APPLE SAUCE

Ham Loaf:
1 pound ground smoked ham
1 pound ground lean pork
3 cups Wheaties
2 eggs, beaten
1 cup milk
1 teaspoon salt
⅛ teaspoon pepper

Sauce:
Glass of apple jelly
Mustard to taste

Ham Loaf: Mix all ingredients thoroughly and pack into 9" x 5" x 3" loaf pan. Bake at 350° for 1½ hours.

Sauce: Combine apple jelly and mustard in blender at high speed. Serve with ham loaf.

Mrs. Clarence J. Edwards

AUNT LUCILLE'S HAM BEEF RICE LOAF

2½ cups ground beef
1½ cups ground ham
1 cup rice, cooked
1 No. 2 can tomatoes
2 teaspoons chili powder
1 teaspoon salt
1 teaspoon Worcestershire sauce
2 teaspoons onion juice

Combine ingredients using about ¾ of the tomatoes. (Save rest to baste with.) Form into a loaf. Bake in 325-350° oven 1½ hours. Baste often.

Makes 6-8 servings.

Mrs. Charles Beaird

JANE'S HAM LOAF

Loaf:
- 2 pounds raw smoked ham (or 1½ pounds ham and ½ pound pork)
- 1 cup bread crumbs
- 2 eggs
- 1 tablespoon chopped onion
- 1 tablespoon green pepper, chopped
- ½ cup catsup
- 1 teaspoon prepared mustard

Sauce:
- Tart jelly (quince, mayhaw. apple, etc.)
- Sharp brown mustard

Loaf: Have butcher grind ham and pork together. Combine all ingredients well, and shape into loaf in baking pan. Cook 45-60 minutes at 425°.

Sauce: Combine equal amounts of mustard and jelly. Strain. Heat for ham loaf. Keeps well and is good on any ham dish or sandwich.

Serves 6. This loaf is equally good hot or cold. Freezes well, either cooked or uncooked.

Mrs. Wesley E. Wheless, Jr.

ZIPPY MUSTARD SAUCE

- 1 cup dry mustard
- 1 cup vinegar
- 2 eggs
- 1 cup sugar
- 1 teaspoon salt
- 1 cup mayonnaise

Combine mustard and vinegar; let stand overnight. Beat eggs, add sugar and salt, mix with mustard preparation. Cook in top of double boiler until custard consistency. Allow to cool. Add mayonnaise and refrigerate.

Makes about 4 cups. Will keep indefinitely in refrigerator.

Dorothy Martin

SWEET SOUR SPARERIBS

- 5 pounds spareribs cut into small (3-inch) pieces
- 1 cup sugar
- 3 to 4 tablespoons soy sauce
- ¾ cup vinegar
- 5 tablespoons green ginger, chopped fine (substitute powdered ginger if necessary, using 1 tablespoon)
- 1 cup crushed pineapple
- Flour, oil, salt, pepper

Flour, salt and pepper spareribs. Brown very lightly in oil. Add green ginger toward end of browning of meat. Add sugar, vinegar, soy sauce. Simmer until tender — 2½ to 3 hours. Add pineapple the last hour. Serve with rice.

Serves 4 to 6.

Mrs. Harold S. Butcher

SWEET AND SOUR PORK

1½ pounds lean pork shoulder, cut in strips
2 tablespoons fat
¼ cup water
¼ cup brown sugar
2 tablespoons cornstarch
½ teaspoon soy sauce
½ teaspoon salt
¼ cup vinegar
Juice from pineapple
1 No. 2 can pineapple chunks, drained
¾ cup bell pepper strips
¼ cup thinly sliced onion
2 cans Chinese noodles

Brown pork slowly in hot fat, add water, cover, simmer until tender (about 1 hour). In saucepan, combine and cook over low heat, stirring constantly until thick, the following: brown sugar, cornstarch, soy sauce, salt, vinegar and pineapple juice. Pour it over hot cooked pork and let stand 10 minutes or longer. Then add pineapple chunks, bell pepper strips and sliced onion. Cook 2 or 3 minutes. Serve over noodles.

Mrs. Anne K. Herold

PORK CHOPS EN CASSEROLE

4 center cut pork chops (1-2 inches thick)
2 medium cooking apples
2-3 tablespoons brown sugar
½ pint sour cream
Salt and pepper to taste
Cooking oil

Salt and pepper chops. Brown in oil in skillet. Drain off fat. Remove and place in casserole. Core and halve apples. Place on each chop. Fill apple centers with brown sugar. Cover chops with sour cream (thin with milk if necessary). Cover casserole. Cook in 350° oven for 40-45 minutes.

Serves 4.

Mrs. Albert Hand

SWEET AND SOUR BUTTERFLY PORK CHOPS

4 butterfly pork chops
3 tablespoons soy sauce
3 tablespoons brown sugar
3 tablespoons wine vinegar
½ lemon, sliced
1 teaspoon ground ginger
1 clove garlic, crushed
½ teaspoon coarsely ground pepper

Combine soy sauce, brown sugar, vinegar, lemon, ginger, garlic and pepper in small skillet. Simmer until sugar melts. Put pork chops in flat pan and pour marinade over them with lemon slice on each one. Marinate 30 minutes to 1 hour. Remove chops from pan and brown in heavy skillet. Lower heat and pour marinade over chops. Add ¼ to ½ cup water. Cover and simmer slowly 30 to 45 minutes, adding water if necessary. Place a lemon slice on each chop while cooking.

Serves 4.

Mrs. R. F. Kayser, Jr.

ITALIAN STYLE STUFFED PORK ROAST

2 cups Italian seasoned bread crumbs
½ cup grated Parmesan or Romano cheese
2 hard boiled eggs, chopped
1 small fresh tomato, chopped fine
1 small fresh bell pepper, chopped
1 cup chopped celery
1 cup chopped onions
1 clove fresh garlic, minced (optional, to taste)
3 tablespoons olive oil
1 raw egg
1 3-pound pork loin (have butcher leave section in one piece and slice chops to bone but not through it — leaving an area between chops to stuff loin)

Saute onion, garlic, bell pepper and celery in oil until golden brown. Drain off excess oil. Mix bread crumbs in a bowl with cheese and eggs (at this time add chopped hard boiled eggs and the raw one). Salt and pepper to taste. Mix all the above into a soft dressing, adding a small amount of water to help hold the dressing together. In a skillet, using only enough oil to cover bottom, brown pork loin and allow to cool so it can be stuffed. Pack dressing firmly between each chop on the loin and cover top with more dressing. Bake at 350° in open pan in about ¼ inch of water for about 2 hours or until brown.

Mrs. Sam R. Fertitta

PORK AND MACARONI BAKE

1 pound ground pork
½ cup chopped onion
½ clove garlic, minced
2 tablespoons oil
1 8-ounce can tomato sauce
1 6-ounce can tomato paste
1 3-ounce can mushrooms with juice
½ teaspoon salt
⅛ teaspoon pepper
1 7-ounce package elbow macaroni, cooked
2 cups grated sharp cheese

Cook pork, onion and garlic in hot oil until onion is golden. Add tomato sauce, tomato paste, mushrooms and seasonings and simmer 15 minutes. Alternate layers of macaroni, cheese and meat in greased 2-quart casserole. Sprinkle top with cheese and bake in moderate oven (350°) for 45 minutes.

Serves 8. May be prepared in the morning of day of serving.

Mrs. Oliver Moore

STRAWBERRY PORK CHOPS

Pork chops, as many as you wish to serve
Lemons, sliced very thin
Soy sauce
Strawberry jam
Bacon grease
Flour and salt

Flour and salt chops. Brown them in a small amount of bacon grease on both sides. Put 1 tablespoon jam on each chop and 2 or 3 slices lemon on top of jam. Put 1 tablespoon soy sauce on each chop and cover. Simmer on low heat.

Mrs. N. E. Liles

BARBECUED PORK CHOPS

8 or 10 pork chops
2 onions, sliced
½ cup catsup
1 cup water
1½ teaspoons salt
¼ teaspoon Tabasco

Line a heavy skillet with foil and cover with a layer of pork chops. Place a slice of onion on each chop. Combine catsup, water, salt and Tabasco and pour half of this mixture over chops. Place another layer of chops and onion slices in skillet and pour remaining sauce over all. Cover and seal with ends of foil and bake at 350° for 2 hours. Uncover for additional 15 to 20 minutes to brown. To serve, lift each chop carefully with spatula to keep whole. Garnish with parsley.

Mrs. Ray Barlow

STUFFED CABBAGE ROLLS

2 small onions, chopped
1 pound hamburger or ground lamb
¾ teaspoon salt
½ cup uncooked rice
1 4-5 pound cabbage
2 tablespoons butter
Dash of cinnamon if lamb is used
Sauce:
3 eggs, separated
½ teaspoon salt
½ cup lemon juice
Hot liquid from meat rolls

Saute onion in butter until soft. Add meat, rice and seasoning and remove from fire. It is not necessary to brown meat. Boil cabbage until tender. Drain. Separate the leaves and if large, remove center vein and cut in 3 x 4 inch pieces. Place a tablespoon of meat mixture on leaf and roll up, tucking in the ends. Place the cabbage rolls in the bottom of a heavy kettle and cover with boiling water. Weight down the rolls with a plate to prevent their moving as they cook. Cover and simmer until rice is tender, about 30 minutes. Remove to a platter and pour the lemon-egg sauce over them.

Sauce: Beat egg whites until stiff. Continue beating and add egg yolks. Still beating, add lemon juice and salt. Finally, very slowly add juice from the meat. The sauce will be light and fluffy, much like a Hollandaise.

George Caragonne, Houston, Texas

CURRIED LAMB

- 2 pounds lean lamb, shoulder or leg, cut into ½-inch cubes
- 2 medium onions, chopped
- 1 clove garlic, minced
- ½ cup butter
- ¼ cup flour
- 4 small apples, chopped
- ½ cup seedless raisins
- 3 tablespoons curry powder
- 1 tablespoon salt
- ½ teaspoon pepper
- ½ teaspoon powdered ginger
- 1 tablespoon Worcestershire sauce
- 2 cups water

Saute onions and garlic in butter until lightly browned; add flour and meat, stirring constantly. Add apples, curry powder, raisins and water and simmer for 5 minutes. Add seasonings, reduce heat, cover and cook 1 hour or until tender. Toward end of cooking time, mushrooms, strips of carrots or slices of bell pepper may be added. Serve over rice. Use chutney, grated coconut, finely chopped hard boiled eggs, bacon and chopped nuts as condiments.

Mrs. James C. Templeton

STUFFED BONED LEG OF LAMB

- 5½-pound leg of lamb (see below)
- 2 cloves garlic
- ¾ teaspoon salt
- ¼ teaspoon pepper
- Bouquet garni for lamb

Stuffing:

- 3 tablespoons butter or margarine
- ¼ cup chopped onion
- ¼ cup chopped celery
- 2 tablespoons chopped green pepper
- ¼ cup canned chopped mushrooms, drained
- 2 tablespoons chopped walnuts
- 1½ tablespoons dried parsley
- ⅛ teaspoon salt
- ⅛ teaspoon pepper
- ¾ teaspoon poultry seasoning
- 2 cups fresh white bread cubes

Ask butcher to make pocket in lamb and tuck in ends to form a pillow. Wipe lamb with damp cloth. Rub surface with cut clove of garlic, insert 2 or 3 slivers of garlic in lamb. Combine salt, pepper and generous amount bouquet garni, rub over surface of lamb and in pocket. Prepare stuffing. Melt butter, saute onion, celery and green pepper until tender, about 5 minutes. Remove from heat. Add rest of ingredients; toss lightly to combine well. Preheat oven to 325°. Stuff pocket in lamb with dressing almost, but not quite, full. Close with skewers. Place roast, fat side up, on rack in shallow roasting pan. Insert meat thermometer, being careful that tip is in meat and not stuffing. Roast about 3¼ hours or until thermometer reads 180° for well done, 175° for medium. Remove to platter and let stand for 20 minutes before carving. Keep warm. Drippings from roast make excellent gravy with or without thickening.

Mrs. Paul W. Winder

ROAST LEG OF LAMB, CREOLE SAUCE

Rub 5½-6-pound leg of lamb with vinegar. Refrigerate overnight. Next day rinse off, dry, rub liberally with salt and red pepper. Sprinkle lightly with flour. Rub top with soft lard. Put in 500° oven for 10 minutes. Then lower heat to 350°. Meanwhile, make roux of 3 tablespoons flour and 3 tablespoons bacon drippings. Brown well. Add 1 cup finely chopped onion, ½ cup chopped celery. Cook until transparent and soft. Add 2 cups water. Bring to a boil, cook down about 10 minutes and pour over roast. In all, cook lamb 20 minutes per pound.

Serve with following sauce:

3 tablespoons tomato catsup
2 tablespoons canned tomato sauce
Juice 1 lemon
½ teaspoon red pepper
1 tablespoon Worcestershire sauce

Bring to a boil; pass separately.

Mrs. Marshall Martin

VEAL PAPRIKA

2 cloves garlic
4 tablespoons butter
3 pounds veal
2 cups water
2 pints sour cream
2 tablespoons paprika
1 teaspoon salt

Have butcher cut veal as for scallopini (very thin and pounded with the flat of the cleaver). Thinly slice the two cloves of garlic and brown lightly in four tablespoons of butter. Add veal and brown well; add two cups of water. Cover pan and let simmer for about 45 minutes. (Do not overcook.) Add sour cream, paprika and salt. Mix well and cook, uncovered, over low heat for another 10 minutes. Serve over noodles immediately.

Makes 8 portions.

M. A. Prescott

STUFFED VEAL CUTLETS

16 slices 4- x 2-inch veal
8 slices boiled ham
8 slices Swiss cheese
1 cup flour seasoned with 1 teaspoon salt, a little pepper
½ cup or more butter
2 cups dry white wine
Lemon slices for garnish

Pound veal slices very thin, cover 8 of the slices with a piece of ham and a slice of cheese (cut slightly smaller than veal). Cover each portion with remaining veal and pound edges with dull edge of knife to seal. Dredge in seasoned flour. Brown in hot butter using a heavy skillet. Add wine and lower temperature, turning once until wine has nearly evaporated. Pour drippings over meat to serve and garnish with lemon slices.

Serves 8. Lemon juice may be substituted for wine, if desired.

Mrs. Thomas E. Stagg, Jr.

THIN VEAL FONESTIER

1½ pounds veal cutlets, cut thin, then pound thinner
1 clove garlic or garlic salt
Flour
¼ cup butter or margarine
½ pound mushrooms (fresh, if possible) sliced thin
Salt to taste
⅓ cup dry vermouth
1 teaspoon lemon juice
Snipped parsley
Pepper to taste

Rub veal with garlic. Dip in flour, coating each side thoroughly. Heat butter or margarine (margarine doesn't brown as quickly as butter) in skillet and saute until golden brown on each side. Heap mushrooms on top of veal. Sprinkle with salt, pepper and vermouth. Cover skillet and cook over low heat about 20 minutes or until fork tender. Be sure veal stays moist. Add a tablespoon of water or vermouth, if necessary. Just before serving, sprinkle with lemon juice and parsley. Delicious and so easy to prepare.

Serves 4.

Mrs. W. W. Lincoln

VEAL IN SHERRY SAUCE

4 veal cutlets
4 tablespoons butter
Salt
Pepper
Flour

Sauce:
1 can sliced mushrooms in butter
4 tablespoons butter
1 green onion, chopped
⅓ cup sherry
1 can prepared brown gravy

Salt and pepper cutlets and flour lightly. Saute in butter until brown. Place in shallow baking dish and cover with sherry sauce. Bake in 350° oven for 30 minutes. Good served with wild rice. May be prepared ahead of time and reheated before serving.

Sauce: Saute onions and mushrooms in butter. Add sherry and brown gravy. Bring to a low boil and cook slowly for 3 to 5 minutes. For a thinner sauce add consomme.

Mrs. Arch Haynes

TERIYAKI SAUCE

½ cup soya sauce
1 tablespoon wine
1 clove garlic
1 tablespoon sugar
1 teaspoon ginger

Put in jar and shake well. Marinate meat in sauce for at least an hour. Wonderful for charcoaled filets. No other seasoning required. Sauce may be put back in jar, refrigerated and used several times.

Mrs. Guido M. Piggott, Jr.

BARBECUE SAUCE

2 tablespoons butter
Medium onion, chopped finely
2 tablespoons chopped celery
2 tablespoons vinegar
1 tablespoon brown sugar
1 cup catsup
1 cup water
3 tablespoons Worcestershire sauce
4 tablespoons lemon juice
½ teaspoon salt
½ teaspoon celery salt, onion salt, garlic salt
1 teaspoon hickory smoke sauce

Brown onion in butter. Add chopped celery and cook for 5 minutes. Add remaining ingredients and cook slowly for 15 minutes.

Makes 1 quart. May be refrigerated and kept for 2 weeks.

Mrs. Paul G. Annan

BARBECUE SAUCE

1 cup catsup
¼ cup vinegar
¼ cup cooking oil
¼ cup water
1 teaspoon chili powder
½ teaspoon red pepper
1 tablespoon dry mustard
½ teaspoon salt
¼ cup sugar
2 cloves garlic, minced

Combine all ingredients in saucepan; bring to boil and simmer for 5 minutes. This sauce imparts a very delicious "sweet and sour" taste to shrimp, chicken and pork. Meat should be generously basted throughout cooking time.

Mrs. Bill Scales

BARBECUE SAUCE

1 onion, chopped
1 tablespoon vinegar
¾ cup water
⅛ teaspoon cloves
¼ teaspoon red pepper
1 teaspoon chili powder
1 cup catsup
2 tablespoons butter
2 tablespoons brown sugar
1 teaspoon mustard
3 tablespoons Worcestershire sauce
1 teaspoon garlic salt

Mix all ingredients and cook over low fire 30-45 minutes. Will keep several weeks under refrigeration.

Makes 2 cups.

Mrs. Pike Hall, Jr.

MUSTARD SAUCE

4 tablespoons dry mustard
½ cup sugar (scant)
2 eggs
½ cup cream or whole milk
½ cup vinegar
Butter, size of an egg
Pinch of salt

Put all in double boiler. Stir constantly, and cook until thick. Cook over medium low heat. Serve with ham.

Makes about 2 cups.

Mrs. R. C. Ridgeway

MARINADE FOR MEATS TO CHARCOAL

Small bottle Worcestershire sauce
½ cup wine vinegar
Juice of 2 lemons
2 bay leaves
2 garlic cloves, sliced
Seasoned salt
Seasoned pepper

Allow steak or meat to marinate at least 2 or 3 hours. A roast should marinate overnight.

Mrs. Robert A. Stacy, Jr.

SEASONED SALT

1 box salt
1 tablespoon corn starch
1 tablespoon monosodium glutamate
2 tablespoons paprika
1 teaspoon mace
1 teaspoon cayenne pepper
2 teaspoons ground celery seed
2 teaspoons black pepper
1½ teaspoons garlic powder
3 teaspoons onion powder
2 teaspoons curry powder
2 tablespoons chili powder
2 teaspoons oregano
1 teaspoon marjoram
1 teaspoon thyme
2 tablespoons dry mustard
¼ teaspoon dill weed or seed (optional)

Combine above ingredients. Pour through fine sieve. Store in sterile jars or shakers.

Philip F. Rosenblath

Cakes & Icings

Pioneer Heritage Center

PIONEER HERITAGE CENTER

Located on the Louisiana State University Campus in Shreveport, authentic buildings from the pioneer days in Northwest Louisiana allow visitors to walk through history and see how early settlers lived in the 1830's through the 1860's.

ANGEL FOOD CAKE

1½ cups egg whites
Pinch of salt
2 level teaspoons cream of tartar
1½ cups sugar
1 cup plus 2 tablespoons flour sifted 5 times
1 teaspoon vanilla

Beat egg whites until stiff (add pinch of salt before beating). Add cream of tartar to whites when they are frothy. Add sugar, flour and vanilla. Bake in slow oven (325°) for 45 minutes or until cake begins to shrink away from sides of pan. Let cool on rack upside down.

Mrs. Marshall Martin

FRESH APPLE CAKE

2 cups sugar
1½ cups salad oil
2 teaspoons vanilla
2 well beaten eggs
Juice of ½ lemon
1 teaspoon salt
3 cups sifted flour
1¼ teaspoons soda
3 cups peeled and chopped apples
1½ to 2 cups chopped pecans

Combine in a mixing bowl the sugar, oil, vanilla, eggs, lemon juice and salt. Beat well, but not too long. Mix the flour and soda, add to the first mixture, and beat well. Stir in the apples and nuts. Bake at 325°, about 1½ hours, in a tube pan which has been buttered and floured. This is a moist cake which keeps well indefinitely.

Mrs. Jackson B. Davis
Mrs. Gilbert L. Hetherwick

FRESH APPLE BUTTER CAKE

1 cup butter, melted and cooled
2 eggs
2 cups sugar
2 cups sifted flour
1½ teaspoons soda
1 teaspoon cinnamon
½ teaspoon salt
2 teaspoons vanilla
1 cup chopped nuts
3 cups chopped apples

Combine in a mixing bowl the melted, cooled butter and sugar. Add eggs. Sift together flour, soda, cinnamon and salt, and add. Add vanilla. Fold in chopped pecans and apples. Bake in a well buttered and floured tube pan, at 325° for about 1½ hours.

Mrs. M. B. Hannah

FRESH APPLE DATE CAKE

2 cups sugar
1½ cups salad oil
3 eggs
3 cups flour
1 teaspoon baking powder
1 teaspoon soda
1 teaspoon cinnamon
1 teaspoon nutmeg
½ teaspoon salt
3 cups chopped, peeled apples (small pieces)
1 cup dates, chopped
2 cups nuts, chopped
2 teaspoons vanilla
½ to 1 cup bourbon (optional)

Cream sugar and oil in mixer. Beat eggs in one at a time. Mix sifted dry ingredients into batter. Fold in chopped dates, apples and nuts. Add vanilla and bourbon. Bake in loaf pan at 325° for 1½ hours.

This is a very large cake. Mrs. Harold Quinn

APPLESAUCE CAKE

½ cup butter or margarine
1 cup sugar
1 egg
2 cups sifted all purpose flour
¼ teaspoon salt
1 teaspoon cinnamon
1 teaspoon soda
½ teaspoon cloves
1 cup applesauce
1 cup raisins
1 cup chopped nuts

Cream butter. Add sugar and cream together until light and fluffy. Add egg and beat well. Sift together dry ingredients and add alternately with applesauce to creamed mixture. Fold in raisins and nuts. Place in greased 9" tube pan and bake at 350° for 50 to 60 minutes. Glaze with simple confectioners' sugar frosting.

Mrs. James W. Middleton

APPLESAUCE SQUARES

½ cup oleo
1½ cups sugar
1 egg
2 cups flour
1 teaspoon soda
¼ teaspoon salt
½ teaspoon allspice
1 teaspoon cinnamon
1 cup applesauce (also good with appleberry sauce)
1½ cups raisins
1 cup pecans

Cream oleo and sugar; add egg. Sift together all dry ingredients; add to creamed mixture alternately with 1 cup applesauce (should be done about ⅓ at a time). Fold in raisins and pecans. Pour into square cake pan which has been greased and floured. Bake at 325° for 50 to 60 minutes. Cut into 9 squares and serve with whipped cream.

Mrs. B. S. Cheesman

BANANA CAKE

½ cup butter
1½ cups sugar
2 eggs
4 crushed bananas
1 teaspoon baking soda
4 tablespoons buttermilk
1½ cups flour, sifted
1 cup chopped walnuts

Melt butter, add sugar and mix well. Add eggs to this and mix well together. Add crushed bananas and mix again. In separate container, mix soda and buttermilk, and add to above. Add chopped nuts and flour and stir well. Pour into greased and floured loaf pan. Bake at 375° for 45 minutes.

Mrs. Otis C. Coles, Jr.

BANANA NUT CAKE

1 cup butter
3 cups sugar
8 tablespoons buttermilk
2 teaspoons baking soda
3 cups sifted flour
4 eggs, separated
5 very ripe bananas, mashed
2 teaspoons vanilla
½ teaspoon salt
1 cup finely chopped pecans

Cream butter and sugar, add milk with soda alternately with flour. Add beaten egg yolks, then the mashed bananas. Add vanilla, pecans and salt. Lastly, fold in stiffly beaten egg whites. Bake in three 9" x 1¼" cake pans, or four 9" x 1" cake pans, at 350° for approximately 40 minutes.

Icing

Cream 1 stick butter with two 1-pound boxes powdered sugar. Add 2 tablespoons heavy cream. Add enough lemon juice to make icing of spreading consistency. (Orange juice may be substituted for lemon.)

Mrs. T. Haller Jackson, Jr.

BROILED BANANA CAKE

½ cup margarine or butter
1½ cups sugar
2 eggs
4 tablespoons sour milk
1 teaspoon soda
1½ cups flour
1 cup mashed ripe bananas
½ cup raisins (optional)
½ cup chopped nuts (optional)

Icing:
½ cup brown sugar
Enough milk to dissolve brown sugar

Cream margarine and sugar, add beaten eggs and milk alternately with sifted dry ingredients. Stir in bananas, raisins and nuts. Bake, in a greased shallow baking dish, at 350° for 65 minutes.

For icing: Combine brown sugar with enough milk to dissolve it, pour over warm cake while still in pan, run under broiler until bubbly and brown. Whipped cream on top really gilds the lily.

Mrs. John G. Wafer, Jr.

BROILED CAKE

½ cup milk
1 tablespoon butter
2 eggs, beaten
1 cup sugar
1 cup flour
1 teaspoon baking powder
1 teaspoon salt
1 teaspoon vanilla

Heat milk and butter, then cool. Beat eggs, add sugar and other ingredients, then add warm milk and vanilla. Bake at 350° for 20 minutes in a greased and lightly floured pan.

Topping

9 tablespoons brown sugar
5 tablespoons melted oleo
4 tablespoons cream
½ cup coconut
½ cup nuts
1 teaspoon vanilla

Mix all ingredients, place on cake and run in oven to broil a few minutes until topping thickens slightly. Or, mixture may be cooked in boiler until it bubbles for a few minutes, then spread while hot.

Mrs. Grady L. Nelson

HOT NORWEGIAN TEA CAKE

2 whole eggs
1 cup sifted sugar
1 cup sifted cake flour
1 rounded teaspoon baking powder
¼ teaspoon salt
1 teaspoon vanilla
½ cup milk
1 tablespoon butter

Beat eggs until thick. Gradually add sugar and beat, then add flour which has been sifted with baking powder and salt. Beat again. Add vanilla and milk which have been brought to a boil with butter and then cooled. Mix thoroughly. Pour into greased and floured pan and cook 30 minutes at 350°.

Topping

5 heaping tablespoons brown sugar
3 tablespoons butter
2 tablespoons heavy cream
Chopped nuts

Cream sugar and butter with cream until consistency of mayonnaise. Spread over cooled cake and sprinkle generously with nuts. Return to hot oven and let bubble. Cut into squares and serve hot.

Mrs. J. Stewart Smith

BLUEBERRY CAKE

½ cup shortening
1 cup sugar
2 eggs
1½ cups all purpose flour
Pinch of salt
1 teaspoon baking powder
1 teaspoon vanilla
1½ cups fresh blueberries

Mix all ingredients except blueberries; fold in berries last. Bake in greased 8" x 10" cake pan in 350° oven for about 35 minutes. Should be served hot with butter.

Mrs. Walter Ritchie, Amherst, Mass.

CARROT CAKE

For Cake:
1½ cups salad oil
2 cups sugar
2 cups grated carrots
4 eggs
2 cups flour
2 teaspoons cinnamon
2 teaspoons soda
1 teaspoon salt

For Icing:
1 8-ounce package cream cheese
1 stick oleo
1 box powdered sugar
1 teaspoon vanilla
1 can WELL DRAINED crushed pineapple

Cake: Cream oil and sugar together; add carrots. Add eggs one at a time; then stir in dry ingredients. Pour into 3 buttered layer pans and bake at 350° for 25-30 minutes.

Icing: Cream the cheese and oleo together. Add sugar and vanilla, then crushed pineapple. Spread between layers and over cooled cake.

Mrs. Weyman H. Oden

BLACK PEPPER CAKE

¾ cup margarine or butter
¾ cup dark brown sugar, firmly packed
1 cup sugar
1 teaspoon vanilla
3 eggs
2¼ cups sifted flour
1 cup buttermilk
1 teaspoon baking powder
¾ teaspoon soda
½ teaspoon salt
½ teaspoon ground cloves
1 teaspoon cinnamon
¾ teaspoon black pepper (½ teaspoon if it is strong)

Cream margarine until it resembles whipped cream. Add brown sugar and stir, then add white sugar and vanilla. Beat well. Add eggs, one at a time, beating well after each addition. Sift together flour, baking powder, salt, pepper and spices. Add this to first mixture alternately with buttermilk to which soda has been added. Beat well after each addition. Pour into well greased and floured pan or pans. May be baked in layers or in a loaf pan. Bake layers 20-30 minutes at 350° to 375°. Bake loaf pan 45-60 minutes at 325° to 350°.

Eleanor Blatterman

BURNT SUGAR CAKE

1¼ cups sugar
½ cup butter
2½ cups flour
2½ teaspoons baking powder
1 cup milk
2 whole eggs
1 teaspoon vanilla
3 or 4 tablespoons burnt sugar syrup

Have ingredients at room temperature. Put all except last two ingredients in mixer and beat well. Then add 3 or 4 tablespoons burnt sugar syrup and vanilla. Bake in two 9" pans which have been greased and lightly floured. Bake at 350° for approximately 30 minutes.

To make Burnt Sugar Syrup: Melt ½ cup white sugar in iron skillet over low heat until dark brown and smooth. Remove from heat and add ½ cup boiling water. Return to heat, stir rapidly until molasses-like syrup is made.

Icing

3 cups white sugar
1 cup milk
Remaining burnt sugar syrup

Boil white sugar and milk until mixture will form soft ball in cold water, add lump of butter and remaining burnt sugar syrup and beat to right consistency to spread.

Mrs. J. Warren Fulton, Jr.

CHOCOLATE CAKE

3 squares unsweetened chocolate
1 stick butter
2 cups sugar
2 eggs
1 cup sour cream
2 cups flour
1½ teaspoons soda
1 teaspoon vanilla
1 cup boiling water

Icing:
1 cup sugar
⅓ cup milk
¼ cup butter
1 square chocolate
Pinch cream of tartar

For Cake: Melt butter and chocolate together and set aside to cool. Place sugar in mixing bowl and add chocolate mixture. Beat well. Add eggs one at a time, beating after each. Add sour cream, flour (with soda in it) and vanilla. Mix well. Turn mixer to "slow" and add boiling water. Bake in well greased and floured pan (10" x 14"). Place batter in cold oven and bake at 350° about 30 minutes or until it springs back when touched lightly.

For Icing: Cook all ingredients together until mixture forms a soft ball when tested in cool water. Add 1 teaspoon vanilla, cool slightly. Beat until creamy and pour over cake while still in the pan and warm.

Mrs. Hewitt H. Wheless

CHOCOLATE CAKE

2 cups sugar
2 sticks butter or oleo
5 eggs, separated
2 squares unsweetened chocolate, melted
1 cup sweet milk
2 cups flour (1 cup plain; 1 cup cake flour)
1 teaspoon baking powder
1 scant teaspoon baking soda
1 teaspoon vanilla

Cream sugar with butter. Add egg yolks and blend. Add melted chocolate, then milk. Gradually stir in flour. Beat egg whites until stiff. Fold baking powder, soda, and vanilla into egg whites. Fold this into batter. Pour into two cake pans which have been greased and dusted well with flour. Bake at 350° about 35 minutes.

Mrs. A. L. Stephens

CHOCOLATE SPICE CAKE

½ cup cocoa
2 cups sugar
½ cup butter
2 whole eggs
⅔ cup buttermilk
2 cups sifted flour
1½ teaspoons soda
1 cup boiling water
1 teaspoon vanilla
Ground cloves, nutmeg, cinnamon — 1 teaspoon altogether

Mix cocoa, sugar and butter well in electric mixer; add eggs. Add soda to buttermilk. Add flour and buttermilk to mixture alternately until mixed well. Add spices and vanilla: pour in boiling water. Place in two greased and floured 9" cake tins. Cook at 350° for 35 to 40 minutes or until done.

Mrs. Guido M. Piggott, Jr.

NORWEGIAN CHOCOLATE UPSIDE-DOWN CAKE

1 cup flour
¼ teaspoon salt
¾ cup sugar
2 teaspoons baking powder
½ cup milk
1 square chocolate
2 tablespoons butter
½ cup white sugar
½ cup brown sugar
2 large teaspoons cocoa
⅞ cup boiling water

Sift together, flour, salt, sugar, and baking powder. Add milk, melt chocolate in butter, add to flour mixture. Spread this mixture in well-greased baking dish. Combine white sugar, brown sugar, cocoa. Pour on top of batter. Over all, pour boiling water. Bake slowly for 40 minutes at 325°-350°. Cool to lukewarm. Turn out of pan, upside down. May be served with whipped cream, if desired.

6-8 servings. Recipe may be doubled and baked in pan 2" x 8" x 12", for 12-15 servings.

Mrs. Walter T. Colquitt

CHOCOLATE COOKIE SHEET

2 cups flour
2 cups sugar
½ teaspoon salt
1 stick oleo
1 cup water
½ cup shortening
3 tablespoons cocoa
2 eggs, beaten
1 teaspoon soda
½ cup buttermilk
1 teaspoon vanilla
Icing:
1 stick oleo
3 tablespoons cocoa
1 box powdered sugar
1 teaspoon vanilla
½ cup chopped nuts
6 tablespoons milk
Pinch of salt

Sift together flour, sugar and salt. In a saucepan put oleo, water, shortening and cocoa. Bring to boil and pour over flour mixture. Mix well. In another bowl beat eggs. Add soda, buttermilk and vanilla. Stir well and add to first mixture. Mix well. Bake in greased and floured cookie sheet (15½" x 10½" x 1") at 350° for 20-25 minutes. Start making icing during last 5 minutes of baking. When cake is done, ice immediately in the pan.

Icing: Using same saucepan as above, melt oleo and cocoa but do not boil. Take off heat and add powdered sugar, vanilla, nuts, salt and milk. Ice cake. Makes 35 squares.

Mrs. C. Lane Sartor

SPECIAL CHOCOLATE CAKE

2 cups flour
2 cups sugar
1 teaspoon soda
1 teaspoon cinnamon
1 stick oleo or butter
½ cup shortening
4 tablespoons cocoa
1 cup water
½ cup buttermilk
2 eggs
1 tablespoon vanilla

Sift dry ingredients together. In saucepan combine and bring to a boil, oleo, shortening, cocoa and water. Pour over sifted dry ingredients. Add buttermilk, eggs and vanilla. Beat well and pour into a buttered 9" x 12" pan. Bake at 400° for 25 to 30 minutes.

Icing

1 stick oleo
4 tablespoons cocoa
6 tablespoons milk
1 box powdered sugar
1 tablespoon vanilla
1 cup chopped pecans (or less)

Melt oleo, cocoa and milk in a saucepan and bring to a boil. Add sugar, vanilla and pecans and beat well while still on the stove. Remove from heat. Beat a little more and spread on cake while still hot.

Mrs. Ray Oden, Jr.

GERMAN CHOCOLATE POUND CAKE

1 bar German sweet chocolate
2 cups sugar
1 cup shortening
4 eggs
2 teaspoons vanilla
2 teaspoons butter flavoring
1 cup buttermilk
3 cups sifted all-purpose flour
½ teaspoon soda
1 teaspoon salt

Partially melt chocolate over hot water. Remove and stir rapidly until melted. Cool. Cream sugar and shortening. Add eggs, flavoring, and buttermilk. Mix well. Sift together flour, soda, salt; add to shortening mixture. Stir well. Blend in chocolate. Pour into greased and floured 9" tube pan. Bake in slow oven for about 1½ hours. Remove from pan while still hot.

Mrs. William M. Sale, Jr.

CHOCOLATE POUND CAKE

1 cup butter
½ cup shortening
3 cups sugar
5 eggs
3 cups cake flour
1 teaspoon baking powder
½ teaspoon salt
½ cup cocoa
1 cup sweet milk
1 tablespoon vanilla

Cream butter and shortening. Add sugar. Add eggs one at a time, beating after each addition. Sift all dry ingredients together. Add to the creamed mixture alternately with milk. Add vanilla and bake in a greased and floured tube pan at 325° for 1 hour and 20 minutes or until done.

Mrs. S. P. Borden, Jr.
Mrs. V. V. Thompson

DEVIL'S FOOD CAKE

½ box unsweetened chocolate (4 squares)
1 cup butter
2 cups sugar
5 eggs, separated
2 cups flour (measure before sifting)
2 teaspoons baking powder sifted with flour
1 teaspoon soda dissolved in 1 tablespoon boiling water
1 cup buttermilk
1 teaspoon vanilla

Melt chocolate over hot water. Cream butter and 1 cup sugar. Add other cup sugar to beaten egg yolks. Add melted chocolate. Sift together flour and baking powder and add alternately with milk. Dissolve soda in hot water and add to cake mixture. Add vanilla. Beat 200 strokes. Fold in stiffly beaten egg whites. Bake at 375° for 30 to 40 minutes. Makes 2 thick layers and one small round layer.

Mrs. D. Y. Smith

MARSHMALLOW-FUDGE CAKE

½ pound butter
2 eggs
2 tablespoons cocoa
1 cup sugar
¾ cup flour
1 cup nuts
1 teaspoon vanilla
Pinch of salt

Frosting:
8 ounces marshmallows, standard size
3 tablespoons butter
⅓ cup evaporated milk
3 cups confectioners' sugar
⅜ cup cocoa
1½ teaspoons vanilla

Melt butter and cocoa. Beat eggs and add sugar. Pour butter and cocoa mixture into eggs. Add flour and salt, nuts and vanilla. Pour into greased 8" x 8" layer cake pan and bake 30 minutes in 350° oven. Cut marshmallows in half horizontally and, placing cut sides down, make a solid layer on cake in pan.

For frosting, bring butter and milk to boil. Sift cocoa and sugar. Pour hot liquid into sugar. Add vanilla. Beat quickly and pour over cake while warm. Keep refrigerated; or, it may be frozen. To serve, cut into thin slices like a pound cake, cutting three rows across pan. This recipe doubles very nicely.

Mrs. W. M. Johnson

LIGHT CHOCOLATE CAKE

1 cup butter
2½ cups cake flour
2 cups sugar
1 teaspoon soda
¼ teaspoon salt
4 squares semi-sweet chocolate, melted
1 cup milk
5 eggs, well beaten
2 teaspoons vanilla

Cream butter. Sift flour, sugar, soda and salt into butter. Add milk and melted chocolate until flour is dampened. Beat 2½ minutes at low speed with electric mixer. Add well beaten eggs and vanilla. Beat 2½ minutes. Pour into two 9" layer pans, lined on bottom with paper. Bake 35 to 40 minutes at 350°.

Frosting

3 egg whites
2 cups sugar
6 tablespoons water
4 tablespoons white corn syrup
4 squares semi-sweet chocolate, melted

In top of double boiler combine egg whites which have been beaten until they stand in peaks, sugar, water and white corn syrup. Put over boiling water and beat with rotary beater or electric mixer until mixture stands in stiff peaks. Swirl chocolate into frosting.

Mrs. Sarah Quigles

WALDORF-ASTORIA CAKE

½ cup shortening
1½ cups sugar
2 ounces red cake coloring
2 eggs
1 teaspoon salt
2 cups all-purpose flour
1 tablespoon cocoa
1 cup buttermilk
1 teaspoon vanilla
1 teaspoon soda
1 tablespoon vinegar

Cream sugar and shortening, then add cake coloring. Add eggs 1 at a time, beating after each. Sift flour, salt, and cocoa 3 times. Add to batter alternately with buttermilk. Add vanilla and beat. Dissolve soda in vinegar and fold into batter. Do not beat. Pour into two pans, greased but not floured. Waxed paper may be used to line pans. Bake in 350° oven 30 to 35 minutes.

Mrs. Will Fullilove

MOCHA CAKE

1½ cups sugar
1 stick butter
½ cup cocoa
2 eggs
1 cup buttermilk
1 teaspoon soda
1⅞ cups cake flour
½ teaspoon salt
2 tablespoons coffee
1½ teaspoons vanilla
1 teaspoon red food coloring

Cream together sugar, butter, cocoa; add beaten eggs. Combine soda and buttermilk. Sift together flour, salt and add remaining ingredients and mix well. Pour batter into 9" x 12" x 2" cake pan and bake in preheated 350° oven for 30 minutes.

Mrs. David H. Walke

CHOCOLATE SYRUP CAKE

8 5-cent chocolate bars
1 large can chocolate syrup
2 sticks butter
2 cups sugar
4 eggs
2½ cups flour
1 cup buttermilk
¼ teaspoon soda
2 teaspoons vanilla
1 cup chopped pecans

Melt candy in double boiler. Cream butter and sugar. Add eggs one at a time. Mix well. Sift flour and soda together and add alternately with buttermilk, syrup and candy. Beat well, add nuts and vanilla. Bake in greased stem pan at 350° for approximately 1½ hours. Chocolate syrup may be omitted if yellow cake is preferred.

Mrs. Hubert Joyner

COCOA GINGERBREAD

¾ cup shortening
½ cup sugar
3 eggs
1 cup dark cane syrup
2½ cups flour
2 level teaspoons soda
½ cup cocoa or less
1 teaspoon cinnamon
2 teaspoons ginger
Pinch salt
1 cup boiling water

Mix the first four ingredients, then sift together all the dry ones and add to the first mixture. Lastly, pour onto the batter one cup of boiling water. Bake in lightly greased pan in 350° oven for 25 to 30 minutes.

Mrs. Melvin F. Johnson

ICEBOX GINGERBREAD

1 cup shortening
1 cup sugar
1 cup dark molasses
3 large eggs
½ teaspoon salt
3 cups sifted flour
2 teaspoons ginger
2 teaspoons cinnamon
1 teaspoon nutmeg
1¾ teaspoons soda
1 cup sour milk

Cream shortening and sugar. Add syrup, mix, add eggs one at a time. Put soda in sour milk and add alternately with dry ingredients which have been sifted together. Put in refrigerator immediately in covered bowl. Batter will keep indefinitely. When ready to bake, pour in greased pan and put in oven at once. Bake in moderate oven (350°) until just done in center when pricked with a toothpick. Serve with a sauce, whipped cream or just plain.

Mrs. Conway Allen

FRUIT COCKTAIL CAKE

1 No. 303 can fruit cocktail (juice and all)
1½ cups sugar
2 cups flour, sifted
2 eggs
2 teaspoons soda
1 teaspoon salt
1 cup chopped nuts
1 cup raisins

Icing:
1 stick oleo
¾ cup sugar
½ cup evaporated milk
½ cup angel flake coconut or nuts
1 teaspoon vanilla

Cake: Mix all ingredients well. Bake in a tube pan in 325° oven for about 1 hour.

Icing: Boil oleo, sugar and milk together three minutes. Remove from fire, add nuts and vanilla. Ice cake while hot.

Mrs. L. C. Allen, Jr.
Mrs. Litt P. Martin

GRAHAM CRACKER CAKE

4 heaping tablespoons butter
2 cups sugar
6 eggs, separated
42 graham crackers, rolled fine
3 heaping teaspoons baking powder
1½ cups milk
1 grated coconut or 1 package frozen coconut
Grated rind of 2 lemons
Grated rind of 2 oranges
2 teaspoons vanilla

Cream butter and sugar, add egg yolks beaten until light. Add cracker crumbs mixed with baking powder alternately with milk. Fold in coconut and grated rinds. Beat egg whites and fold into batter with vanilla. Bake in three layer pans at 350° for 30 minutes. If fresh coconut is not available, frozen coconut may be used.

Icing

3 cups confectioners' sugar
4 tablespoons melted butter
4 tablespoons bourbon
4 tablespoons whipping cream

Beat all ingredients until creamy. Let cake cool before icing.

Mrs. John B. Hutchinson

BLACKBERRY JAM CAKE

1¼ cups cake flour
¼ teaspoon salt
1 teaspoon cinnamon
1 teaspoon allspice
¾ cup sugar
1 stick oleo
2 eggs
½ teaspoon baking soda
¼ cup buttermilk
1 cup seedless blackberry jam
½ cup chopped pecans
½ cup seedless raisins (optional)

Sift flour, salt and spices together. Cream sugar and oleo. Add eggs one at a time to this mixture. Dissolve soda in buttermilk and add buttermilk alternately with flour mixture to creamed mixture. Mix well. Fold in jam and then add nuts and raisins. Bake in greased and lightly floured loaf pan at 350° for 1 hour and 10 minutes or until done.

Serves 8-10.

For variation, triple this recipe, omit raisins, and bake it in 6 coffee tins. Shorten cooking time to 50 minutes, test and continue baking, if necessary. Excellent at Christmastime.

Mrs. Sterling Bigner

JELLY ROLL

3 eggs
1 cup sugar
3 tablespoons cold water
1 cup flour
1 teaspoon baking powder
⅓ teaspoon salt

Beat eggs and sugar until thick. Add water, then dry ingredients, which have been sifted together twice. Line sheet pan with waxed paper. Bake at 375° for 12 minutes. Cool, then spread cake with large jar of grape jelly. Start at one end and roll cake up into a jelly roll. Put damp towel around roll for a while, until it sets.

Mrs. J. Claiborne Cook

LEMON JELLO CAKE

1 package white cake mix
¾ cup water
¾ cup salad oil
1 package lemon Jello
4 eggs
Juice of 1 lemon

Beat all ingredients together. Bake in 13" x 9" x 2" loaf pan at 350° for 30 minutes.

Icing

1 cup powdered sugar
1 stick butter, melted
Juice of 1 lemon

Mix all ingredients together. Spread icing on cake immediately upon taking it out of oven, while it is still hot. Ice in pan. Cool and serve.

Mrs. Matthew H. Miller

JELLO CAKE

1 package yellow cake mix
1 4-ounce package lemon or orange Jello
4 eggs
⅔ cup salad oil
⅔ cup water or apricot nectar

Mix ingredients and beat well. Bake at 350° for 50 minutes in greased and floured tube pan. Remove from pan shortly and pour icing over warm cake.

Icing

½ stick oleo, melted
Juice of 1 lemon
Juice of 1 orange

Stir in enough powdered sugar to make a thick liquid, pour over warm cake. A rotary egg beater keeps the sugar from lumping.

Mrs. John G. Wafer, Jr.
Mrs. William Peacock
Mrs. James L. Moore
Mrs. W. B. Ogilvie

EXTRA SPECIAL YELLOW CAKE

½ pound butter
2 cups sugar
4 eggs, separated
1 cup sweet milk
3½ cups cake flour
2 teaspoons cream of tartar
1 teaspoon soda
2 teaspoons vanilla

Cream butter, add sugar gradually. Add egg yolks one at a time. Sift cake flour twice before measuring. Add cream of tartar and soda and sift at least one more time. The more you sift, the lighter the cake will be. Add this to butter mixture alternating with the milk. Add flavoring and fold in stiffly beaten egg whites. Pour into layer pans or large tube pan and make a slight X across batter to insure even rising. Bake at 350° for 20-25 minutes or until toothpick inserted in center comes out clean. When cool, ice with 7-Minute Icing.

7-Minute Icing

(Will ice a two-layer 8" cake)

5 tablespoons water
⅛ teaspoon salt
1½ cups sugar
1½ teaspoons white corn syrup
2 egg whites
1 teaspoon vanilla (or use ½ teaspoon almond or peppermint, or a few drops of black walnut flavoring, if coconut is not used)
Fresh or canned coconut (optional)

Put first five ingredients in top of double boiler and blend with beater. Have water in lower boiler boiling rapidly, but avoid letting it touch bottom of top boiler. Beat constantly with rotary beater for seven minutes. An electric mixer at high speed may take less time. When frosting stands in stiff peaks and clings to beater, remove from heat, add flavoring and/or coconut, and continue beating only until thick enough to spread.

Mrs. K. J. Heddons

WHITE CAKE

1 cup butter
2 cups sugar
3 cups cake flour
½ teaspoon salt
3 teaspoons baking powder
1 cup milk
2 teaspoons vanilla
6 egg whites

Cream butter and sugar thoroughly. Sift flour, salt and baking powder 4 times. Add flour mixture alternately with milk and vanilla to butter and sugar. Beat at medium speed for not more than 2 minutes. Fold in by hand stiffly beaten egg whites. Pour into two 9" square pans. Bake at 350° for 30-35 minutes.

Mrs. Ed Minor

BRIDE'S CAKE

2½ cups sugar
1 cup butter
4 cups sifted flour
2 teaspoons baking powder
⅛ teaspoon salt
1 cup sweet milk
1 teaspoon flavoring (vanilla or almond)
8 egg whites

Cream butter until very light, then add sugar gradually until both have been well creamed. Combine remaining dry ingredients and add them alternately with milk to first mixture. Add flavoring and blend. Add egg whites (unbeaten) one at a time, beating well after each one. Pour into well greased and floured tube pan. Bake at 350° for one hour and 15 minutes or until done. This recipe is over 100 years old.

Mrs. Weyman H. Oden

PINEAPPLE UPSIDE-DOWN CAKE

Use one 9" x 9" x 1¾" cake pan
Part One:
¼ cup butter
1 cup brown sugar
3-5 slices pineapple
5 or 6 maraschino cherries
About 6 pecan halves (optional)

Grease pan with 2 tablespoons of the butter. Pat brown sugar over butter, firmly; dot with remaining butter. Place pineapple slices on top, whole one in center. Halves may go around edges. Put cherry in center of slices. Decorate with pecan halves if desired.

Part Two:
½ cup butter
1 cup sugar
2 eggs
1 teaspoon vanilla
2 cups sifted cake flour
3 teaspoons baking powder
½ teaspoon salt
¾ cup cold water

Cream butter until soft. Add sugar gradually, continuing to cream until light and fluffy. Add eggs, vanilla; beat thoroughly. Sift flour, baking powder and salt together. Alternately add, in thirds, flour mixture and water; beat well after each addition. Pour over pineapple; spread evenly. Bake for 55 to 65 minutes in 350° oven. (Test by inserting wooden toothpick in center.) When done, remove from oven; let stand just 3 or 4 minutes. Then, loosen sides from pan; place platter over cake; invert onto platter at once. Serve preferably while warm, either plain or with whipped cream.

Mrs. John L. Rhea, Jr.

POUND CAKE — MACE FLAVORED

1 cup butter or oleo at room temperature
1⅔ cups sugar
5 eggs, room temperature
2 cups sifted cake flour
¼ teaspoon salt
1 level teaspoon mace

Lightly grease and flour a tube pan about 9" in diameter at top, or grease and use waxed paper cut to fit the bottom. Preheat oven. Sift flour, salt, and mace together. Cream butter and sugar well. Add eggs, one at a time, beating well after each addition. Add flour, about ¼ at a time; beat well after each addition. After all is mixed, beat 10 minutes. The secret is in the beating. Bake at 325° for 1 hour and 10 or 15 minutes. Check after one hour and remove from oven when cake separates from pan and springs back when touched, not leaving an indentation. Cool in pan 10 or 15 minutes. Run thin knife around tube and inside of pan before turning out on rack to cool. It looks pretty sprinkled with confectioners' sugar, using a sifter. Place a sprig of holly in the center at Christmas time. A cool weather cake.

For variation, instead of mace try 1 teaspoon lemon extract, 1 tablespoon lemon juice, and grated rind of about ¾ lemon.

Mrs. W. A. Fortson, Jr.

POUND CAKE

1 pound butter or margarine
1 box powdered sugar
6 eggs
Sifted cake flour to fill powdered sugar box
Lemon and almond flavoring to suit taste

Cream margarine with sugar in mixer. Add eggs, one at a time, while continuing to cream. Add flour and mix well. Stir in flavorings. Bake in a greased and floured stem pan. Bake 1 hour at 375°.

Eleanor Blatterman

BUTTERMILK CAKE

3 cups sugar
2 sticks oleo (or butter)
5 eggs
3 cups plain flour
1 teaspoon salt
1 cup buttermilk
¼ teaspoon soda dissolved in 1 tablespoon hot water
2 teaspoons vanilla

Cream sugar and oleo (or butter), then add eggs, one at a time. Add flour (sifted with salt) and buttermilk. Beat well; add soda and vanilla. Pour into greased tube pan and bake 1 hour and 20 minutes at 300°. The crust on this cake makes icing unnecessary.

Mrs. C. Walker Weston

CONNIE HURD'S ORANGE CAKE

Cake:
1 cup sugar
½ cup butter
2 eggs
1 cup sour milk or cream
1 teaspoon baking soda
2 cups regular flour
Pinch of salt
½ cup raisins
Orange rind

Icing:
Juice of 1 lemon
Juice of 1 orange
½ cup sugar dissolved in these juices

Cream butter and sugar. Add eggs and sour milk. Sift flour, soda and salt together and add. Put raisins and orange rind through small blade of meat chopper, then add. Bake for 1 hour in a greased tube pan at 350°. When finished, turn out, and pour icing mixture over cake. Let stand overnight before serving. This cake stays moist and fresh for several days.

Mrs. Stanley P. Clark, Jr.

DUCHESS OF WINDSOR CAKE

1 whole egg
6 eggs, separated
4½ cups confectioners' sugar, sifted (1 box)
1¼ cups medium coarse chopped walnuts
¾ cup chopped almonds
1 cup sifted cake flour

Preheat oven to 325°. Butter three 9" round layer cake pans. Line bottoms with buttered paper. Beat egg yolks with one whole egg and sugar, until mixture doubles in volume and sugar is dissolved. Beat egg whites stiff but not dry, and add to yolk mixture. Combine almonds, walnuts, and flour. Add to egg mixture, ⅓ at a time, folding in gently. Pour into pans and bake 25 to 30 minutes. Cool pans on rack. When ready to serve put layers together with Cream Chantilly.

Cream Chantilly

1½ cups heavy cream
1½ cups sifted confectioners' sugar
1½ teaspoons vanilla

Whip cream in bowl, set in ice water for 5 minutes. Add sugar and vanilla. Cake may be prepared day before serving, but filling must be prepared on the day needed. Be sure to keep cake covered tightly and wrapped in cloth if prepared ahead of time.

Mrs. Andrew Querbes, Jr.

NATCHEZ CAKE

- 3 cups sugar
- ½ cup shortening
- 1 stick butter
- ½ teaspoon salt
- 3 cups sifted all-purpose flour, sifted 3 times
- 6 eggs
- 1 cup buttermilk (with ¼ teaspoon soda added)
- 1½ teaspoons vanilla

Cream sugar, shortening and butter. Add flour and salt. Add eggs, one at a time, alternately with buttermilk. Beat well. Add vanilla. Use ungreased tube pan. Do not preheat oven, but turn on only after cake has been put in oven. Bake at 300° for 1½ hours. When done, place on a rack to cool slightly before removing from pan.

Mrs. Murphy Yearwood

SOUR CREAM POUND CAKE

- 3 cups sugar
- ½ pound butter
- 6 very fresh whole eggs
- 3 heaping cups cake flour
- ¼ teaspoon soda (add to sour cream)
- 1 8-ounce carton sour cream
- 1 teaspoon flavoring (vanilla, lemon or almond)

Cream sugar and butter well, then add eggs, one at a time. Alternately add flour and sour cream (with soda). Add flavoring. Use a Bundt cake pan to make an unusually pretty cake. Bake at 350° for 1 hour and 15 minutes or until done.

Mrs. B. H. Shepherd
Mrs. Robert Evans, Monroe, La.

ALMOND POUND CAKE

- 1 cup butter or oleo
- 1 cup granulated sugar
- 1 cup powdered sugar
- 4 egg yolks
- 1 teaspoon vanilla
- 1 teaspoon almond extract
- 4 egg whites
- 3 cups flour, sifted three times
- Pinch salt (⅛ to ¼ teaspoon)
- 2 teaspoons baking powder
- 1 cup milk (skim milk may be used)

Cream butter or oleo well, sift both sugars together and add slowly to butter. Add unbeaten egg yolks, one at a time, and beat until smooth. Mix both extracts. Sift flour, baking powder and salt three times. Add flour mixture and milk alternately to batter, beginning and ending with flour. Beat egg whites until stiff and fold into mixture. Use a well greased cake mold or pan. If using a mold, put large dabs of butter or oleo in creases and put almonds in butter dabs. Pour batter in pan and cook for 1¼ hours at 350°. When done, let cool in pan 15 minutes before turning out.

Makes 24 pieces. Will freeze well. Mrs. Tom Hope, Jr.

GEORGIA POUND CAKE

3 sticks butter or margarine
2½ cups sugar
3 cups flour
½ teaspoon salt
8 whole eggs
1½ teaspoons cream of tartar
1½ teaspoons lemon extract
2 tablespoons lemon juice
Grated rind of 1 lemon

Cream well the butter and sugar. Add well-beaten eggs and cream of tartar. Sift flour twice, then add salt and sift again. Add to butter mixture. Add flavoring and rind. Now beat for 10 minutes. Bake in a lightly greased and floured tube pan about 10" across. The heavy aluminum Bundt pan is perfect. Preheat oven to 300°. Bake for 1 hour and 15 minutes, then test. It may need 5, 10 or 15 minutes more. It must separate a bit from the pan and when touched, spring back and leave no depression. Let cool in pan for 15 minutes. Run thin knife around tube and outer rim. For Bundt pan, jar on bottom, invert on rack and jar again. If cake sticks, cover inverted bottom with wet cloth a time or two until it comes loose, jarring the edge meanwhile. Good plain or may be glazed with the following:

Orange Glaze

¾ cup sugar
1 teaspoon cornstarch
½ cup orange juice (apricot juice is good, too)
1 pinch salt

Boil mixture 3 or 4 minutes. Brush on cake while both are hot.

VARIATION: For Rum Cake, substitute 1½ or 2 teaspoons rum flavoring for the lemon in cake and use the following glaze:

½ cup brown sugar
½ cup white sugar
1 teaspoon cornstarch (optional)
½ cup water
1 teaspoon or more rum flavoring, or 1 tablespoon rum

Mix all together, except flavoring, and boil well 3 or 4 minutes if cornstarch is used. Add flavoring. Brush on cake while both are hot.

Mrs. J. V. Hendrick

SOUR CREAM CAKE

½ pound butter
2½ cups sugar
6 large eggs, separated
1 cup sour cream
3 cups flour
¼ teaspoon soda
½ teaspoon salt
2 teaspoons vanilla

Cream butter, add sugar and cream well. Add sour cream and blend well, then add egg yolks and mix. Sift dry ingredients and add. Beat egg whites until stiff, add vanilla to whites and fold very gently into batter. Bake in large steeple pan for 1 to 1½ hours at 325°.

Mrs. Clint Gamble

TIPSY CAKE

5 eggs, separated
1 cup sugar
1 cup sifted flour
½ teaspoon baking powder
Grated rind of ½ lemon

Sherry Glaze:
½ cup sugar
½ cup cream sherry

Beat egg yolks until thick, then slowly add sugar, beating until fluffy. Sift the combined flour and baking powder over yolk mixture and beat just to blend thoroughly. Stir in the lemon rind. Beat egg whites until stiff; gently fold yolk mixture into whites. Pour into lightly greased tube pan. Bake at 350° for 30-35 minutes until cake springs back when pressed. Cool in pan for 10 minutes, then turn out on cake plate and add Sherry Glaze.

To make Sherry Glaze, combine sugar and sherry, bring to a boil and cook until thickened, about 4 minutes. Pour this syrup over top of cake. When glaze has cooled, place lace paper doily over top, sprinkle with a mixture of equal parts cinnamon and sifted confectioners' sugar. Remove doily. To enjoy this cake fully, serve with glasses of cream sherry.

Mrs. James M. Turner

FEATHER SPONGE CAKE

6 egg yolks
½ cup cold water
1½ cups sugar
½ teaspoon vanilla
½ teaspoon orange or lemon extract
¼ teaspoon almond extract
1½ cups cake flour
¼ teaspoon salt
6 egg whites
¾ teaspoon cream of tartar

Beat egg yolks until thick and lemon colored, add water and continue beating until thick. Gradually add sugar, then extracts. Fold in flour, sifted with salt, a little at a time. Beat egg whites until foamy, add cream of tartar and beat until they form peaks. Fold into egg yolk mixture. Bake in ungreased tube pan in 325° oven for 1 hour. When done, invert to cool, then frost.

Icing

1 pound box confectioners' sugar
½ stick butter
Grated rind of large orange
⅓ cup orange juice

Cream butter and sugar; add juice and rind of lemon or orange and beat until creamy consistency for spreading is reached.

Mrs. Leroy Kirby

PINEAPPLE UPSIDE-DOWN CAKE

Topping:
- ½ cup butter or oleo
- 2 cups brown sugar (packed)
- 1 No. 303 can sliced pineapple
- 1 cherry for center of each pineapple ring
- ½ cup chopped pecans

Batter:
- 4 eggs
- 4 tablespoons pineapple juice (may use ½ cherry juice)
- ½ cup white sugar
- 1 cup flour
- ¼ teaspoon salt
- 2½ level teaspoons baking powder

Preheat oven to 350°. Melt butter in heavy cast iron skillet 3" deep. Add brown sugar and stir. Arrange pineapple slices side by side. Add pineapple juice if mixture is too thick. Place cherry in center of each slice and sprinkle nuts over mixture. Let bubble over low heat. Beat eggs in mixing bowl until light and foamy. Add pineapple juice and sugar. Sift together flour, salt, and baking powder and add to beaten eggs. Beat batter just until smooth. Pour into skillet over bubbling mixture and shake skillet to level and distribute batter. Place skillet in preheated oven for 20 to 30 minutes. When done, cool 10 to 12 minutes, and turn cake out on a plate or tray.

Makes 8 servings.

Mrs. Harmon Egger

DELICIOUS OLD-FASHIONED SPONGE CAKE

- 3 cups sifted cake flour
- 2 teaspoons baking powder
- 6 large eggs at room temperature
- ¼ teaspoon salt
- 2 cups sugar
- 1 cup hot milk (bring to a boil just a short while)
- 1 teaspoon vanilla

Resift flour with baking powder. Put salt in eggs and beat 2 minutes with mixer at high speed until light and fluffy. Gradually add sugar and blend well. Add ¼ of hot milk and blend. Fold in by hand the remaining milk alternately with flour. Take a spoon and mix thoroughly to be sure milk is blended; then add vanilla. Bake in a 12" x 8" x 2" pan lined with waxed paper, greased and floured. Bake at 300° for 15 minutes, then turn oven to 350° and bake for 45 minutes more.

24 servings.

Mrs. Paul E. Sippel, Jr.

LEMON SPONGE CAKE

4 eggs, separated
1 cup sugar
1 tablespoon baking powder
Juice of 1 lemon
1 teaspoon vanilla
1¼ cups flour
Grated rind of 1 lemon
Whipped cream to cover
Coconut or nuts for garnish

Beat egg yolks with sugar until lemon colored, then add lemon juice, ¼ cup hot water and flour sifted with baking powder. Fold in stiffly beaten egg whites, add lemon rind and vanilla last. Pour into buttered square cake pan. Bake 30 minutes at 350°. When cool, cut into squares, cover with whipped cream and finely grated coconut or chopped nuts.

Serves 9. Sherman, Chef of Charlton Lyons, Sr.

BIZCOCHO DE ESPECIES (SPICE CAKE)

3½ cups sifted cake flour
3 teaspoons baking powder
½ teaspoon salt
2 teaspoons each of cinnamon, ground cloves, nutmeg (The original recipe calls for 1 tablespoon of each spice but you must LOVE spice for that amount. You may prefer 1½ teaspoons of each)
1 cup butter or oleo
2¼ cups dark brown sugar, well packed
6 eggs, unbeaten
1 cup milk
⅓ cup sweet Madeira wine, or other sweet wine
Confectioners' sugar

Sift together first six dry ingredients (including spices). Cream butter, while gradually adding brown sugar, with electric mixer at medium speed. Beat until well blended. Add eggs, one at a time, beating after each addition. Add alternately flour mixture and liquids (milk and wine) beginning and ending with flour, beating until just well mixed.

Pour into a Bundt pan which has been well greased and floured or into any tube pan which is about 10" in diameter. Bake at 350° for 1 hour. Or bake at 300° for 1 hour and 20 minutes. Cool cake in pan on wire rack for 10 to 15 minutes. Loosen edges and turn out. When cool, dust top with confectioners' sugar. This cake keeps nicely and improves in flavor when stored in cake container. This is an Israeli recipe.

Mrs. W. A. Fortson, Jr.

PRUNE SPICE CAKE

2 cups sifted flour
½ teaspoon salt
1 teaspoon soda
½ teaspoon baking powder
1½ teaspoons cinnamon
1 teaspoon nutmeg (optional)
1 teaspoon allspice (optional)
½ cup salad oil
1½ cups sugar
3 eggs, unbeaten
1 cup cooked prunes
1 cup buttermilk
1 cup pecans

Sift together, flour, salt, soda, baking powder and spices. Beat eggs, adding oil and sugar. Add cooked prunes, then add sifted flour mixture, alternately with buttermilk. Scrape sides of bowl. Add pecans, blending thoroughly. Pour into greased tube pan, place in preheated 350° oven and bake for about 1 hour, or use 2 greased loaf pans, and bake at 350° for about 30 minutes. Let cool for 10 minutes before turning out of pan. The following sauce may be poured over the cake, but it is not necessary:

1 cup sugar
½ teaspoon soda
1 teaspoon light syrup
½ cup buttermilk
1 stick butter or margarine

Combine all ingredients in saucepan. Cook until butter melts. (Start about 5 minutes before cake is done so it may be poured over warm cake.)

Cake freezes very successfully.

Mrs. Albert L. Dietz, Jr.
Mrs. John L. Rhea, Jr.

ENCORE CAKE

½ cup butter
2 cups brown sugar
2 egg yolks
1¼ cups buttermilk
1 scant teaspoon soda
2⅓ cups flour
1 teaspoon baking powder
1 teaspoon cinnamon
1 teaspoon ground cloves
¾ teaspoon salt
1 teaspoon vanilla

Blend butter, sugar and egg yolks. Dissolve soda in milk. Add milk alternately with dry ingredients. Add vanilla and mix thoroughly. Pour into 8" x 12" greased and floured pan and spread with icing.

Icing

2 egg whites
1 cup brown sugar
½ cup broken pecans

Beat egg whites until stiff, add sugar slowly and beat until smooth. Spread over cake and sprinkle with nuts. Bake 45 to 50 minutes at 350°.

Frances Koch

FRESH SWEET POTATO CAKE

1½ cups cooking oil
2 cups sugar
4 eggs, separated
4 tablespoons hot water
2½ cups flour
3 teaspoons baking powder
¼ teaspoon salt
1 teaspoon cinnamon
1 teaspoon nutmeg
1½ cups finely grated sweet potatoes
1 cup nuts
1 teaspoon vanilla

Combine oil and sugar, and beat until smooth. Add egg yolks and beat well, then add hot water. Add remaining dry ingredients which have been sifted together. Stir in potatoes and nuts. Add vanilla and beat, then fold in stiffly beaten egg whites. Bake in greased tube pan about 1 hour at 350°.

If desired, this cake may be made in three 9" greased and floured pans and put together in layers with the following icing:

1 large can evaporated milk
1 cup sugar
1 stick margarine
3 egg yolks
1 teaspoon vanilla
1½ cups coconut

Combine milk, sugar, margarine and egg yolks and cook over medium heat, stirring constantly until thick, about 12 minutes. Remove from heat and add rest of ingredients. Cool, then ice layers.

Mrs. Boyd Holley

PLANTATION PECAN CAKE

3 cups finely chopped pecans
2 tablespoons cake flour
2 teaspoons baking powder
¼ teaspoon salt
6 eggs, separated
1½ cups sugar
Frosting:
1 pint whipping cream
¼ cup confectioners' sugar
1 teaspoon vanilla

Chopped pecans should resemble fine corn meal. Combine flour, baking powder, and salt with pecans. Beat egg yolks with sugar until thick and lemon-colored. Fold beaten egg whites into nuts. Fold egg white-nut mixture into yolk-sugar mixture. Pour into two greased paper-lined 8" round cake pans. Use either waxed paper or brown paper. Bake in a moderate oven, 350°, for 20-25 minutes. Cool. For frosting, whip cream with confectioners' sugar and vanilla. Spread between cooled layers and over top of cake.

Mrs. Edgar Galloway

AUNT HATTIE'S DATE-NUT CAKE

1 cup butter
2 cups sugar
7 eggs, separated
3½ cups flour
3 teaspoons baking powder
1 cup whiskey or brandy
4 packages dates, cut up
1 quart shelled pecans, broken

Cream butter and sugar together. Add egg yolks, one at a time, stirring well after each addition. Sift flour and baking powder together and add. Stir in whiskey. Beat egg whites until stiff and fold in gently. Add chopped dates and nuts carefully. Use a greased loaf pan or tube pan lined with brown paper. Bake at 300° for 1-1½ hours. This is an expensive cake to make, but it is a wonderful "Christmas" cake and keeps well for some time.

Mrs. M. C. Bubenzer

CHOCOLATE DATE CAKE

1 package dates
1 cup hot water
1 teaspoon soda
½ cup shortening
1 cup sugar
2 eggs, beaten
1 teaspoon vanilla
1⅓ cups flour
1 teaspoon cocoa
1 package chocolate morsels
1 cup pecans

Cut up dates and pour hot water over them. Let cool 1 minute. Then add soda and let stand. Cream shortening and sugar, add eggs and vanilla and mix thoroughly. Sift flour and cocoa together. Add to shortening mixture and beat. Add dates (do not drain them) and mix well. Pour into greased 8" x 11" pan and sprinkle chocolate morsels and pecans over top. Bake at 350° for 30-35 minutes.

Mrs. Will J. Fullilove

DATE LOAF CAKE

1 package dates
1 cup boiling water
1 teaspoon soda
1½ cups pecans
½ cup shortening
1 cup sugar
2 eggs
1 teaspoon vanilla
Pinch of salt
2 cups flour

Cut up dates, add soda to boiling water and pour over dates. Cool. Cream shortening, sugar, salt, eggs and vanilla. Roll pecans in flour. Mix dates and shortening, then add flour, ½ cup at a time, until all flour has been added. Add nuts and fold into mixture. Pour into loaf pan which has been greased and floured. Bake at 350° for 45 minutes.

Mrs. W. T. Whisner

ORANGE DATE CAKE

1 cup butter
2 cups sugar
4 eggs
1 teaspoon soda
1⅓ cups buttermilk
4 cups sifted flour
2 tablespoons grated orange rind
1 pound chopped nuts
1 pound chopped dates
¼ teaspoon salt

Cream butter and sugar, then beat in eggs, one at a time. Dissolve soda in buttermilk. Dredge orange rind, dates and nuts with some of the flour. Add remaining sifted flour in about 3 parts, alternately with milk mixture, to butter mixture. Beat batter until smooth. Add orange rind, dates and nuts dredged in flour, and salt. Grease and flour 1 tube or 2 loaf pans. Bake in slow oven 300°-325° for 1½ hours. When cake is done, pour orange sauce over hot cake and let cool in pan.

Orange Sauce

2 cups sugar
1 cup orange juice
2 tablespoons orange rind

Mix these ingredients together until sugar is dissolved. If desired, top with whipped cream on individual servings.

Mrs. Edward N. Henderson

RAISIN-NUT LOAF WITH HARD SAUCE

For 2 Loaf Cakes:
2 cups raisins
2¼ cups water
½ cup shortening
2 cups sugar
4 cups flour
1 teaspoon salt
1½ teaspoons cinnamon
1 teaspoon nutmeg
1 teaspoon ground cloves
1 teaspoon soda
1 cup water
¾ cup finely chopped nuts

Hard Sauce:
4 tablespoons butter
2 teaspoons vanilla
Confectioners' sugar

Loaf Cakes: Simmer raisins and the 2¼ cups water for 15 minutes. Cream shortening and sugar together. Sift flour, salt, soda and spices together and add to shortening mixture. Add sugar mixture alternately with 1 cup water. Add the raisin-water mixture and beat lightly until well blended. Add nuts and bake at 350° for 1 hour in 2 greased loaf pans.

Hard Sauce: Cream butter and vanilla with enough confectioners' sugar to give the desired consistency. Serve with raisin-nut loaf.

These loaf cakes are ideal for freezing. They also remain fresh for a long time unfrozen.

Mrs. Ray Barlow

OLD FASHIONED PECAN CAKE

½ pound butter
1 pound sugar
6 eggs
1 pound flour
2 teaspoons baking powder
1 tablespoon nutmeg
1 cup bourbon whiskey
1 quart broken pecan meats
1½ boxes seedless raisins

Coat raisins with flour. Cream butter and sugar. Add eggs, one at a time. Gradually add flour (to which baking powder and nutmeg have been added) alternately with whiskey. Add nuts and raisins. Bake in a greased and floured loaf or Bundt pan. Do not preheat oven. Bake at 300° for 3 hours.

Mrs. Roy C. Stringfellow

BIG MAMMA'S FRUIT CAKE

1 cup butter
2 cups sugar
6 eggs, separated
4 cups flour (save 1 cup for flouring fruit)
Pinch of salt
2 teaspoons baking powder
1 cup bourbon (good brand)
2 teaspoons fresh grated nutmeg
2 teaspoons vanilla extract
1 pound candied cherries
1 pound pitted dates
1 pound raisins
1 pound pecans
½ pound English walnuts
1 pound candied pineapple

Cream butter thoroughly, then add sugar gradually. Beat until light and fluffy. Add egg yolks one at a time. Sift and measure 3 cups flour; resift 3 times with the baking powder and salt. Add alternately (flour first and last) with the whiskey. Add nutmeg and vanilla. Flour fruit with the remaining cup of flour (sifted) and fold into the batter. As this needs a very large container, I use my roasting pan, and use my hands to mix fruit into batter thoroughly. Lastly, fold in egg whites, which have been beaten stiff but not dry. This recipe makes one large and two smaller cakes; may be cooked in tube, loaf and assorted deep pans, greased and lined with wax paper. Makes wonderful Christmas presents to "special" people. Bake at 275° for 2 or more hours. Test with a straw or toothpick for doneness of batter; you do not want cake to be too dry.

Mrs. William S. Evans

Try making your favorite "boxed" cake in your prettiest mousse or salad mold. Be sure to double the baking time.

WHITE NUT FRUIT CAKE

1 cup sugar
¼ pound butter
3 eggs, well beaten
2 cups flour
1 teaspoon baking powder
2 ounces whiskey
1 pound nuts (1 quart chopped)
½ pound dates
½ pound candied cherries
½ pound candied pineapple

Cream butter and sugar together and add eggs. Add flour, sifted with baking powder. Add whiskey, nuts and fruit (floured for better mixing). Pour into two loaf pans about 2½" x 4½" x 8½". Cook at 350° approximately 1 hour and 20 minutes. It is also extra good if poured in thin layer and cut into cookie squares when done.

Faerie Marston

BILLIE'S FRUIT CAKE

2 sticks butter
2 cups sugar
6 eggs, separated
1 iced tea glass of bourbon whiskey (12 ounces)
Grated rind of 1 orange and 1 lemon
4 cups sifted flour
1 teaspoon baking soda
1 teaspoon baking powder
2 tablespoons nutmeg
2 pounds white raisins
1 quart shelled pecans, chopped
4 slices crystallized pineapple, cut in bits

Dredge raisins, pineapple and pecans well in some of the flour. Cream butter and sugar together; add egg yolks one at a time, beating after each addition. Sift flour, baking soda, baking powder and nutmeg together and add, alternately with whiskey, to creamed mixture. Then add batter to fruit, and mix well. Fold in beaten egg whites. Bake in slow oven (250°) until lightly brown.

This recipe makes 2 loaf cakes. When using loaf pans, grease pans; cut brown paper to fit bottom of pans and put in place; then grease paper. This also makes about 150 bite-size cakes, baked in tiny paper cups.

Mrs. W. E. ("Ned") Wilson

ICEBOX CAKE

1 large box vanilla wafers
1 can condensed milk
1 pound pecans, chopped
1 pound raisins
1 pound crystallized cherries or pineapple (or 1 pound of each)

Crush vanilla wafers and chop nuts finely. Combine wafer crumbs, nuts and milk and mix well. Add raisins and fruit. Roll in waxed paper and place in refrigerator until firm.

Mrs. Sidney E. Cook

WHITE RAISIN POUND CAKE

- 1 pound butter
- 2 cups sugar
- 6 eggs
- 3½ cups flour
- 1 teaspoon baking powder
- 1 pound white raisins
- 2 cups pecans
- 2 ounces lemon extract

Cream butter and sugar. Add eggs, flour and baking powder, then raisins and chopped nuts. Mix well, and add extract. Bake at 250° for about 4 hours.

Mrs. William J. Atkins

CHRISTMAS NUT CAKE

- 2 pounds shelled pecans
- 2 packages puffed seeded raisins
- 1½-inch pieces lemon peel (4-ounce package, chopped)
- 1½-inch pieces orange peel (4-ounce package, chopped)
- 1½ pounds flour (5 cups)
- 1 rounded tablespoon baking powder
- 1 rounded tablespoon nutmeg
- ½ tablespoon salt
- ¾ pound margarine
- 1½ pounds white sugar (3 cups)
- 1 10-ounce glass apple jelly or any tart jelly
- 9 eggs
- 1¼ scant cups cider or apple juice

Chop pecans, not too fine. Add lemon peel, orange peel and raisins. Measure flour and sift twice. Then sift about half the flour into fruit. Dredge well, making sure that each piece of fruit is covered with flour. Sift remaining half of flour the third time with baking powder, nutmeg and salt. Set aside. Cream margarine and sugar together well. Add jelly. Add eggs, two at a time, mixing well after each addition. Add dry ingredients alternately with apple juice, ending with some of the apple juice. (Batter will be heavy.) Then add batter to fruit, and mix well.

Grease cake pans and cut brown paper to fit bottom of each pan. Grease paper, place in pan, and flour paper and sides of pans. This recipe makes two large loaf cakes and two small loaf cakes. Fill them with batter to one inch from top. Bake in 250° oven. Large cakes take about 4 hours; small ones, about 3 hours. Watch closely toward end of cooking time. Cakes are done when they shrink from sides of pan, and when they spring back when touched in the middle. When they are done, cool thoroughly on racks. Cakes will keep indefinitely when wrapped in a bourbon-soaked cloth, then in heavy foil.

Mrs. H. Clay Garrison

CHOCOLATE-COFFEE ICED CUPCAKES

1 stick oleo or ½ cup shortening
1 cup sugar
2 eggs
¼ teaspoon salt
2 cups all purpose flour
2 teaspoons baking powder
½ cup plus 2 tablespoons milk
1 teaspoon vanilla
Icing for Cupcakes:
1 stick oleo
¾ box powdered sugar
4 tablespoons cocoa
2 tablespoons brewed coffee
4 tablespoons light cream
½ teaspoon vanilla

For cupcakes, cream together oleo and sugar. Add eggs and salt, and cream all together. Sift flour and baking powder together, and add to creamed mixture alternately with milk. Then add vanilla and beat until smooth. Grease muffin pans and fill about half full with batter. Bake in 375° oven 10 to 15 minutes, until brown around edges.

Makes 18 cupcakes.

For icing, cream softened oleo, then stir sugar in. Add cocoa, then coffee. Add cream until mixture reaches right consistency to spread. Add vanilla. Let cupcakes cool before icing.

Mrs. August C. Erickson

BLACK FRUIT CAKE

2 pounds white raisins
1 pound black raisins
1 pound candied pineapple
1 pound candied cherries
½ pound citron
1 quart chopped nuts
1 pound butter or margarine
1 pound sugar
1 pound flour
2 rounded teaspoons baking powder
1 tablespoon cinnamon
1 tablespoon cloves
1 tablespoon ginger
1 tablespoon nutmeg
12 eggs
1 cup syrup
1 cup coffee
1 cup whiskey

Cut fruits into small pieces. Use some of flour to dredge fruits and nuts. Cream butter and sugar together. Add flour, baking powder and spices. Add eggs one at a time, stirring after each addition. Add syrup, coffee and whiskey, then fruits and nuts. Grease pans and line bottom of each with two thicknesses of brown paper. Bake at 325° for approximately 2½ to 3 hours, depending upon size of pan. Cakes may be made weeks or days before Christmas and stored in closed containers. They should be wrapped in foil to prevent drying.

Recipe makes 12 pounds of fruit cake.

From the recipes of Mrs. J. A. Bell

WHITE FRUIT CAKE

½ pound butter
3 cups sugar
6 eggs
3 cups cake flour
1 teaspoon soda
1 teaspoon nutmeg
1 jelly glass bourbon
1 pound white raisins
1 pound cherries and pineapple
2 pints broken pecans

Cream butter and sugar; add eggs, one at a time, beating after each addition. Add flour, which has been sifted with soda and nutmeg, alternately with bourbon. Fold in chopped fruit and nuts. Grease and flour miniature muffin pans well, and spoon batter into them. Bake at 325° for about 15 minutes. Cakes will keep well when stored in tin boxes.

Mrs. D. Y. Smith

RAISIN GEM CUPCAKES

½ cup shortening
1 cup brown sugar
1 egg
1 cup buttermilk
2 cups flour
1 teaspoon soda
1 teaspoon cinnamon
1 teaspoon nutmeg
1 teaspoon cloves
1 cup raisins
½ cup chopped nuts

Blend shortening, sugar and egg together. Add buttermilk, and stir in dry ingredients which have been sifted together. Add raisins and nuts. Pour into greased cupcake tins and bake in 350° oven for 15 or 20 minutes.

Makes about 18 cupcakes or 5 dozen tiny muffins, which you would bake 10 minutes.

Mrs. Thomas McElroy

WACKY CUPCAKES

1½ cups flour
1 cup sugar
3 tablespoons cocoa
½ teaspoon salt
1 teaspoon baking soda
1 teaspoon vanilla
1 teaspoon vinegar
5 tablespoons melted shortening
1 cup cool water

Sift dry ingredients together into bowl and make 3 grooves in this mixture. Pour vanilla into one, vinegar into one, and shortening into one. Pour cool water over all, and mix together until smooth. Place cupcake papers in muffin tins, and pour batter into them. Bake at 350° for 30 minutes.

Makes 3 dozen small or 12-14 large cupcakes.

Mrs. Charlotte Merriam

APPLESAUCE CUPCAKES

2½ cups flour
2 cups sugar
¼ teaspoon baking powder
1½ teaspoons soda
1½ teaspoons salt
¾ teaspoon cinnamon
½ teaspoon cloves
½ teaspoon allspice
½ cup soft oleo or butter
¼ cup rum
1 cup raisins, cut up
½ cup nuts, chopped
1½ cups applesauce
1 very large egg

Sift first 8 ingredients together. Add next four and beat 2 minutes. Add applesauce and egg and beat 2 more minutes. Pour into muffin tins which have been well greased and floured. Bake at 325° for 17 to 20 minutes.

Icing:
1 stick butter
1 whole egg
¼ to ½ cup cream
1 box powdered sugar

Beat all ingredients until well blended. Spread on top of cupcakes and decorate each with a pecan half. These are nice to serve at a coffee or tea, as they look pretty and taste delicious. They freeze beautifully.

Makes 100 to 150 tiny muffins.

Mrs. Harry A. Johnson, Jr.

INDIVIDUAL NUT CAKES

1½ boxes white raisins
Bourbon whiskey
1 pound sugar (2 cups)
6 eggs, separated
1 pound butter (2 cups)
1 pound flour (4 cups)
1 teaspoon baking powder
4 cups pecans, coarsely chopped

Examine raisins carefully and discard any dark ones; pull stems from good ones, and pour bourbon over these just to cover; let soak overnight. Next day, make cakes by creaming sugar and egg yolks well. Melt butter and let it cool, then add it to sugar and yolks. Sift flour before measuring, then sift with baking powder. Add to creamed mixture. Add raisins and bourbon, then add pecans which have been lightly floured. (To do this, place a small amount of flour in a paper bag, and shake pecans in it.) Whip egg whites stiff and fold into batter until well blended. Pour batter into fluted paper muffin liners and fill a little more than half full. Bake at 325° for 20 or 25 minutes. Cool well and store in tightly covered tins. With a teaspoon, drip extra bourbon on each cake every 2 or 3 days for a week. This is not necessary, but it makes cakes that much better.

Mrs. W. J. O'Brien, Jr.

UNCOOKED CHOCOLATE ICING

¾ stick butter or margarine
3½ squares unsweetened baking chocolate
⅓ cup evaporated milk
1 pound confectioners' sugar
1 teaspoon vanilla
⅛ teaspoon salt

Melt butter and chocolate in top of double boiler. To this mixture, add sugar and milk, stirring constantly until mixture is smooth and thick. Add vanilla and salt and beat about 15 minutes. Mixture should remain over hot water at least 15 minutes altogether to remove any uncooked taste. Add more milk if icing is too stiff to spread.

This will ice a 2-layer 9" cake.

Mrs. Vernon W. Woods

ONE-MINUTE CHOCOLATE ICING

2 cups sugar
1 stick butter
½ cup cocoa
¼ cup corn syrup
½ cup sweet milk
1 teaspoon vanilla

Bring ingredients to a good boil, and let boil one minute. Remove from heat; add vanilla. Allow to cool a few minutes, then beat to spreading consistency.

Mrs. David H. Walke
Mrs. Walter Hawkins

ROASTED ALMOND COFFEE ICING DELIGHT

1 package plain gelatin
¼ cup cold water
1 cup confectioners' sugar
2 tablespoons strong coffee (instant coffee may be used)
6 egg yolks
1 teaspoon vanilla
1 pint whipped cream
1 package almond halves, roasted

Soften gelatin in cold water and place over hot water to dissolve. Add sugar and coffee. Beat yolks until very light, and add gelatin mixture to these. Add vanilla and whipped cream. Store in icebox for at least four hours. Stir well before spreading on cake; after spreading, sprinkle with roasted almonds.

Mrs. H. D. Lawrence

CHOCOLATE FROSTING

4 squares unsweetened chocolate
1 stick butter
1 box powdered sugar
1 small can evaporated milk
Pinch of salt

Melt chocolate and butter. Mix well and add salt. Then add sugar and milk alternately.

This makes enough frosting for a 2-layer 9" cake.

Mrs. Robert Paul Wear, Jr.

LAPLANDER FROSTING

2 eggs
3 squares unsweetened chocolate
4 tablespoons butter
1¾ cups sugar
5 tablespoons cream
1 teaspoon vanilla

Beat eggs in saucepan, then add all other ingredients except vanilla. Bring to boiling point, stirring constantly. Let cook 2 or 3 minutes. Add vanilla and beat until thick.

Ices a 2-layer cake.

Mrs. Marshall Martin

WHITE ICING

4 or 5 egg whites
2½ cups sugar
1 cup water
¼ teaspoon cream of tartar
1 teaspoon vanilla

Boil 2 cups sugar and water until mixture threads (220°). Beat egg whites until foamy; add cream of tartar. Continue beating until stiff. Add remaining ½ cup sugar gradually, beating continually until whites are very stiff. Gradually add sugar syrup, pouring very slowly. Add vanilla. This may be made in electric mixer.

Mrs. D. Y. Smith

SAUCE FOR ANGEL FOOD CAKE

¾ cup sugar
Juice of 1 orange
Grated rind of 2 oranges
4 egg yolks
1 pint whipping cream

Combine all ingredients except cream in top of double boiler and cook over hot water until thick. Let cool. Whip cream and fold into custard.

Half of this recipe is sufficient for one angel food cake.

Mrs. Paul R. Winder

Pies

ADVOCARE 100 INDEPENDENCE BOWL

The spirit of the nation's independence is celebrated annually during the Advocare 100 Independence Bowl, and what better way to celebrate the American Dream than with football—the all-American Sport. The bowl features a weeklong party with two top college teams competing on the gridiron in Independence Stadium. Each year the bowl honors an outstanding U.S. citizen who epitomizes the bicentennial spirit in which the game was formed with the awarding of the General Omar Bradley Spirit of Independence Award.

Recipients have included Bob Hope, John Wayne, Paul Harvey, and Danny Thomas. Activities prior to the game include a riverfront rally with spirit contests between the two teams' supporters, a Battle of the Bands and dance. A "Red, White, and Blue Tailgate Party" is held on the day of the game with music and plenty of Louisiana cuisine.

EASY STIR-N-ROLL PASTRY

2 cups sifted enriched flour
1½ teaspoons salt
½ cup salad oil
2 tablespoons evaporated milk
2 tablespoons water

Mix flour and salt. Measure oil, milk and water in same cup (but don't stir). Pour all at once into flour; stir until mixed. Press into smooth ball. Cut in halves; flatten slightly. Place one half between 2 sheets waxed paper, 12" square. Roll out gently to edges of paper. (Dampen table top to prevent slipping.) Peel off top paper. If dough tears, mend without moistening. Lift paper and pastry by top corners. Place paper-side-up in 9" pie pan. Peel off paper and fit pastry into pan. Roll out top crust the same way.

Mrs. Clarence B. Erickson, Jr.

FLAKY PIE CRUST

1½ cups flour
½ cup shortening, chilled
½ teaspoon salt
4 to 6 tablespoons ice water

Sift flour and salt. Cut chilled shortening into flour until shortening particles are about the size of a pea. Add just enough ice water to make a paste which will clean bowl. Roll on floured board, fold and refold, then roll again. Continue this until dough is smooth. Handle quickly but gently.

Makes two 8-inch crusts.

Mrs. W. T. Whisner

APRICOT TARTS

Pastry:
2 cups flour
1 cup shortening
½ teaspoon salt
⅓ cup cold water, plus 2 tablespoons

Prepared pie crust mix may be used.

Filling:
1 8-ounce package dried apricots
⅛ teaspoon salt
1½ cups water
¾ cup sugar

Pastry: Sift flour and salt, cut in shortening and add water. Roll and cut with 2½-inch biscuit cutter, roll very thin.

Filling: Cover apricots with water and boil briskly 5 minutes with cover off. Cover and simmer slowly for 15 minutes. Add sugar and salt for last 5 minutes of cooking. Put through ricer and chill.

Put ½ teaspoon apricots in dough and fold over, then crimp with fork. Prick tarts one time with fork, brush with melted oleo or butter and sprinkle with sugar. Bake in 350° oven for 25 minutes or until brown.

Freezes very well. Do not brush on sugar or butter until ready to bake. Cook while still frozen.

Mrs. F. L. Housh

AMBER PIE

¼-½ cup mayhaw jelly
¾ cup sugar
4 eggs
4 level tablespoons flour
1½ cups buttermilk
1 pinch salt
1 teaspoon vanilla
1 tablespoon butter
1 cooked pie shell

Separate eggs, setting whites aside. Into top of double boiler put egg yolk, jelly, sugar, flour, buttermilk, salt, vanilla and butter. Mix well and cook over boiling water until thickened. Pour into pie shell, and top with meringue. Bake in 250° oven until meringue is brown. (Any tart jelly, such as plum, may be substituted for mayhaw.)

Mrs. E. Rupert Campbell

APPLE PIE

6 tart juicy apples (first choice: Jonathan; second choice: Winesap)
¾ cup sugar
½ teaspoon cinnamon
¼ teaspoon nutmeg
¼ teaspoon apple pie spice
⅛ teaspoon lemon rind
2 tablespoons flour
½ lemon
½ cup melted butter

Wash, peel and core apples. Cut apples into quarters and thinly slice into bowl. Mix ½ cup sugar, all spices, lemon rind, and flour together. Coat apples with sugar mixture. Squeeze lemon over apples. Let set while lining 9-inch pie shell with crust. Pinwheel apples as regularly as possible in pie shell. Pour melted butter over apples, sprinkle remaining sugar on top and for spicy taste sprinkle with more nutmeg and apple pie spice. Place strips of crust on top of pie and dot crust with butter. Bake in hot oven at 450° for 15 minutes or until crust begins to brown. Turn heat to moderate (350°) and continue baking for about 25 minutes or until apples are tender.

Mrs. Tom Perry

SOUR CREAM APPLE PIE

6 or 7 tart apples
Juice of ½ lemon
¾ cup sugar
⅓ cup flour
1 teaspoon cinnamon
¼ teaspoon nutmeg
½ teaspoon apple pie spice
¼ cup butter
1 cup sour cream

Arrange pared apples in unbaked pastry shell. Use a deep 9" pan. Sprinkle combined ingredients over apples, and spoon sour cream on top. Bake 30 minutes at 400°, then reduce heat to 350° and bake 45 minutes longer. Whenever sour green apples are available, use them. They add so much flavor!

Mrs. Sinclair Kouns

FRESH BERRY PIE

Wash fresh wild dewberries; add small amount of water and cook until berries are soft. Remove from fire and put through ricer. Return juioe to fire, sweeten to taste and thicken with small amount of flour dissolved in cold water. Mixture should be slightly thickened but not firm. This may be prepared ahead of time—in fact, I do this at berry season and freeze until needed.

When ready to serve, heat this mixture until very hot. Add fresh boysenberries (these may be frozen also) and fill small individual cooked pastry shells.

Top with hard sauce made from equal parts of butter and powdered sugar creamed together with a small amount of vanilla added.

Mrs. C. N. Frierson

BLUEBERRY PIE

1 3-ounce package cream cheese, softened
½ pint whipped cream
½ cup powdered sugar
1 teaspoon vanilla
½ can blueberry pie filling
1 teaspoon plain gelatin

Combine whipped cream, cream cheese, sugar and vanilla. Pour into prepared pie shell. Heat blueberry pie filling with gelatin and cool. Spread over pie and chill. This is good served in a graham cracker crust, made as follows:

Graham Cracker Crust

1¼ cups graham cracker crumbs
3 tablespoons sugar
⅓ cup melted margarine
¼ cup chopped pecans

Combine crumbs and sugar. Stir in melted butter and blend. Pack in a 9" pie pan. Pat pecans into crust. Bake in 350° oven for 5-8 minutes. Cool, then add filling.

Mrs. James Herndon
Dallas, Texas

BLUEBERRY ICEBOX PIE

1 bag graham crackers (⅓ box)
1 8-ounce package cream cheese, softened
1 egg
⅓ cup sugar
1 teaspoon vanilla
1 can blueberry pie filling
½ pint whipping cream

Make graham cracker crust using softened oleo or butter. Whip together cream cheese, egg, sugar, and vanilla and pour on crust. Bake for 25 minutes at 325°. Cool. Add blueberry pie filling. Top with whipped cream. (May be prepared a day ahead.)

Number of servings—8.

Mrs. Frank Green, Jr.

CARAMEL PIE

¾ cup sugar
1 tablespoon butter
2 tablespoons flour
4 eggs, separated
1 cup milk
¾ cup sugar (to be caramelized)
⅓ stick butter
1 tablespoon cream

Cream sugar, butter and flour. Add egg yolks and milk. Heat this mixture in double boiler while browning sugar, butter and cream in heavy skillet. Pour browned ingredients into first mixture and cook until thick and smooth. Remove and cool. When thoroughly cool, pour into cooked pie shell and cover with meringue made of stiffly beaten egg whites. Brown.

Mrs. Jack Elgin

YUM-YUM PIE

1 8-ounce package cream cheese
1½ cups confectioners' sugar
1 package powdered whipping cream
1 teaspoon vanilla
1 can cherry or raspberry pie filling
Whipping cream or sour cream for garnish if desired

Bake a very deep 9" or 10" pastry shell, and set aside to cool. Blend and whip cream cheese and 1½ cups confectioners' sugar. No need to sift sugar. Mix powdered whipping cream with vanilla (and milk), according to box directions. Combine the two mixtures and fill pastry shell. Top with cherry or raspberry filling. Use directly from can, with nothing added. Top with whipping cream or sour cream when served, if desired. Should be chilled over night. (Freezes well.)

Will make 8 servings.

Note: Fresh strawberries make a good topping. Add when ready to serve, and then top with whipped cream.

Mrs. John W. Paylor, Jr.

KARO PECAN PIE

1 cup dark corn syrup
½ cup sugar
1 tablespoon flour
3 eggs
1 teaspoon vinegar
3 tablespoons butter
1 cup whole pecans

Mix all ingredients together and pour into unbaked pie shell. Bake 10 minutes at 450°; reduce heat to 300° and bake 35 minutes longer.

Laura Ann Brooks

CHERRY CREAM PIE

2 tablespoons butter
1 cup sugar
¼ cup cornstarch
½ teaspoon salt
1 cup evaporated milk
1 cup water
3 egg yolks (beaten)
2¼ teaspoons vanilla
1 large can sour pitted cherries (drained)

Combine sugar, cornstarch, and salt. Melt butter and add the sugar mixture. Stir in evaporated milk which has been mixed with water. Cook in double boiler, stirring frequently for 20 minutes. Remove mixture from heat and stir into 3 beaten egg yolks. Return to heat and cook for 2 minutes. Add vanilla. Pour cherries (drained) in bottom of lightly baked pie crust, pour custard over top and bake at 325° until set.

Mrs. James Claiborne Cook

CHERRY PIE

2 cups canned sour red pie cherries, drained
1 cup cherry juice
1 cup sugar
Pinch salt
1½ tablespoons tapioca
1 tablespoon melted butter
⅛ teaspoon almond flavoring
2 drops red food coloring

Combine ingredients and allow to stand while preparing pie crust. Use any good pie crust recipe. Roll out half of dough, fitting into bottom of a 9" pie pan. Roll out remaining dough, cut in strips. Pour well-mixed filling into pie shell. Lay strips of dough diagonally across, in both directions. For decoration, cherries and leaves may be cut from excess dough, and put in center of lattice. Trim and fold under excess dough, then flute edges of crust. Bake in hot oven, 450° for 8-10 minutes, then reduce heat and cook for an additional 30 minutes at 350°. Watch to prevent edges from burning. It is best served at room temperature without refrigeration, with ice cream on top of each serving.

6-7 generous servings.

Mrs. James M. Turner

MACAROON PIE

9 saltine crackers
1 teaspoon baking powder
1 cup pecans, cut fine
3 egg whites
1 cup sugar
1 tablespoon almond extract

Crush crackers; add baking powder and pecans to them. Beat egg whites until very stiff, adding sugar gradually. Add almond extract, and combine the two mixtures. Place in buttered pie plate and bake 20 minutes in 325° oven. (Meringue may crack). Serve with ice cream topped with raspberries.

Mrs. Harold Bicknell

CHESS PIE

8″ or 9″ unbaked pie crust
For Filling:
2 cups sugar
1 tablespoon flour
1 tablespoon melted butter
¼ teaspoon nutmeg
3 egg yolks
1 whole egg
1 cup sweet milk
Pinch of salt

For Meringue:
2 egg whites
2 tablespoons sugar

Combine all ingredients for pie mixture adding milk last. Pour into unbaked pie crust and bake in 325° oven for approximately 45 minutes. When knife blade comes out clean, add meringue and return to oven until brown on tips. Make this on the day that it is to be served.

Will make 8 small or 6 large servings.

Mrs. T. M. Williams

CHESS PIE

Pastry:
1 cup flour (all purpose)
1½ teaspoons baking powder
¼ teaspoon salt
⅓ cup shortening
⅓ cup milk

Sift together flour, baking powder and salt. Cut in shortening, add milk. Roll dough very thin and place in a deep 9″ pie pan. Place in a 450° oven for a few minutes, allowing it to crust over but not brown. Set crust aside and let oven cool to 300°.

Filling:
4 eggs
2 cups sugar
½ cup butter (melted)
½ cup whipping cream (not whipped)
1 lemon (juice and grated rind)

Beat eggs thoroughly, add sugar and melted butter and stir in cream, lemon juice and rind. Pour into pastry shell and bake 1 hour at 300° or until inserted knife comes out clean and pie is brown.

Mrs. Claude Beene

CHOCOLATE PIE

Prepare a 9″ pie shell
1 cup sugar
2 tablespoons cocoa
2 tablespoons flour (all purpose)
3 eggs (separated)
1½ cups milk
3 tablespoons butter
1 teaspoon vanilla

Combine sugar, cocoa, and flour. Beat 3 egg yolks and milk thoroughly and add to first mixture. Cook in boiler until very thick, stirring constantly. Remove, add butter and vanilla, and cool. Pour into 9″ pie shell and use remaining 3 egg whites for meringue. Bake in moderate hot oven (400°) until a delicate brown, 8 to 10 minutes.

Mrs. Dayton Waller, Jr.

CHOCOLATE CHIFFON PIE

1 envelope gelatin
¾ cup cold water
2 squares unsweetened chocolate
½ cup sugar
¼ teaspoon salt
3 egg yolks, slightly beaten
1 teaspoon vanilla
3 egg whites, stiffly beaten
½ cup sugar
8" baked pastry shell or graham cracker crust

Soften gelatin in cold water. Add chocolate, ½ cup sugar and salt. Cook in double boiler until chocolate melts and gelatin is dissolved. Beat with egg beater until blended. Pour slowly over egg yolks. Cook and stir until mixture thickens. Chill. Gradually beat remaining ½ cup sugar into beaten egg whites. Fold into gelatin mixture with vanilla. Turn into baked pastry shell or graham cracker crust. Chill until firm. Decorate with whipped cream and shaved chocolate, if desired.

Makes one 8" pie. Serves 6 generously or 8.

Mrs. Michael W. Eiser

CHOCOLATE ICEBOX PIE

1 graham cracker or vanilla wafer pie crust (according to directions on box), in 8" or 9" pie pan
1 ounce square unsweetened chocolate (melted)
¼ pound butter
¾ cup sugar
1 teaspoon vanilla
2 eggs
1 cup heavy cream—whipped, sweetened, and flavored with vanilla to taste

Cream soft butter and sugar together. Add chocolate and vanilla; mix well. Add 1 egg. Beat with electric mixer 5 minutes. Add the other egg; beat 5 minutes more. Pour into crust, top with whipped cream, and chill in refrigerator. The filling will be soft and fluffy when poured into crust, but will be firmer when cold.

Will serve 8. Mrs. Donald M. Ewing

FUDGE PIE

2 squares unsweetened chocolate
1 stick oleo
1 cup sugar
¼ cup flour
2 eggs
1 teaspoon vanilla

Melt chocolate in double boiler; add oleo, turn off heat, and add sugar, flour, eggs and vanilla. Stir well, and pour into small buttered pie pan. Cook 25 minutes at 350°. Serve warm. This is very good topped with vanilla or pistachio ice cream. If prepared a day or two in advance, place unbaked pie in refrigerator and bake shortly before ready to serve.

Will serve about 6. Mrs. William Lynch

FRENCH SILK PIE

Filling:
½ pound butter (at room temperature)
1 cup sugar
2 eggs
2 squares bitter chocolate, melted
1 teaspoon vanilla
Pinch of salt
1 cup whipping cream, plus 1 or 2 tablespoons sugar

Crust:
1¼ cups crushed graham crackers
3 tablespoons sugar
⅓ cup margarine, melted
Pinch or two of mace
¼ cup chopped pecans (optional)

Beat together butter and sugar about 30 minutes. Add eggs and beat until well blended. Add chocolate and vanilla and beat again. Then rub mixture between fingers until smooth. This is the secret of the pie. It must be absolutely velvety. Pile in cold crust. Top with whipped cream and grated chocolate. Chill.

Crust: Blend crust ingredients and pack into 9" pie pan. Bake in 350° oven 5-8 minutes. Cool. About ¼ cup chopped pecans patted in bottom of pie shell before baking is a nice addition.

Mrs. Charles H. Jeter

CREAM PIE

1 baked 8" or 9" pie shell
⅓ cup flour
⅔ cup sugar
¼ teaspoon salt
2 cups scalded milk
3 slightly beaten egg yolks
½ stick butter
½ teaspoon vanilla

Mix flour, sugar and salt. Place in top of double boiler and gradually add scalded milk. Cook and stir until smooth. Add this mixture a little at a time to the beaten egg yolks, then return all to pan. Cook until thick, remove from heat and add butter and vanilla. Cool. Coconut may be added to this. Pour into cooked pie shell. Top with meringue made from egg whites and 6 tablespoons sugar. Bake in 350° oven until brown.

This cream filling may be used to make banana pudding by placing in an ovenproof dish a layer of vanilla wafers, sliced bananas and cream filling, repeating layers until all filling is used. Top with meringue; bake at 350° until brown. To make fresh peach pie, pour cream filling in cooked pie shell. Place fresh sliced peaches solid on top of filling, sprinkle with powdered sugar and cover with whipped cream. Chill.

For Banana Ice Box Pie—place sliced bananas in bottom of cooked pie shell, cover with filling, put whipped cream on top and chill.

Mrs. Dayton H. Waller, Jr.

GRASSHOPPER PIE

1½ cups of crushed chocolate wafers
¼ cup butter, melted
¼ cup sugar
1½ teaspoons gelatin
⅓ cup cream
4 egg yolks
¼ cup sugar
¼ cup green creme de menthe
¼ cup white creme de cacao
1 cup cream, whipped

Crush wafers with a rolling pin and force through sieve to make fine crumbs. Mix with butter and ¼ cup sugar. Butter a pie plate generously and pat crumbs thickly over bottom and sides. Bake in a very hot oven (450°) for 5 minutes and cool.

Soften 1½ teaspoons gelatin in ⅓ cup cream and dissolve over hot water. In another bowl, beat egg yolks until thick. Add ¼ cup sugar. Stir in creme de cacao, creme de menthe and gelatin mixture. Chill until slightly thickened. Fold in 1 cup cream, whipped. Pour filling into crust and chill until firm. Sprinkle with crushed mint-flavored chocolate, or top of pie may be covered with whipped cream swirled with creme de menthe.

Will serve 6.

Julia Dehan
Mrs. Keith Begbie

CUSTARD PIE

2 cups milk, scalded
4 eggs, separated
¾ cup sugar
3 tablespoons cornstarch
⅛ teaspoon salt
1 teaspoon vanilla
5 drops almond flavoring

Beat egg yolks, sugar and cornstarch. Add milk to egg yolk mixture one half at a time. Add salt, vanilla and almond flavoring. Cook this in top of double boiler until mixture thickens, stirring constantly. Make meringue, using egg whites, 4 tablespoons sugar, ⅛ teaspoon cream of tartar and salt. Pour custard into pie pan lined with crust made of ¾ box Holland Rusk crumbs, tossed with 1 stick butter and ½ cup sugar. Pat this crust firmly into place. Top pie with meringue and bake at 325° until golden brown. Refrigerate.

Mrs. R. G. Smitherman

LEMON PIE

4 eggs (separate 3 eggs)
1¾ cups sugar
2 lemons (juice of both, ½ teaspoon of rind)
2 tablespoons butter, softened
3 tablespoons flour
4 tablespoons milk
1 baked pastry shell

Put 3 egg yolks and 1 whole egg in mixing bowl. Add sugar gradually and cream until light and lemon-colored. (The secret to this pie is creaming the sugar and eggs long enough.) Add other ingredients and mix well. Pour into pastry shell which has been baked for 10 minutes in a 400° oven. Then bake whole pie in 350° oven for about 30 minutes. Make a meringue of remaining 3 egg whites. Add very slowly 6 tablespoons of sugar. Beat until mixture will stand in peaks. Cover baked pie with meringue; return to oven and brown at 350°.

Mrs. J. S. Douglas

LIME CHIFFON PIE

1 envelope plain gelatin
1 cup sugar
½ cup water
1 teaspoon grated lime rind
½ cup lime juice
4 eggs, separated
Green food coloring
1 tablespoon creme de menthe
½ teaspoon salt
Graham cracker crust
Fresh lime slices

In top of double boiler, mix gelatin and ½ cup sugar. Beat in lime rind, egg yolks, lime juice and water. Stir over simmering water until mixture thickens enough to coat spoon. Remove from heat and add a few drops of food coloring and creme de menthe. Chill until mixture begins to set. Beat egg whites with salt until foamy; gradually add remaining ½ cup sugar and beat until stiff. Fold into first mixture, pour into pie shell and chill until firm. Decorate with whipped cream and lime slices.

Mrs. Dudley R. Meier
Mrs. John D. Harrell

ORANGE CHIFFON PIE

1 envelope plain gelatin dissolved in ¼ cup cold water
4 eggs, separated
1 cup sugar
⅓ cup orange juice (frozen or fresh)
2 tablespoons lemon juice
1 tablespoon grated orange or lemon rind
¼ teaspoon salt
1 baked pie shell

Cream egg yolks with ½ cup sugar; add juices and rind. Cook in double boiler until thick. Add gelatin and cool. Beat whites with ¼ teaspoon salt and ½ cup sugar. Fold into egg yolk mixture. Put in large baked pie shell. Cover with whipped cream when ready to serve.

Makes 1 large pie.

Mrs. Albert L. Dietz, Jr.

ORANGE-ANGEL PIE

1 tablespoon butter
1 cup flaked coconut
1 cup orange juice
1 envelope gelatin
½ cup sugar
½ teaspoon salt
3 egg yolks, slightly beaten
1 teaspoon grated orange rind
½ teaspoon grated lemon rind
3 egg whites and ⅓ cup sugar
1 cup diced orange sections
1 cup heavy cream

Heat oven to 325° Spread butter over bottom, up sides, and over rim of 9" pie plate; pat coconut into butter evenly. Bake 10 minutes or until light golden brown; cool. Combine gelatin in orange juice, add ½ cup sugar, salt and slightly beaten egg yolks in top of double boiler. Cook while stirring over hot (not boiling) water until slightly thickened. Stir in orange and lemon rinds. Refrigerate until partially set, stirring occasionally. Beat egg whites until soft peaks form; gradually beat in ⅓ cup sugar until stiff peaks are formed. Fold into gelatin mixture; fold in diced orange sections (drained of juice). Refrigerate mixture until it mounds when dropped from spoon. Then pour into coconut pie crust and refrigerate until set. Before serving, top with whipped cream and sections of oranges.

Makes 6 large or 8 small servings.

Mrs. Will Fullilove

PECAN PIE

3 eggs
1 cup sugar
3 tablespoons flour
1 cup white corn syrup
1 cup shelled pecans
3 tablespoons butter or oleo
1 tablespoon vanilla
1 unbaked pastry shell

Beat eggs thoroughly in pan or bowl; add sugar, flour and syrup gradually. Add pecans and soft oleo, then vanilla last. Pour into unbaked pastry shell. Bake in 350° oven for approximately 45 minutes.

Mrs. Warren Ogden
Baton Rouge, La.

OSGOOD PIE

1 cup sugar
2 eggs, separated
½ cup raisins
½ cup chopped nuts
½ teaspoon cinnamon
½ teaspoon cloves
½ tablespoon butter
1½ teaspoons vinegar

Beat egg yolks and add sugar. Add all other ingredients and fold in beaten egg whites. Pour in pastry shell and bake slowly in 325° oven for 45 minutes or until done.

Mrs. John R. Murphy

SWEET POTATO PIE

2 cups cooked mashed sweet potatoes
½ cup butter at room temperature
2 egg yolks
1 cup brown sugar
¼ teaspoon salt
½ teaspoon cinnamon
½ teaspoon nutmeg
½ teaspoon ginger
½ cup milk
2 egg whites
¼ cup sugar

Mix first eight ingredients while potatoes are still warm. Add milk. Beat egg whites until stiff, gradually adding sugar. Fold into the potato mixture and pour into an unbaked pie shell. Bake at 400° for 10 minutes, then lower heat to 350° and bake until set.

Mrs. Sinclair Kouns

PUMPKIN PIE

1½ cups pumpkin
1½ cups brown sugar
3 eggs
1 cup milk
1 teaspoon cinnamon
½ teaspoon allspice
¼ teaspoon ground ginger
1 tablespoon bourbon
3 tablespoons butter or margarine
1 uncooked pie crust

Beat eggs until light. Add brown sugar, beat well. Add all other ingredients. Pour into unbaked pie crust and bake at 325° for 1 hour or until set.

Serves 6 to 8, depending on size of cut.

Mrs. John Guth

ANNIE'S PUMPKIN PIE

1 small can pumpkin (No. 303)
3 eggs, lightly beaten
1½ cups sugar
½ teaspoon nutmeg
¼ teaspoon cinnamon
Dash of ground cloves
¾ stick butter or margarine
½ cup sweet milk

Beat eggs in mixing bowl. Add pumpkin and mix well. Add all other dry ingredients. Next, put in melted butter and milk and mix thoroughly. Bake in a 9" pie pan lined with an unbaked pie crust. Bake 45-50 minutes in 300° oven until brown.

Topping for pie, if desired: Sprinkle ⅔ cup broken pecans mixed with ⅔ cup brown sugar and 3 tablespoons melted butter. Slide under the broiler (or place in hot oven) just until the topping begins to melt.

Mrs. Rand Metcalfe

FRENCH STRAWBERRY PIE

1 cooled 9" baked pie shell
1 8-ounce package cream cheese
1 quart strawberries
1 cup sugar
3 tablespoons cornstarch
Sweetened whipped cream

Soften cream cheese with a little cream. Spread over bottom of pie shell. Dip largest berries in sugar and set close together on the cheese. Place remaining berries in a blender and puree. Add enough water to make 1 cup of juice. Bring to a boil. Add remaining sugar which has been mixed with cornstarch. Cook slowly for 10 minutes, stirring frequently. Cool and pour over berries. Chill. Spread pie with whipped cream. Easy to make. Add a few sesame seeds to flour when making pie shell, if desired.

Makes a 9" pie.

Mrs. Clarence J. Edwards

FRESH PEACH OR STRAWBERRY PIE

¾ cup sugar
4 tablespoons cornstarch for peach, 5 to 6 tablespoons cornstarch for strawberry
Dash of salt
1 cup boiling water and 2 tablespoons water
2 tablespoons lemon juice
Red or yellow food coloring
6 to 8 sliced peaches or 1½ pints strawberries
1 baked pie shell

Mix sugar, cornstarch and salt with 2 tablespoons water into a paste. Pour 1 cup boiling water over, cook slowly, stirring constantly until thick. Remove from heat, add lemon juice and food coloring. Cool, add fruit (sliced), and put into baked pie shell. Chill. An hour or so before serving, cover with whipped cream and chill.

Mrs. Roger Naus

FRESH PEACH PIE

1 cup sugar
1 stick butter
1 egg
1 teaspoon vanilla
1 pie crust
fresh halved peaches

Beat first four ingredients together. Bake pie crust and have slightly cool. Place fresh halved peaches, cup shape up, on crust. Put sauce from above in cavity of peaches and any left over around peaches. Bake slowly for about 30 minutes. Top with ice cream or whipped cream.

Mrs. W. G. McElroy

ANGEL BERRY PIE

Meringue crust:
3 egg whites
1 cup sugar
2 teaspoons white vinegar

Beat egg whites until stiff, add sugar gradually, then vinegar. Bake in greased 9" ovenproof pie dish for 1½ hours at 300° on second rack of oven.

Filling:
3 egg yolks, beaten
½ cup sifted sugar
1 heaping tablespoon sifted flour
1 cup milk
1 teaspoon vanilla
Pinch of salt

Cook in top of double boiler, stirring constantly, until thick. Pour into meringue when cool. Let set for awhile, then cover custard filling with cut-up strawberries. Cover strawberries with ½ pint whipped cream and garnish with whole strawberries.

Mrs. Walter Chandler

Cookies

Shreveport Captains

SHREVEPORT CAPTAINS

Home runs, fly balls, double plays and calls are part of the action during the Shreveport Captains season, which runs from April to September. This local team has featured several big names in baseball during the early days of their careers.

PECAN TASSIES

Pastry:
1 3-ounce package cream cheese
½ cup butter or margarine
1 cup sifted flour
Filling:
¾ cup brown sugar
1 egg
1 tablespoon soft butter or margarine
1 teaspoon vanilla, or 1 teaspoon grated orange rind and ½ teaspoon orange flavoring
Dash salt
⅔ cup coarsely broken pecans

Pastry: Allow cream cheese and butter to soften at room temperature; blend. Stir in flour, chill slightly for one hour. Shape into 2 dozen 1-inch balls; place in tiny ungreased 1¾-inch muffin cups. Press dough against bottom and sides of cups.

Filling: Beat together egg, sugar, butter or margarine, flavoring and salt, until just smooth. Divide half of pecans among pastry-lined cups; add egg mixture and top with remaining pecans. Bake at 325° for 25 minutes or until filling is set. Cool, remove from pans. Makes 24 pastries.

These are delicious, resembling tiny pecan pies. They are wonderful to serve for open house, receptions, etc., and make a nice twosome served with little cream puffs filled with chicken salad.

They may be frozen, or made several days ahead.

Mrs. Olin P. Oden
Mrs. Robert B. Horner
Bristol, Va.

BROWN LACE COOKIES

2 cups brown sugar
½ stick butter
2 eggs
1 teaspoon baking powder
½ cup flour
1 teaspoon vanilla
2 cups pecans, whole or coarsely chopped

Cream butter and sugar. Add eggs and beat well. Add flour and baking powder, then vanilla. Mix with pecans and place in refrigerator until firm. Drop by ½ teaspoon three inches apart on buttered and floured cookie sheet. Cook at 400° for 5 minutes. Remove while warm.

Note: These cookies may be made almost instantly as dough keeps well in refrigerator. Do not place them any closer than three inches or they will run together.

Mrs. Charles Samuel Newson
Tampico, Mexico

BOHEMIAN APRICOT KOLACHY

Pastry:
- ½ pound butter or margarine
- 2 3-ounce packages cream cheese
- 2 cups sifted flour
- ½ teaspoon baking powder

Filling:
- 1 12-ounce package dried apricots
- 1 cup sugar
- ½ cup water

For filling: Soak apricots in water for 1 hour; drain off all water except ½ cup. Simmer apricots in water until tender, adding sugar. Allow to cool and then mash before using.

For pastry: Cream together cream cheese and butter. Add flour, sifted with baking powder. Mix all together and refrigerate for several hours or overnight. Roll pastry to ¼-inch thickness and cut into small rounds or squares. For rounds, place on ungreased cookie sheet, and put a scant teaspoon of filling in the middle of each. If using squares, put a small amount of filling in middle and bring up opposite corners, forming a filled roll. Place rounds or squares on ungreased cookie sheet and bake at 375° for 15 minutes. When cool, sift with powdered sugar. These cookies should be baked just a short while before using.

Mrs. Curtis D. Sims
Mrs. J. B. McCullough

GRANNY'S BUTTERSCOTCH SQUARES

- 1 stick oleo
- 1 cup sugar
- 1 whole egg
- 2 egg yolks (reserve 2 whites for topping)
- 1½ cups cake flour
- ½ teaspoon salt
- 1 teaspoon baking powder
- 1 teaspoon vanilla

Topping:
- 1 cup light brown sugar
- 2 egg whites, beaten
- 1 cup pecans

Cream oleo, add sugar, beat in egg and yolks. Sift flour with salt, baking powder, add to mixture. Stir in vanilla. Pack this mixture into a pan 11" x 14", lightly greased. Spread topping over cookie mixture and bake 30 minutes in 325° oven. Allow to cool. Cut while still warm.

Mrs. Juanita Ford

APRICOT BALLS

- 2 cups dried uncooked apricots, ground
- 1 cup pecans, chopped fine
- 1½ cups sugar
- 4 tablespoons orange juice
- Grated rind of 1 orange

Mix all ingredients. Roll into small balls, and then roll in granulated sugar.

Mrs. John B. Entrikin
Mrs. Marvin Turner

PECAN BARS

4 eggs
1 pound dark brown sugar
1½ cups flour
½ teaspoon baking powder
⅛ teaspoon salt
1 teaspoon vanilla
2 cups broken pecan meats

In top of double boiler, beat eggs. Stir brown sugar into eggs. Cook over boiling water 10 to 15 minutes, stirring often. Remove double boiler from water. Sift into sugar mixture the dry ingredients. Stir until fairly well mixed. Add vanilla and broken pecan meats. Stirring in pecans will dissolve the last of the lumps. Pour into a buttered 8" x 10" pan. Bake at 325° for 35 minutes or until cookies begin to pull away from sides. Allow to cool. Cut into 48 small bars. May be prepared in advance and covered well with foil until needed.

Mrs. James E. Smitherman, Jr.

BROWN SUGAR SQUARES

1 pound brown sugar
¼ pound butter
2 eggs
1½ cups flour
1¼ teaspoons baking powder
2 teaspoons vanilla
2 cups chopped pecans

Melt butter and sugar in saucepan. Cool slightly. Beat in whole eggs, flour, baking powder, nuts and vanilla. Pour into a greased 8" x 10" pan. Bake about 45 minutes at 325°. Let cool and cut into squares.

Mrs. Robert U. Goodman

TOFFEE SQUARES

1½ sticks oleo or ¾ cup lard
1 cup brown sugar, packed
1 egg
1 teaspoon vanilla
2 cups sifted enriched flour
½ teaspoon salt
8 to 12 ounces semi-sweet chocolate chips (Milk chocolate silver bells may be substituted, if you prefer)
1 cup chopped nuts

Cream lard and sugar until light and fluffy. Add egg and blend. Add vanilla. Sift flour and salt together and add, mixing thoroughly. Spread batter on ungreased 10" x 15" pan. Bake in moderately hot oven (350°) for 20 minutes. Top with chocolate chips, melt in oven 5 minutes. Spread chocolate with knife to cover top completely. Sprinkle with nuts. Cut while warm. Makes 40 squares.

Mrs. M. Alton Evans, Jr.

BROWN SUGAR BROWNIES

½ cup butter
1 cup brown sugar
1 egg
1 teaspoon vanilla
½ cup chopped pecans
½ cup coconut
1 cup flour
¼ teaspoon salt
1 teaspoon baking powder
½ box penuche frosting

Melt butter and add sugar. When well blended, remove from heat and cool until lukewarm. Add unbeaten egg, then vanilla. Stir well and add dry ingredients. Mixture will be very thick. Bake in shallow pan (7 or 8 inches square) for 20 minutes at 350° or until slightly brown and away from the sides of the pan. When cool, frost with ½ box penuche frosting.

Mrs. Edward S. Peterson

BROWNIES

1 cup oleo or butter
2 cups sugar
4 eggs
4 squares unsweetened chocolate
1½ cups cake flour
½ teaspoon salt
½ teaspoon baking powder
2 cups pecans
1 teaspoon vanilla

Cream oleo and sugar, then mix in eggs. Stir in chocolate, which has been melted over warm water. Sift flour, baking powder and salt. Add all at once and mix. Add pecans and vanilla. Bake at 350° for 25 to 30 minutes in two 9" square pans, removing from oven while batter is still just barely moist.

Mrs. Joe Loftus

CHOCOLATE BROWNIES

1 stick margarine or butter
2 squares unsweetened chocolate
2 eggs, well beaten
1 tablespoon light corn syrup
1 cup sugar
¾ cup sifted all-purpose flour
½ teaspoon baking powder
1 teaspoon vanilla
1 cup pecans

Melt butter and chocolate together over hot water and let cool. Beat eggs until light and beat in corn syrup, sugar and cooled chocolate mixture. Sift together flour and baking powder and stir into first mixture. Stir in vanilla and nuts. Bake in well-greased 8" square pan at 350° for 25 minutes or until top crust is dull. Makes sixteen 2" squares.

Mrs. Clyde Minor, III

BROWNIES

2 cups sugar
1 cup butter or shortening
1 cup flour
4 squares unsweetened chocolate, melted
4 eggs, well beaten
½ teaspoon salt
2 teaspoons vanilla
2 cups chopped nuts

Cream butter and sugar. Add flour, melted chocolate, eggs and other ingredients. Bake at 325° for 25 to 30 minutes.

Mrs. John B. Atkins, Jr.

BUTTER COOKIES

1 cup sugar
1 stick butter
1 stick oleo
1 egg yolk
1 unbeaten egg white
1 teaspoon vanilla
2 cups flour
About 1½ cups chopped nuts (optional)

Cream butter, oleo and sugar. Add egg yolk and flour. Mix well and then add vanilla. Put into cookie press. Make cookies small. (I use disc that makes shape of a flower.) Press cookies on well-greased cookie sheet. (Don't put cookies too close to edge of sheet, because the edges burn easily; also, don't put too close together, as they will almost double in size when cooked.) Spread unbeaten egg white lightly over top of cookies and then sprinkle with chopped nuts, if desired. Bake in 350° F. oven about 10 to 15 minutes. Makes about 45 cookies.

If your dough gets too soft, chill in refrigerator by putting cookie press and dough in refrigerator.

Mrs. S. P. Borden, Jr.

BUTTER CRUNCH COOKIES

2 sticks butter
¾ cup white sugar
¾ cup light brown sugar
1 egg
1½ to 2 cups sifted all-purpose flour
Pinch soda
Pinch salt
2 tablespoons buttermilk
Cinnamon-brown sugar mixture (in sprinkle jar)

Cream butter and sugars well. Add egg. Combine flour, soda and salt and add to the butter-sugar mixture alternately with buttermilk. The batter should be fairly stiff. Drop ½ teaspoon at a time on a greased cookie sheet. Bake about 8 to 10 minutes at 350°, leaving plenty of space between these cookies so they will have room to spread and have a slightly brown edge. Let cool just a moment after removing from oven. Then put on a cookie rack and sprinkle with the cinnamon-brown sugar mixture.

Rosemary Davis

PLAIN ROLL-OUT COOKIES

Cream together:
2 sticks butter
⅓ cup shortening
1 cup white sugar
¼ teaspoon salt
1 egg
3 tablespoons milk
1 teaspoon vanilla
½ teaspoon lemon juice

Sift together:
3½ cups flour sifted 4 times
1 teaspoon soda
1 teaspoon cream of tartar

Add dry ingredients to creamed ingredients slowly. Chill and roll out. Cook at 350° until lightly brown. Makes approximately 3 dozen cookies.

This recipe is especially good for making decorative cookies.

Mrs. F. C. Boykin

ICEBOX COOKIES

½ pound butter
1 pound brown sugar
2 eggs, beaten
4 cups flour
1 tablespoon cinnamon
1 tablespoon baking powder
½ pound pecans, chopped fine

Sift together flour, cinnamon and baking powder. Cream butter and sugar; add beaten eggs. Add sifted dry ingredients and pecans. Shape into four long rolls, wrap in waxed paper and place in icebox overnight. Cookies should be sliced thin. Cook on a lightly greased cookie sheet 8-10 minutes at 375°.

4-5 dozen thin cookies. Dough may be prepared and frozen successfully for 2 or 3 weeks. Needs to be thawed just enough to slice.

Mrs. A. B. Killgore

OLD-FASHIONED TEA COOKIES

2 cups sugar
1 cup butter or oleo
1 scant teaspoon soda
Pinch salt
4 cups flour
2 eggs
1 teaspoon vanilla

Blend sugar and butter. Sift dry ingredients together. Add alternately with beaten eggs to sugar mixture. Add vanilla. Roll out on board very thin and cut with cookie cutter, or make a long thin roll, chill, and slice very thin. Bake in 350° oven, until lightly brown, approximately 15 minutes.

Mrs. James B. Harris

EGGLESS TEA CAKES

1 cup butter
1½ cups sugar
¾ cup heavy cream
1 teaspoon soda
Flour to make a stiff dough (approximately 4 cups)

Cream butter and sugar. Add other ingredients. Chill dough. Roll thin and cut in any desired shape. Bake at 375° until lightly browned.

Mrs. Joe LeSage

CHINESE CHEWS

1 cup granulated sugar
¾ cup sifted flour
½ teaspoon baking powder
¼ teaspoon salt
2 eggs
1 teaspoon vanilla
1 cup chopped dates
1 cup chopped walnuts or pecans
½ cup powdered sugar

Sift granulated sugar, flour, baking powder and salt together. Beat eggs; add vanilla. Add to sifted dry ingredients. Mix well. Add dates and walnuts. Mix thoroughly. Spread mixture on greased baking sheets and bake at 350° for 30 minutes. While still hot, cut into small squares. Drop several squares at a time into paper bag containing powdered sugar, and shake to coat in sugar. Repeat until all are sugared.

Makes 2 dozen chews.

Mrs. William M. Sale, Jr.

CHOCOLATE MERINGUES

2 egg whites
⅛ teaspoon salt
⅛ teaspoon cream of tartar
1 teaspoon vanilla
¾ cup sugar
1 6-ounce package (1 cup) semi-sweet chocolate pieces
¼ cup chopped pecans

Beat egg whites, salt, cream of tartar, and vanilla until soft peaks form. Add sugar gradually, beating until peaks are stiff. Fold in chocolate pieces and nuts. Cover cookie sheet with plain paper. Drop mixture on by rounded teaspoons. Bake in slow oven (300°) about 25 minutes. Cool slightly before removing from paper.

Makes about 2 dozen cookies.

Mrs. John H. McKee

CINNAMON COOKIES

2 sticks butter
1 cup sugar
2 cups flour
1 teaspoon cinnamon
1 egg, separated
1 cup finely chopped pecans

Cream butter and sugar. Sift flour and cinnamon together and add; then add egg yolk. When thoroughly mixed, spread as thinly as possible on greased cookie sheet or 10" x 15" baking pan. Brush over top with beaten egg white. Sprinkle nuts on top of this evenly. Bake in 350° oven, until slightly brown, 10 to 15 minutes. Cut into thin bars to serve.

Mrs. Jack McLean

CINNAMON STICKS

Thinly sliced bread
Melted butter or oleo
1 cup powdered sugar
3 teaspoons cinnamon

Cut crusts off bread and cut into 3 or 4 "sticks" per slice. Melt butter and brush each side of bread. Place powdered sugar and cinnamon in a paper bag. Drop buttered bread sticks into bag and shake. Place on cookie sheet and bake at 300° for 10 minutes, then turn over and bake about 10 minutes longer.

Susan Patricia Davis

CORN FLAKE COOKIES

3 egg whites
1 cup sugar
4 cups corn flakes
1 tablespoon vanilla
1 cup pecans, chopped

Beat egg whites until stiff. Add sugar slowly, then corn flakes, pecans and vanilla. Drop by teaspoon on greased cookie sheet. Bake in slow oven (275°) for 10 to 15 minutes.

Mrs. James C. Gardner

DATE DELIGHTS

3 egg whites
¾ cup sugar
½ cup flour
½ teaspoon baking powder
1¾ cups nuts, ground fine
1 small package dates, chopped fine

Sift flour and baking powder together. Beat egg whites until stiff, adding sugar gradually. Fold in flour and baking powder mixture, then nuts, then dates, and drop from a teaspoon onto cookie sheet. Bake at 360° approximately 10 to 12 minutes. Watch closely. These are very chewy and good.

Mrs. Joe LeSage

SOUTHFIELD GINGER COOKIES

1 cup ribbon cane syrup
1 teaspoon soda
2 teaspoons powdered ginger
½ teaspoon salt
½ cup lard
3 cups flour (or enough to be stiff)

Combine all ingredients and mix thoroughly. Form in small balls, then press flat on buttered cookie sheet with a spatula. Cook approximately 30 minutes at 300°. Do not try to brown.

Makes about 5 dozen cookies.

Mrs. Melvin F. Johnson

HOLIDAY DATE STICKS

1 cup flour
1 cup sugar
½ teaspoon salt
⅓ teaspoon soda
½ teaspoon cinnamon
¼ teaspoon vanilla
1 cup chopped dates
1 cup chopped pecans
2 eggs, slightly beaten

Sift together dry ingredients; add vanilla, eggs, dates and pecans. Pour mixture into greased oblong cake pan (about 9" x 11"). Cook in slow oven, 325°-350° for about 25 minutes. While still very warm, cut into bars and remove from pan. Mold the sticks with your hands, and roll in powdered sugar. These are really delicious around Christmas or any other holiday.

Makes about 2 dozen sticks.

Mrs. Harmon Chandler

HONEY DROPS

⅓ cup shortening
½ cup honey
1 egg, unbeaten
½ teaspoon vanilla
1¼ cups all-purpose flour
½ teaspoon soda
1 teaspoon baking powder
½ teaspoon salt
½ cup finely chopped nuts
1 package (7-ounce) chocolate bits or 1 square unsweetened chocolate, coarsely grated

Cream shortening and honey together; add unbeaten egg and vanilla and mix thoroughly. Sift flour, soda, baking powder and salt together and add. Stir in nuts and chocolate bits. Drop from teaspoon on greased cookie sheet. Bake at 375° for 10 to 12 minutes.

Makes 4 dozen cookies.

Mrs. Leroy Scott, Jr.

LAYER COOKIES

Bottom Layer:
¼ pound butter
1 cup flour
2 tablespoons sugar

Top Layer:
2 eggs
1½ cups brown sugar
2 tablespoons flour
1½ cups chopped nuts
½ teaspoon vanilla

Icing:
1 tablespoon butter
¾ cup powdered sugar
1 or 2 teaspoons hot water

Cream together ingredients for bottom layer and pat in 9" x 13" pan. Bake 20 minutes at 375°. Beat together all ingredients for top layer except nuts, then fold in nuts. Pour over bottom layer and bake an additional 30 minutes at 375°.

Icing: Cream together butter and sugar and add water. Allow cookies to cool approximately 15 minutes before icing.

Mrs. Van Lindley
Oklahoma City, Okla.

HALLIE'S COOKIES

½ cup butter
1½ cups sugar
¼ teaspoon vanilla
2 eggs
1½ cups flour
1 teaspoon baking powder
Dash salt
2 tablespoons sweet milk
1 cup pecans, chopped

Cream sugar and butter. Add vanilla and eggs. Sift together dry ingredients (flour, baking powder and salt) and add alternately with milk. Fold in pecans. Pour into buttered and floured 8" x 10" pan. Bake at 350° for approximately 30 minutes; as much as 45 minutes may be required in a gas oven. Cut into bars when cool. These may be stored in cake tins for a day of two.

Makes about 20 squares.

Mrs. Hugh King

LEMON STICKS

½ cup butter
½ cup confectioners' sugar
2 egg yolks, lightly beaten
1 cup flour
2 teaspoons grated lemon rind

For topping:
2 egg whites
½ cup sugar
1 tablespoon lemon juice
½ cup chopped pecans

Cream butter; add confectioners' sugar gradually. Add egg yolks. Stir in flour and grated rind. Mix until smooth, and spread evenly in bottom of ungreased 9" x 13" pan. Bake in 350° oven 10 minutes.

While this is baking, beat egg whites until stiff; gradually add sugar. Beat in lemon juice and fold in pecans. Spread this meringue topping over baked mixture, and bake 25 minutes longer. Cool. Cut into 1" x 3" sticks.

Yield, 32 sticks.

Mrs. Ed J. Crawford, Jr.

MINCEMEAT SQUARES

1 9-ounce package condensed mincemeat
¾ cup sifted cake flour
¾ teaspoon baking powder
1 cup granulated sugar
¼ teaspoon salt
1 cup finely chopped walnuts or pecans
2 eggs, beaten
1 teaspoon of either: rum or rum extract, or lemon extract, or vanilla extract
½ cup confectioners' sugar (for dusting)

Break mincemeat into small pieces in mixing bowl. Sift together flour, baking powder, sugar and salt. Add to mincemeat. Stir to mix. Add nuts, eggs and flavoring. Mix well. Spread in very well greased square pan (8" x 8" x 2" or 9" x 9" x 2"). Bake at 350° about 45 minutes. When cool, cut into squares. Dust with confectioners' sugar. Store in covered container.

Mrs. Towner J. Pringle

SCOTCH SHORTBREAD

1½ cups sugar
1 pound butter
1 teaspoon vanilla
6 cups sifted flour
2 egg yolks

Cream butter and sugar; add vanilla. Add flour with hands until all trace of flour is gone. Add whole egg yolks one at a time, kneading dough well until all trace of egg yolk is gone. Divide dough into eight parts and pat each into a circle. Prick with fork. Bake at 350° for 15 minutes. Reduce heat to 300° and bake until golden brown. Cut each piece into eighths and return to oven until edges are brown.

Mrs. W. C. Wilkins, Jr.

SPICY MOLASSES COOKIES

1 cup sugar
1 cup butter or margarine
½ cup molasses
1 teaspoon cloves
1 teaspoon ginger
1 teaspoon cinnamon
½ teaspoon vanilla
1 egg
1 teaspoon soda in a little water
3 cups flour

Cream butter and sugar together; add other ingredients in order. Chill dough at least 24 hours. Roll dough very thin, cut with cookie cutter, and bake at 350° until golden brown (about 10 to 12 minutes).

Makes about 4 to 5 dozen cookies. This dough keeps well in refrigerator.

Mrs. Towner J. Pringle

WILLY MAY'S COOKIES

2 cups Rice Krispies
2 cups one-minute oatmeal
2 cups flour
1 cup coconut
1 cup chopped nuts (pecans are best)
½ cup brown sugar, and
½ cup white sugar or,
1 cup brown sugar
½ pound hot butter
1 teaspoon soda
2 well beaten eggs
1 teaspoon vanilla

Combine thoroughly first six ingredients, through sugar, then put baking soda on top. Pour hot butter over soda, add beaten eggs, and mix well; then add vanilla. Taking small amounts of the dough, form balls, and pat flat on a greased cookie sheet. Leave enough room to spread. Bake at 350° for 10 to 12 minutes, or until golden brown. Remove from cookie sheet while hot. These cookies tend to season, and are better the day after baking than they are fresh from the oven.

Mrs. William J. Nesbitt

OATMEAL COOKIES

2 cups oatmeal
2 cups flour
½ teaspoon soda
1 teaspoon baking powder
1 teaspoon spices (cinnamon, cloves, etc.)
1 cup shortening (it's good to use ½ cup bacon grease and ½ cup shortening)
1¼ cups sugar
2 teaspoons sweet milk
2 eggs
1 teaspoon vanilla
1 cup nuts
1 tablespoon vinegar
1 cup raisins

Mix all dry ingredients. Cream shortening and sugar, then add dry ingredients. Stir in remaining items, adding raisins and nuts last. Drop from teaspoon onto greased cookie sheet and bake in 350° oven until brown, 8 to 10 minutes.

Makes 5 dozen good-sized cookies.

Mrs. B. S. Cheesman

PECAN CHEWIES

3 egg whites
3 cups pecans
1 pound light brown sugar
1 teaspoon vanilla
¼ teaspoon salt

Beat egg whites until stiff. Fold in chopped pecans and all other ingredients, mixing well. Drop scant teaspoons of mixture onto well-greased cookie sheet. Bake at 300° for 20 minutes.

Mrs. T. W. Robinson

PINWHEEL COOKIES

2 cups flour
1 teaspoon baking powder
½ teaspoon salt
½ cup butter
½ cup sugar
1 beaten egg yolk
1 teaspoon vanilla
3 tablespoons milk
1 square (2 ounces) unsweetened chocolate, melted
Sugar

Sift first three ingredients together. Cream butter, add sugar; add egg yolk and vanilla. Add flour mixture alternately with milk, beating constantly. Divide dough into two parts; to one part add the melted chocolate. Roll each part into rectangles. Place chocolate sheet on plain sheet, and roll tightly. Wrap in waxed paper and chill in refrigerator overnight. When ready to bake the next day, slice roll ¼-inch thick. Sprinkle slices lightly with sugar. Bake on lightly greased cookie sheet 10 to 12 minutes in 400° oven.

Makes approximately 4 dozen cookies.

Mrs. Marshall Martin

SKILLET COOKIES

1 stick oleo
¾ cup sugar
2 egg yolks
½ pound dates, cut fine
1 teaspoon vanilla
1 cup chopped nuts
2 cups Rice Krispies
1 can angel flake coconut

Melt oleo in skillet. Add sugar, egg yolks and dates, constantly mashing dates, over low heat about 10 minutes. Set off burner and add vanilla, nuts and Rice Krispies. As soon as you can work with mixture, pull off balls of it and roll in angel flake coconut.

Mrs. Marshall Martin

PECAN BALLS

1 stick butter
1 cup flour
2 tablespoons sugar
1 teaspoon vanilla
⅛ teaspoon salt
1 cup chopped pecans
Confectioners' sugar

Combine all ingredients except confectioners' sugar. Mix with hands, and roll into bite-size balls. Place on ungreased cookie sheet and bake at 375° for 20 minutes. Remove from pan and roll each ball in confectioners' sugar.

Makes about 3 dozen balls.

Mrs. F. A. Moore
Mrs. Richard Langford

SAND TARTS

1 cup butter
⅓ cup confectioners' sugar
1 tablespoon vanilla
3 cups cake flour
2 cups finely chopped pecans
⅔ box confectioners' sugar

Cream butter and ⅓ cup confectioners' sugar well. Add vanilla, flour and pecans. Roll into small cocoons. Bake on ungreased cookie sheet at 300° for one hour or until the bottoms are slightly browned. Roll in confectioners' sugar immediately and let cool before putting away.

Makes about 72 cookies.

Mrs. Paul Sippel
Mrs. James C. Gardner

THIMBLE COOKIES

¾ cup shortening
½ cup light brown sugar
½ cup peanut butter
½ teaspoon salt
1 egg
½ teaspoon orange extract
1¾ cups sifted flour

Cream shortening, sugar and peanut butter. Add salt, egg and orange extract. Mix well and add flour. Stir and shape into 1-inch balls, making thimble-shaped dent in top. Bake at 350° for 12 to 15 minutes. Remove from oven and fill holes with different kinds of jelly.

Makes four dozen cookies.

Mrs. Conway Allen

WHISKEY BALLS

2½ cups vanilla wafers, crushed (1 large box)
1 cup pecans, ground
2 level tablespoons cocoa
½ cup rum
3 tablespoons bourbon or brandy
3 tablespoons corn syrup
1 cup powdered sugar

After crushing vanilla wafers, add nuts and cocoa and mix well. Then add rum and brandy or bourbon and slowly add corn syrup; mix thoroughly. Roll into small balls. Roll balls in powdered sugar and store carefully. They improve with age!

Mrs. Hall S. Morehead

Desserts

RED RIVER REVEL ARTS FESTIVAL

Hundreds of the country's top artists, craftsmen, entertainers, and culinary masters come together for this annual festival of the arts. Street performers entertain the crowds, juried artists display and sell their paintings, sketches and sculptures and craftsmen demonstrate and sell fork art, including leather work, basket weaving, woodwork and pottery. There's also a remarkable variety of food with German, Polish, Greek and other culinary delicacies among those offered. Hands-on arts activities are a special feature for children.

RED RIVER REVEL

For eight days and nights a true "Celebration of the Arts" is held on the banks of the Red River. Four outdoor stages provide hours of free entertainment including jazz, country, gospel, rock, and story telling. A Photography workshop, a Photo Scavenger Hunt and 24 food booths run by non-profit organizations provide a variety of choice. The Red River Revel, co-sponsored with the Shreveport Regional Bicentennial Commission, was the Junior League's bicentennial gift to the Shreveport and Bossier communities in 1976.

APPLE DUMPLINGS

2¼ cups flour
¾ teaspoon salt
¾ cup shortening
7 or 8 tablespoons ice water
6 medium tart, juicy apples
½ cup sugar
1½ teaspoons cinnamon
1 tablespoon butter
Syrup:
1½ cups sugar
½ teaspoon cinnamon
6 tablespoons butter
3 cups water

Sift flour and salt directly into bowl. Add most of shortening and cut in with pastry blender or knives until mixture resembles meal. Add remaining shortening and mix until particles are size of giant peas. Sprinkle water lightly over all, blending with fork until dough can be pressed together. Roll out to ⅛-inch thickness. Cut into 7-inch squares. Pare and core apples, and place an apple on each square. Fill cavity of apples with sugar and cinnamon combined, and dot with butter. Moisten points of pastry and bring opposite corners up over apples, sealing well. Place about 2 inches apart in an 8" x 12" pan. Chill thoroughly in refrigerator.

Prepare syrup by mixing sugar, cinnamon, butter and water in saucepan; boil for 3 minutes. Pour syrup around dumplings. Bake immediately for 5 to 7 minutes (until crust begins to color) in a very hot oven (500°), then reduce temperature to 350° and bake for 30 to 35 minutes. Serve warm with hot syrup and cream if desired. Total baking time, about 40 minutes.

Serves 6.

Mrs. Tom B. Conerly

APPLE TORTE

½ cup sugar
2 well-beaten eggs
½ cup sifted enriched flour
½ teaspoon cinnamon
½ teaspoon baking powder
¼ teaspoon salt
1 cup chopped tart apples, pared
½ cup chopped pecans

Gradually add sugar to well-beaten eggs, beating until thick and lemon-colored. Sift together dry ingredients; fold into egg mixture. Then fold in apple and nuts. Grease bottom of 8 x 8 x 2-inch pan. Pour in batter and bake in slow oven (325°) about 45 minutes. Cool. Cut in squares and serve with whipped cream spiced with a bit of cinnamon.

Makes 6 servings.

Mrs. John H. McKee

CANDIED APPLES ON STICKS

3 cups sugar
⅔ cup white corn syrup
⅔ cup margarine
1 cup water
1 teaspoon salt
2 teaspoons vanilla
12 Delicious apples

Combine ingredients in 2-quart saucepan. Using candy thermometer, cook to 240° (until a hard ball forms in cold water). Stir constantly after it starts cooking to prevent scorching. Take off flame and cool until thick. Quickly coat 12 apples, speared on sticks. Drain on well-greased waxed paper.

Mrs. William G. Scarborough, III

BANANAS FOSTER

6 tablespoons dark brown sugar
3 tablespoons butter
3 bananas, peeled and sliced lengthwise
1½ ounces creme de banana liqueur
3 ounces white rum
Cinnamon
Vanilla ice cream

Melt brown sugar and butter in chafing dish. Add bananas, sprinkle with cinnamon, add banana liqueur and saute until tender. Pour rum all over and flame-baste with warm liquid until flame burns out. Serve immediately over ice cream.

Makes 6 servings.

Mrs. May Hendrick Chidlow
Mrs. J. Bennett Johnston, Jr.
Mrs. Jackson B. Davis

ANGEL FOOD WALDORF

10-inch angel food cake
1½ pints whipping cream
6 tablespoons sugar
6 tablespoons cocoa
⅛ teaspoon salt
⅔ cup toasted almonds

Whip cream and fold in sugar, salt, and cocoa. Chill for at least one hour. This allows cocoa to dissolve. Cut entire top from cake one inch down. Cut trough in bottom section, leaving 1-inch wall outside, center and bottom of cake. Fill the cavity with ⅓ of the chocolate whipped cream mixture to which has been added half the almonds cut up coarsely. Replace top and spread remaining mixture on top and sides. Shave remaining almonds and sprinkle over cream. Chill 2 or 3 hours before serving. This may be prepared a day ahead.

Makes 12 to 16 servings.

Mrs. Wesley E. Wheless, Jr.

AVOCADO CREAM

2 large avocados
Juice of 4 or 5 limes
Powdered sugar to taste
Creme de cacao or curacao

Put avocados through blender. Add juice of limes and powdered sugar to taste. Serve in sherbet glasses with creme de cacao, curacao or other liqueur to pour over.

Makes 4 servings. Mrs. Melvin F. Johnson

BLACK FOREST CAKE

Meringue Discs:
1 cup egg whites
2⅛ cups sugar
1 small pinch cream of tartar
1 teaspoon vanilla
½ cup finely chopped almonds
½ cup finely chopped hazelnuts

Whip egg whites until foamy and add cream of tartar. Continue whipping whites until stiff enough to follow the beater around. Whip in sugar (with vanilla) just to blend. Do not let sugar melt whites. Add almonds and hazelnuts, **but fold them in with a wooden spoon.**

Have in readiness 2 well-greased cookie sheets. Preheat oven to 225°. Place above mixture in a pastry tube and squeeze gently onto four 9" brown paper discs on the cookie sheets. Cook for 2½ hours at 225° and leave in oven for about 5 or 6 hours with the door closed so that the discs can dry thoroughly. Don't peek.

Chocolate Filling:
2 egg whites
½ cup sugar
2 tablespoons breakfast cocoa
2 ounces German sweet chocolate, melted
½ pound butter, slightly melted

Whip egg whites over hot but not boiling water. Add sugar and whip until stiff. Add cocoa and whip in very well. Take off fire. Add German chocolate, then fold in butter. Let chocolate mixture get cold enough to spread. Then smooth it right on top of each disc and set in the icebox to chill.

Whipped Cream Icing:
1½ packages gelatin
2 tablespoons vanilla
⅔ quart heavy whipping cream
⅓ cup sugar

Melt gelatin in a small amount of hot water with vanilla. Whip cream very stiff, add sugar, then add gelatin and vanilla mixture, which has cooled thoroughly.

Remove meringue discs from icebox. To build the cake, simply ice the first disc with whipped cream, then place the second on top of this and ice it, and so on until all four layers are arranged. Then ice the sides and top with remainder of whipped cream and sprinkle all over (liberally) with grated chocolate. Store in icebox.

Serves 18 to 20. The Shreveport Club

BABA AU RUM

Baba:
1½ cups sugar
2 eggs
2 tablespoons heavy cream
⅛ teaspoon salt
1 cup plus 2 heaping tablespoons sifted flour
1½ teaspoons baking powder
1 teaspoon vanilla
½ cup hot (not boiling) milk

Sauce:
1½ cups sugar
1 cup cold water
⅓ cup rum (light or dark)

Topping:
½ pint whipping cream
⅓ cup sugar
1½ teaspoons almond flavor

Baba: Mix sugar, eggs, cream and salt until smooth. Sift in flour and baking powder and mix well. Add vanilla. Add hot milk, stir well and immediately pour into buttered 7" x 11" cake pan. Bake 30 minutes at 360°. When done, remove from pan, place in larger pan, and let cool until warm. Pour rum sauce over baba, letting it soak in well. Cover with waxed paper, not foil. Let stand overnight.

Sauce: Combine sugar and water and boil 3 minutes. Let cool. When cool, not before, add rum. Let stand until ready to use.

Topping: Whip cream, add sugar and flavoring.

Cut baba in squares. Ice each square with topping.

Makes 8-10 servings. Mrs. Jerome H. Ferguson, Jr.

RUM ICE BOX CAKE

1½ dozen ladyfingers
72 large marshmallows
¼ cup sweet milk
2 pints whipping cream
5 tablespoons white rum or more to taste

Crust: Split ladyfingers lengthwise and stand around buttered 10 spring mold; place close together. Crumble ladyfingers in bottom of pan until completely covered.

Cake: Place marshmallows and milk in a double boiler and cook over a slow fire, stirring often. When marshmallows are completely melted, remove from fire and water and set aside to cool. Whip cream until it stands in peaks. Add rum slowly to the marshmallow mixture; fold into the whipped cream. Pour in mold and set in freezer for thirty minutes. Remove and leave in refrigerator overnight. Remove spring mold band before cutting. This is a beautiful cake to serve at the table.

Serves 12 to 16.

Julia Dehan
Loryne Martin

BLITZ TORTE

Cake batter:
½ cup butter
½ cup sugar
4 egg yolks
½ cup plus 2 tablespoons flour
¼ teaspoon salt
1 teaspoon baking powder
4 tablespoons milk

Meringue:
4 egg whites
¾ cup sugar
1 teaspoon vanilla
¾ cup chopped pecans

Filling:
½ pint whipping cream
1½ teaspoons powdered sugar
¼ teaspoon vanilla
1 No. 303 can crushed pineapple or 1 pint fresh strawberries, washed, cleaned and slightly crushed

Cake: Cream butter and sugar, add egg yolks and beat well, then add flour, which has been sifted with salt and baking powder, alternately with the milk. Pour into two lightly buttered 8" cake pans.

Meringue: Beat egg whites stiff, add sugar and vanilla. Put meringue on top of batter in the two cake pans. Sprinkle with chopped pecans. Bake 20 to 30 minutes at 325°. Remove from oven and let cool.

Filling: Whip cream, add powdered sugar and vanilla and fold in well-drained fruit.

When cakes are cool, turn one out upside down, put whipped cream filling on this layer, then top with other layer right side up. Place in refrigerator until ready to serve.

Mrs. John William Patton, Jr.

MERINGUE SHELLS

4 egg whites
Pinch of salt
1 cup sugar
1 teaspoon lemon juice

Beat egg whites until stiff. Add salt. Sift sugar and add gradually. Beat well after each addition. When about ½ the sugar is added, add lemon juice, a little at a time, alternating with remaining sugar. Beat until very stiff and glossy. Drop by a big kitchen spoon onto brown paper on baking sheet. Form hollow in the center of each with the back of the spoon. Bake in a slow oven 275° for 40 to 60 minutes or until lightly browned. Allow to cool. Remove from paper and store in airtight container. Fill shells with ice cream and top with fruit.

Mrs. R. H. Nelson, Jr.

BUTTER ROLL DELICIOUS

- ½ cup butter
- 1 cup sugar
- 1 cup milk
- ½ cup water
- ½ teaspoon nutmeg
- 1 teaspoon vanilla
- 1½ cups flour
- 3 teaspoons baking powder
- ½ teaspoon salt
- 5 tablespoons shortening

Cream together butter with ½ cup sugar. Mix together and bring to a boil ½ cup milk, ½ cup sugar, water, nutmeg, and vanilla. Make a dough of flour, baking powder, salt, shortening and ½ cup milk, and roll ⅛-inch thick. Spread butter and sugar mixture over this, then roll dough as for jelly roll. Cut into 1-inch rolls, and place in a large shallow greased baking dish. Pour the syrup mixture over this and bake at 375° until syrup thickens, about 20 minutes. Sprinkle with cinnamon before baking if desired.

Makes 12 servings. Mrs. J. B. McCullough

CHARLOTTE RUSSE

- 2 whole eggs
- 2 cups milk
- 1 cup sugar
- 1 teaspoon vanilla
- 1 envelope gelatin dissolved in ½ cup cold water
- ½ pint whipping cream
- 8-10 ladyfingers, halved

Beat eggs well, stir in milk and sugar. Cook in top of double boiler until mixture coats spoon. Add vanilla. Remove from fire, add dissolved gelatin, and cool. When mixture is completely cold, fold in whipped cream. (Crumbled macaroons may be added before whipped cream if desired.) Line serving bowl with halved ladyfingers and pour custard mixture over them. Place in refrigerator for several hours. Ladyfingers may have a sprinkling of sherry before the custard is poured, if desired. Very attractive if served with whipped cream on top.

8 servings. Mrs. Walter E. Hawkins, Jr.

REFRIGERATOR CHEESE CAKE

- 1 4-ounce package lemon gelatin
- 1 cup hot water
- 1 8-ounce package cream cheese
- ¾ cup sugar
- Juice of one lemon
- 1 13-ounce can evaporated milk, whipped stiff (chill before whipping)
- 20 graham cracker squares
- ¼ pound butter, melted

Dissolve gelatin in hot water. Cool. Cream together cream cheese and sugar. Add lemon juice and cooled gelatin to cream cheese mixture gradually, while beating. Fold the above mixture into whipped evaporated milk. Crush graham crackers and mix with melted butter. Press graham cracker crumbs into bottom of a 10" x 14" pan and pour cream cheese mixture on top. Refrigerate.

Makes 16 servings. Mrs. Neil Dixon

CARAMEL CROQUEMBOUCHE

1 cup water
½ cup (1 stick) butter or margarine
1 cup sifted flour
¼ teaspoon salt
4 eggs
Caramel Cream
Caramel Syrup
¾ cup (3-ounce package) walnut pieces

The first five ingredients are for puffs, to form a 12-inch high tree, or about 20 servings of 3 puffs each. To make them, heat water and butter or margarine to boiling in medium-size saucepan. Add flour and salt all at once and stir hard with a wooden spoon about 2 minutes, or until batter forms a thick smooth ball that follows spoon around pan. Remove saucepan from heat and cool slightly. Then add eggs, 1 at a time, beating each in well until mixture is shiny and thick. Shape small mounds, with 2 teaspoons, 1 inch apart on ungreased cookie sheets. (One rounded teaspoonful of batter is enough for each, but measure carefully so puffs will be about the same size; recipe will make about 5 dozen.) Bake in hot oven (400°) 25 to 30 minutes, or until shells are puffed, crisp, and lightly golden; remove at once from cookie sheets with spatula, and allow to cool completely on wire cake racks.

When ready to make tree, cut a slit in side of each puff, being careful not to cut off top; fill each with a teaspoonful of chilled Caramel Cream. Arrange a single layer of filled puffs to cover bottom of a 9-inch serving dish (use dish with a slightly raised edge to hold the puffs in place); drizzle with warm Caramel Syrup; scatter a few walnut pieces over layer of puffs. Make a second slightly smaller layer the same way; drizzle with syrup; continue to make layers of decreasing size, drizzling each with syrup, until all puffs are used and last puff crowns the top; drizzle with any remaining Caramel Syrup; stud all over with remaining walnuts.

To serve, remove puffs with 2 forks, starting at the top (tree will come apart easily); place 3 in each dessert dish. Serve plain; they are lusciously rich.

Caramel Cream: Scald 2½ cups milk in top of double boiler over hot water while making caramelized sugar, by heating 1½ cups sugar in heavy 3-quart saucepan, over medium heat, stirring constantly with a wooden spoon until melted and golden. Remove from heat. Pour scalded milk, **very slowly** (mixture may spatter), into melted sugar, stirring constantly; cook over medium heat until melted sugar is dissolved. Smooth 4½ tablespoons cornstarch and ⅛ teaspoon salt to a paste with ½ cup cold milk; stir into caramel mixture. Cook over medium heat, stirring constantly, until mixture thickens and boils 3 minutes; remove from heat. Stir in 6 tablespoons butter or margarine and 1½ teaspoons vanilla; chill at least 1 hour before filling puffs. Makes about 3½ cups.

Caramel Syrup: Melt 1½ cups sugar in medium-size heavy frying pan or saucepan, stirring constantly with wooden spoon until golden, remove from heat. Stir in ½ cup boiling water very slowly (mixture may spatter); cook about 3 minutes, or until a teaspoon of syrup dropped into cold water forms a hard ball (250° on a candy thermometer). Keep warm over hot water while assembling Caramel Croquembouche. Makes 1½ cups.

Mrs. John D. Caruthers, Jr.

CHEESE CAKE PIE

Crust:
1¼ cups crushed graham crackers
⅓ cup sugar
⅓ cup melted butter

Filling:
2 tablespoons butter
1 large package cream cheese, softened
½ cup sugar
2 tablespoons flour
1 egg
⅔ cup milk
¼ cup lemon juice
2 tablespoons lemon rind, grated

Crust: Mix crust ingredients with fork and pat into greased 9" pie pan. Save 2 tablespoons for top of pie.

Filling: Cream together butter, cream cheese and sugar. Add flour, egg, milk, lemon juice, and lemon rind. Pour into graham cracker crust. Bake at 350° for 35 minutes. When done, sprinkle remaining crumbs on top. Chill 2 hours.

6 servings.

Mrs. Robert S. Hendrick

CHOCOLATE DELIGHT

2 bars German sweet chocolate
4 tablespoons water
3 tablespoons powdered sugar
4 eggs, separated
1 teaspoon vanilla
1½ dozen ladyfingers
1 cup pecans
½ pint whipped cream

Melt chocolate in double boiler. Add water and sugar. Beat over hot water until smooth. Beat egg yolks until very creamy, add them to chocolate mixture, then remove from stove. Beat egg whites very stiff and fold them into this mixture. Add vanilla.

Line 9" x 9" mold with halved ladyfingers. Pour ½ chocolate mixture over ladyfingers and sprinkle with half of the pecans. Cover with remaining halved ladyfingers, rest of the mixture and top with nuts. Refrigerate overnight. Unmold and cover with sweetened whipped cream.

Six to eight servings.

Mrs. Arch Haynes
Mrs. Tandy Lewis
Mrs. Charles DeBardeleben, III

CHOCOLATE ANGEL DESSERT

1 oblong angel food cake
1 package semi-sweet chocolate bits
1 pint whipping cream
1 tablespoon vanilla
1 can shredded coconut

Slice cake in 1" slices. Add ½ cup water to chocolate bits and melt in double boiler. Whip cream lightly. Divide and add ½ cream to melted chocolate. Add vanilla. Spread cream and chocolate mixture between cake slices and arrange in 6" x 10" ovenproof dish. Whip remaining cream until fluffy and spread over cake. Sprinkle with coconut. Place in refrigerator for about 8 hours before serving.

Serves 8. Mrs. A. S. Cooper

CHOCOLATE CHIFFON DESSERT

⅓ cup sugar
½ teaspoon salt
1¾ cups milk
1½ packages German sweet chocolate
3 beaten egg yolks
1 tablespoon gelatin softened in ¼ cup cold water
1 teaspoon vanilla
3 egg whites
⅓ cup sugar
1 un-iced layer devil's food cake
1 cup whipping cream
Chocolate curls for decoration

Combine sugar, salt, milk in medium saucepan, add chocolate and cook over medium heat, stirring constantly, until chocolate is completely melted. Blend mixture with egg beater. Add small amount of hot mixture to beaten egg yolks and then add remaining hot mixture, stirring constantly; return mixture to saucepan and cook over low heat until slightly thickened, about 5 minutes. Remove from heat and add softened gelatin and stir until dissolved. Pour into large mixing bowl and chill until partially thickened.

Beat egg whites until foamy, add vanilla and sugar, 2 tablespoons at a time, and continue beating until stiff peaks form. Fold into chilled chocolate mixture. Spoon into a 1½-quart mixing bowl and chill until firm, about 2½ hours.

Place un-iced devil's food cake on large plate. Loosen mold of chocolate at top edge with sharp knife, and place in bowl of warm water for a few seconds. Remove from water and shake bowl gently to loosen. Place one edge of bowl 1 inch from edge of cake layer and unmold on cake. Whip cream and spread over molded mixture and cake. Garnish with chocolate curls, if desired.

Makes 8-10 servings. This may be prepared the day before needed, but should be iced the same day. It also may be prepared in individual molds and turned out on squares of cake and topped with spoon of whipped cream.

Mrs. Sterling Bigner

MOUSSE AU CHOCOLAT

½ pound semi-sweet chocolate
½ cup sugar
¼ cup water
5 egg yolks
1 teaspoon vanilla
5 egg whites

Melt together in the top of a double boiler the chocolate, sugar and water. Stir until smooth and thoroughly blended. Then remove pan from heat to a pan of cold water. Stir occasionally until the mixture is cool. Add well-beaten egg yolks and vanilla. The mixture should be semi-fluid. If it is too firm, add 4 or 5 tablespoons of tepid milk. Beat egg whites until stiff and fold the chocolate mixture gently but thoroughly into them. Pour the mousse into individual glasses or coupes and chill for 6 to 8 hours.

Mrs. G. P. Disosway

CHOCOLATE SOUFFLE

3 tablespoons butter
3 tablespoons flour
½ cup sugar
1 cup milk
3 squares unsweetened chocolate, broken into bits
Dash salt
5 beaten egg yolks
7 stiffly beaten egg whites

In the top of a double boiler, melt butter and mix with flour. Cook a moment. Then add milk, and continue cooking, stirring constantly, until the mixture is rich and creamy. Add sugar and stir until dissolved. Add chocolate. The mixture will appear grainy for a while, but, as you keep stirring, the chocolate will suddenly combine and you will have a smooth, thick, sauce. Take this off the fire. Add a dash of salt and beat the mixture for a minute. Allow to cool a bit, then add beaten egg yolks to it, and beat until smooth. Beat egg whites until stiff. When chocolate sauce is really cool, take a large spoonful of egg whites and fold vigorously in the chocolate mixture until it appears slightly foamy. Dribble this sauce over the remaining egg whites, and fold thoroughly and carefully. Slide all this into a buttered and sugared souffle dish and place in a 350° oven. Bake for 20 minutes.

Simple Sauce to top off the souffle: Beat a half pint of heavy cream until it is stiff. Allow a half pint of vanilla ice cream to soften (not melt). Then beat these together. Add about 2 tablespoons of good brandy.

6 or 8 servings.

Mrs. James A. Latham

CHOCOLATE TOFFEE

2 cups vanilla wafer crumbs
2 cups pecans, finely chopped
2 cups powdered sugar
2 sticks butter
6 eggs, separated
4 squares unsweetened chocolate
1 teaspoon vanilla

Mix crumbs and nuts and line buttered pan with half of mixture. Cream powdered sugar and butter; add egg yolks (beaten) and melted chocolate. Cool chocolate mixture. Beat egg whites until they peak. Fold into chocolate mixture; add vanilla. Pour on top of crumb mixture and top with remaining crumb mixture. Refrigerate overnight. Top with whipped cream to serve.

10 to 12 servings.

Mrs. Tandy Lewis
Mrs. William Kalmbach

FRUIT COBBLER

1 stick margarine
1 cup flour
1 cup sugar
2 teaspoons baking powder
½ teaspoon salt
1 cup milk
Canned fruit (such as cherries or peaches)

Melt margarine. Sift together all dry ingredients and stir milk into them. Then pour mixture over melted margarine. Do not stir. Pour one regular size can of any fruit into the mixture; again, do not stir. Bake in 350° oven for 45 minutes. Serve warm.

Approximately 3 or 4 servings.

Mrs. Clyde Minor, III
Mrs. Walter Hawkins
Mrs. Larry Teague

COFFEE BAVARIAN

1 cup fine graham cracker crumbs
¼ cup melted butter or margarine
1 envelope unflavored gelatin
½ cup cold water
½ cup sugar
1 tablespoon instant coffee
¼ teaspoon salt
1⅔ cups evaporated milk
1 cup shaved chocolate

Mix cracker crumbs and melted butter. Line bottom of 8" square pan with mixture and chill. In 1-quart saucepan, soften gelatin in cold water. Add sugar, coffee and salt. Stir over low heat until sugar and gelatin dissolve. Remove from heat. Stir in 1 cup of the evaporated milk. Pour into small bowl of electric mixer and chill until firm. Then beat at low speed until mixture is just broken up. Add ⅔ cup evaporated milk. Beat at high speed until mixture fills bowl, then pour it over crumbs in pan. Sprinkle shaved chocolate over top and chill until firm. To serve, cut into squares. This may be prepared several days ahead.

Mrs. Gilbert L. Hetherwick

COCONUT BLANC MANGE

Custard:
2 cups milk
⅓ cup cornstarch or less
½ cup sugar
⅛ teaspoon salt
1 teaspoon vanilla
½ cup shredded coconut
2 egg whites

Lemon Sauce:
2 tablespoons cornstarch
1 cup sugar
2 cups hot water
Juice of lemon
1 egg yolk
1 tablespoon butter

Scald milk. Add cornstarch mixed with sugar and salt, dissolved in 3 tablespoons milk. Cook in top of double boiler until mixture thickens, about 10 minutes. Add coconut and vanilla. Pour mixture slowly into stiffly beaten egg whites, beating constantly. Pour into individual molds and chill. Serve with lemon sauce.

Sauce: Mix cornstarch and sugar and add water slowly. Cook for 8 minutes, stirring constantly. Add lemon juice, butter and lightly beaten egg yolk. Cook three minutes and then chill slightly.

Serves 6.

Mrs. D. E. Flowers

CRACKER PIE

3 egg whites
½ teaspoon baking powder
  or cream of tartar
1 cup sugar
1 cup chopped pecans
1 teaspoon vanilla
20 Ritz crackers, crushed

Topping:
½ pint whipped cream
2 tablespoons sugar
½ teaspoon vanilla

Beat egg whites with baking powder (or cream of tartar) until stiff, gradually adding sugar, as for meringue. Add vanilla, and fold in crushed cracker crumbs and pecans. Spread in a well buttered 9" pie pan or medium-size baking dish. Bake at 350° for 30 minutes. Cool and cover with whipped cream with sugar and vanilla added. Pie may be garnished with angel flake coconut, or shaved bitter chocolate, or crushed peppermint candy; or mix several tablespoons of drained crushed pineapple into cream before spreading on pie. Fresh crushed or frozen strawberries may also be used. (Add at the last.) Chill pie for several hours before serving.

Will serve 8 from a pie pan, or make 12 squares if baked in a rectangular pan. This same batter may be dropped from a spoon onto a greased cookie sheet and baked as separate meringues.

Mrs. William T. Murphy, III
Mrs. Ernest H. Turner, Jr.
Mrs. Jack Murrell

COFFEE DESSERT CAKE

2 dozen ladyfingers
1 10-ounce package large marshmallows
1 pint whipping cream, unwhipped
¼ cup extra strong coffee
2 cups chopped pecans

Melt marshmallows in strong coffee in a double boiler. Stir in chopped pecans and ½ pint of cream, whipped. Place a layer of ladyfingers in a 1½-quart buttered loaf pan and cover with marshmallow mixture. Repeat layer of ladyfingers and marshmallow mixture to fill loaf pan. Refrigerate. When mixture is firm, remove from pan. Serve frosted with the remainder of the whipping cream. May be garnished with cherries.

Mrs. Dosite Perkins, Jr.

A simple Coffee Mousse may be prepared from the above recipe, omitting ladyfingers and pecans, and increasing coffee to 1 cup. Simply melt marshmallows in coffee, and allow to cool. Fold mixture into 1 pint whipping cream, unwhipped. Pour into a shallow mold and allow to become firm. This will take about 7 hours.

Mrs. Darrell E. George

COFFEE CHIFFON

1½ cups milk
1 cup light cream
2 tablespoons instant coffee
5 eggs, separated
1⅙ cups sugar
2 envelopes plain gelatin
½ cup cold water
½ teaspoon salt
Grated German sweet chocolate
Whipped cream

Mix together and scald first three ingredients. Beat egg yolks until thick. Add ½ cup sugar slowly, beating well after each addition. Add egg mixture to scalded mixture and cook in top of double boiler until it coats spoon. Remove from heat and add gelatin which has been softened in cold water. Chill until thickened but not set. Beat egg whites and salt. Gradually beat in remaining sugar. Fold whites into chilled mixture and pour in lightly greased mold. At serving time, garnish with chocolate and whipped cream. Always make a day before needed.

Serves 12.

Mrs. T. Haller Jackson, Jr.
(nee Huldah Edens)

BEST BAKED CUSTARD

6 eggs, beaten whole
2 cups sugar
2 teaspoons vanilla
1 quart milk, scalded

Beat eggs; add sugar and vanilla, then milk. Mix well and pour into cups placed in pan of water. Bake in moderate oven for an hour. A dash of nutmeg on top is optional.

10 servings.

Mrs. Daniel John Shea

BAKED CUSTARD

2 eggs
Pinch of salt
½ cup sugar
1½ cups milk
1 teaspoon vanilla
Lump of butter (1 tablespoon)

Beat eggs well, add sugar gradually, then salt, milk and vanilla. Stir until well mixed, then place in one-quart casserole dish. Put lump of butter in and place dish in a pan of warm water. Place in 350° oven and cook until knife inserted in center comes out clean or when you shake it, center portion about the size of a demi-tasse cup is not quite set. This takes about 1 hour.

4 servings. This is best if prepared about 4 hours before serving, as it is best served at room temperature.

Mrs. Robert S. Hendrick

CUP CUSTARD

2½ cups milk
3 eggs, separated
1 cup sugar
1 tablespoon butter
1 teaspoon vanilla
Nutmeg

Scald milk. Beat yolks with sugar. Add milk and fold in beaten egg whites. Add vanilla and butter; then pour in custard cups. Sprinkle nutmeg on top before baking. Bake in a pan of water in 300° oven for 1 hour.

Makes about 8 cup custards. Mrs. Bert Kouns

Variation: Caramelize ½ cup white sugar in heavy iron skillet until a rich golden brown. Pour a small amount in each custard cup before adding custard mixture. You may also use coffee for an interesting variation.

Mrs. Earl Harter

VELVET CUSTARD

3 egg yolks
1 whole egg
½ cup sugar
2 level tablespoons cornstarch
⅛ teaspoon salt
3½ cups milk, scalded
2 teaspoons vanilla
Meringue:
3 egg whites
3 tablespoons sugar
Pinch of salt

Cream egg yolks and whole egg with sugar which has been blended with cornstarch and salt. Add scalded milk. Cook in double boiler until thick. Add vanilla and pour into custard cups.

Beat meringue ingredients together and top custards with the mixture. Cover completely with meringue and brown on lowest rung of broiler slowly and carefully.

Makes 8 cup custards. Mrs. G. Randell Whitmeyer

DAYLIGHT, DARKNESS PUDDING

1 package large, round chocolate wafers
1 stick butter or margarine
1 cup sifted confectioners' sugar
⅛ teaspoon almond extract
1 egg, well beaten
½ pint whipping cream
1½ tablespoons granulated sugar
1 teaspoon vanilla
1 cup chopped pecans

Crumble chocolate wafers and spread half of them in bottom of 8" x 8" pan. Cream butter and gradually add confectioners' sugar, then beat in the egg and almond extract. Spread over chocolate wafers. Beat cream until stiff, fold in granulated sugar, vanilla and pecans, and spread over egg mixture. Add remaining chocolate wafers, cover with waxed paper and let stand in refrigerator for 24 hours. Cut in squares and serve as is; or add a dab of whipped cream to the top of each square.

Mrs. W. F. Conway

EGGNOG RING

8 eggs, separated
1 cup granulated sugar
½ cup water
2 envelopes gelatin
¾ cup bourbon or brandy
½ cup slivered salted almonds, toasted
1 pint whipping cream

Beat egg yolks until thick and lemon colored. Add sugar and beat until no longer gritty. Add bourbon or brandy. Let gelatin stand in cold water for 15 minutes. Then melt thoroughly over hot water. Pour gelatin slowly into stiffly beaten egg whites. Lightly fold in yolk mixture with whites. Add slivered almonds. Pour in ring mold (rinsed in cold water first) and chill. When ready to serve, add whipped cream to center of ring. Decorate with more almonds, if desired.

Mrs. W. W. Lincoln

GRAHAM SURPRISE

20 graham crackers
¼ cup cocoa
⅓ cup sugar
½ pint whipping cream

Whip cream. Add sugar and cocoa. Start stacking graham crackers, putting a layer of the whipped cream between each one. (After the stack gets too high, place it on its side, continuing to add icing and crackers.) When this is done, ice the outside with remaining cream. Wrap in waxed paper and freeze. When ready to serve, remove from freezer and slice diagonally from one corner.

Mrs. Sinclair Kouns

BOILED CUSTARD ICE CREAM

1 quart milk, scalded
10 egg yolks
1 cup sugar
½ teaspoon salt
1 teaspoon vanilla
½ pint whipping cream
1 pint half and half

Beat eggs, add sugar and salt, then add hot milk gradually, stirring constantly. Cook in double boiler; stir constantly until mixture thickens and coats spoon. Add cream and vanilla and chill.

Makes ½ gallon.

Mrs. David H. Walke

CARAMEL ICE CREAM

2 cans sweetened condensed milk
5 cups milk
1 pint whipping cream
⅛ teaspoon salt
1 cup sugar
1 cup boiling water
2 teaspoons vanilla

Remove labels from condensed milk cans. Place cans in a pan, and cover with water. Place pan on heat, and when water is boiling, turn heat to low and let cans cook for three hours. Be sure the cans are always covered with water. Cool. Over low heat, melt sugar. Cook until it is light brown, stirring as needed. Do not let sugar burn, or it will be bitter; you just want it to have the caramel flavor and color. Pour the cup of boiling water on the melted sugar and cook until all sugar is dissolved. Be careful of the burning steam. Cool the syrup. In a blender mix the caramelized condensed milk with some of the milk. When smooth, add together all the ingredients, including all the milk, the caramel syrup, salt, vanilla and whipping cream (whipped a little if desired). Pour in a gallon ice cream freezer and freeze.

Yields 3 quarts of ice cream.

Chopped pecans are excellent in this. They may be slightly toasted before adding to the ice cream after freezing, or used without toasting.

Mrs. James E. Smitherman, Jr.

LEMON ICE CREAM

Juice of 8 lemons
4 cups sugar
2 quarts of milk (or enough to fill freezer container ¾ full)
1 pint heavy cream
Grated peel of 1 orange
Pinch of salt

Mix all ingredients together and freeze in hand or electric ice cream freezer.

Mrs. John R. Murphy

FIG ICE CREAM

3 cups milk
1½ cups granulated sugar
4 tablespoons flour
Few grains of salt
4 eggs, slightly beaten
3 teaspoons vanilla
3 cups heavy cream
3 cups sieved figs, combined with ½ cup granulated sugar
1 teaspoon almond extract

Scald milk in double boiler. Mix sugar, flour and salt together. Stir in enough milk to make smooth paste. Then stir in rest of milk in double boiler. Add eggs. Stir until mixture thickens. Cover and cook ten minutes on medium heat. Cool mixture, then add figs, almond extract, vanilla and heavy cream and freeze in 2-quart ice cream freezer. Use 8 parts crushed ice to one part ice cream salt.

This makes 2 quarts. Mrs. Jack Tullos, Jr.

MACAROON ICE CREAM

½ dozen almond macaroons, toasted
⅓ cup sherry
12 maraschino salad cherries
½ cup whipping cream
1 quart vanilla ice cream, softened
½ cup pecans

Break macaroons into pieces and soak them in sherry. Add sliced cherries. Whip cream; fold it into softened ice cream. Add nuts and cherry-macaroon mixture. Put in pan in freezer and when half-frozen, stir and let refreeze.

6 to 8 servings. Mrs. Robert U. Goodman

SIMPLE ICE CREAM

8 eggs
2 cups sugar
1 can evaporated milk
1 can condensed milk
Dash flour
Dash salt
Homogenized milk

Beat eggs with mixer until you can "cut them with a knife" or about 20 minutes. Continue beating while adding sugar, both kinds of milk, salt and flour. Pour into ice cream freezer, filling rest of container with homogenized milk and flavor, such as peaches, pineapples, strawberries, etc.

Makes 6 quarts ice cream. Mrs. Ernest H. Turner, Jr.

TART BUTTERMILK SHERBET

1 quart buttermilk
½ pint whipping cream
Juice of 3½ lemons
2 pinches salt
1⅛ cups sugar

Combine all ingredients and place in freezer tray until mixture attains a soft consistency. Take from freezer tray and place in cold bowl. Beat thoroughly and return to freezer, freezing until firm.

Mrs. Robert G. Chandler

LEMON CUPS

2 tablespoons butter
1 cup sugar
3 eggs, separated
1½ cups milk, slightly scalded
4 tablespoons flour
Pinch salt
5 tablespoons lemon juice
Grated rind of 1 lemon

Cream butter and sugar. Add flour, salt, rind, and juice. Pour on mixture of well beaten egg yolks and slightly scalded milk, stirring well. Fold in stiffly beaten egg whites, and pour into ovenproof custard cups. Place in pan of water and bake at 350° for 45 minutes. Watch closely to be sure crust does not brown too quickly.

Makes 6 or 7 cups.

Rufus Youngblood
Harriet Blish McGee

LEMON ICEBOX CAKE

8 eggs, separated
1 cup sugar
1 cup lemon juice
2 envelopes gelatin
½ cup cold water
1 teaspoon lemon rind
1 cup sugar
Angel food cake (10-inch)
½ pint whipping cream

Beat egg yolks with 1 cup sugar and lemon juice until creamy. Cook until of custard-like consistency. Have gelatin dissolved in cold water and add to custard while warm. Add lemon rind. Let stand until cool. Beat egg whites, gradually adding second cup of sugar, and fold into cooled mixture. Break cake into medium chunks, add to above mixture and pour into tube pan. Set in icebox until stiff. Remove from pan and ice with whipping cream to which a little vanilla and sugar have been added.

Mrs. M. Z. Piper

LEMON FROMAGE

2 envelopes gelatin
½ cup cold water
6 eggs, separated
1 cup sugar
Grated rind of 1 lemon
Juice of 2 large lemons
½ pint heavy cream, whipped

Have all ingredients ready, as this sets quickly. Soften gelatin in cold water, dissolve over hot water. Set aside to cool until lukewarm. Beat egg yolks with sugar until light and almost white. Add lemon juice, rind, and cooled gelatin. Fold in beaten egg whites. Continue beating, and when mixture holds its shape when stirred with a spoon, pour into a 1½-quart oiled ring mold. Chill until set. Serve with whipped cream.

Serves 8.

Mrs. W. Edward Wilson

LEMON ORANGE CAKE

Make 1 lemon custard angel cake, using your own recipe or a mix. When cool, slice cake into 3 layers and fill and ice with the following:

- 1 cup orange juice (you may use frozen orange juice)
- ¾ cup sugar
- 2 tablespoons flour
- 3 whole eggs
- 1 pint whipping cream
- Angel flake coconut

Cook first four ingredients in top of double boiler, stirring constantly until thick. Set aside and cool. When cold, fold in cream (which has been whipped) and ½ cup angel flake coconut. Keep in refrigerator.

Mrs. Jerome Bryan
Houston, Texas

ORANGE PINEAPPLE CREAM CAKE

- 1 orange chiffon cake
- 1 box instant vanilla pudding
- 1 8½-ounce can crushed pineapple
- 1 pint heavy cream, whipped
- 2 to 3 tablespoons sugar
- Mandarin orange sections

Split cake in 3 crosswise layers (if frozen, cake cuts better). Mix pudding and well drained pineapple thoroughly. Fold sweetened whipped cream into mixture. Spread between cake layers and over entire cake. Garnish with orange sections on top. Refrigerate until used. It may be frozen ahead of time. Orange sections may be omitted.

Mrs. Louis Planchard

LEMON SURPRISE

- 3 eggs, separated
- ½ cup sugar
- 4 tablespoons lemon juice
- ½ pint whipping cream
- Vanilla wafers

Beat egg yolks. Add sugar and lemon juice. Heat if necessary to blend. Cool. Fold in whipped cream. Beat egg whites, and fold in last. Roll enough wafers into crumbs to form crust in buttered icebox tray. Line bottom of tray with crumbs and pour in mixture, sprinkling top with a few additional crumbs. Freeze.

8 servings.

Mrs. C. Lane Sartor

LEMON TORTE

Crust:
2 tablespoons sugar
2 sticks softened butter or oleo
2 cups flour

Custard:
1 envelope gelatin soaked in
⅔ cup water
1 cup sugar
8 eggs, separated
2 lemons (rind and juice)
½ pint whipping cream

Crust: Mix sugar, butter and flour with pastry blender. Press or pat into a 10" x 14" pan. Bake 30 minutes at 325° or until brown.

Custard: Mix sugar with the egg yolks and beat well. Add to this the lemon juice and rind. Cook in a double boiler until thick. Cool slightly and add dissolved gelatin. Cool. Beat egg whites and fold into custard mixture. Spread over crust and refrigerate. Top with whipped cream just before serving.

15 or 16 servings.

Mrs. Peyton Kelley

NUT TORTE

2 cups pecans, ground
2 tablespoons flour
4 eggs, separated
1 cup sugar
1 teaspoon salt
½ teaspoon baking powder
1 tablespoon orange juice

Grind pecans. Beat egg yolks, then add sugar, flour, salt, baking powder and orange juice. Add to pecans. Beat egg whites and fold in. Bake 25 minutes at 350°. Cut in half and add filling. To make filling, combine ⅔ cup whipping cream, whipped, and 1½ teaspoons orange rind, grated. After filling cake, frost it with icing made by mixing together one 6-ounce package semi-sweet chocolate dots, melted, ½ cup sour cream and pinch of salt. It may be garnished with whole pecans on top.

Mrs. Edward J. Crawford, Jr.

BROWNIE PARFAIT—Cut your favorite brownie in small pieces and alternate with softened ice cream in parfait glass. Freeze. Before serving, garnish with a dollop of whipped cream to which a little instant coffee has been added.

ORANGE LADYFINGER DELIGHT

1 cup sugar
5 tablespoons flour
3 eggs, separated
1 cup orange juice
1 cup milk
⅓ cup butter
Grated rind of 1 orange
Sections from 2 oranges
8 ladyfingers
½ pint whipping cream

Mix together sugar and flour, add slightly beaten egg yolks, then orange juice and milk, stirring until smooth. Cook in top of double boiler over water until mixture thickens, then add butter while mixture is hot. Allow to cool. Fold in stiffly beaten egg whites. Add orange sections and grated rind. Line a dessert bowl with split ladyfingers. Pour in pudding, garnish top with whipped cream. Allow to chill for several hours before serving.

8 servings. Mrs. Robert Brown

PARADISE PUDDING

12 almond macaroons
12 maraschino cherries
1 cup pecans
1 cup tiny marshmallows
1 envelope plain gelatin (use 2 in hot weather)
1 pint heavy cream, whipped
¼ cup sugar
1 teaspoon vanilla

Break macaroons into small pieces; add marshmallows and cut-up cherries and pecans. Dissolve gelatin in small amount of cold water; then add enough hot water to make ¾ cup in all. Add this to first mixture. Whip cream with sugar and vanilla and fold into this; refrigerate. Make the day before serving.

Serves 8 well. Mrs. R. G. Lawton, Jr.

ANGEL PARFAIT

⅓ cup sugar
4 tablespoons water
2 egg whites
½ pint whipping cream
1½ teaspoons vanilla

Put sugar and water in saucepan, stir until sugar is dissolved and boil until syrup spins a thread when dropped from tip of spoon. Remove from fire. Beat egg whites until stiff. Add syrup slowly, continuing to beat mixture until light and fluffy. Chill, stirring occasionally. Beat cream until thick, add vanilla, then beat in egg mixture with a few turns of an egg beater. Freeze. This may be frozen in parfait glasses. It is also pretty and good if layered with fruit before freezing.

Mrs. Jerry Howard

CHERRY CUSTARD PARFAITS

5 tablespoons flour
½ cup sugar
½ teaspoon salt
2 cups scalded milk
2 slightly beaten eggs
1 teaspoon vanilla
1 No. 2 can cherry pie filling

Mix flour, sugar and salt; slowly stir in scalded milk. Cook in double boiler until thick. Add a little of the hot mixture into eggs, then pour eggs into hot mixture. Cook 3 minutes longer, then add vanilla and let cool. Alternate layers of cherry filling and custard in parfait glasses, beginning and ending with cherry filling. Garnish with whipped cream and a cherry. Chill until serving time.

Serves 4 to 6.

Mrs. Larry Burke

PECAN SLICE TORTE

There are 3 parts to this recipe:

1. Crust:
   1 cup flour
   ½ cup butter
2. Filling:
   2 eggs, slightly beaten
   1½ cups brown sugar
   ¾ cup coconut
   1 cup chopped nuts (pecans or walnuts)
   2 tablespoons flour
   ¼ teaspoon baking powder
   ½ teaspoon salt
   1 teaspoon vanilla
3. Icing:
   2 tablespoons butter
   1½ cups powdered sugar
   3 tablespoons orange juice
   1 tablespoon lemon juice

Later: **½ cup nuts**

1. Mix to a paste the flour and butter. Press on bottom of buttered 9" x 9" square pan. Bake 15 minutes at 350°, until a very light brown.

2. While crust is baking, mix filling ingredients in order given above. Pour this filling on the baked crust and again bake at 350° for 20 minutes. Remove from oven and cool. When cool, spread the icing.

3. Mix icing ingredients, spread on torte, and sprinkle top with ½ cup finely chopped nuts.

Let this cool in the pan you bake it in. Cut it in small squares to serve, as it is very rich and delicious.

16 or more servings.

Mrs. Gene Fleming

MAXIM'S PEARS

6 fresh table pears
Vanilla syrup (simple syrup flavored with vanilla)
9 egg yolks
1 cup sugar
¼ to ½ cup good brandy
1 pint heavy cream, whipped
Vanilla ice cream
½ pint heavy cream, whipped

Peel pears and empty cores from the bottom to remove all pits. Poach pears in light vanilla syrup. Do not cook too long, as fruit should remain firm. Let pears cool, then remove from syrup and drain on paper towels.

Prepare mousse as follows: Beat egg in top of double boiler and add sugar. Cook, over hot water, until the mixture is firm and has the consistency of a ribbon. Remove from fire and continue beating over ice until it is completely cold. Add brandy and fold in the pint of whipped cream.

Pour mousse into a deep dish and chill. When serving, fill centers of pears with vanilla ice cream, then place them on the mousse and decorate with slightly sweetened whipped cream.

Mrs. Edward H. Jackson, Jr.

PEPPERMINT TWIST

2 cups vanilla wafer crumbs
½ cup melted butter
¾ cup butter
3 cups sifted confectioners' sugar
5 eggs, slightly beaten
4½ squares melted chocolate
1½ cups whipping cream, sweetened and whipped
Dash vanilla
1 8-ounce package tiny marshmallows
½ cup crushed peppermint candy

Mix first two ingredients and press into 13" x 8" x 2" dish. Cream butter and sugar, add beaten eggs and chocolate and beat well. Spoon over crumbs and set in freezer while whipping cream. Whip cream with a little confectioners' sugar and dash of vanilla. Fold marshmallows into whipping cream and spread over chocolate. Crush peppermint stick candy with rolling pin and sprinkle over whipped cream-marshmallow mixture. Place in freezer uncovered and when frozen, remove and cover with plastic wrap or foil. Return to freezer. Thirty minutes before serving, transfer it from freezer to refrigerator. Cut in squares to serve.

12 servings.

Mrs. Oliver Moore

FROZEN PINEAPPLE DELIGHT

½ cup melted butter
1 cup powdered sugar
2 eggs, separated
1 cup crushed pineapple, drained
1 cup chopped pecans
1 cup whipping cream
Graham cracker crumbs

Combine butter, sugar and egg yolks. Add pineapple, pecans, egg whites (beaten to form peaks), and whipped cream. Line bottom of 8" x 10" pan with graham cracker crumbs. Pour in pineapple mixture. Sprinkle remainder of crumbs on top. Place in freezer.

8 to 10 servings. Keeps well in freezer.

Mrs. Edward N. Henderson

PINEAPPLE MOUSSE

1½ dozen ladyfingers (split in half)
½ cup pineapple juice
1 small can crushed pineapple
1 envelope gelatin
1 cup cold water
4 eggs, separated
½ cup sugar
1 teaspoon vanilla
½ pint whipping cream

Line two pans with halved ladyfingers. (Use layer cake pans.) Heat pineapple juice and add gelatin which has been dissolved in cold water. Set aside to cool. Cream egg yolks with sugar. Beat vanilla and the cooled juice mixture into yolks. Let stand until this begins to congeal. Add drained crushed pineapple. Add whipped cream and stiffly beaten egg whites. Pour mixture into the two pans. (It is also pretty made in loaf pans and iced with whipped cream.) Refrigerate.

Serves 10 to 12.

Mrs. Peyton Kelley

HOLIDAY PUDDING

1 cup ground suet
1 cup sugar
1 cup buttermilk
1 egg
1 teaspoon soda
2 teaspoons cinnamon
1 teaspoon allspice
1 teaspoon cloves
2 cups flour
1 cup raisins
1 cup pecans

Beat egg until light. Gradually beat in sugar, then stir in ground suet. Add alternately buttermilk and flour which has been sifted with soda and spices. Fold in raisins and pecans. Steam on top of stove for two hours. If you don't have regular steamed pudding containers, improvise with pressure cooker, rack and a coffee can for the pudding.

Serves 8 to 10. Good served with hard sauce or lemon sauce.

Mrs. William T. Murphy, III

FROZEN RASPBERRY DELIGHT

1 cup boiling water
2 tablespoons sugar
⅛ teaspoon salt
2 tablespoons lemon juice
1 tablespoon lemon peel
2 cups heavy cream, whipped
1 package lemon gelatin
1 package frozen raspberries (strawberries may be used if preferred)
1 tablespoon Cointreau
1 teaspoon grated orange peel

Add hot water, sugar and salt to gelatin. Let cool a little, then add lemon juice, grated orange and lemon peel and whipped cream. Whip until light and foamy. Put in mold and chill. When ready to serve, unmold and pour raspberries mixed with Cointreau over the top.

8 servings. Mrs. E. D. Klinger

RED CHERRY PUDDING

Pudding:
1 can sour red cherries
1 teaspoon soda
2 cups sugar
1½ cups flour
2 eggs
1 tablespoon red food coloring
4 tablespoons melted butter
1½ teaspoons vanilla
1 cup chopped nuts

Sauce:
1 cup light brown sugar
2 tablespoons flour
Pinch salt
1 cup hot water
1 tablespoon butter

Drain cherries and reserve juice. Mix soda with cherries and let stand. Mix sugar, flour, well beaten eggs, juice, and food coloring. Combine this mixture with cherries. Mix. Add butter, vanilla, and chopped nuts. Bake in ungreased ovenproof pan (11" x 7" x 2½") at 300° for 45 minutes. While pudding is cooking, combine sauce ingredients in saucepan and cook over low heat about 25 minutes, stirring occasionally. When done, pour over hot pudding. Cool and refrigerate. Serve with whipped cream if desired.

10 servings. Mrs. C. Cody White, Jr.

STRAWBERRIES CAVIARE

2 pints fresh strawberries, washed and hulled
2 or more tablespoons sugar
¾ cup sweet red wine
¼ cup brandy or rum
Coffee ice cream

Drain berries. Sprinkle with sugar and let stand for at least one hour. At serving time, combine berries and wine in chafing dish and heat. Pour warm brandy or rum over berries and ignite. Stir to keep flaming and spoon over coffee ice cream.

6 servings. Mrs. Keith Begbie

STRAWBERRY MOUSSE

1 10-ounce package (standard size) frozen strawberries
1 8-ounce carton sour cream
½ cup sugar
1 tablespoon vanilla

Place all ingredients in electric blender, turn on high speed and allow to mix thoroughly. Pour in refrigerator tray and freeze solid. An electric mixer may also be used successfully.

6 servings.

Mrs. T. O. Perry

STRAWBERRIES NINA

(Easy and Festive Summer Dessert)

2 quarts sugared strawberries (use powdered sugar, if desired)
½ pint heavy cream, whipped
1 pint vanilla ice cream
2 ounces Cointreau
1 ounce rum
Juice of one lemon

Place berries in a large bowl. Whip ice cream slightly and fold in whipped cream; add lemon juice and liquors and pour over strawberries.

Mrs. Staunton Sample

STRAWBERRY SHORTCAKE

Cake:
2½ cups flour
2 tablespoons sugar
2 teaspoons salt
5 teaspoons baking powder
6 tablespoons shortening
1½ cups milk

Filling:
¼ pound butter
2 quarts strawberries
1½ cups sugar
1 pint whipping cream
Sugar to taste (about 3 tablespoons)

For cake, sift together dry ingredients. Cut shortening in fine, then stir in milk. Mound batter on slightly greased cookie sheet, and bake at 450° for 12 minutes. Split immediately after removing from oven. Butter with the ¼ pound butter on both insides of split cake. For filling, crush strawberries with hands and add the 1½ cups sugar at the very last minute, just as you are ready to serve. Put between layers of shortcake and on top of cake. Serve with sweetened whipped cream.

Makes 6 large servings, or 8 smaller ones. This will melt in your mouth, but must be attended to immediately before eating it, with cake served while quite warm. It is well worth the trouble.

Mrs. Elizabeth H. Baynum
Wilmington, Del.

SHORTCAKE

6 tablespoons butter, oleo or shortening
¾ cup sugar
1 egg
3 tablespoons milk
1½ cups sifted flour
2 teaspoons baking powder
¼ teaspoon salt
1 teaspoon vanilla

Cream butter well, then add sugar, beating thoroughly. Add egg and beat. Add milk alternately with flour which has been sifted with baking powder and salt; then add vanilla. Grease a jelly roll pan, or use a large ovenproof baking dish. Press cake batter down on pan with hands, making a very thin layer. Bake at 350° for 10 minutes. Cut in squares and alternate with berries and whipped cream.

Makes about 16 squares.

Mrs. William T. Murphy, III

TRIFLE DESSERT

3 egg yolks
3 cups milk
3 teaspoons flour
½ cup sugar
1 teaspoon vanilla
2 dozen ladyfinger cookies
1 dozen almond macaroons
½ cup black walnuts
Whipped cream

Make a custard by cooking the first five ingredients together until thick, then allow to cool. In a large ovenproof bowl, place a layer of ladyfingers and crumbled macaroons, add black walnuts and pour some of the boiled custard over this. Repeat layers until all ingredients are used. Top with whipped cream and refrigerate several hours.

Mrs. George D. Wray, Jr.

"STEWED" WATERMELON

Make a marinade consisting of:
1 jigger apricot brandy
1 jigger peach brandy
1 jigger orange curacao
4 jiggers rum

Make a plug in a medium-sized watermelon and pour the marinade into the hole. Replace plug and seal with toothpicks. Stand plug-side up in chopped ice. Chill for at least 2 hours. When ready to serve, cut into wedges and serve in soup bowls. Dry champagne may be substituted for rum, for an even more elegant dessert.

Mrs. H. Whitney Boggs, Jr.

WINE JELLY

1 package gelatin
¼ cup cold water
1 cup boiling water
⅓ cup sugar
1 tablespoon strained lemon juice
1 cup good sherry
⅛ teaspoon salt
Whipping cream
Toasted almonds or coconut (optional)

Soften gelatin in cold water. Add boiling water to dissolve. Add sugar and stir until dissolved. Add salt, lemon juice and sherry. Pour into individual sherbet glasses. When set, garnish with whipped cream, sprinkle with fine toasted almonds or toasted coconut, if desired.

6 servings.

Mrs. Jerome H. Ferguson, Jr.
Mrs. John W. Paylor, Jr.

CHOCOLATE SAUCE FOR ICE CREAM

1 tablespoon butter
1 square unsweetened chocolate
½ cup boiling water
1 cup sugar
½ teaspoon vanilla

Melt chocolate and butter over very low heat. Gradually add boiling water. Bring to a boil. Add sugar gradually and boil 5 minutes. Cool. Add vanilla; broken pecans may be added also, if desired.

Mrs. D. Y. Smith

CHOCOLATE SAUCE

1 stick oleo or butter
8 tablespoons cocoa
1½ cups sugar
Salt
2 small cans evaporated milk
2 teaspoons vanilla

Cream cocoa and butter. Add other ingredients and mix thoroughly. Bring to a boil, stirring constantly. Let boil for 7 minutes, then cool sauce and add vanilla.

Mrs. Claude Cunningham

CHERRY SAUCE

1 can sour pitted cherries, drained
½ cup sugar
2 tablespoons cornstarch
½ teaspoon salt
½ teaspoon cinnamon

Combine dry ingredients. Stir in cherry juice and cook until thick. Let boil for 4 or 5 minutes, then add cherries and let come to a boil again. Take off heat and add 2 tablespoons butter. This is very good with baked ham, as well as with desserts.

Mrs. George N. Gray

LEMON SAUCE

6 egg yolks
Juice of 6 lemons
1½ cups sugar
¼ pound butter

Beat all ingredients together thoroughly and cook in double boiler until thick. This will keep well in refrigerator. It may be mixed with whipped cream and used as a pie or cake filling, or it may be poured over angel food cake.

Mrs. E. Obering
Oklahoma City, Okla.

ORANGE SYRUP

1 cup sugar
¼ cup orange juice concentrate
½ cup butter

Combine these 3 ingredients and bring to a boil. This syrup is delicious with hot cakes.

Mrs. Ralph F. Pullen

TAHITIAN ICE CREAM SAUCE

¾ cup preserves—pineapple and apricot combined
1 cup rum

Combine preserves and rum, and set on "back of stove." Heat slightly, but do not cook. Or, you may set mixture in a pan of boiling water to heat it. To serve, take sauce to the table in a chafing dish, and ignite. (Rum must be warm to blaze.) Have vanilla ice cream already in serving dishes at the table, so all is ready for the "flame." After sauce is burning, stir it and ladle it until the flames are about to go out, and serve over the ice cream.

8 servings.

Mrs. Melvin F. Johnson

Candy

The Strand Theatre

THE STRAND THEATRE

No matter what is being staged, Broadway's award-winning "CATS," "GYPSY," or "ZIEGFELD'S FOLLIES," a night at the Strand is memorable. Built in 1925, this ornate theatre is listed on the National Register of Historic Places.

AUNT BILL'S BROWN CANDY

- 3 pints white sugar
- 1 pint whole milk (or cream)
- ¼ teaspoon soda
- ¼ pound butter
- 1 teaspoon vanilla
- 2 pounds nut-meats

Pour 1 pint sugar into heavy aluminum or iron skillet and place over low heat. Begin stirring with wooden spoon, and keep sugar moving, so it will not scorch at all. It will take almost a half hour to melt this sugar completely, and at no time let it smoke or cook so fast that it turns dark. It should be about the color of light brown sugar syrup.

While you are melting the sugar in the skillet, pour the remaining 2 pints of sugar, together with milk, into a deep heavy kettle and set it over low heat to cook slowly.

As soon as all the sugar in skillet is melted, begin pouring it into the kettle of boiling milk and sugar, keeping it on very slow heat and stirring constantly. Now the real secret of mixing these ingredients is to pour a stream no larger than a knitting needle and to stir across the bottom of the kettle all the time.

Continue cooking and stirring until the mixture forms a firm ball when dropped into cold water. After this test is made, turn off the heat and immediately add soda, stirring vigorously as it foams up. As soon as soda is mixed, add butter, allowing it to melt as you stir. Now, set off the stove, away from drafts, for about 20 minutes, then add vanilla and begin beating. Use a wooden spoon and beat until the mixture is thick and heavy, having a dull appearance instead of a glossy sheen. Add the broken nut-meats and mix. Turn into tin boxes or into square pans where it may be cut into squares when cooled slightly. This keeps moist and delicious indefinitely and is most attractive when decorated with a sprig of holly, candied cherries and halves of pecans.

Mrs. P. F. O'Brien, Jr.

FOURS

- 1 cup butter
- 1 cup white sugar
- 1 cup brown sugar
- 1 cup cream
- 1 cup dark corn syrup
- 1 cup whipping cream
- 1 cup pecan meats
- 1 tablespoon vanilla
- Dipping chocolate

Place first five ingredients in medium large vessel and bring to a boil. Add whipping cream (unwhipped). Cook to medium hard ball, or 236° F. Add nuts and vanilla and pour into two greased pans, 9 inches square. Cool and cut in squares of desired size. Dip in melted dipping chocolate.

Mrs. Harrel Mulkey, Jr.

MARTHA WASHINGTON CANDY

½ pound butter
1 large can sweetened, condensed milk
2 pounds confectioners' sugar
1 quart pecan meats
2 packages semi-sweet chocolate "dots" or one 12-ounce package
⅔ block paraffin

Mix butter, milk and sugar. Add chopped pecans and roll into small balls. Chill thoroughly (at least 2 hours). Melt chocolate and paraffin in double boiler, and dip balls into this. (If chocolate hardens, heat it again.) Place on waxed paper. Makes about 150 pieces.

Mrs. Dixon Carroll

AUNTIE'S CHOCOLATE-COVERED CREAMS

This is an old-fashioned recipe which has been in my family for years and takes "a lot of doing." But for some extra special occasion (such as Christmas), they are well worth the effort.

3 cups sugar
1 cup milk
1 tablespoon butter
1 teaspoon vanilla
Pinch salt
½ cup pecans

Boil together all ingredients except pecans, until mixture forms soft ball in cold water. Do not stir. Cool to lukewarm. Beat until very stiff. Add pecans. Knead on board. Form into small balls on waxed paper.

8 squares bitter chocolate
1 tablespoon butter, cocoa butter if possible

Melt chocolate and butter over hot water. Dip balls in chocolate with fork (do not pierce) and drop into bowl of ice water. Leave 10 minutes. Store in cool place (not necessarily refrigerator).

Makes about 100 balls.

Mrs. Lilbourn G. Morgan

DATE LOAF

3 cups sugar
¼ teaspoon salt
½ stick butter
1½ cups milk
1 8-ounce package pitted dates (chopped)
¾ teaspoon vanilla
1½ cups broken pecans

Cook sugar, salt, butter and milk to form soft ball in cold water. Add chopped dates and cook slowly, stirring constantly, until mixture forms hard ball in cold water. Remove from fire and add vanilla and broken pecans. Beat until cool. Pour on wet cloth and shape into loaf. Let get completely cold, then slice.

Mrs. Dayton H. Waller, Jr.

DIVINITY CANDY

2 cups sugar
⅔ cup white corn syrup
½ cup water
2 egg whites
1 teaspoon vanilla
1½ cups pecans

Combine sugar, syrup and water and cook to 270° F. on candy thermometer. While this is cooking, beat egg whites in large bowl with electric mixer until very stiff. Pour hot syrup over egg whites in a thin stream and beat constantly until all syrup is used. Add vanilla and continue beating until candy mixture stands in peaks. Add nuts and beat by hand until candy loses its gloss. Drop it in small amounts on waxed paper. If first few pieces don't hold their shape, beat candy some more and then drop it on waxed paper.

Mrs. Dayton H. Waller, Jr.

DIVINITY

½ cup light corn syrup
2½ cups sugar
Pinch salt
½ cup water
2 egg whites
1 teaspoon vanilla extract
1 cup nuts, chopped

Mix corn syrup, sugar, salt and water in saucepan, stirring over heat until sugar is dissolved. Continue cooking, without stirring, until a small amount of mixture forms a firm ball when dropped in cold water, or 248° F. Beat egg whites until stiff but not dry. Pour half the syrup slowly over whites, beating constantly. Cook remainder until a small amount forms hard threads in cold water, or 272° F. Add slowly to first mixture and beat until mixture holds its shape. Add vanilla and nuts. Drop by teaspoon onto waxed paper. This can be made on a rainy day, by using candy thermometer, and will keep several days in a tight tin box.

Mrs. John Hearne
Mrs. Sidney L. Carroll

DIVINITY FUDGE

3 cups sugar
1 cup water
Pinch salt
¾ cup white corn syrup
3 egg whites
Chopped nuts
1 teaspoon vanilla

Mix sugar, water, salt and corn syrup and boil until very firm when dropped in cold water. Remove from fire and pour gradually over very stiffly beaten egg whites. (Heat sugar mixture once or twice during pouring.) Beat vigorously until it begins to thicken. Then add nuts and vanilla and pour onto greased platter or drop by teaspoon on glass.

Linda Laskey

SEAFOAM

3 cups sugar
½ cup white corn syrup
⅔ cup water
2 egg whites
⅛ teaspoon salt
½ teaspoon vanilla
1 cup nuts

Boil sugar, corn syrup and water together until it will form a hard ball when dropped in water (250° F. on candy thermometer). Beat egg whites and salt at high speed on mixer for 3 minutes. Pour syrup slowly into beaten egg whites while beating at high speed. Continue beating until mixture passes the glossy stage. Add nuts and vanilla and continue beating until mixture forms a peak when beater is raised. Drop by teaspoon on waxed paper. Let dry overnight before storing in tin boxes between layers of waxed paper.

Mrs. Charles Beaird

FUDGE

3 cups sugar
3 tablespoons cocoa
3 tablespoons dark corn syrup
1½ cups milk
4 tablespoons butter
1 teaspoon vanilla
1½ cups nuts

Cook sugar, cocoa, syrup and milk over low fire in heavy kettle. Stir only until sugar melts. Cook to 234° F. on candy thermometer or until candy forms soft ball in cup of cold water. Remove from fire, add butter and cool until you can touch sides of pan. Add vanilla, then beat until candy loses gloss. Add nuts and pour into greased 9" x 13" pan.

Mrs. Earl M. Harter, Jr.

OATMEAL FUDGE

2 cups sugar
2 tablespoons cocoa
½ cup milk
2 teaspoons vanilla
2 tablespoons butter (or oleo)
½ cup peanut butter
2 cups 3-minute oatmeal or 1 cup oatmeal and 1 cup nuts

Mix first three ingredients, boil one minute, and take off stove. Add butter, peanut butter, vanilla and oatmeal. Cool about 30 minutes and drop on waxed paper from teaspoon. Makes about 2 dozen pieces.

Mrs. Robert Hankinson
Mrs. John B. Entrikin

CHOCOLATE FUDGE

2 cups sugar
4 tablespoons cocoa
1 small can evaporated milk
2 Hershey Bars
½ cup nuts
Lump of butter

Mix sugar and cocoa. Add milk. Boil about 5 minutes, then cool. Add Hershey Bars, nuts and butter. Beat slightly and pour into greased pan.

Mrs. Frank Green

GOLD BRICK

1 tall can evaporated milk
4½ cups sugar
½ stick butter
4 6-ounce packages chocolate chips
4 cups pecans
1 8-ounce jar marshmallow cream

Boil milk and sugar for 6 to 8 minutes or to soft ball stage. Take off fire and add butter, stirring until melted. Next add chocolate chips, pecans and marshmallow cream, stirring until well blended. Pour into greased pan, and cut into squares when cool.

Mrs. Marshall Martin

FUDGE

3 cups sugar
3 tablespoons cocoa
3 tablespoons white corn syrup
1½ cups milk
¾ stick butter
1 teaspoon vanilla
2 cups pecans

Mix first four ingredients and cook until mixture forms firm ball in cold water. Remove from fire and add butter, vanilla, and pecans. Beat until cool and candy loses gloss. Turn into a buttered pan.

Mrs. Dayton H. Waller, Jr.

NEVER-FAIL PEANUT BRITTLE

3 cups white sugar
1 cup white corn syrup
½ cup water
3 cups RAW peanuts
3 teaspoons butter
1 teaspoon salt
2 teaspoons soda

In deep pan boil sugar, syrup and water until thread spins. Add peanuts and stir continuously. Cook until mixture turns brownish and peanuts look cooked. Take from fire. Add butter, salt and soda. Pour immediately onto well-buttered platter. When cool, break into pieces.

Mrs. Saunders Gregg
Mrs. Clarence J. Edwards

FRUIT ROLL

2 cups brown sugar
4 cups white sugar
1 cup evaporated milk, diluted with ½ cup sweet milk
Scant ½ cup corn syrup
Large lump butter
1 teaspoon vanilla
1 cup grated coconut
1 cup chopped figs
1 cup chopped dates
1 cup chopped raisins
2 cups chopped nuts

Cook brown sugar, white sugar, evaporated milk, sweet milk and corn syrup until soft ball is formed when a little candy is dropped in cold water. Remove from fire, add butter and vanilla, let cool, then beat until creamy. Add fruit and nuts. Pour onto brown paper and knead repeatedly until well mixed. Shape into rolls and wrap in brown paper. This may be stored for days. It does not need to be refrigerated. Slice from roll as needed.

Mrs. A. M. Shaw

HOLIDAY CANDY

3 cups sugar
1½ cups coffee cream
1 cup white corn syrup
1½ teaspoons vanilla
1 pound Brazil nuts
1 pound English walnuts
½ pound each candied pineapple and cherries
½ pound pecans

Combine sugar, cream and corn syrup, and cook to soft ball stage. Remove from heat and begin beating immediately. Add vanilla and continue beating. Have fruit and nuts chopped finely and add to candy mixture, combining well. Mixture will be thick and sticky. Pack in pans lined with waxed paper, pressing with a wet spoon. After a few hours the syrup will become firm and almost white in color. Slice after 24 hours into finger-length pieces.

Nancy Walker

JANUARY THAW

2 cups brown sugar (light or dark)
½ cup milk
2 level teaspoons butter
1 cup chopped pecans

Combine sugar, milk and butter in very small saucepan. Bring to a boil, stirring constantly, and cook until a small ball of candy is formed when mixture is dropped into a cup of cold water. Remove from fire and beat until very thick and stiff. Add nuts, beat another minute, and pour onto well-greased platter. Let cool and cut.

Mrs. Ernest H. Turner, Jr.

ORANGE PECANS

2 cups sugar
¾ cup milk
3 tablespoons grated orange peel
3 tablespoons orange juice
2 cups pecans

Combine sugar, milk and orange peel in saucepan and cook to soft ball stage. Let cool a few seconds, then add orange juice. Beat this mixture until cloudy, then add pecans. Continue beating until mixture begins to sugarize. Pour into buttered pan. Let cool, then break nuts apart.

Leaoto Martin

PECAN CANDY

1 can sweetened condensed milk
1 cup sugar
⅓ stick butter
1 teaspoon orange rind
1 teaspoon vanilla
Pinch salt
3 tablespoons milk
2 cups pecans

Cook first six ingredients over a medium fire, stirring constantly to keep from burning. When golden brown in color, add milk gradually. Bring to a rolling boil once more, and let boil about ½ minute. Remove from fire, and add pecans. Drop by teaspoon onto waxed paper. If too much milk is used, candy will not harden.

Mrs. M. B. Hannah

CREAMY PRALINES

1 cup brown sugar
2 cups white sugar
3 tablespoons white corn syrup
1 cup milk (whole or evaporated. The latter makes richer pralines.)
½ stick butter
2 or 3 cups pecan halves
2 teaspoons vanilla

In heavy pot blend together well the sugars, corn syrup and milk. Cook slowly, stirring constantly. Add half the butter when the candy first comes to a boil, then continue to cook until it reaches 236° F. Remove from heat, add remaining butter and beat, using about 150 vigorous strokes. Add vanilla and pecans and continue beating until candy becomes slightly lighter in color and is more creamy. This is the most important step. While candy is still hot, drop onto buttered waxed paper so that it will form smooth, creamy pieces. This will make approximately 18 pralines, depending on size.

Mrs. Paul E. Sippel, Jr.

OLD MISSISSIPPI PRALINES

2 cups light brown sugar
⅓ cup water
½ stick butter
1½ cups pecan meats
1 teaspoon vanilla

Bring sugar and water to a quick boil over high heat. Add butter and pecan meats. Stir constantly. Cook until candy thermometer reaches 236° F., or the mixture forms a soft ball when tested in a cup of water. Remove from fire. Beat slightly and add vanilla. Drop on ungreased foil or a buttered cookie sheet.

Mrs. Jackson B. Davis

MAMA'S PRALINES

3 cups sugar
1 cup buttermilk
1 teaspoon baking soda
½ stick butter
1 teaspoon vanilla
3 cups pecans

Put all ingredients except pecans into a big boiler and boil until mixture turns brown and forms soft ball in cold water. Add one teaspoon vanilla and beat a little. Stir in pecans and drop on waxed paper.

Mrs. J. B. Haynes, Jr.

OLD-FASHIONED BUTTER CRUNCH TOFFEE

2 cups finely chopped almonds
1 cup butter
1¼ cups sugar
2 tablespoons light corn syrup
2 tablespoons water
1 12-ounce (large) package semi-sweet chocolate chips, melted

Spread almonds in shallow pan and toast until golden. Melt butter in heavy pan. Add sugar, corn syrup, and water. Stir often and cook to hard crack stage (300° F.) Remove from heat and stir in 1 cup almonds. Pour quickly into 12" x 8" x 2" pan. Cool completely. When set, pour half the chocolate over top and spread with ½ cup almonds. Let set. Turn candy over and repeat. Break up.

Mrs. T. Warren Ogden, Jr.
Baton Rouge, La.

Condiments

The Times Fourth of July Celebration

THE TIMES FOURTH OF JULY CELEBRATION

Spectacular fireworks, patriotic music and family fun highlight this annual event, which was begun during the nation's bicentennial year as a gift from the Shreveport newspaper to the citizens of the area. Activities begin around dusk with excitement building up to the finale — the fantastic fireworks extravaganza highlighted with music by the Shreveport Symphony.

DILLED OKRA

1 teaspoon dill seed
1 hot red pepper
1 hot green pepper
2 cloves garlic
1 quart white vinegar
1 cup water
½ cup uniodized salt
Okra

Place ½ teaspoon dill seed in bottom of each jar, then pack fresh washed okra in as tightly as possible, being careful not to bruise okra. Add ½ teaspoon dill seed, peppers and garlic. Bring to boil the vinegar, water and salt. Cover okra with mixture; seal jars and allow to stand 2 weeks. Serve icy cold.

Mrs. F. L. Housh

BREAD AND BUTTER PICKLES

12 medium cucumbers, unpeeled but sliced
6 medium onions, sliced thin
1 cup salt
2½ cups vinegar
2 cups sugar
2 teaspoons mustard seed
2 teaspoons turmeric
2 teaspoons celery seed

Combine cucumbers, onions and salt. Cover with cold water, let stand two hours. Drain through colander. Combine vinegar, sugar and seasonings; bring to a boil. Add cucumbers and onions and boil ten minutes. Seal immediately in hot sterile jars.

Mrs. W. C. Sibley

DILL PICKLES

2 gallons water
1½ cups salt
1 teaspoon red pepper
2 cups vinegar
2 large bundles fresh dill (or more)
2 heads (whole clusters) of garlic, undivided and unpeeled, cut across in halves
1 peck cucumbers

In a large container, make a brine of the first four ingredients. Then arrange cucumbers, dill and garlic in alternating layers in a large earthenware crock. Pour brine over and be sure all layers are well covered. "Weight" them down. Cover crock with a dishcloth. Let set for three or four days. Pickles have "made" when a heavy white scum forms. This should not be removed. Pack pickles in sterilized jars, putting some dill weed and garlic in each jar. Cover well with brine.

Keep refrigerated. This type pickle is best when first made. It stays crisp 2 or 3 months. It softens after this, but is still edible.

John L. Rhea, Jr.

CUCUMBER ICICLE PICKLES

7 pounds cucumbers
1 bottle slaked lime
6 quarts vinegar
8 pounds sugar
8 teaspoons salt
1 box pickling spices

Wash cucumbers well and cut in slices ⅛-inch thick. Soak for 24 hours in mixture of 3 gallons water and slaked lime. Drain and wash well. Then soak in clear ice water for 3 hours. Drain. Soak for 24 hours more in mixture of vinegar, sugar, salt and spices. Next day, cook slowly, boiling for two hours. Seal in sterile jars.

Makes about 15 pints. Recipe may be halved, if smaller amount is desired.

Mrs. W. E. McKee

DILLED GREEN TOMATO PICKLES

1 peck small firm green tomatoes
1 bunch celery
6 bell peppers
12 hot peppers
1 pod garlic
1 gallon water
½ gallon vinegar
2 cups salt
1 bunch dill

Wash tomatoes and pack into sterilized quart jars. To each quart jar, add 1 bud garlic, 1 stalk celery, 1 hot pepper and ½ bell pepper, cut into long strips for easy handling. Make a brine of water, vinegar and salt and boil with dill for 5 minutes. A piece of dill may be added to each jar to give a stronger flavor if desired. Pour the hot brine over the tomatoes in jars and seal immediately. Allow to set for 4 to 6 weeks to season.

Makes about 12 quarts.

Mrs. Lilbourn G. Morgan

WATERMELON RIND PICKLES

1 watermelon rind, cut up
1 tablespoon slaked lime
1 tablespoon alum
1 teaspoon ginger
16 cups sugar
8 cups vinegar
5 cups water
2 sticks cinnamon
1 package allspice

Mix lime in 1 gallon water and soak watermelon rind in this overnight. Drain and rinse. Add alum to 1 gallon water and soak rind for 10 minutes in this mixture. Drain off liquid, add 1 gallon water and ginger. Boil for 30 minutes. Drain and rinse 7 times in cold water. Combine sugar, vinegar, water and spices tied in a bag. Boil rind in this solution for 4 hours. Pack in hot sterile jars and seal.

Mrs. D. E. Smitherman

GRANDMOTHER'S CHILI SAUCE

30 large tomatoes
10 large onions
5 large sweet peppers (bell)
1 teaspoon cinnamon
1 teaspoon allspice
1 teaspoon cloves
3 tablespoons salt
1½ cups sugar
2 cups vinegar

Peel tomatoes. Chop all vegetables medium size. Cook all ingredients for two hours. Pack in hot sterile jars and seal.

Makes about 13 pints. Mrs. M. Allen Dickson

CHILI SAUCE

2 gallons ripe tomatoes
4 red peppers
5 large onions
4 tablespoons salt
8 tablespoons sugar
1 tablespoon celery seed
1 tablespoon black pepper (scant)
1 tablespoon mustard seed
6 cups vinegar

Boil peeled tomatoes, onions, peppers and vinegar until thick. Add seasonings and seal while hot in sterilized jars.

Mrs. Phillip Bishop

GREEN PEPPER JELLY

2 cups ground bell peppers
7½ cups sugar
1½ cups white vinegar
1 bottle liquid fruit pectin
Few drops green food coloring

Boil peppers, sugar and vinegar together for 6 minutes. Add the liquid pectin and boil for 3 minutes. Add 2 or 3 drops food coloring, if desired. Pour into sterilized jars. Cover with paraffin and store.

Makes about a dozen half-pint jars. Mrs. John R. Mills

CORN RELISH

24 large or 36 small ears corn
2 bunches of celery hearts
1 medium sized head cabbage
4 medium bell peppers
4 large Spanish onions
6 cups brown sugar
5 bottles prepared English mustard
½ cup salt
½ pint water
1½ pints cider vinegar

Cut corn from cob, chop vegetables and add remaining ingredients. Cook 30 minutes. Seal while still hot in sterile jars.

Makes about 12 pints. Mrs. E. Bernard Weiss

ROSY RELISH

1½ cups vinegar
2¾ cups sugar
1 tablespoon salt
1 3-inch stick cinnamon
2 tablespoons mustard seed
8 whole cloves
2 cups ripe peeled tomatoes, chopped
2 cups tart apples, peeled and chopped
1 cup onion, chopped
1 cup celery, chopped
1 cup green pepper, chopped
2 tablespoons red pepper, chopped

Combine vinegar, sugar, salt and seasonings and bring to a rapid boil. Add fruit and vegetables and simmer until mixture is thick and clear (about 30 to 45 minutes). Pour into hot sterilized jars and seal at once. Red food coloring may be added, if desired.

Makes 2 pints. Mrs. W. H. North

MEXICAN TOMATO RELISH

8 cups chopped ripe tomatoes
4 cups chopped bell peppers (use some red ones)
3 cups chopped onions
3 cups vinegar
2 cups sugar
2 tablespoons cinnamon
2 tablespoons salt
2 tablespoons celery seed

Blend all ingredients together and simmer 1 hour or until mixture is as thick as you like it. Seal in hot sterilized jars.

Makes approximately 3 pints. Mrs. Robert A. Taliaferro

PEAR RELISH

18 hard pears
4 bell peppers
4 lemons
1 cup seedless raisins
1 cup brown sugar
2 cups white sugar
½ teaspoon cayenne pepper
2 tablespoons onion flakes
1 cup cider vinegar
1 tablespoon salt
1 tablespoon powdered ginger
1 tablespoon dry mustard

Peel, core and slice pears; seed and slice bell peppers; slice lemons (remove seeds when possible). Combine these and add raisins. Put into kettle with brown and white sugar, vinegar, mustard, ginger, onion flakes, salt and cayenne. Simmer gently until pears are translucent and tender and syrup is thick (about 2 hours). Seal in sterile jars. This is a rather unusual, but delicious chutney-type relish.

Elizabeth Friedenberg

PEAR CHUTNEY

9 pounds firm, unripe pears, peeled, cored and chopped (about 30)
5 onions, chopped
5 garlic pods, chopped
1 quart cider vinegar
1 pound seedless, golden raisins
1 pound currants
1 pound light brown sugar
1 pound white sugar
2½ tablespoons salt
1 teaspoon cayenne pepper
2 teaspoons paprika
4 ounces mustard seed
1 cup orange marmalade (or frozen orange juice undiluted)
1 tablespoon grated orange rind
2 limes (or lemons) sliced thin
2 tablespoons curry powder
3 tablespoons candied ginger, chopped
1½ teaspoons each of:
cinnamon
cloves
allspice
nutmeg

Simmer vinegar and sugar in large enamel pot for about 15 minutes, then add all above ingredients and cook slowly for 1 hour.

Add ½ pound dried apples, chopped, and ½ pound dried apricots, chopped. Cook about 30 minutes until thick. The dried fruit thickens the chutney and gives it texture. 1 cup sherry wine may be added after chutney is off the fire, if desired. Put into sterilized jars and seal.

Makes approximately 20 half pints. Philip F. Rosenblath, Sr.

HOT PEPPER RELISH

4 pounds white onions
50 hot peppers
2 cups sugar
3 tablespoons salt
3 cups vinegar

Grind onions and peppers together. Heat sugar, salt and vinegar and bring to a boil, add onion-pepper mixture and cook for three minutes. Fill hot sterile jars with mixture and seal.

Makes about 6 pints. Mrs. Douglas F. Attaway

FIG PRESERVES

2 pound figs
2 pounds sugar (white or raw)
1 lemon
1 cup water for white sugar (1½ cups water if raw sugar is used)

Wash and peel figs. Make syrup by boiling sugar and water together. Add figs and thinly sliced lemon, and boil one minute. Lower heat and cook slowly 30 minutes. Let stand 12 hours. Pour in cold sterile jars and seal.

Mrs. John A. Walden

BRANDIED PEACHES

3 cups sugar
2 cups water
5 pounds small peaches
Brandy

Bring 3 cups sugar and 2 cups water to boil, stirring down crystals from sides of pan. Cover peaches with boiling water; let stand 1 minute; cool quickly under running water. Peel and put in pan of slightly salted water to prevent browning. Do not let stand more than 15 minutes. Add 8 to 10 peaches at a time to sugar syrup; simmer 10 minutes, or until tender. Lift out into 4 or 6 hot, sterilized pint jars, filling to ½" from top. Put lids on to keep peaches hot. Spoon 2 to 4 tablespoons brandy into each jar. Bring syrup to boil and fill jars all the way to top; seal.

Mrs. Jerry Waters

ORANGE MARMALADE

1 large grapefruit
1 large navel orange
1 large lemon
8 cups sugar (4 pounds)
11 cups water

With a single-edge razor blade, slice around fruit which has been cut in half. The slice should be paper thin. Use every bit of rind and pulp. Cover with water and let stand overnight. Then, boil until tender and add sugar. Let stand overnight again, then boil until mixture thickens. Use white enamel container for preparation, if possible. Fill hot sterile jars and seal.

Mrs. D. Y. Smith

SWEET PEAR CONSERVE

1 pound ground pears
½ lemon
1 large orange
1 No. 2 can crushed pineapple
Sugar
Large bottle maraschino cherries, drained

Peel, core and grind pears until you have one pound. This will be a large bowl-full. Grind lemon and orange, combine with pear mixture, and add crushed pineapple. Cook about 30 minutes. Add 3 cups sugar for every 4 cups cooked fruit. Cook until clear and thick, about 30 more minutes. Add maraschino cherries to fruit while cooking. Seal in hot sterile jars.

Makes about 9 pints

Mrs. M. Allen Dickson

PEAR PRESERVES A LA SANDEL

The ingredients are pear slices, sugar, and water. The main thing to remember is to use **two** cups of pear slices to **one** full cup of sugar. This ratio is really just right.

Pare the pears, slice them, measure two cups of pear slices and one cup of sugar and place in a large pan. (I use the bottom half of my turkey roaster.) Continue adding two cups of pear slices to each cup of sugar until all pear slices are gone. Remember the ratio of two to one if you only have a few pear slices left over. After you have sliced and measured pears, put enough water in the roaster pan to cover pear slices fully. Stir sugar around and place on top of stove. Turn burners on full to begin heating the water, pears, and sugar. After a full boil is reached, turn burners down until a slow boil is reached. Continue stirring throughout the entire cooking time. Test frequently by removing a spoonful of juice and cooling. A rich reddish brown color usually indicates a good jar of pear preserves. The time limit varies depending on how full the pan is. When preserves have finished cooking, run hot water over and in the jars you are planning to use. Pour preserves, **while hot,** into jars. (Place a spoon inside jar while pouring preserves.) Seal immediately after filling.

A gallon of fruit yields about 2 dozen pint jars.

Mrs. Arthur James Ferguson

STRAWBERRY PRESERVES

4 cups sugar
1 cup water
4 cups whole strawberries

Boil together 2 cups sugar and 1 cup water until syrup spins a thread. Add 2 cups whole strawberries. Boil 10 minutes. Add 2 more cups strawberries and 2 more cups sugar. Boil 10 more minutes. Skim and set aside until following day. Stir well and seal cold in sterile jars.

Makes about 4 half pints. Mrs. Mike Tipps

TO TEST FOR MAYHAW JELLY

Mix 1 tablespoon grain alcohol with 1 tablespoon mayhaw juice. Let set 1 minute. If quite thin and runny, use ½ cup sugar to 1 cup juice. If fairly thin, use ¾ cup sugar to 1 cup juice. If firm, use 1 cup sugar to 1 cup juice. The best jelly is made when cooked in small amounts, with no more than 3 cups of juice at a time.

Mrs. Whitfield Jack

INDEX

BEVERAGES

BEEF

BREAD

CAKES

CANDY

CASSEROLES

CHEESE AND EGG DISHES

CHICKEN

CONDIMENTS

COOKIES

DESSERTS

DRESSINGS

GAME

HAM

HORS D'OEUVRES

LAMB

MEAT–pages 183-219

See Also: Beef, Ham, Lamb, Pork or Veal

PIES

PORK

SALADS

SAUCES

SEAFOODS

SOUPS

TURKEY

VEAL

VEGETABLES

A Cook's Tour of Shreveport

2601 Line Ave., Shreveport, Louisiana 71104

Please send __________ copies of your book at $19.95 plus 8.6% tax and $4.50 postage.

Enclosed is my check or money order for $ ____________.

Name ______________________________

Street ______________________________

City __________________ State ______ Zip ______

Compiled and published by the Junior League of Shreveport

A Cook's Tour of Shreveport

2601 Line Ave., Shreveport, Louisiana 71104

Please send __________ copies of your book at $19.95 plus 8.6% tax and $4.50 postage.

Enclosed is my check or money order for $ ____________.

Name ______________________________

Street ______________________________

City __________________ State ______ Zip ______

Compiled and published by the Junior League of Shreveport

A Cook's Tour of Shreveport

2601 Line Ave., Shreveport, Louisiana 71104

Please send __________ copies of your book at $19.95 plus 8.6% tax and $4.50 postage.

Enclosed is my check or money order for $ ____________.

Name ______________________________

Street ______________________________

City __________________ State ______ Zip ______

Compiled and published by the Junior League of Shreveport